BRITISH ECONOMIC HISTORY
1870-1914

COMMENTARY AND DOCUMENTS

T0340288

BRITISH
ECONOMIC HISTORY
1870-1914

COMMENTARY AND DOCUMENTS

BY

W.H.B.COURT

Professor of Economic History in the
University of Birmingham

CAMBRIDGE
AT THE UNIVERSITY PRESS
1965

CAMBRIDGE UNIVERSITY PRESS
Cambridge, New York, Melbourne, Madrid, Cape Town, Singapore, São Paulo

Cambridge University Press
The Edinburgh Building, Cambridge CB2 8RU, UK

Published in the United States of America by Cambridge University Press, New York

www.cambridge.org
Information on this title: www.cambridge.org/9780521047319

© Cambridge University Press 1965

First published 1965
Re-issued in this digitally printed version 2008

A catalogue record for this publication is available from the British Library

Library of Congress Catalogue Card Number: 65–19045

ISBN 978-0-521-04731-9 hardback
ISBN 978-0-521-09362-0 paperback

For A. K. C.
without whom, nothing

CONTENTS

LIST OF DOCUMENTS

List of Documents

List of Documents

List of Documents

List of Documents

List of Documents

PREFACE

History is the essence of innumerable lives and as such beyond our understanding. We can only, as people say, form an idea of it. To sort out in every generation our ideas of history and to test them against the evidence available is the task of the historian. Unless this is done, human society remains without true knowledge of its past and presumably indifferent to its future.

The concern of this book is with the economic characteristics and transformations of British society in the thirty or forty years before 1914, within the lifetime of men and women who had already reached middle-life when the First World War broke out. The war marked the end of the social order, as well as of the political system, of nineteenth-century Europe. The period of violent change so introduced may be said to have lasted thirty years, until it closed under vastly altered circumstances in the Europe of 1945. These were years which seem likely to affect permanently the destinies of mankind. Therefore it becomes a matter of considerable interest to examine the resources with which Britain entered upon the war in August 1914 and the movements of her economy and society in Late Victorian and Edwardian times. In that pre-war generation, the direction and ordering of policies, the economic and political decisions which lay behind them, which were to do so much to settle the large outline of later events, were still in the making.

This book is not another narrative of the economic changes of the years with which it deals. One or two such already exist, notably those written by Sir John Clapham and William Ashworth,[1] and the number may soon be increased. It is rather an attempt to interest students and others who wish to understand those years in the documentary evidence for economic history and in the problems of its interpretation. Contemporaries have been left, as far as possible, to speak for themselves. They can best explain their intentions, the conditions under which they worked, what they expected and what they did not expect.

A certain amount of statistical material is included in some of the documents quoted. But it has been assumed that the central statistics of British economic development are already available and will be consulted elsewhere.[2] Meanwhile, there seemed to be room for a

---

[1] Sir John Clapham, *An Economic History of Modern Britain*, vol. III (1938) and William Ashworth, *An Economic History of England, 1870–1939* (1960).

[2] See especially B. R. Mitchell and P. Deane, *Abstract of British Historical Statistics* (1962), and P. Deane and W. A. Cole, *British Economic Growth, 1688–1959* (1962).

collection of documents, in addition to the statistical measurements. Both are indispensable to the serious study of economic change.

There are some things which documents, with all their inadequacy and untidiness, can do to aid our understanding of history which statistical series can hardly perform. Economic events are the consequence of economic decision, private or public, that is, of the resolve to use resources in one way and for one purpose rather than in another way and for another purpose. It is hoped the documents here gathered may throw some light, admittedly neither steady nor without shadow, upon the processes by which decisions in these years came to be taken of a kind which involved the use of the national resources between competing ends, the manner of the execution of those decisions and the consequences to the nation in terms of the size and distribution and expenditure of incomes. These documents relate to a time when this country was at the height, not of her population and national product, for both are larger now, but of her power and influence in the world, on the eve of the supreme crisis of modern Western history.

The main problem for the editor was the arrangement of the documents. A purely chronological order would have been meaningless. Nor would it have been enough to use them to throw light upon passing complexities and confusions of opinion, although these are important for our understanding of situations as they unfolded themselves to view at the time. In the last ten or fifteen years, economists and historians have studied with great intentness the events of this momentous period, when Victorian certainties were passing away and many modern problems were coming into sight for the first time. Their professional discussions have done much to give the book its present shape. This has been directed towards two main topics, much discussed both at the time and later. One of these is the extent and causes of economic change in Great Britain at this period. The other is the effect of those changes upon what was coming to be called about the turn of the century economic welfare, that is, men's notion of what was desirable and rational in the way of making an income and a living, given the current development of resources. The national product between 1870 and 1914 had to provide not only for a rising population but also for the growing expectations of individuals and classes, with all the hope of a widened personal choice in life and the massive drive of democratic politics behind them. It had, besides, to sustain the country's defence, in an era of intense armaments competition in Europe between the Great Powers, and to protect the most populous and extensive of Western colonial empires. These great themes in the economic history of the period are illustrated here in a manner, it is hoped, sufficiently broad to give an adequate view of the working of the highly complicated system of relationships which formed the national economy as a whole.

It has proved impossible to illustrate every aspect of economic life. Some important and interesting subjects, such as the organization of the great produce markets and the structure of banking, come off badly here, although the existence of Sir Theodore Gregory's *British Banking Statutes and Reports* (1929) makes the financial gap less painful than it might otherwise be. But it seemed necessary to make some sacrifice even of significant and useful knowledge for the sake of what is vital towards an understanding of the main economic interactions of industrial society and of what it meant to live in the British national community, in those days one of the richest and most powerful in the world, before general war in Europe made it necessary to contemplate what seemed incredible, the destruction of the social arrangements of peace time.

The interpretative essays, if they may be called so, which introduce the chapters of documents, are intended to relate the chapters to one another and the documents to modern discussions of the period. They are not intended to be exhaustive or to do away with the need for further reading on the part of students. Notes for further reading are attached to the essays. The notes do not form in any way a bibliography—a true bibliography of the period would be as long as this book—but it is hoped they may be useful. The essays and the documents are intended to lend support to one another. The hope has been that, out of both, the reader might collect something like a coherent and reasonably balanced picture of the British economy, although it will be seen that great gaps exist in the material available for a satisfactory economic portrait of this age.

Brief annotations have been attached to the documents. These are intended sometimes to throw light on the personality and the intentions of the writer of the document quoted, sometimes to illustrate the wider context of the problems which it reflects, and always to give the source of the document, so that this may be sought if required. References to the Parliamentary papers follow the system of P. and G. Ford's *Select List of British Parliamentary Papers, 1833–1899* (1953).

Particular thanks are due to two institutions of learning abroad. A book on this phase of modern British history was first meditated on a visit to the Institute of Advanced Studies at Princeton, in walks among the fields and woods of New Jersey. A fellowship to the Australian National University at Canberra in 1959 provided the leisure for a much-needed revision of the original plan.

The book owes much, I am sure, to two men neither of whom has seen it or bears any responsibility at all for it. Sir Keith Hancock, now in Australia, probably has forgotten many conversations about

xvii

Preface

colonies and the economic meaning of Empire. The profound knowledge of Lance Beales, formerly of the London School of Economics,
of the sources of British history in the nineteenth century, is only
matched by his generosity in imparting it to other people.

In the actual search for, transcription and checking of documents, I
owe a great debt to three research assistants who have at one time or
another been on the strength of the Faculty of Commerce and Social
Science at the University of Birmingham. They are Miss Janet Black-
man, Mr M. F. Miles and Mr J. H. Treble. Without their help, an
inquiry of this kind would have been impossible. Equally indispensable
have been the labours, at different times, of Mrs Mary Wightman, Mrs
Judith Moseley and Mrs June Malone, who typed the book. On their
shoulders, and on those of Miss Helen Berry, also of the Faculty of
Commerce and Social Science, a great load fell. For the final results,
both in the main and in detail, I remain responsible.

I have been much indebted throughout to the care and interest
and forbearance shown by the Cambridge University Press during
the long composition of this book.

W. H. B. C.

Birmingham
November 1964

xviii

PART I
THE PATHS OF ECONOMIC CHANGE

CHAPTER I

THE CLIMATE OF ECONOMIC EXPECTATIONS

In the 'sixties and early 'seventies of last century, the British economy was one of the fastest growing in the world.[1] Conditions were unusually favourable at that time in all of its great departments, in agriculture, industry, transport and foreign trade, for an exceptionally wide and rapid advance in output and incomes. Between 1875 and 1914 the increase of national product and of output per head continued, although at a rate which declined sharply in the early years of the present century. When the inhabitants of the British Isles went to war in August 1914 they were, although a third more numerous than they had been in 1871, on the average of their incomes more than one third richer. This is a statistician's average. It is not intended to deny that many people were little, if at all, better off than before or that deep poverty existed upon a most serious scale. But the increase of the national income as a whole over this period was important. Under late Victorian and Edwardian conditions, it had the most immediate social and political consequences.

The continued growth of incomes in a country where population was still rising—for the United Kingdom as a whole in 1871 it was 31,484,000 persons, in 1911 45,221,000—and, no less, the remarkable fall in the rate of that economic growth which took place at the beginning of this century, a slackening which lasted through the First World War down to the 1930's, raise economic questions which require an answer. How were incomes made and how were they increased? World conditions in 1914 were clearly very different from those of 1871. How did these affect the earning of a wage, a profit, a rent, or an interest payment? The expansion of British incomes obviously went on at all times under limitations and constraints, which seem to have increased their power in the early 1900's. What was the character of those constraints and limitations? Were they internal or external to the national economy?

To try to answer these and similar questions would be out of place in a selection of documents. No collection could cover the ground nor

[1] For an international comparison, see D. C. Paige, F. T. B. Blackaby and S. Freund, 'Economic Growth: the last hundred years', *Economic Review* (National Institute of Economic and Social Research), July 1961, p. 35.

would it be complete without statistical evidence which is more conveniently to be sought elsewhere. Neither would documents and statistics go far towards solving such problems without analysis. What will be attempted in the following chapters, in relation to agriculture, industry, foreign trade and overseas investment, is to show how the business of earning a livelihood and an income looked to those persons who for one reason or another found themselves closely connected with the organization and direction of production. For the whole movement of the highly developed industrial economy which Great Britain was running at the end of the nineteenth century depended upon the views of such men. It was a capitalistic economy, in the sense that it relied, far more exclusively in those days than now, when public investment and control of the economy have become so important, upon the investment of private capital. The willingness of those who disposed of savings to put them into production or transport or distribution or banking turned in the long run upon their hope of a profit or their fear of a loss. The movement of the economy therefore depended at any given moment on the state of men's economic expectations.

Those expectations were strikingly mobile. Perhaps the most remarkable feature of them was the swiftness with which they could change. The business world of the early 1870's lived in a state of pleasurable excitement, induced by the most powerful international investment boom that had been known for many years. A few months of financial crisis on the Continent and in the United States in 1873 sufficed to bring that mood to an end, although production continued to rise for some time. The swings of the late nineteenth-century trade cycle, from the crest of activity in 1874 to the depths of unemployed resources in 1879, from the comparative cheerfulness of 1882–3 to the gloom of 1886, broke down an unthinking confidence in the future of British industry which had been built upon the experience of twenty years of unprecedented industrial expansion. Heavy fluctuations in prices and production set men talking about depression and decline through the 1880's and 1890's, until the vigorous investment revival of the late 1890's. For many years, members of the business and professional classes referred in a general way to the period after 1873 as depressed. The last quarter of the nineteenth century was in fact, as Marshall and other economists pointed out, a time of improvement and quiet prosperity for most of the nation. The period that followed 1905 saw, on the other hand, a marked return of hopefulness and investing confidence among the same investing classes. The mass of people were finding it more difficult to live in those years before the war, as prices and the cost of living rose, unless their trade union did an unusually effective job in securing a rise of wages for them. But the memory of the late Edwardian and the first Georgian

years which men of the business and professional classes carried into
the First World War, and, if they survived, looked back to with
nostalgia, was that of a prolonged and cheerful investment boom. The
dismal years of the early 1890's and of the period immediately after the
Boer War had been forgotten.

How are we to account for these astonishing swings of opinion,
which were often swift and transient, but sometimes deep and long
lasting? Contemporaries would have said that they were to be explained by what happened to the general level of prices. Certainly
prices in the markets varied widely from time to time, often over a
wide range of commodities. The last quarter of the nineteenth century
saw a world-wide tendency of prices to fall and the years after 1896 a
tendency equally general for prices to rise. These events profoundly
impressed opinion both in Britain and in many other countries. For
economically about this time the Western world was becoming one.

The incomes of important groups and institutions were sharply
affected. In the price fall, when the market value of many farm
products and of some metals was declining continuously and heavily,
it was farmers and silver producers and merchants and governments
with payments to make between countries which in those days used
silver coins and those who used gold ones, who felt their interests to be
hurt by this state of affairs. On the other hand, during the years of
strongly rising prices before 1914 it was the social classes and groups
whose incomes did not follow the cost of living up or did not follow
it fast enough to maintain the value of their incomes who complained
bitterly. General price movements gave rise therefore to a great deal
of public discussion and led to much official and private inquiry. The
documents in this first chapter will illustrate how strong this tendency
to debate prices was in Britain, which stood at the centre of many of
the most important world markets. Other documents in later chapters,
for example, on farming, will show how influential at the time and, up
to a point, how instructive such economic argument could be. They
will also display what is perhaps difficult to understand today, the
constant tendency in men's minds to connect price movements with
the gold coins which were in general daily use before 1914 and to discuss
general problems of the working of the economic system in terms of
what was happening to the value of the precious metals. The events of
a later economically far more disturbed age between the two world
wars first forced British public opinion to penetrate beyond money and
to think of economic processes in more consistently real terms.

Late Victorian and Edwardian business opinion was little troubled by
questions about the volume of effective demand. Such questions shook
the economic thinking of the 1930's, in the midst of a depression of
incomes and demand more serious than anything which the nineteenth

century knew. Perhaps the earlier age was not troubled enough, Victorian opinion was certainly prepared to tolerate an amazing waste of the national resources at regular intervals, under the impact of what it had learned to call the trade cycle. One might wonder too, with later experience in mind, whether the pressure of high prices upon the working class cost of living in the early 1900's and its effect upon the margins of expenditure of large masses of people may not have retarded the growth of those home markets as distinct from export outlets which it would have been useful for the country to possess later. But the opinion of fifty and sixty years ago was chiefly conscious, less of fluctuations and the constant changes in the economy, than of living in an age of amazing economic expansion. The rate of growth of the British economy—so far as it could be measured, and how fast it was growing was mostly a matter of popular impression—seemed only a little less impressive than that of, say, Germany and the United States, which were the two other highly industrialized countries of the day. Supporters of the reigning economic system agreed with its critics that the waste and unemployment brought by the trade cycle was lamentable. But this was generally regarded, except always by organized labour, as the price to be paid for an economic development which it was assumed must necessarily be uncertain. In any case, men were inclined to argue, was not the trade cycle much less of a curse than it had been, now that the Bank of England and the banks managed credit so much better than they used to do? There seemed little to worry about. The supreme concern of the investor was only where and how much to invest.

If we wish to understand today how the economy of 1914 grew out of that of 1870 and why it took the shape and direction that it did, we have to ask what happened to that relatively small part of the total national income which was neither consumed nor hoarded but was invested, either at home or abroad. Much of the movement of prices and much of the stir of opinion which meditated on market values was a consequence rather than a cause of the economic development which arose out of investment and the process of capital accumulation. The prime cause of growth, or of stagnation, where that occurred, lay in the decisions of the relatively few men who had savings to invest. It was they who, in building up their own capital and income, settled what the capital and the income of the nation as a whole were to be for years to come.

The major economic events of the age were therefore the product of great capital movements, the result of the consensus of investing minds. The true dimensions of these movements could only be guessed at the time, and they cannot be exactly known today. It is in these terms, of the rate of economic expansion due to capital investment and the

6

relation between rates of investment in the industrial and the primary producing countries of the world, that historians would explain nowadays the late nineteenth-century price fall and the subsequent rise of world prices. It was the varying and uneven pressure upon real resources, as economic development proceeded in country after country, which was important, rather than the rate of gold output in the world's mines. The general movement of prices, however important it was to people socially and politically, was the consequence rather than the cause of these processes of fundamental economic change.

Great Britain, still in 1870 indisputably the leading manufacturing state, but yielding place by 1914 in the value of her industrial output to Germany and the U.S.A., stood very much at the centre of this world in course of transformation. Her capital history in these forty-four years was dominated by the remarkable fact that two strikingly different paths lay before her investing classes. They could invest at home or they could lend their capital overseas. Many Englishmen could not understand how other Englishmen could invest in any country but their own. Given Britain's position, however, throughout most of the nineteenth century as the centre of world trade and given the network of knowledge, personal connexions and credit established in London, the development of foreign investment was a natural step. Much investment of capital overseas was complementary to the industrial development of Britain herself. Other countries could produce the raw materials and the foodstuffs which she increasingly required. It became profitable to invest in such foreign production. Hence recurrent lending booms, when capital moved abroad, sometimes on a great scale, as in the periods 1871–4, 1886–90, and again 1905–13. These tended also to be the years of expanding commodity exports, as countries abroad increased their equipment with the aid of money raised in London. Between the capital export booms came long periods when it was home investment that was vigorous rather than foreign. Such were the years 1875–84 and 1895–1905. Home investment and foreign were to this extent both complementary and competitive with one another.

The competition between foreign and home borrowing ran, however, within strict limits, which were set not only by investment opportunities, but also by the structure of the British capital market. It would be misleading to think of the course of British economic history during this period as determined by a simple transfer of resources from home to foreign borrowers and back again[1] by the

---

[1] W. W. Rostow, *British Economy of the Nineteenth Century* (1948) seems to make this over-simple assumption. The importance of the distinction between the two types of investor was first pointed out, I think, by Dr C. H. Feinstein.

decision of a single body of investors, calmly reckoning the line of maximum profit and pursuing the critical path between competing investment opportunities. The home and the foreign paths, if one may stick to that analogy, were traditional beaten tracks. They were habitually pursued by different men. Investors often moved most unwillingly outside the field of their best knowledge. The line of distinction was particularly important between those who put capital by custom and preference into home industry and agriculture on the basis of their personal knowledge, and those who did not. Home industrial and agricultural investment followed its own rules. It depended on the decisions of local men who often neither knew nor cared what foreign countries were doing or what merchant bankers in London might be offering. Foreign lending was an alternative to home investment largely as an alternative to house building, not to investment in industry. The years when foreign investment flourished at the expense of home were years when house construction in this country suffered. The early 1890's, for example, saw a house building boom, after the foreign lending of 1886–90 fell away. They were not particularly profitable years for home industry. Again, when overseas investment revived after 1905, the housing industry in some cities, such as Birmingham, felt a sharp setback. It was in this way that Great Britain took a housing shortage into the First World War which was in part the consequence of Edwardian capital export.

Industrial (including farm) investment, foreign loans and house construction formed the three dominant and interacting influences in the formation of new capital between 1870 and 1914. In the economic history of those years, there are few questions more important than this. Were the nation's savings used to best advantage? A proper answer would need to take into account all three forms of investment, for they formed the basis of the expansion of the economy. The record of their interaction, looked at cursorily, is interesting. Two phases of high total investment came at the beginning and the end of the period in the years 1870–2 and 1911–13. These were times of active capital export, fast rising prices, optimistic expectations and high employment. Something like 20 per cent of the gross national income was being invested, with home and foreign investment competing strongly for available savings. The twenty years of falling prices, 1875–96, which were also the time of recurrent complaints of depression, were a period when home and foreign investment together formed a smaller proportion of the gross national income than they did for the 1870–1914 years taken as a whole. Men became used in these twenty years to a rate of new capital formation rather lower than it could have been. Industrial investment stood up, it is true, fairly well in the decade 1873–83 when there were great developments in the steel industry.

Economic Expectations

The gay 1890's were industrially not at all gay, at least not until after 1895. The early and middle 1890's showed the poorest investment record of all these forty-four years. The ten years 1895–1905 saw a remarkable recovery of investment. Based upon industrial expansion and city building at home, it was largely concentrated in a few years and did not last, for reasons which are still unclear.

The course of investment in farming and industry cannot be understood without going into much tiresome detail. It depended upon a multitude of conditions internal to each industry. Some of these special conditions are illustrated here, in the documents contained in chapters 2 and 3. They cover farming, mining and manufacturing industry. The outward facing side of the national economy represented by overseas trade and foreign investment and the incomes which they earned abroad come in for attention in chapter 4. Whether industrial capital was invested under monopolistic or competitive conditions bore directly on the expectations of investors. It receives some documentary treatment in chapter 5.

Capital was not all-important, even in a capitalistic age. Perhaps it never had been. In the Industrial Revolution of the eighteenth century, which laid the foundations of Britain's industrial power, the greatest productive advances had been made, not by mere accumulation of capital, but by the deliberate investment of savings in what were essentially new ideas. If technical innovation was important then, it was certainly no less so at the end of the nineteenth century. Great Britain was by this time no longer a solitary industrial state. She competed hotly for world trade with half a dozen other nations. The direction and quality of industrial investment was no less vital to her future development than its quantity. In her new and uncertain situation, an open mind to scientific ideas and a capacity to turn them to practical account were more urgent than the accumulation of capital along accepted lines. If technology had acquired a new significance, so too had management. The task of tying together the factors of production became more and more large scale and complex every year. Under the new conditions, could rule of thumb administration survive any more than the rule of thumb of the craftsman?

These aspects of the economic life of pre-1914 Britain have received much attention of late years from economists and historians. They have pointed out that, towards the end of the nineteenth century, the range of industrial techniques with which the prosperity of Victorian Britain had been identified, steam and iron and the railway, were beginning to exhaust their possibilities. The industrial future lay with new forms of power and transport and raw materials. Whether and how quickly British industry could adapt itself to a fast-changing situation was a question debated at the time, as an examination of some of the documents printed here will show. The pressing importance of industrial innovation was connected with another trend of the times. This was the change in Great Britain's international position. For many years she had occupied an exceptional position in the trade of the world, based in the long run on her industrial advantages. As these comparative advantages over other nations declined towards the end of the century so too did her easy dominance in commerce. The change was marked from the 'seventies onwards. New problems then began to come into sight. Where was the incentive to industrial change to come from which in the recent past had arrived so regularly in the form of overseas demand? Could the home market take its place? If so, where were the production and the new industries to come from to serve and to provoke demand from within the economy? These questions are easier to put now than they were at the time. The basic issues were at that date obscure. Much of the interest of the history of this period lies in seeing how men approached them, by what stages, and how clarification arrived, if it came at all. In the chapters which follow, an attempt has been made to set down side by side some of the evidence concerning the state of economic expectations from time to time; some of the evidence as to what men thought was happening, at the time it happened; and some of the evidence of what appeared to have been the outcome, looking back. It is only by entering into these shifting points of view that we can, however imperfectly, appreciate the rational and the irrational elements which entered into men's expectations and understand the decisions which determined the use of the nation's resources.

Economic questions which are posed fifty, sixty and seventy years after the events to which they relate may appear to be of little human interest. To think so would be a mistake. Questions of the best use of resources take their rise and, strictly speaking, they only possess a meaning in terms of the ends which are to be served. The problem of economic welfare, i.e. what the British economy in late Victorian and Edwardian days produced in the way of incomes for the individual and the State and how far personal and communal purposes were satisfied, is the other side of the allocation of resources. It will be approached through a different range of documents in the second half of this volume. The failures and wastes of the economy—the recurrent standstill of a proportion of all resources in the trade cycle, the decline in the rate of growth of industrial investment after 1870, the depression of the 1890's—require to be considered against this general background of individual and social need. For the price of any resources which may have been wasted, the real cost of idle men and idle machines, was not transmitted to posterity. It was paid at the time, day by day and hour by hour, in the conditions of those who lived through these years, not least by that great number of people, the majority of the nation, who had no income to save and no savings to invest, and who never made an economic decision in that sense in the whole course of their lives.

FURTHER READING

The place of capital in British economic history and of the conditions surrounding its formation during these years have been much discussed. Many of the basic economic statistics are in B. R. Mitchell and P. Deane, *Abstract of British Historical Statistics* (1962) and P. Deane and W. A. Cole, *British Economic Growth 1688–1959* (1962). There are estimates of income and investment for the period in C. H. Feinstein, 'Income and Investment in the United Kingdom 1856–1914', *Economic Journal* (June 1961).

W. W. Rostow, *British Economy of the Nineteenth Century* (1948) began the modern discussion of the problem but also seriously over-simplified it. Compare J. Saville, 'A Comment on Professor Rostow's British Economy of the 19th Century', *Past and Present* (1954), pp. 66–81.

A. K. Cairncross, *Home and Foreign Investment 1870–1913* (1953) is indispensable for an understanding of the relation between capital accumulation and economic expansion. See also the useful sketch by J. H. Lenfant, 'Great Britain's Capital Formation 1865–1914', *Economica*, New Series, XVIII (1951), 151–68.

For the highly important influence of technical change on both capital growth and economic expansion, E. H. Phelps Brown and S. J. Handfield Jones, 'The Climacteric of the 1890's', *Oxford Economic Papers*, New Series, IV (1952), 266–307. See also, however, D. J. Coppock, 'The Climacteric of the 1890's: A Critical Note', *The Manchester School*, XXIV (1956), 1–31. The observations in the earlier chapters of A. K. Cairncross, *Factors in Economic Development* (1962) are relevant.

The other great influence on economic expansion and capital growth, the change in markets, was discussed by W. A. Lewis, *Economic Survey 1919–1939* (1949), ch. 5. See also D. J. Coppock, *ibid.*

For the problem of adaptation as a whole in the British economy in the generation before the First World War, J. Saville, 'Some Retarding Factors in the British Economy before 1914', *Yorkshire Bulletin of Economic and Social Research*, XIII (1961), 51–60.

The relation between economic expansion and price-levels came in for a good deal of attention, both at the time and later. See, for example, A. Sauerbeck, *Prices of Commodities and the Precious Metals* (1886) now available in E. M. Carus-Wilson (ed.), *Essays in Economic History*, vol. 3 (1962) and W. T. Layton, *Introduction to the Study of Prices* (1912). For a modern view, G. Maynard, *Economic Development and the Price Level* (1962).

The Paths of Economic Change

I. THE BOOM OF 1868–73

Source: 'The Economist' (vol. XXXI), 4 January 1873, pp. 1–2.

This article represents the views of Walter Bagehot (1826–77), the editor of the paper. Bagehot explains why industrial life tends to move in cycles of prosperity and depression and that the country is now approaching the later stages of such a cycle, when some depression may be expected. For comment, in relation to later discussions of the trade cycle, see W. W. Rostow, "Bagehot and the Trade Cycle", in 'The Economist 1843–1943, a Centenary Volume' (1943).

THE main cause of these cycles in price and trade is, as we have often shown, the different amounts of loanable capital which are available at different times for the supply of trade. After great panics like 1847, 1857 and 1866, for a very long period enterprise is so slack and credit so bad that there is no possibility of employing an increasing capital to advantage. Trade continues much as it was, whereas the savings of the country are accumulating constantly. Accordingly there is at such seasons a constant excess in the supply of loanable capital over good bills and other accredited securities; the rate of interest, which is the barometer of the relative supply of these articles, continues very low generally through a series of years. After a certain period some circumstance more or less powerful occurs to augment trade; and then the effect of that capital is felt. Enterprise revives as credit grows, and that capital is lent largely....But when from some cause peculiar to itself trade does revive, bankers are only too eager to lend, and trade, so far from wanting the money which it requires, finds the accumulated capital of bankers lying ready and waiting to be used by it. The development of one trade, too, is never isolated. If any one great industry—say the iron trade—starts into sudden prosperity, the purchasing power of all persons connected with the iron trade is largely augmented, and all the dependent trades, and all the trades in which those concerned in the iron trade lay out their money increasingly, thrive in consequence. And these second and dependent trades quicken other third trades dependent on them, and so on through the industrial world. The first period of every industrial cycle is a period of immense new production, and of great prosperity running through and permeating all trades.

This period is also one of very high price. The loanable capital—the deposits which have accumulated in the years of depression—are then poured into trade. These have the effect of new money. They are a new purchasing power, which augments all prices dealt in, and especially the prices of wholesale articles, which are those upon which enterprise most acts, and in which speculation is quickest and most constant....

But elevations in price so caused are sure to have corresponding depressions, and any dilation of trade so caused is sure to have its corresponding contraction....

And though nothing can be more mischievous or more untrue than to hold and teach that each period of depression ends in or coincides with a panic, yet it is undeniably true that all such periods of depression are times of great difficulty....

...The panic of 1866 was the most formidable blow to credit and enterprise since 1825. The distrust which it occasioned was much deeper and larger than that of 1857, and somewhat greater even than that of 1847. The amount of unused savings which accumulated in the country after 1866 was much greater than at any previous period. And to this accumulation was added the stimulus given by long continued cheap corn—the greatest stimulus known to industry. The result was our past prosperity—that the country went forward, as Mr Gladstone expressed it, not by steps, but by 'leaps and bounds'.

The danger was very great that this sudden prosperity might be abused. To the mercantile community such periods have generally been very fatal; even wise and cautious heads are usually turned at such times. And to bankers and other distributors of loanable capital, such periods have been even more fatal still. The ordinary guides of bill-brokers and bankers are lost at such times. New people start into prominence with wonderful rapidity, and it is not easy to tell whether their apparent wealth is real or not....

In the case of the present period the danger is greater, because two checks have arisen which will probably diminish our prosperity. First the cause which stimulated trade—a cheapness and abundance in the food of the people—now is no longer likely to stimulate it. The last harvest in England was defective...in 1873, as far as we can see now, the conditions of the harvest all over Europe will be unfavourable....

Industry too is checked in an unusual degree by a rise in the price

13

of the great "instrumental articles", coal and iron. This diminishes profits, and so tends to produce a slackening of trade just when an augmentation in the price of corn would also tend to produce it.

If therefore we were to expect the usual course of the commercial cycle, if we were to expect that in 1873 'loanable capital' would become exceedingly scarce...the prospect of the coming year would not be happy, but very dismal....

We do not expect it....

2. TRADE RECESSION IN THE 1870's

Source: Robert Giffen, 'Essays in Finance, First Series', 5th ed., 1890, pp. 111–17.

Giffen was head of the statistical department of the Board of Trade from 1876 to 1897 and a well known economic writer of his day. In this essay, dated 1877, he was explaining to the businessmen of the late 1870's why the trade depression which they so much complained of had come about. He was countering, among other things, the common belief that prosperity and depression had been due to the Franco-Prussian war of 1870–1.

THE next important characteristic [*the first had been its universality*] of the depression, and, perhaps, the most important characteristic of all, appears to be that the conspicuous industry which has failed is that of the 'exploitation' of new countries with little surplus capital, and whose business is mainly that of producing raw materials and food for export, by old countries which have large surplus capital, and are largely engaged in manufacturing; in other words, the investment in new countries by the capitalists of old countries. Much bad business is brought to light in every depression; but it is the peculiarity of the commercial cycle, as we have noted, that there is a change from time to time in the favourite business, so that every period has its special trade development, and special trade disease. The favourite business for many years before 1873 had become that of foreign investment, and now the depression occurs where there was the greatest expansion....

The order of events in the crisis affords of itself a very striking confirmation of the assumption. The difficulties commenced in the countries more or less farmed by the capital of England and other old countries; whose industries are nourished by public loans from England,

and by the investment of private English capitalists within their territories, principally in the form of English iron and manufactures. The crisis in Austria, which was the first in the whole series, was a crisis in a country answering this description to some extent. To the United States, where the next great crash occurred, the description is still more applicable. The South American countries, whose prolonged suffering was the special feature of 1874, are almost a domain of England; and Russia, too, is largely 'developed' by English capital. Some of these countries, especially Austria and Russia, have not been exclusively dependent on English capital. They have also benefited by the accumulation of capital in Holland, Belgium, and France, which had been drawn largely to Germany before 1873, through the French indemnity, and had overflowed thence into Austria and Russia; but the indemnity payments, though they helped to precipitate and aggravate the crisis in Austria, did not alter the power of that crisis to react on England. No doubt, in 1873, as already noticed, the collapse of the foreign loan financing had been foreshadowed; but the anticipatory events of that year were in themselves comparatively unimportant, so that down to 1875 what chiefly happened was a succession of monetary and commercial crises in countries dependent on England, but from which England by comparison escaped. In 1875 these crises were succeeded by a crisis in England itself of very great intensity, naturally leading to a renewal of crisis and distress elsewhere, though not of actual panic, and the whole culminating in the financial disorders of the foreign loan collapses, which will probably form, in after years, the most conspicuous feature of the whole series of liquidations....

We have next to adduce in evidence the fact of the great expansion of the business of investment in foreign countries previous to the depression. The great multiplication of foreign loans in the period is now familiar. Not to speak of Turkish and other loans, which were so largely mere borrowings to pay interest, there was a loan of £32,000,000 for Egypt, after there had been large loans in 1868 and 1870; Chili [*sic*] in the same time (1867–73) borrowed £5,250,000; Peru, £24,000,000; Brazil, £10,000,000; Russia, £77,000,000; and Hungary, £22,000,000—exclusive of minor borrowings by guaranteed companies and otherwise. These were the nominal amounts of the loans, and the real money or money's worth ever transmitted to those countries in respect of them must have been much less; but, making all deductions, they indicate an immense direct credit opened up in this country in favour of the States named. The minor borrowings we have referred to were equally important, if not more important, and, especially in the case of the United States, the aggregate of small loans for railways and other purposes was immense. All this direct borrowing likewise implied a great investment of capital privately in foreign countries. Merchants and traders were induced to set up establishments abroad to facilitate the business which the loans brought into existence, and accommodate the wants of emigrants to the new fields of industry. The result was a luxuriant industrial growth in the new countries by means of this vast direct and indirect credit which old countries were giving. Thus in the United States, immediately before 1873, the length of the whole railway system had been doubled in seven years; in Russia almost the entire system of 12,000 miles has been created since 1868; in Austria there had been an increase from 2200 miles in 1865, to over 6000 miles in 1873; and in South America, Brazil, the River Plate Republics, Chili [*sic*], and Peru, had all been endowed with railways in a very few years—the loans for these countries above enumerated, and especially the above loan of £24,000,000 for Peru, being avowedly all for railways. And never was there a more rapid development of the foreign trade of the United Kingdom. The total import and export trade, which was £500,986,000 in 1867, had risen in 1873, or in six years only, to £682,292,000, or 36 per cent; and the trade per head from £16 1s. 3d. to £21 4s. 9d., or 32 per cent.... And in one or two trades the increase of business was even greater than the general increase. Thus the quantity of our iron and steel exports rose from 2,042,000 tons in 1868 to 3,383,000 tons in 1872, or 66 per cent in four years; while there was simultaneously a rise of price which made the increase in values immense, not only in these, but in other articles where there was no such increase of quantity.... The expansion of our foreign trade was thus manifestly in connection with the general expansion of our foreign investment business, and not the result of the accidental or temporary causes which have been assigned.

That there has been a most disproportionate stoppage of the foreign investment business, which would go far to account for the present depression, is also very obvious....There has also been a diminution of singular magnitude in our export trade. That trade has frequently fallen off in times of general depression, but never to such an extent as has lately been witnessed. The diminution altogether in the exports of home produce and manufactures has been from £256,257,000 in 1872 to £200,639,000 in 1876, the change being partly due as usual, and perhaps rather more than usual, to a fall in price, but only partially to that cause. There has not since the free trade period been such a decline in our foreign trade, just as there had been no previous example of so great an expansion. The decline has also been mainly in the exports to such countries as the United States, which had been our great borrowers—the falling off to the United States alone being from £40,737,000 in 1872 to £16,834,000 in 1876, this latter figure being the lowest since 1864. It has also been mainly in such articles as iron and steel; the exports of which diminished from 3,383,000 tons and £35,996,000 in value in 1872, to 2,224,000 tons and £20,737,000 in value in 1876; while the exports to the United States alone fell from 975,000 tons in 1872 to only 160,000 tons in 1876....

The embarrassments in the new countries were also connected with the excessive development of their capabilities which had been attempted. A very considerable amount of the railway and other speculation during the last few years, has been proved to have been wholly in anticipation of the wants of the world, the evidence of this being an over-production of raw materials and food, the characteristic products of the new countries. Of this over-production the most significant sign was the low price of wheat in 1875, notwithstanding the bad harvest of that year in several countries....The result of what appears to be excessive cultivation is an unremunerative price, which leaves merely agricultural communities in distress, and disturbs their whole system of industry....

3. AN OFFICIAL INQUIRY INTO TRADE DEPRESSION, 1886

Source: 'Final Report of the Royal Commission appointed to inquire into the Depression of Trade and Industry 1886,' C. 4893, XXIII, pp. xv, xxiii.

After the liquidations of the 1870's, trade and industry picked up again and ran through a new cycle, first of prosperity, then of depression, between 1879 and 1886. The return of serious depression at the end of these years upset business and political opinion and led to the appointment in 1885 of a royal commission, which reported in the next year. The holding of an inquiry of this sort was novel and disapproved of by strict adherents to the ideas of economic liberalism, for whom trade prosperity and depression were matters for business, not for government. The commissioners, headed by Lord Iddesleigh, a prominent although undistinguished politician of the day, had little difficulty in showing that the depression so much complained of by business men did not amount to a decline in national production and that it had in fact a number of remarkable features of its own.

This inquiry into trade depression, together with the Gold and Silver Commission of 1888 (no. 6) and two royal commissions on agricultural distress (nos. 9 and 10) helped to give the years from 1874 to 1886 and even those from 1874 to 1896 the somewhat misleading title of "the period of the Great Depression", conferred upon them by later historians. But depression was a word of special meaning within the limited circles of those who publicly debated economic questions in late Victorian times. It is certainly not to be identified with a decline in the real income of the nation as a whole. See the comment by Alfred Marshall in the next extract (no. 4) and H. L. Beales' critical essay, "The 'Great Depression' in Industry and Trade", 'Economic History Review' (October 1934), vol. v, no. 1, pp. 65–75.

W E may therefore sum up the chief features of the commercial situation as being—

    (a) a very serious falling off in the exchangeable value of the produce of the soil;

    (b) an increased production of nearly all other classes of commodities;

    (c) a tendency in the supply of commodities to outrun the demand;

    (d) a consequent diminution in the profit obtainable by production;

and (e) a similar diminution in the rate of interest on invested capital.

The diminution in the rate of profit obtainable from production, whether agricultural or manufacturing, has given rise to a widespread feeling of depression among all the producing classes.

Those, on the other hand, who are in receipt of fixed salaries or who draw their incomes from fixed investments have apparently little to complain of; and we think that, so far as regards the purchasing power of wages, a similar remark will apply to the labouring classes.

We must, however, point out that the displacement of labour, which is always proceeding owing to the increased use of machinery or other changes in the methods of production, cannot fail to create a certain amount of distress of a more or less temporary character among the working classes, who are naturally less able to adapt themselves to sudden changes than those whose capital is in a more moveable form. This distress, which is to some extent at all times inevitable, was aggravated during the last winter by the exceptional severity of the weather. On this point we may refer to the results of an inquiry instituted by the Local Government Board in the early part of the year, from which it would appear that the winter of 1885–86 was marked by a general want of employment such as has not been felt for five or six years.

The demand for labour must of necessity be always fluctuating and uncertain, and within the last year or two this irregularity has been more marked than usual; but, notwithstanding the occurrence of periods of temporary distress, such as that above referred to, we think that the statistics of pauperism and the increasing consumption of the commodities most in demand by the working classes prove that their thrift has increased, and that their general prosperity has not materially diminished in recent years.

. . . .

We have now reviewed the more prominent features of our commercial position, and the forces which have contributed to bring it about.

We have shown that while the general production of wealth in the country has continuously increased, its distribution has been undergoing great changes; that the result of these changes has been to give a larger share than formerly to the consumer and the labourer, and so to promote a more equal distribution; that the condition of the large class who depend upon the produce of the soil is unsatisfactory, and the number of the unemployed is a matter of serious importance; but that the general condition of the country affords encouragement for the future; that trade, though less profitable, shows little tendency to diminish in volume; but that owing to the nature of the times the demand for our commodities does not increase at the same rapid rate as formerly; that our capacity for production is consequently in excess of our requirements, and could be considerably increased at short notice; that this is due partly to the competition of the large amount of capital which is being steadily accumulated in the country, partly to the stimulus given to production by the events of 1870–71, which has been maintained longer than was warrented by the demand for commodities, and partly to a falling off in the purchasing power of at least one important section of the community; that our position as the chief manufacturing nation of the world is not so undisputed as formerly, and that foreign nations are beginning to compete with us successfully in many markets of which we formerly had a monopoly.

4. WHAT SORT OF DEPRESSION?
AN ECONOMIST'S COMMENT

Source: 'Official Papers by Alfred Marshall' (published for the Royal Economic Society) 1926, pp. 98–99.

Alfred Marshall (1842–1924), one of the best economists of his genera-tion, was a frequent witness at official investigations into economic affairs. In this instance, he was speaking, on 16 January 1888, to the members of the Gold and Silver Commission (see no. 6) and was answer-ing a question by Henry Chaplin, M.P.

9823. Do you share the general opinion that during the last few years we have been passing through a period of severe depression?— Yes, of severe depression of profits.

9824. And that has been during a period of abnormally low prices? —A severe depression of profits and of prices. I have read nearly all the evidence that was given before the Depression of Trade and Industry Commission, and I really could not see that there was any very serious attempt to prove anything else than a depression of prices, a depression of interest, and a depression of profits; there is that un-doubtedly. I cannot see any reason for believing that there is any considerable depression in any other respect.

5. THE PROBLEM OF ALTERING PRICE LEVELS

Source: Alfred Marshall, "Remedies for Fluctuations of General Prices", 'Contemporary Review', March 1887, reprinted in 'Memorials of Alfred Marshall', ed. A. C. Pigou, 1925, pp. 189–90, 192.

The long fall of prices between 1874 and 1896 was the subject of much discussion, both popular and expert. Alfred Marshall here states why he thought the problem of general stability of prices was important. The

*reasons he gives afford some clue to the nature of a debate which affected,
in more or less degree, almost every country in the Western world. In
the United Kingdom it led directly to a government inquiry illustrated
by the next extract, no. 6.*

M UCH of the importance of having a good standard of deferred
payments is peculiar to modern times. In early stages of civilization business arrangements seldom looked far ahead; contracts to
make definite payments at distant times were rare and unimportant.
But a good deal of our modern business life is made up of such contracts. Much of the income of the nation goes to its ultimate recipients
in the form of fixed money payments on Government bonds, on the
debentures of private companies, on mortgages and on long leases.
Another large part consists of salaries and wages, any change in the
nominal value of which involves great friction; so that as a rule the
nominal rate remains unchanged, while the real rate is constantly
fluctuating with every change in the purchasing power of money.

And lastly, the complex nature of modern trade and industry puts
the management of business into the hands of a comparatively small
number of men with special ability for it, and most people lend the
greater part of their wealth to others instead of using it themselves. It
is therefore a great evil that whenever a man borrows money to be
invested in his business he speculates doubly. In the first place, he runs the
risk that the things which he handles will fall in value relatively to others
—this risk is inevitable, it must be endured. But in addition he runs the
risk that the standard in which he has to pay back what he has borrowed
will be a different one from that by which his borrowing was measured.

We are vaguely conscious that an element of speculation is thus
unnecessarily introduced into life, but few of us, perhaps, realize how
great it is. We often talk of borrowing or lending on good security at,
say, 5 per cent. If we had a real standard of value that could be done;
but, as things are, it is a feat which no one performs except by accident.
Suppose, for instance, that a man borrows £100 under contract to
pay back £105 at the end of the year. If the purchasing power of
money has meanwhile risen 10 per cent (or, which is the same thing,
general prices have fallen in the ratio of ten to eleven), he cannot get
the £105 which he has to pay back without selling one-tenth more
commodities than would have been sufficient for the purpose at the

beginning of the year.... While nominally paying 5 per cent for the use of his money, he has really been paying 15½ per cent.

On the other hand, if prices had risen so much that the purchasing power of money had fallen 10 per cent during the year so that he could get £10 for things which cost him £9 at the beginning of the year—that is, £105 for things which cost him £94 10s. at the beginning of the year—then, instead of paying 5 per cent for the loan, he would really be paid 5½ per cent for taking charge of the money.

. . . .

A distinction must be made between fluctuations of general prices which come and go quickly and those whose period is long. Short-period fluctuations practically efface themselves when we compare the mean prices of successive decades, but are conspicuous when we compare prices in successive years. Long-period fluctuations do not show themselves clearly from year to year, but stand out prominently when the mean prices of one decade are contrasted with those of other decades.

6. THE GOLD AND SILVER COMMISSION, 1888

Source: '*Final Report of the Royal Commission appointed to inquire into the Recent Changes in the Relative Values of the Precious Metals 1888*' C. 5512, vol. XLV, pp. 1, 92, 104–5.

Falling prices were regarded by many, during the quarter century 1875–1900, as responsible in a general way for depression, both agricultural and industrial. This was misleading, for they were not inconsistent with economic development on the great scale. But the view was widespread among those whose living depended on the state of markets and who judged that state by current prices. The tendency of prices in general to fall was in turn attributed by many to monetary causes. This opinion seemed to have the sanction of the best economic analysts of the day, according to whom not only short but also long-term price movements might be the product of the current relation between the number of market transactions to be financed and the quantity of money available to make purchases. The quantity of money, in the gold-and-silver coin using society of Victorian England, was assumed to depend on the output of the precious metals. Hence the anxiety with which the British government examined in the 1880's, following the inquiry into trade depression, the values of gold and silver and their possible connexion with prices and depression.

Behind the royal commission of 1888 lay the urgings of a number of large and important interests. They were in particular the agricultural

*landowners in the United Kingdom, dismayed by the fall of agricultural
prices and rents; the government of India and British bankers and traders
interested in India and China, countries whose currencies were on a silver
standard. The heavy fall in the value of silver seriously inconvenienced
those who had important financial transactions to make across the exchanges between the gold-using West and the silver-using East. Silver's
depreciation finally led to the closing of the Indian mints to silver and
the abandonment of the silver standard by the government of India in
1893. The remedy proposed by these interests was an international
bimetallic standard, i.e. an international monetary standard which should
be neither gold standard nor silver standard but a gold-and-silver standard.
This would, bimetallists hoped, raise prices by rehabilitating silver as
legal tender and so adding to the world's stock of money.*

*These discontents died away in the late 1890's when prices began to
rise again, but they represented a powerful agitation in their day. For
some of the difficulties of British business in the East owing to the depreciation of the silver currencies, see Compton Mackenzie's 'Realms of Silver
One Hundred Years of Banking in the East' (1954). For the international monetary discussions of 1878, 1881 and 1892, H. B. Russell,
'International Monetary Conferences' (New York, 1898). For the
highly interesting contemporary silver agitation in the United States,
A. B. Hepburn, 'A History of Currency in the United States' (revised
edition, New York, 1924).*

[*Final Report—Part I*]

May it please Your Majesty, we, the undersigned Commissioners
appointed to inquire into the recent changes in the relative values of the
precious metals, desire humbly to submit to Your Majesty our final
Report upon the several matters which we have been directed to
investigate.

2. The recent changes above referred to have been of a twofold
character:

I. There have been extensive *fluctuations* in the relative values of
gold and silver.

II. There has been a considerable *fall* in the gold price of silver.

3. We are directed to inquire whether these changes have been caused
by (*a*) the depreciation of silver, or (*b*) the appreciation of gold, or (*c*) a
combination of both these causes; and further whether such depreciation or appreciation has been caused by (*a*) an increased supply of, or
diminished demand for, silver, (*b*) a diminished supply of, or increased
demand for, gold, or (*c*) a combination of two or more of these causes.

4. We are then directed to investigate the bearing of these changes upon the general interests of the United Kingdom and India; and finally if we are satisfied that such changes have been prejudicial to any of those interests, we are to suggest any remedies likely to remove or modify the evils which may be found to exist, without injustice to other interests, and without causing evils equally great.

. . . .

[Final Report—Part II, being the Majority Report]

138. Though unable to recommend the adoption of what is commonly known as bimetallism we desire it to be understood that we are quite alive to the imperfections of standards of value, which not only fluctuate, but fluctuate independently of each other; and we do not shut our eyes to the possibility of future arrangements between nations which may reduce these fluctuations.

One uniform standard of value for all commercial countries would no doubt, like uniformity of coinage or of standards of weight and measure, be a great advantage. But we think that any premature and doubtful step might, in addition to its other dangers and inconveniences, prejudice and retard progress to this end.

We think also that many of the evils and dangers which arise from the present condition of the currencies of different nations have been exaggerated, and that some of the expectations of benefit to be derived from the changes which have been proposed would, if such changes were adopted, be doomed to disappointment.

Under these circumstances we have felt that the wiser course is to abstain from recommending any fundamental change in a system of currency under which the commerce of Great Britain has attained its present development.

All which we humbly submit for Your Majesty's gracious consideration.

(*Signed*) HERSCHELL

C. W. FREMANTLE

JOHN LUBBOCK

T. H. FARRER

J. W. BIRCH

LEONARD H. COURTNEY

. . . .

[*Final Report—Part III, being the Minority Report*]

33. ...Failing any attempt to re-establish the connecting link between the two metals, it seems probable that the general tendency of the commercial nations of the world will be towards a single gold standard.

Any step in that direction would, of course, aggravate all the evils of the existing situation, and could not fail to have a most injurious effect upon the progress of the world.

A further fall in the value of silver might at any moment give rise to further evils of great and indefinite magnitude in India, while a further rise in the value of gold might produce the most serious consequences at home.

34. No settlement of the difficulty is, however, in our opinion, possible without international action.

The remedy which we suggest is essentially international in its character, and its details must be settled in concert with the other Powers concerned.

It will be sufficient for us to indicate the essential features of the agreement to be arrived at, namely—

(1) Free coinage of both metals into legal tender money; and

(2) The fixing of a ratio at which the coins of either metal shall be available for the payment of all debts at the option of the debtor.

35. The particular ratio to be adopted is not, in our opinion, a necessary preliminary to the opening of negotiations for the establishment of such an agreement, and can, with other matters of detail, be left for further discussion and settlement between the parties interested.

We therefore submit that the chief commercial nations of the world, such as the United States, Germany, and the States forming the Latin Union, should in the first place be consulted as to their readiness to join with the United Kingdom in a conference, at which India and any of the British Colonies which may desire to attend should be represented, with a view to arrive, if possible, at a common agreement on the basis above indicated.

36. We have indicated what appears to us to be the only permanent solution of the difficulties arising from the recent changes in the

relative value of the precious metals, and the only solution which will
protect this and other countries against the risks of the future....

． ． ． ． ． ． ．

All of which we submit to Your Majesty's gracious consideration.

(*Signed*) LOUIS MALLET
ARTHUR JAMES BALFOUR
HENRY CHAPLIN
D. BARBOUR
W. H. HOULDSWORTH
SAMUEL MONTAGU

7. RISING PRICES AND THE COST OF LIVING, 1912

Source: W. J. Ashley, 'Gold and Prices' (London, 1912), pp. 3, 10, 16–17.

William James Ashley, economist (1860–1927), discussed the rise of prices in the early 1900's at a time when it was beginning to influence very much the cost of living and the state of industrial relations. Like many contemporaries, he found the main cause in the supply of gold, i.e. additions to the world's monetary stock and its supposed influence upon credit since the gold discoveries in South Africa at the end of the nineteenth century. This was in tune with the economic thinking of Ashley's day, which tended to conceive of general and long-term price movements as the result of a plenty or a shortage of the precious metals, the basis of currency. No mention is made by him of investment or of great additions to the world's stock of real capital as a possible cause of rising prices. For an example of this very different line of argument, see no. 8.

THE extent of the rise of prices has recently been indicated by an interesting return issued by the great Co-operative Wholesale Society. This shows, for certain years from 1898 onward, the cost to the Society, at wholesale prices, of what it calls 'an average weekly family grocery order'. The order consists of 1 lb. bacon, 2 lb. butter, ½ lb. cheese, 12 lb. flour, ½ lb. lard, 1 lb. meal, 4 lb. sugar, ½ lb. tea. The secretary has been good enough to furnish me with additional figures for 1895 and 1896; and the whole series is as follows:

	d.			*d.*
1895	58·38		1908	70·61
1896	59·48		1910	72·38
1898	63·85		1911	71·00
1906	67·28			

The figures, it will be seen, for 1911 are 19 per cent above those for 1896; and this tallies exactly with the estimate of the Board of Trade as to retail food prices in London.

. . . .

Taking the prices of 1900 as 100, the Board of Trade's index number for 1896 is 82·2, and for 1911 109·3. This is a rise of some 24 per cent. Or we may take some other year or average of years for our starting-point. The price inquiries both of the American and Canadian Governments take the average for 1890–99 as their basis; and, if we follow their example, the rise by 1910 from the average of 1890–99 works out at 13 per cent. That the Board of Trade method does not exaggerate the rise is shown by the fact that the well-known index numbers of Mr Sauerbeck, based on a slightly different list of commodities, and with a different original starting-point, gives us a rise of 18 per cent. in 1910 as compared with 1890–99.

The statistics of other countries witness to the existence of a similar rise over the whole commercial world. Everywhere there has been an upward tendency, clearly distinguishable from fluctuations within the trade cycle.

. . . .

Brief cycles of trade, extending over seven to eleven years, have, as we have already seen, obviously a great deal to do with contemporary cycles of price. But this is not a case of cyclical fluctuations, but of a much more protracted lift upward of the price level, about which the short-period movements do but oscillate. Good trade cannot explain the movement since 1896 for the same reason that bad trade could not explain the movement before 1896. We did not suffer from continuously bad trade in the earlier period, and we have not enjoyed continuously good trade in the later.

In the business circles it is sometimes asserted that the rise of prices has been the result of a rise of wages. If this were so, one could expect that the fall from 1873 to 1896 was the consequence of a fall of wages. But we know that during that period money wages went up some 12 per cent in England, and that they also rose in the United States, Germany, and France. It requires but little knowledge of business conditions and of human nature to show us that wages are much more likely to lag behind than to precede prices; and this expectation has been confirmed by so much experience that it has become an economic commonplace. [*Ashley then draws attention to a chart showing 'the general course of wages in the United Kingdom', here omitted.*] This indicates that the movement of wages has fallen behind that of retail food prices since 1900, and of wholesale prices since 1903....

We are thus compelled to look round us, and ask what other big force can there have been which began to operate in the nineties, and has been working continuously ever since. Surely the only answer is the vast increase in the output of gold. That output began to increase from 1890 onward by a value of from two to four million pounds sterling a year; in 1897 the increase over the preceding year leapt up to seven millions, and in 1898 to ten millions more. It was checked by the South African War; yet in 1901–2 it remained well above what it had been in 1897. In 1903 its upward march was resumed; and in six years it reached its present figure of well over 90 millions annually, or between three and four times as much as the annual output during the forty years 1850–1890.

8. CAPITAL FORMATION—A CANADIAN VIEW

Source: 'The Rise in Prices and the Cost of Living in Canada 1900– 1914: a Statistical Examination of Economic Causes' (Statistical Branch, Department of Labour) Ottawa, 1915, pp. 17–20, 24–5, 28.

In a country like Canada, the connexion between prices and gold output after 1896 was less obvious than their relation with other things, especially the rapid economic development of the country and the con- nexion between this and the investment activity of Great Britain. The Government Statistician of the Dominion, R. H. Coats, offers his view, which treats gold as subordinate. He regarded general price movements as a part of the whole process of economic growth or stagnation. This point of view would now be accepted as a better approach to an understand- ing of the events of the period than the gold-explanation represented by Ashley (above, no. 7), although the latter view was dominant at the time. Coats supplied elaborate statistical material which is here omitted.

Outline of General Economic Conditions—Economic Trends and Prices

Now this [*the fact that in countries where prices have risen fastest, food prices have risen faster than other prices*] is very significant, for it yields a working hypothesis as to the nature and origin of the influences that have had the greatest effect on prices since 1896 and particularly during the past ten years. The period, speaking broadly, and with the purpose only of the most general characterization, has been one of great prosperity: 'good times' have been everywhere the rule. The immediately preceding period, on the contrary, was one of exceedingly 'bad times'—a period when, the world over, a bitter agitation was in progress against low prices (1896 saw the 'cross of gold' campaign in the United States.) The price rise, in fact, in its earlier stages was two-thirds reaction from the lowest level in over 100 years—lower even than during the great depression of the eighteen-forties. (Incidentally it may be added that at their highest, recent prices fall below those of 1870–1872, and still further below those of 1812–1815.) For a quarter of a century prior to 1896, supply had steadily gained on demand, until 'overproduction' brought on stagnation. Credit was exceedingly contracted. The situation worked its cure first and partially through a great increase in consumption. But this soon gave way to a more positive stimulus. A period of marked expansion set in, based as usual upon credit extensions. (To the exceptional financial conditions involved, reference will be made later on.) With agriculture once more on a paying basis, and with population rapidly increasing, there began early in the present century a great forward movement to extend the areas devoted to the production of foods and raw materials. Capital in large amounts began to flow from Great Britain, the home of investment funds, in the direction of the 'new' countries, notably, Canada, Argentina and Brazil. France sent large sums to Russia, Austria and Turkey. Germany made considerable investments abroad, notably in Austria and America. All the capital producing countries, including now the United States, spent large sums within their own boundaries mainly on industrial development. But it is with the export of capital by Great Britain during the past few years that we are here primarily concerned. Great Britain as above stated is not only the home *par excellence* of investment capital in general, but on account of her more adventurous financial policy is peculiarly the source of loans for the 'new' countries and is accordingly the major factor in the expansion as affecting Canada. Sir George Paish, Joint Editor of the London *Statist*, has estimated that since 1907 alone approximately $5,500 millions have been sent abroad from the British Isles, for investment primarily in undertakings having for their object the bringing into the international trade scheme of new productive areas.

It has been pointed out in some detail in the Introduction that prices reflect the general economic trend and that the phenomenon known as 'prosperity' or 'expansion' is almost invariably accompanied by a rise in prices. This is primarily because 'expansion' involves in the first instance a turning aside from the usual activities of production to the providing of additional 'plant' or 'equipment'. Equipment in the making does not 'produce' at all in the economic sense and not to full capacity often for long periods thereafter, being always planned to a degree against the future. Hence in the meantime a stimulating effect on general prices, seeing that the demand for materials and labour thus created has for the time being no offset in the form of additional supply. That effect is of course greatly aggravated when the new activity takes the form of opening up remote areas to settlement, with an extensive programme of railway construction, town building, road-making and general industrialization. Such operations are not only of the largest of their kind and thus the longest in becoming fully productive, but they are carried out in comparatively undeveloped communities, where the disturbance they create economically is at its maximum. Hundreds of millions may be expended on such enterprises in a highly industrialized country like England with little influence on prices, where a less expenditure in a small agricultural community would be followed by a considerable rise. It is important to note, therefore, that according to the observations of Sir George Paish, no less than four of the five and a half billions of capital above mentioned as having been exported from the British Isles since 1907 have been devoted to enterprises of just this character, namely, the construction of railway lines and municipal improvements in new countries, the countries to which Great Britain is looking more and more for her supplies of food and raw materials. Altogether 140,000 miles have been added to the railways of the world since 1900—an increase of 47 per cent—in new countries alone. The tonnage of vessels in the world has increased almost as rapidly.

Applying the above to the international price situation previously defined, it will be remarked that it is precisely where expansion has been in progress that the rise in prices has been accentuated, and especially where the expansion has been of the kind just mentioned. England, France, Belgium and Holland, have witnessed no revolutionary changes economically during the past decade and have maintained comparative stability of prices. These countries have, of course, added materially to their industrial resources, but the additions have been to systems already large and complex. Countries like Japan and Germany on the other hand, have gone forward industrially to a much greater relative degree, and the same is true of India, New Zealand and Australia, where prices have been considerably more buoyant than in the countries first named. Austria-Hungary is an example of a European country largely agricultural under process of rapid industrialization by imported capital; her prices have been very buoyant. In the United States the process of industrialization has, likewise, been exceedingly rapid since the beginning of the century. When therefore it is stated that of the great export of capital from Great Britain above described, a full quarter has been poured into Canada alone, making her second only to the United States as the field of British investments abroad, (the United States, Argentina, Brazil and India, being the countries next in order affected) and there devoted to a scheme of railway, municipal and industrial development on a scale without parallel in her previous experience, and without parallel relatively in any other country, it will not be a matter for surprise if in Canada is seen in maximum intensity the phenomenon always associated in an outstanding way with such a process, namely a great rise in prices. This, to repeat, is for the simple reason that upon the regions contiguous to areas under rapid development in this manner naturally falls the chief share in providing labour and materials for creating the new railways, towns, elevators, agricultural implements, etc. etc., which a process of the kind makes necessary.

. . . .

The Increase in Gold Production

The above brief analysis of the general situation leaves one factor in abeyance—gold. It is an old and orthodox view that the general level of prices is the result of a balance between the total amount of money and the total amount of commodities—or rather between the amount of the medium of exchange (taking into account its rapidity

31

of circulation) and the number and magnitude of the transactions it is called upon to effect—and that a great increase in the gold supply, through its influence on credits, sets in motion an industrial and trade boom precisely of the kind above described. Since the year 1890 the annual production of gold—the standard 'money metal' of practically the entire civilized world—has gone up from about 113 millions to about 460 millions, or nearly four times, (the result of the discovery of the cyanide process and its application chiefly in South Africa) with the result that the total accumulated stocks of gold available for monetary purposes have considerably more than doubled. This, as has been well said, 'almost bludgeons the understanding' into the belief that we have here the underlying cause of the rise in world prices—especially in view of the similar experience after the Australian and Californian discoveries and on other occasions.

But the primary purpose of this memorandum is to seek an explanation why prices have risen higher in Canada than in other countries like England and France. As above stated, the increased Canadian gold supply would not appear to have entered into that difference as a *primary* factor, seeing that it has been brought here largely because we have sought and obtained a plentiful supply of long-time credit abroad—the latter a product largely of reorganized financial apparatus. That the increased gold production, however, facilitated this movement, and that its effect has been to assist materially in the enlargement of world credits and in one way and another to stimulate the world-buoyancy, may be accepted.

CHAPTER 2

CHANGE ON THE FARM

Agriculture, the oldest occupation in Great Britain, was already in mid-Victorian times descending from the high position it had enjoyed at the beginning of the century, when it had supplied perhaps a third of the national income. By 1871 it had become far less important than mining, manufacturing and building as an earner of incomes. But it was an industry still retaining an immense social prestige and political influence, perhaps more appropriate to its old than to its new condition. It was also a vocal industry, given to discussing its state of health in public; and while it seldom felt itself to be really well, it was beginning towards the end of the 1870's to complain in a manner which caused even the more sceptical of its friends to take notice.

Agricultural questions in the last quarter of the nineteenth century in all western countries bore a certain common character but preserved at the same time the stamp of national history and institutions. The common character derived from influences which were felt throughout Europe: the rise in other continents of new and important sources of food supply, particularly in wheat and meat; the extension and cheapening of world communications by railway and steamship; the constant movement of people from the countryside into the cities, and the effect of these developments upon the general structure of farm prices and costs. But the existing systems of cultivation and of landholding varied greatly from country to country, so that the consequences of the great changes which were going on in world agriculture varied immensely.

In Great Britain, with the important exceptions of large parts of Ireland and Gaelic Scotland, the agricultural system of the mid-Victorian age had passed through a period of exceptional prosperity, lasting from the 1850's to the early 1870's. This was due partly to an increase in farming efficiency but even more to the growth of population, of city demand and incomes, at a time when the state of international communications did not allow of large food imports. Mentally, the industry was ill-prepared for the age of strenuous competition which followed. It possessed a structure of landholding for which there were few parallels in western Europe. Agricultural properties were largely concentrated in the hands of a relatively few men who, although great landowners, were not themselves the main cultivators of their estates. They let the land, or most of it, to substantial tenant farmers, who themselves put much money into their farms. The day-to-day cultivation was for the most part in the hands of a large class of agricultural labourers, who lived by their wages. There was plenty of room here for conflicts of interest if difficult times came.[1]

The impact of the great changes of the 1880's and 1890's was taken hard by many landowners and farmers, but not by all. Agriculture was less an industry than a bundle of industries, serving different markets, all making use of the soil but in many ways and for a variety of purposes. There were possibilities of growth and innovation, which the mid-Victorian agriculturist had already begun to explore.[2] Much of the farming history of the years 1870-1914 consisted of the transfer on a large scale of men, land and equipment from types of farming which no longer paid to those which did, above all from arable to stock farming. The depression was a time in which long-term technical and business changes were reshaping the structure of British agriculture, through the medium of those falling prices for products and those relatively fixed wages for labour, which many farmers and landowners found it hard to face. It was a period of severe hardship for some, of quiet prosperity for others and for all of unavoidable change.

The presence of influences which would take years to work themselves out was less easily seen and understood at the time than it is now. Over a long series of puzzling years, men had to sort out the long-term factors from the short, weather and bad harvests from American grain, animal and vegetable epidemics from Argentine herds, rail and sea freights from Indian silver currency. Much of the interest of the literature of the time lies in watching people adjust themselves to a fast-changing situation and in seeing what mistakes were possible. After 1900 a moderately prosperous and substantially altered farming emerged from the phase of painful transition, partly because prices recovered but mainly as a result of successful adaptation of the industry's methods and costs.

It is difficult for anyone who reads the discussions of the time not to feel that the complaints of depression arose from social as well as economic change. Questions of income are seldom distant from those

[1] See the interesting passage in the speech by Hartington, the heir to the Duke of Devonshire's estates, in the House of Commons on 4 July 1879, beginning vigorously, 'We talk about the land of this country going out of cultivation; Sir, I believe that to be utter nonsense. All that is meant is, that it cannot be cultivated under the present system, so as to return a profit to everyone concerned'. (*Hansard's Parliamentary Debates* 3rd Series, vol. 427, cols. 1527-8). Hartington did not expect serious conflicts of interest to arise, if the landlords as the directing class on the land did their duty.

[2] E. L. Jones, 'The Changing Basis of English Agricultural Prosperity 1853-73', *Agricultural History Review* (1962), pp. 102-119.

of status in a money-using society, which gets into the habit of judging men and things in money terms. So it was here. There was a feeling among the landowners and farmers who had held their heads high in mid-Victorian England that the agricultural interest was losing ground to manufacturing industry and to the city and that the special difficulties of the corn-growers among them were accelerating that decline. There certainly was a sharp fall in the position of agricultural incomes relative to those of the nation as a whole after 1870 as the industrialization of Britain became complete and countries abroad became more efficient at supplying her with foodstuffs in return for her manufactures. In early and mid-Victorian times, agricultural incomes had formed a substantial part of all British incomes. They had been about 20 per cent of the aggregate national income late in the 1860's, by the estimates of modern statisticians, but were no more than 8–9 per cent of it in the late 1890's and early 1900's. The decline in the proportion of the national income earned in agriculture after 1880 was greater than the decline in the number of persons occupied in the industry. This had the effect of opening up a disparity between the average income earned in agriculture and the national average of incomes per head. Late in the 1860's and in the early 1870's, the average income earned per head of persons employed in agriculture seems to have been about the same as the national average of all incomes. This parity of agricultural and other incomes never returned, partly because the exceptional agricultural rents and profits of the mid-century did not recur, partly because of the success of industry in improving industrial incomes of all kinds.[1] The consciousness of a relative decline in the national importance of agriculture, brought home in many ways, economically, socially, politically, was an important element in the impression among landowners and farmers in the last quarter of the century that a Golden Age was coming to an end.

These strong sentiments of nostalgia were not shared by the farmworker. His economic position, although still weak, had been strengthening both before and during the years of depression. This improvement took place at the expense of other groups living by agriculture, to the extent that the amount going to wages remained constant or slowly grew, while farm rents and profits suffered a check. The slow emergence of the great group of farm-workers and their families out of the deep poverty which had surrounded them in the early Victorian age was in its own unspectacular way one of the most impressive events of its time. It had little to do with trade union action, which was rare and not very successful. It was far more closely connected with one of the most constant features of Victorian society, the

[1] E. M. Ojala, *Agriculture and Economic Progress* (Oxford, 1952), pp. 128–9.

movement of people from country to town in the search for a better wage, a more congenial occupation and a freer life. This migration, bigger than any emigration to lands overseas, had been taking men from the farms and increasing the town population compared with that of the country since the early years of the century without, however, bringing about a fall in rural population, so quick was the increase in Victorian families. The attraction of the towns had created by the 1890's a relative scarcity of labour on the farms in many parts of the country, compared with the wasteful plenty of it in earlier years. This improved the bargaining position of the country labourer. It also caught many farmers in an economic scissors, between receipts which were falling and wage rates which were maintained, although even then too low to keep men on the land.

The same generation which saw a wide redistribution of farm resources between one product and another saw, therefore, also a striking redistribution of incomes between different social groups within the farming industry. The labourer's success in obtaining a greater share of the gross profit of agriculture, modest as it was, was resented by many of his employers who disliked both the improvement in his wage rate and the greater independence this gave him, so offensive to long-standing conceptions of rural rank and propriety. But it had to be accepted, for it was as unavoidable as American wheat. On the national stage, the changing economic position of the farmworker was one of the most striking proofs so far given of the enhanced value of labour brought about by the strongest process at work in British society in that era—the advance of industry and of the occupations and urban life that went with it.

Most of the documents here quoted deal with events in England and Lowland Scotland, where a strongly commercial and highly capitalized type of landowning and farming prevailed. The forces of economic and social transformation produced a more devastating effect in Highland Scotland and Ireland. Here were men farming at near subsistence level, without the resources or the knowledge to move easily from one style of production to another. Their economic problems were mixed in Ireland with issues of nationality and religion, a highly explosive compound in the days of Gladstone and Parnell. It is not possible here to do more than indicate the presence of the Irish and Scottish land questions, although they played a role for many years in British politics.

FURTHER READING

The standard account of British farming in the nineteenth century is still Lord Ernle, *British Farming Past and Present*, but it needs to be read in the sixth edition, in the light of the comment and bibliography supplied by one of its editors, O. R. McGregor. The history of agriculture in these years needs to be rewritten, by product, by farm and by district. For a model example of a critical monograph see the chapter by F. M. L. Thompson, 'Agriculture since 1870', in the *Victoria County History of Wiltshire*, vol. IV (1959). Essential statistics are to be found in E. M. Ojala, *Agriculture and Economic Progress* (1952).

A number of visitors from abroad recorded their impressions of British farming. An acute and well-informed observer in the 1890's was P. H. Koenig, *Die Lage der Englischen Landwirtschaft* (Jena, 1896). Englishmen, in their turn, visited the United States and watched with interest in the 1850's the vast expansion of mid-Western farming which was to mean so much for European farmers in the near future. Among the witnesses were James Caird, *Prairie Farming in America* (1859) and Richard Cobden, the Free Trade leader, whose *American Diaries* (Princeton, N.J. 1952) edited by Elizabeth Cawley, go back to the same year, 1859.

The stupendous changes in the world wheat market which followed the opening up of the American Mid-West and West and other granaries of the late nineteenth century, have been studied by W. Malenbaum, *The World Wheat Economy, 1885–1939* (Harvard University Press, 1954). They have also been the subject of valuable papers in the *Wheat Studies* of the Stanford University Food Research Institute: e.g. Helen Farnsworth, 'Decline and Recovery of Wheat Prices in the Nineties', *Wheat Studies*, X (1933–4), 289–352 and the same author's 'World Wheat Stocks 1890–1914 and 1922–1939', *ibid.* XVI (1939–40), 39–66 and 'Wheat in the Post Surplus Period 1900–1909, with recent analogies and contrasts', *ibid.* XVII (1940–1), 315–86.

On the drift of population from country to town, John Saville, *Rural Depopulation in England and Wales 1851–1951* (1957) is instructive; also the paper by Lord Eversley on 'The Decline in the Number of Agricultural Labourers in Great Britain', *Journal of the Royal Statistical Society*, vol. LXX (1907). On agricultural profits at this time, C. H. Feinstein, 'Income and Investment in the United Kingdom, 1856–1914', *Economic Journal*, vol. LXXI (1961). On agricultural rents, R. J. Thompson, 'An Inquiry into the Rent of Agricultural Land in England and Wales during the Nineteenth Century', *Journal of the Royal Statistical Society*, vol. LXX (1907). On the wages of agricultural labour, A. Wilson Fox, 'Agricultural Wages in England and Wales during the last Half Century', *ibid.* vol. LXVI (1903). On the land market, F. M. L.

Thompson, 'The Land Market in the Nineteenth Century', *Oxford Economic Papers*, New Series, vol. 9 (1957) and in a more general way, the same author, *English Landed Society in the Nineteenth Century* (1963).

9. COMPLAINTS OF AGRICULTURAL DEPRESSION, 1882

Source: 'Final Report from Her Majesty's Commissioners on Agriculture, 1882', C. 3309, vol. XIV, pp. 28–33.

Complaints of serious agricultural depression first began to be heard towards the end of the 1870's. The immediate causes were a run of bad seasons affecting the harvests, outbreaks of cattle and sheep disease, and a simultaneous inflow at the ports of agricultural products, especially from the United States, attracted by good prices in British markets. These conditions led to strong complaint from the more suffering and politically minded farmers, who demanded protection from foreign competition. This was refused them in 1879 by the Disraeli administration which, however, went so far as to set up a commission of inquiry in August of that year. This commission became known as the 'Richmond Commission' from the name of its chairman, Charles Henry Gordon-Lennox, sixth Duke of Richmond, an agriculturist and landowner. The commissioners, who also inquired into Irish agriculture, issued their report upon conditions in England and Scotland in 1882. An inconclusive document, it is chiefly interesting from the difficulty which the commissioners evidently felt, and which was shared by their contemporaries, in distinguishing between long-term trends in the industry, such as stretched back into the 1860's, and incidental events such as the outstandingly poor harvest of 1879. The findings of the commissioners and the debate which surrounded their activities led to an official step which might have been of more importance than it was, the establishment of the Board of Agriculture, the forerunner of the present Ministry of Agriculture and Fisheries, in 1889. The report was also followed in 1883 by an Agricultural Holdings Act designed to protect the interests of tenants under conditions when many of them were having to leave their farms. Now that tenants were becoming harder to get, the principle was allowed that an outgoing tenant who had improved the holding was entitled to compensation to the extent of the value of the improvement to the new tenant. In mid-Victorian times, custom and the law and the competition among tenants for holdings had favoured the landlord on this and other points.

IN obedience to Your Majesty's command, we now desire to report the conclusions at which we have arrived upon the effect of the evidence which has been submitted to us as to:

1. The depressed condition of the agricultural interest, and the causes to which it is owing;

2. Whether those causes are of a permanent character, and how far they have been created or can be remedied by legislation.

Whatever difference of opinion may exist as to the causes of agricultural depression, or as to remedies which be suggested for it, it will be observed that there prevails complete uniformity of conviction as to the great extent and intensity of the distress which has fallen upon the agricultural community. Owners and occupiers have alike suffered from it. No description of estate or tenure has been exempted. The owner in fee and the life-tenant, the occupier, whether of large or of small holding, whether under lease, or custom, or agreement, or the provisions of the Agricultural Holdings Act—all without distinction have been involved in a general calamity. It is important that this should be clearly understood, so that undue stress may not be laid upon suggestions for legislative changes, which, whether expedient or not, have no direct or immediate connexion with the distress of the present time.

The two most prominent causes which are assigned for that distress are bad seasons and foreign competition, aggravated by the increased cost of production and the heavy losses of live stock.

The extent to which agriculture has been injuriously affected by an unprecedented succession of bad seasons is very clearly shown by the abundant evidence to which we have referred in a preceding part of this Report....

Whereas formerly the farmer was to some extent compensated by a higher price for a smaller yield, he has had in recent years to compete with an unusually large supply at greatly reduced prices. Evidence to this effect has been already referred to under the head of 'Foreign Competition'.

On the other hand, he has had the advantage of an extended supply of feeding stuffs, such as Indian corn, linseed and cotton cakes, and of artificial manures imported from abroad.

Disastrous as the combined effect of bad seasons and foreign competition has been, the witnesses who speak in the interest of agriculture fully recognise the advantage to the community that food should be cheap. They contend, however, that the low price of agricultural produce, beneficial as it is to the general community, lessens the ability of the land to bear the proportion of taxation which has heretofore been imposed upon it.

Local Taxation

The history of the various imposts that are now levied for local purposes is very fully given in the evidence to which we have already referred. The first and the most important of these is the rate for the relief of the poor. [*The Commissioners were of the view that part of the cost of the poor rate should be borne, either by a contribution from the central government, or by local personal property, and that a certain proportion of local taxes should be assigned to local authorities in aid of local expenditure.*] . . . .

Agricultural Labour

The difficulties of farmers during the last few years have been greatly aggravated by the condition of agricultural labour.

Owing to a variety of causes, labour has been more costly and less efficient, so that the average labour bill of an arable farm is at least 25 per cent higher at the present time than it was some 20 years ago.

This condition of things is undoubtedly attended with serious embarrassment to the agricultural interest.

So far as the high price of agricultural labour results from the competition of other industries it must be accepted, just as the low price of agricultural produce must be accepted as the effect of foreign importation.

While the difficulties of the farmers have been thus increased, higher wages and more general employment have proportionately improved the condition of the labourer. It is most satisfactory to be assured that the labouring class has been scarcely, if at all, affected by the distress which has fallen so heavily upon owners as well as occupiers. Provisions have been cheap and employment abundant, while wages in a few districts only have been slightly reduced. . . .

Agricultural Education

We have received a good deal of evidence upon the subject of agricultural education in Great Britain and foreign countries, and the desirableness of encouraging scientific together with practical instruction has been urged by several witnesses.

We concur in these opinions, and, whilst we are not prepared to suggest the manner in which this instruction should be supplied, we are of opinion that the subject is well worthy of consideration. . . .

Rent

It has been suggested in the course of this inquiry that for many years previous to 1875 rents had been unduly raised. The weight of evidence, however, satisfies us that such a practice was exceptional, especially on large estates, and might be attributed in a great measure to imprudent competition on the part of tenants....

Cultivation of Land

Among the suggestions that have been made for the amelioration of the prospects of the tenant farmer, the extension of the growth of market garden crops on a portion of the farm, and as a part of one or more of the courses in the usual rotation, deserves notice. The extent to which this suggestion is applicable varies necessarily in different country districts; but it seems probable that on some farms, hard fruit, and the less tender kind of vegetables might be grown to advantage, if sufficient capital were applied to the fertilisation and cultivation of the land, and an adequate amount of attention were given to the management of the crops. But the success of husbandry of this description must mainly depend upon suitability of soil and climate, as well as upon facility of railway carriage and proximity to large centres of population. Where these conditions are wanting, small farming, the *petite culture* of continental countries, has but slight chance of success.

Dairy Farming

There appears to be a general agreement that although agricultural depression has been less intense in dairy than in arable districts, the yield of milk was much diminished, and the quality deteriorated owing to the inferiority of grass due to the continuance of wet weather during the past few years.

The price of ordinary cheese has been seriously lowered by unusually large imports from abroad.

Sufficient attention does not appear to have been hitherto devoted to first-class dairy products, and thus many dairy farmers have suffered considerably.

The production and sale of milk are largely on the increase; it is now sent by railway in considerable quantities to London and other populous centres, and this branch of farming is assuming much larger proportions. The growing demand for milk has apparently had great influence in directing the attention of landowners and farmers to the importance of dairy farming as possibly a profitable branch of husbandry, and to the desirableness of laying down land to grass....

Compensation for Unexhausted Improvements

We are of opinion that notwithstanding the beneficial effects of the Agricultural Holdings Act,[1] there are many parts of Great Britain in which no sufficient compensation for his unexhausted improvements is secured to the tenant. In many cases landlords have not offered, and tenants have omitted to ask for the fair compensation which we believe it is the interest of both that the tenant should enjoy, and to which we think he is entitled....

Upon the most careful consideration of the evidence before us, we have arrived at the conclusion that further legislative provision should be made for securing to tenants the compensation to which they are equitably entitled in respect of their outlay, and we recommend that the principles of the Agricultural Holdings Act relating to compensation should be made compulsory in all cases where such compensation is not otherwise provided for....

Railway Rates

In a preceding part of this Report we have directed attention to the complaints of producers, not only of the inequality of railway rates as affecting home producers, but of the still more serious disadvantage arising from preferential rates for foreign commodities.

The present law clearly contemplates that similar treatment should be accorded to similar goods carried under similar conditions, but the evidence before us shows that in many cases such equality does not exist; and we would recommend that the law should be so amended as to provide a cheap and speedy means of securing the equality contemplated by the existing law.

We are not, however, prepared to recommend that railway companies should be debarred by legislative enactment from offering special terms for through traffic from abroad.

[1] [*The reference is to the Agricultural Holdings Act, 1875. Ed.*]

Minister of Agriculture

With reference to the appointment of a Minister of Agriculture, we believe that a system corresponding to that which prevails in foreign countries would be attended with advantage, and we recommend that the administration of all matters connected with agriculture should be vested in one public department.

In submitting to Your Majesty the preceding recommendations we desire, in conclusion, to observe that:

Of the immediate causes of agricultural depression it cannot be said that any one of them is necessarily of a 'permanent character'. Bad and good seasons appear to come in cycles, and with them alternations of agricultural prosperity or depression.

This, the main cause of depression, no legislation can control.

How far foreign competition may affect the home producer in the future it is impossible to calculate with any degree of certainty. That its effect will continue to be felt may be assumed as certain. . . .

We have already indicated various matters upon which legislative interference can benefit directly the agricultural classes of this country. But no interference between classes, between owners and occupiers, or between employers and labourers, can render any one of them independent of the other. We cannot recall a period in our history in which the relations of these classes have been more severely tried than during the existing depression. Owners have, as a rule, borne their share of a common calamity, and they, as well as occupiers, have done much to avert the distress from the class who are least able to bear it. It is satisfactory to know that, as we have already observed, upon the labourer it has fallen more lightly than upon either owner or occupier. The best hope for the prosperity of agriculture lies in the mutual confidence and friendly relations of the three classes directly engaged in it, and in the common conviction that their interests are inseparable.

10. THE AGRICULTURAL PRICE-FALL

Source: 'Final Report of Her Majesty's Commissioners appointed to inquire into the subject of Agricultural Depression,' 1897, C. 8540, vol. xv, pp. 43, 52–3.

Renewed depression of agricultural prices, especially for wheat, led in the 1890's to a demand that "something should be done" for agriculture. A new commission of inquiry was appointed in 1893 by the fourth Gladstone administration and sat under the chairmanship of Lord Eversley, a noted Liberal politician. The commissioners grasped the importance of the price-fall of the previous twenty years. Nor does it appear from later estimates of agricultural income, uncertain as these are, that they were substantially mistaken in thinking that agriculture as an industry had become relatively unprofitable, compared with the exceptional prosperity of mid-Victorian times.[1] But they were divided among themselves on policy and their practical recommendations lacked clarity and distinction. The influence of those who were losing money on arable farming and arable land seems to have been strong among them[2] and secured the Agricultural Derating Act of 1896, which remitted one half of the farmer's rates. This was no more than a palliative. As a remedy, it was out of scale with the transformation coming over the agricultural industry, which required a more scientific and economical use of its resources both in the way of men and land. The protection demanded by many corn growers was deemed impossible, perhaps undesirable too. In this extract, lengthy footnotes referring to the evidence before the Commissioners have been omitted.

ONE conclusion which cannot fail to be drawn from a perusal of the evidence before us, is that among all classes of agriculturists there is a consensus of opinion that the chief cause of the existing depression is the progressive and serious decline in the prices of farm produce. So unanimous has been the testimony from nearly all parts of the country on this point that we consider it unnecessary to quote from the general statements of individual witnesses on the subject, but we propose to deal in some detail with the statistics of prices which have been put before us in the course of our inquiry....

[*The Commissioners, after discussing the evidence for falling prices as regards different agricultural products, cereals, meat, wool, dairy produce and so forth, came to this verdict.*]

Conclusions

Summarizing briefly the facts demonstrated in the foregoing paragraphs, we have arrived at the following general conclusions:

[1] Table 4 in C. H. Feinstein, 'Income and Investment in the United Kingdom 1856–1914', *Economic Journal*, LXXI (1961), 384.

[2] On this, see T. W. Fletcher, 'The Great Depression of English Agriculture 1873–1896', *Economic History Review*, XIII (1961), 427–31.

(a) That the changes in the prices of grain during the past 20 years represent a fall of over 40 per cent in the three staple cereals, and over 50 per cent in the case of wheat.

(b) That in the price of beef there has been in the same period a fall ranging from 24 to 40 per cent according to quality.

(c) That the prices realised for mutton since 1882–84 have exhibited a progressive decline of from 20 to 30 per cent.

(d) That there has been a fall in the price of wool amounting to upwards of 50 per cent during the past 20 years.

(e) That dairy produce has participated in this depreciation, and that, taking the changes in the prices of milk, butter, and cheese as a whole, there has been a fall approaching 30 per cent.

(f) That the fall in the staple products already referred to has been accompanied by a decline of at least 20 to 30 per cent in the price of potatoes.

(g) That although there have been fluctuations in the prices of hops, they have exhibited in recent years a general tendency to fall to an unprofitable level.

One of the gravest features of the depreciation which has been so manifest in the course of prices of agricultural products during the period under review has been its persistency.

II. FARM LOSSES ON THE CORN-LANDS

Source: James George Cornish, 'Reminiscences of Country Life' (1939), pp. 62–3, 83, 85–90.

These recollections of agricultural depression in the 1870's and 1880's come from a country rector, who had been brought up as a boy and young man in the parish of Debenham, on the Suffolk heavy clay, and at Childrey among the downlands of North Berkshire. They suggest both how genuine depression was in such wheat-and-barley and corn-and-wool districts and how farmers and landowners adapted themselves, in one way or another, to the new conditions.

Now when the hard times came [*in Suffolk*] the wiser men weathered the storm while the unwise were wrecked. The former had been saving money during the good years and could draw on their bank balances. They had lived quietly and so needed to make little change in their home budget and they had not more land to farm than they could attend to well. With lower rents and extra care they managed to make both ends meet. One new thing many of them now began: namely, the keeping of accounts. Formerly their bank passbooks were the sole record they possessed, and not one in ten had the foggiest notion of whether the corn or the cattle or the poultry were *each* paying their way.

...Economy, careful attention, and the keeping of accounts pulled them through many hard years. The personal factor in success comes to the fore when difficulties and changes arise in agriculture, and this was shown in the fact that every here and there a man was able to increase the area that he farmed with profit. There was more than one man in our district who succeeded in this way. How he did it is not easy to say, but the following is an attempt at explanation. If there be four men in the parish all quite competent to carry on one farm each, not more than one of them will have the character and ability to succeed with two farms, and as for running three farms at a time, I should say that not one man in ten can do it....

The many years of plenty for the farmers and landowners [*in Berkshire*] had ceased in 1883, but one heard much about those times when corn and wool fetched such high prices and labour was so plentiful and cheap. In the 'sixties many of the tenants who rented large farms under good landlords made great profits, and not a few of them saved money steadily. Even in the 'seventies many were still thriving. 'I never can put by two thousand a year', one of them said to his Parson in a moment of confidence. 'They did not have to make money, it was brought home and shot down at their doors', was a remark I heard later when it was most difficult to make farming pay. It was like the good times in Suffolk on a more lavish scale. The contrast between the lot of the owners and farmers on the one hand and the labourers on the other was too great; for bread and sugar and tea were all dear....

When the parish of Childrey was 'Enclosed' early in the nineteenth century and the holdings of land consolidated, the Rector was given 'an allotment of land in lieu of tithes'...no doubt both the Rector and the landowners were pleased with the arrangement. No less than 540 acres were assigned to the living, about sixty acres of meadow land in the Vale [*of White Horse*], a small portion of the best Black Land, a long strip of White Land up to the Downs, and a great stretch on the hilltop. Up there stood a barn and cottage; under the hill the farmhouse and its buildings; and another great barn close to the Rectory. For many years the Rectory of Childrey was most comfortably endowed, for the rent of the farm was once as much as £1000 a year....

There were many anxious years for my father while great stretches of the glebe-land lay waste and only the meadows and the best of the arable were let, and if his upbringing as the son of a Devonshire landowner had not taught him how to manage land even his courage could not have taken us through those lean years....

...The area of unlet farms extended far and wide in the Down country, and the landlords must either allow them to be waste or work the farms themselves. There was no money to spare for repairing cottages and they deteriorated fast....

Lord Wantage[1] took the keenest interest in farming and kept a large area of land under his own control. When the hard times came and tenant after tenant gave notice to leave, he resolved not only to farm the land himself but even to increase the yield from it. Three things were absolutely needful for success: courage, capital, and ability, and Lord and Lady Wantage possessed all of them. But all three might not have been enough had they not also known how to choose the right man for their various parts....Gradually he took in hand 6000 acres of Lockinge, Ardington and West Hendred, and before many more years had passed the area on the Downland was equally large. At the head of this vast undertaking was Mr C. H. Eady, with a sub-agent for the hill-farms and a foreman, John Robey by name, to superintend the lower land.

12. ARE THERE ALTERNATIVES TO WHEAT?

Source: Henry P. Dunster, 'How to Make the Land Pay' (1885), pp. 1–4.

There was a disposition among many farmers and landowners to regard wheat as a staple of farming for which there could be no substitute

[1] [*Robert James Lindsay, Baron Wantage (1832–1901), whose career is here briefly mentioned by J. D. Cornish in a footnote, was a soldier who had served in the Crimea and been awarded the Victoria Cross. He married the heiress of the banker, Lord Overstone, became a leading agriculturist in Berkshire and one of the founders of Reading University. Ed.*]

and the existing pattern of land-use as something which could not be changed without loss. But there were also men in the country districts who pointed out that, given the circumstances of Great Britain, the possibilities of profitable innovation in agriculture were far from having been exhausted. Henry Dunster, one of the many who wrote at this time about farming and its problems, lived in a corn-growing county, being vicar of Wood-Bastwick, in Norfolk. He was one of a number of country clergymen who displayed a keen practical concern for agriculture, with which their own interest as well as that of their parishioners was bound up.

THAT the growth of wheat in this country at the present low prices, induced by foreign competition, is unprofitable alike to landlords and tenants is acknowledged by every one; and there are few persons who are not prepared to admit that these low prices will be permanent...on the general run of farms in England one or more substitutes must be provided, either wholly or partially, for unprofitable wheat. In the several industries here dwelt upon, it is hoped that some compensation may be found for losses sustained by foreign competition in this particular product, which hitherto has been regarded as the most important and best paying of the farm crops.....

It is a very common, but faulty objection, when any substitute for unprofitable wheat is proposed, to urge that the country would be overdone with that particular product, as if wheat everywhere would cease to be grown, and as if that one product would everywhere and wholly take the place of it. Whoever will give himself the trouble to consult the yearly returns issued by H.M.'s Custom House, will find that a sum of money little short of thirty-eight millions is being paid yearly to foreigners because our farmers do not provide a sufficiency, viz:

	£
Bacon and ham	9,539,039
Pork, salted and fresh	729,041
Poultry and game	591,064
Butter	11,505,015
Cheese	4,739,664
Eggs	2,731,332
Lard	2,079,719

Vegetables

	£
Chicory	55,016
Hops	891,560
Onions	437,447
Potatoes	1,582,938
Tares	125,286
Vegetables unenumerated	363,741

Fruits

Apples	552,385
Nuts	397,007
Fruit preserved without sugar	123,533
Ditto raw unenumerated	1,261,477
Ditto dried unenumerated	185,828

In addition therefore to the present home produce an amount valued at nearly thirty-eight millions of money of the above-named commodities must be forthcoming before the home supplies can ever satisfy the present demand of the home markets; and this demand, it must be remembered, is ever on the increase. The effects of this increase have long been showing themselves in increased and increasing prices. Upon this point it is instructive to notice that while wheat, in consequence of foreign competition, has been falling in price, all these other items of farm produce viz. butter, cheese, bacon, eggs etc., notwithstanding foreign competition, have been advancing. And that the demand for such items will continue to increase is certain, for the customers of these particular commodities increase in numbers so rapidly, that it has been calculated on the best authority, from the data of the last census, that our city populations will double themselves in the next forty years, and our rural population in fifty.

13. CHANGING USES OF THE SOIL

Source: R. H. Rew, 'An Agricultural Faggot' (1913), pp. 36–7.

Fortunate in soil and climate, with capital at its disposal and great city markets at its door, much English and Scottish agriculture had adapted itself successfully to the great changes in the market for agricultural products by the end of the century. As some types of farming ceased to be profitable and other types took their place, a widespread alteration took place in the use of agricultural land. The general nature of the movement was already clear by the 1890's. This particular statement is from a paper read to the Farmers Club in December, 1897. It is worth noticing that in the opinion of Rew, whose knowledge of the agricultural industry was great, the changes he is referring to had been going on since the middle years of the century. In this he was undoubtedly correct. Henry Rew (1858–1929), one of the best agricultural statisticians of his time, became Secretary of the Central Chamber of Agriculture in 1890 and joined the staff of the Board of Agriculture and Fisheries in 1898.

THE change which has taken place during the past half-century might perhaps be concisely summed up by saying that the balance of power has shifted from the corn grower to the stock breeder and the dairy farmer. In some calculations which I made in 1895 I estimated the annual receipts for the farm crops of the United Kingdom at £64,000,000, for meat and live stock at £89,000,000, and for dairy products and eggs at £41,000,000. The development of stock-breeding has been very great, in spite of the disastrous and discouraging effects of outbreaks of rinderpest, foot-and-mouth disease, pleuro-pneumonia and other diseases. The increase in the national herds and flocks has been already noted, but still more remarkable has been the improvement in their general character. Among the sciences to which agriculture has been indebted mention should be made of physiology and, particularly, veterinary science. To a fuller grasp of scientific principles is probably attributable the great development of early maturity, and consequently of economical meat production. It is sometimes doubted whether a knowledge of the principles of breeding farm stock has really advanced greatly beyond what was known and practised by Collings, Bakewell, and other heroes of the last century, but there can be no doubt whatever that there has been a wide diffusion of knowledge and a general levelling-up of the character of the farm stock of the country. One striking fact—at once a cause and an effect of this tendency—is the multiplication of societies for the publication of breed registers and the protection of the interests of particular breeds. The Shorthorn Herd Book dates from 1822 and the Hereford Herd Book from 1845, but with these exceptions and that of the Thoroughbred Stud Book, I believe all the present breed-register societies have come into existence since 1846, and most of them within the last twenty years.

The extension of dairying has been alluded to, but mention might also be made of the equally remarkable development of other branches of farming, which fifty years ago would hardly have been recognised as coming within the scope of agriculture, such as the cultivation of fruit and vegetables, and the keeping of poultry.

14. THE COST AND STATUS OF AGRICULTURAL LABOUR

Source: 'Royal Commission on Labour; General Report on the Agricultural Labourer by Mr W. C. Little, 1893–4', C. 6894-xxv, vol. XXXVII, part II, paras. 5, 104–5, 377, 381.

The setting up of a Royal Commission on Labour under the chairmanship of the Duke of Devonshire,[1] by the Salisbury administration in 1891, was a consequence of the labour unrest of the late 1880's and of current political concern. The commissioners devoted most of their time to labour and industrial relations in mining and manufactures. But they also carried out the fullest inquiry into labour in farming since the commissioners who had examined the employment of children, young persons and women in agriculture in the years 1867–70. The investigators of the early 1890's found that in the past twenty years the farm-worker and his wife had strengthened their bargaining position against agricultural employers, not so much by anything that others had been able or willing to do for them as by their own incessant search for alternative employments for themselves and their children. W. C. Little, writing the report, did not share the opinion of some employers that this was a bad thing. He saw that it brought stresses and an altering system of industrial relations.

IT is no exaggeration to say that in the quarter of a century which has elapsed since the inquiry of which I have been speaking was in progress, [*the reference is to the government inquiry into the employment of children, young persons, and women in agriculture of 1867 and the years immediately following*] a quiet economic revolution, accomplished with little aid from legislation, has transferred to the labourers from one-fourth to one-third of that profit which the landowners and farmers then received from the cultivation of the land.

. . . .

The fact that less labour is generally employed on farms cannot be disputed, and the main causes of the decrease are not in doubt. What is disputable is the share which each cause has had in bringing about the result.

[1] Spencer Compton Cavendish, eighth Duke of Devonshire (1833–1908), a former leader in the Liberal party, had joined forces with the Conservatives over Irish Home Rule a few years before, in 1886.

I venture to express the opinion that a change in the system of farming in all the arable districts of the country was originated by the agricultural lock-out of 1874. Farmers were then compelled to sub-stitute machinery for manual labour wherever possible, and they were induced to lessen the area of those crops which required most labour.

The great rise of wages which then occurred led farmers to employ fewer men and to leave undone all work which could be abandoned. The period was one of great unrest, and many labourers left their native villages and either emigrated or were absorbed in the town populations.

The wet and disastrous seasons of 1878–1881...and since that time a still lower general level of prices of cereals has augmented the difficulties of farmers, and reduced the volume of demand for labour.

It is undoubtedly the opinion of many persons that want of employ-ment was the cause of the labourers migration to the towns, but I venture to maintain...that the reduction of the working staff on farms was the consequence, and not the cause, of migration.

. . . .

Mr Chapman [*one of the Assistant Commissioners who had gone out into the districts*] reports as follows:

'The relations of employers and employed are marked everywhere by a want of cordiality, and in a great many places by mutual suspicion. The familiar and quasi-patriarchal terms upon which farmers used to live with their men are fast giving way to mere contractual relations. Things are at present in a transition stage; farmers resent the notion of men being independent of them and dread being left in the lurch at busy seasons. They begin to see that nothing but money will keep a man upon a farm, and money is more than ever difficult to get....'

Mr Aubrey Spencer states his conclusions on the point in the follow-ing terms:

'In all the districts visited labourers were said to be more "indepen-dent" than they used to be, by which is meant, I think, that they regard their relation to the farmer more in a strictly commercial light than they used to, and that the quasi-family tie which used to exist between farmer and labourer has nearly ceased to exist. I do not, however, gather that there is much real hostility....'

It need be no matter of surprise if what I had previously described as an economic revolution has disturbed and dislocated the old ties which formerly connected the employers and employed. The farmer has been losing ground; while the labourer has been advancing the resources of the employer have diminished. The labourer has been able to make better terms for himself, to reduce the hours of work, and, as is generally alleged to be the case, he works less diligently than formerly; his ideas have been expanded, and his demands have increased; he will not be contented with what his father accepted, and, if he consents to remain an agricultural labourer, he exacts conditions which his employer finds it difficult to comply with.

15. SPLENDOUR AND MISERIES OF LIFE ON THE LAND, 1901–2

Source: H. Rider Haggard, 'Rural England' (1902), vol. I, pp. 135–6, 148–9, 287–8, 298, 335, 344, 349–50, 462–3, 465–6, 509–11; vol. II, pp. 186, 259, 267–8, 279–80.

Henry Rider Haggard (1856–1925), best known as a novelist and the author of 'King Solomon's Mines' (1885), was also a landowner and farmer, at Ditchingham, in Norfolk. His agricultural researches were connected with his views on social and political questions and with the so-called 'flight from the land', which at the turn of the century aroused concern in many circles, for a number of reasons. His 'Rural England' represented the product of personal inquiries in twenty-six English counties. It is not a work of systematic analysis but a series of personal impressions. For Haggard's life and personality, see Lilias Rider Haggard, 'The Cloak that I Left' (1951).

Sussex

My general conclusion on this district is that were it not for the fowl industry, and for the fact that many rich men from London occupy large houses, which absorb much produce at a good price, it would go very hardly both with tenants and with landlords. As it is, the latter are much crippled, while, save in exceptional instances, the farmers make no more than a bare living. Those who are left of the labourers, however, are more prosperous than their class has ever been before.

Kent

I had a very interesting conversation with Mr Wacher, of the firm of Messrs Cooper and Wacher, who for many years has had to do with the management of estates in the district. He estimated the average fall since 1875 in the rental value of land at 33 per cent and in the fee simple value at 50 per cent, instancing farms. . . .

As regarded the landlords, he was of opinion that they were 'like the eels which are said to grow accustomed to being skinned'. They had resigned themselves to their misfortunes. . . .

On the whole, farmers of fruit, hops, and stock were moderately prosperous. He thought that the best of them might perhaps make rent, interest on capital, and a living, but that none did more. . . . Labour he believed to be very scarce everywhere, and although there were some good men to be had near the towns, their number was few.

Herefordshire

Herefordshire has always been famous for its fruit, and of late the culture of strawberries has been added to its industries. For the actual profits of this crop I must rely upon the information given me by growers. . . . One gentleman, a large farmer, told me that in 1900 from six and a half acres of strawberries he netted £200 clear profit. Another plot of sixty acres was said to have produced 150 tons, which sold at £25 a ton, the net profit on this parcel amounting to £1500. How often does an ordinary cultivator of the soil clear £1500 profit in these days, even from a farm of, let us say, 1000 acres. . . . My question leads to another. How many English farmers can grow a strawberry, or, being ignorant, will take the trouble to learn the craft?

. . . 'Labour', said one, 'is becoming scarcer and scarcer. . . . The tenant farmer, even in the face of reduced rents, complains bitterly, and seems to have lost heart.' 'Labour', said another, 'is very scarce, days shorter, men more independent, women and boy labour almost nil.' 'Labour', declared Mr Britten, whose opinion is perhaps as valuable as that of anybody in the county, 'is very short. The position is most acute.'

Worcestershire

In the course of my stay in these Western Midlands I had the great advantage of inspecting the accounts, carefully kept over a number of years, of a very large grower of hops. . . . Now comes the amazing part of the statement. The average profits of the previous ten or twelve years, after deducting every charge and providing for every expense, amounted to something over £30 an acre net. Until I had seen these incontestable figures, I confess I would not have believed that anything which the land could grow in England, was capable of producing so splendid a return.... I believe also, although for this I have but a general authority, that similar profits are earned by sundry other growers....

[*Vale of Evesham*] The usual results of high culture on small-holdings are not wanting in this instance—general prosperity and an increase of population. Thus the census returns for 1901 of the Evesham Union show that the population has grown from 13,891 in 1841 to 17,629 in 1901, the increase over the return of 1891 being 1560, and this in the face of the fact that a good many of the purely rural parishes show a decrease. The general prosperity cannot be doubted—it is borne witness to by the numbers of comfortable homesteads and the hundreds of plots of highly tended gardens.

The present depression would doubtless cause a check, but this, he thought, [*Mr Jones 'the well-known Evesham fruit expert' speaking*] would right itself in another year or so. The market for apples and pears was splendid, and it was only lately that they had come to appreciate the value of their soil, both as regards aspect and protection from the east. Also the average price of fruit during the last ten years was higher than it had ever been before. Mr Jones added that he introduced tomato-growing for market purposes into Evesham in 1887, and had grown them ever since with but one failure.

Essex

I believe the Hon. Edward Strutt, who manages the large Essex estates of his brother, Lord Rayleigh, to be one of the most skilful farmers in England. Certainly in the course of my somewhat extended experience I have met no one who impressed me as being quite so thoroughly master of his business, or, I may add, so successful in combating the difficulties of the times and prices. Of course there are reasons for this success. To begin with, he farms an enormous extent of land, in all some 10,000 acres, most of which is in excellent heart.... Further, there is no lack of capital; also London, which lies within thirty miles, furnishes a ready market for all sorts of produce, and especially for that of the cows, of which about 700 are kept.

Its true inner cause in my opinion, however, is to be found in the agricultural talent—if I may use the term—of Mr Strutt himself, with which he combines a business ability that is really remarkable. Never before had I seen such books as those that he keeps. One of them, which he had playfully christened the 'Bailiff Tormentor'—a tillage book—actually treats each field as if it were a separate farm. By this I mean that every expense, including proportion of rent, tithe, taxes, labour, manure, etc., is charged against that field and deducted from the value of what it produces, so that the farmer can tell at a glance whether the crop has or has not been profitable, and the exact extent of the gain or loss....

I do not think that during all my agricultural wanderings I have made any more deeply interesting journey than that upon which we were most kindly conducted by Mr Edward Strutt through what are called the 'black' districts of Essex. Between Billericay and Althorne we saw hundreds, or rather thousands, of acres of strong corn lands which have tumbled down to grass. I can only describe the appearance of this land as wretched: it did not look as though it would support one beast upon ten acres of it, although, oddly enough, here and there we saw also a well-farmed and productive-looking holding. Much of this soil, which is only suitable to the growth of corn, beans, and lucerne, is in the hands of Scotsmen, who take it at a small price.

Hertfordshire

After the examination of various districts in Hertfordshire, were I asked what struck me most in that county I think that I should answer, the submergence of the Hertfordshire farmer. 'But where are the home people?' I inquired after visiting a long succession of Scotch and Cornish agriculturists. 'You must look for them in the backwoods', was the reply....

In Hertfordshire, I think, almost for the first time in the course of all my journeying, except in the case of those who practise some special industry, when I have put to farmers the question of how their business did, I have in various instances received the reply: 'Well, sir, I have no reason to complain'—which, coming from the lips of an agriculturist, means a very great deal....The newcomers have thrown over the old shibboleths. The Scotchman introduced potato growing, which he has brought to a fine art, and practises in conjunction with dairying, the cows consuming all the unmarketable tubers, that are pulped and fed to them like roots. Also he imports from London vast quantities of manure purchased from the collecting merchants, with which he doses his potato lands....Further he makes use of all the newest and best labour-saving machinery, and pays the highest wages for the pick of the men.

The Cornishman practises a system of three-year layers, which at the end of that time are ploughed up and put under other crops in rotation. In this way he saves labour, although in most instances, to a greater or less degree, he imitates the potato growing and dairying of his Scotch neighbours. It must be remembered that to be successful this style of farming is dependent upon proximity to the railway, without which it is impossible to import the necessary manure.

Lincolnshire

...The Isle of Axholme is one of the few places I have visited in England which may be called, at any rate in my opinion, truly prosperous in the agricultural sense, the low price of produce notwithstanding, chiefly because of its assiduous cultivation of the potato. Also, as in the case of the Marsh lands [*between the Humber and the Wash*] which we saw subsequently, it has benefited much from the recent dry seasons that have brought disaster to many parts of England. On those deep saline soils our poison is their meat.

Of course values and rents have fallen since the good times; thus a farm of 200 acres which thirty years ago was let at £5 the acre in 1901 fetched, I believe, under £3, about the top rent in these days; and land which used to sell at perhaps £100 the acre has come down in proportion. But it still both sells and lets readily; indeed, the smallholders take up all that can be had, if it be of the right quality.

Rutlandshire

...My informant thought that agriculture was not prosperous in Rutlandshire in 1901. In a good year Bass bought the barley grown in the eastern part of the county, but in 1900 the firm had taken little, and he feared that in 1901 it would not be good enough for them.

Also the grazing was very bad that season, although in the centre of the county, where there was more stiff soil, the crops would be better than elsewhere. Of the farmers he said that he could not put his finger on a man who had made money of late years, and many of them had been spending capital. Taking the average of the land, rents had fallen about 25 per cent since the good times. Arable alone had, however, come down 50 per cent; but, on the other hand, the grass where cheese was made had not fallen at all, and the mixed farms only about 25 per cent.

In Rutlandshire 400 acres was a large farm, and such there was some difficulty in letting at from 25s. to 30s. an acre; but the small farms were well applied for, and fetched 40 per cent more than the big ones, as the little men, who depended upon their own labour only, paid a heavier rent. The pick of the feeding lands in the south of the county brought in from £2 to 50s., and the mixed farms from 15s. to 25s. an acre. Of the labour he said that he thought the exodus from the country very serious, as in Rutlandshire, as elsewhere, the young folk went away.

Leicestershire

At Leicester I had the pleasure of seeing two of the leading graziers in the county, Mr Henry Burgess, of Middleton, Market Harborough, and Mr W. H. Kendall, of Goadby. Both these gentlemen informed me that grazing was not a profitable occupation, especially in dry seasons, as they were unable to compete with the American meat. At the best, graziers in Leicestershire could scarcely hold their own. It was impossible to produce beef at 6d. a pound, and many had been obliged to look to sheep as their mainstay, but the price of wool was ruin. It had to come to this, that they had to bolster up their farming businesses out of private capital.

Nottinghamshire

Mr Turner, of the firm of Bradwell and Son, auctioneers, valuers, and land agents in Nottingham, whom I saw, said that those farmers did best who worked their holdings with the help of their families. The large sheep farmers in the west of the county were not flourishing. He thought that some of the biggest of them would give up, and it was doubtful whether their holdings would be relet in all cases. Land with heart in it—that is, medium loams suitable for wheat and grazing— still sold fairly at from £30 to £45 the acre, but the latter price would be for small holdings with buildings on them. In the seventies this same land would have fetched £70 the acre...rents had not varied appreciably. There were not many failures among farmers, but they lived from hand to mouth.

16. THE BRITISH FARMER ON THE EVE OF WAR, 1912

Source: A. D. Hall, 'A Pilgrimage of English Farming' (1913), pp. 145–7, 150–3, 437.

Daniel Hall (1864–1942) an agricultural scientist, who became a notable figure in British agricultural education and research, toured farms throughout Great Britain in the years 1910, 1911 and 1912. He described the farming methods of the various regions and the new and more prosperous agriculture which had come into being in the past decade, the result both of the great change in farm products and practices and also of the general rise in prices in the early 1900's. This rise conferred an unexpected bonus upon the better run farms and estates and also upon others which, as Hall points out, were not so well managed. For Hall, see H. E. Dale, Daniel Hall (1956).

WHAT, perhaps, we had hardly been prepared for was the great variety presented by British farming and the diversity of the methods that are practised. Great Britain is not a very large country, and the variations of climate and soil which occur within its limits might be considered trifling by men accustomed to continental areas, yet every few miles of our journey we found ourselves in a totally different country from a farming point of view. This indicates that the British farmer has learnt, partly by old tradition, partly by his personal skill, to adapt his methods very nicely to his particular environment, whether of soil, or of markets, or of climate. One sometimes felt inclined to disagree with the local practices, which a wider experience of other districts might have taught the farmer to modify with advantage; but one cannot be too diffident in advancing such opinions, so great is the value of tradition and experience in the workaday matters of agriculture....

But if the methods of British agriculture are very diverse, they seemed uniformly to be meeting with a very fair measure of success, for one could not but conclude that the industry as a whole was in a prosperous condition and had healthily and stably recovered from the great depression that lay upon it as recently as fifteen years earlier.... Next, it was noticeable that nearly all the advanced and skilfully adapted farming we saw was being done by tenants. Large tenant farming has for the last century or more been the special characteristic of British agriculture; under this method has been built up our supremacy in production per acre and in live stock, and today it still seems the most effective form of dealing with the land on a wholesale scale. As a system it offers many points for criticism; it is often illogical, but its prime justification is that it works well, when the landlords and tenants are such as we find them in this country. In the majority of cases the tenant stands entirely on the side of the landlord and backs him politically and privately, however contrary their interests may appear to be....

As a feature in the prosperity of the modern farmer we have put his adaptability to his conditions. In the main, the men who could not alter their system to meet the low prices prevailing only a few years ago have been shaken out of the industry, and the most capable have survived to take advantage of the recent rise in prices. But though the best of these men still maintain the supremacy of British farming over that of any other country, nothing is more striking than the contrast between them and some of their neighbours. In every district we visited we found good and bad farmers close together, men who are earning good incomes on one side of the hedge, and on the other men who are always in difficulties, who in many cases are only kept going through the tolerance of their landlords.... We may fairly say that the ordinary farmer is a pretty good master of his craft; he knows how to manage his land, he has an instinct for stock, and he gives very little away in the practical day-to-day management of his business. He is, however, very closely bound inside the routine of his district, he has little acquaintance with the methods by which other people attain the same ends, and is impatient of even attempting to think whether he cannot introduce modifications into his own system. He is apt to regard his style of farming as inevitable, something that nature imposes upon him and that he ought not to attempt to alter. It is just this lack of flexibility of mind, this power to look abroad and consider his business in a detached fashion as a whole, putting aside for the time details which are otherwise essential, that marks the imperfection in the education of the farmer today. The same defects may be seen in his organizations for social and political purposes.... For all these reasons we feel justified in concluding that the average British farmer is not educated up to his position or his opportunities; but it is not so much technical education that is lacking as an awakening to ideas, and that, probably, is more likely to come in the next generation from the general tuning-up of the country grammar schools than from the growth of agricultural colleges.... In one technical detail, also, the British farmer's education is defective: he has never learnt a system of book-keeping adapted to the farm, a system which will show him the profit and loss on each branch of his business—cattle raising, milk producing, crop growing—instead of merely his indebtedness or otherwise to A, B, and C with whom he trades. It is true that the teachers of book-keeping have never put such a system before him, but it is a problem that our schools and colleges ought seriously to take in hand, and it is a problem capable of solution.

If by 1910 the farmer had succeeded in readjusting his position since the depression, the condition of the labourer was still not satisfactory. ... On far too many of our farms labour is still being employed wastefully. The farmer allows his men to work clumsily and slowly by hand rather than take the trouble to teach them labour-saving contrivances. Five men may be found receiving 15s. a week when the ideal to be aimed at should be two men earning 30s. each and doing the same work with the aid of machines. It is less, not more, labour we want on most of our farms, but then the labour should be of the best and paid at rates competing with the wages of the artisan....

. . . .

If we consider the men who are engaged in this business of agriculture, we must conclude that the owners, however kindly and helpful to their tenants, are yet deficient in leadership.... The great opportunities of leadership they might exercise in the way of drawing their tenants into co-operative marketing and purchase, or improved methods of farming, are rarely or never exercised; at their worst landlords become mere rent receivers and must inevitably become crowded out unless they take some higher view of their function. The model farms that were not uncommon a generation ago were justly discredited as only instructive in their expensiveness; what we do lack are examples of large-scale capitalist farming distinguished by its rigorous application of science and business to the real purpose of the industry—making money.

17. AGRICULTURAL DEPRESSION AND AGRARIAN CRISIS IN IRELAND, 1881

Source: 'Preliminary Report from Her Majesty's Commissioners on Agriculture, 1881', C. 2778, vol. xv, pp. 6–9.

The impact of bad seasons and falling prices, with a partial failure of the potato harvest, produced a sharp agrarian crisis in Ireland at the end of the 1870's and in the early 1880's. The situation there was very different from that in England and Scotland, although something resembling it existed on a much smaller scale in the Scottish Highlands. In Ireland, owing to the lack of industry, there were few alternatives to a life on the land. Ireland was a land of estates which were sometimes very large, the owners of which were often absentees. There were many tenants farming in a very poor way. In the west of Ireland particularly a large population lived on barren soil, without knowledge or capital or easy access to markets, deriving from their tiny holdings one of the poorest livings in Europe. But it was the only life they knew and emigration to the United States or some other distant country seemed the only alternative. Elsewhere in Ireland, the elastic demand of English markets had helped to better the position of the Irish farmer. But the older generation could remember and never forget the famine years 1846–7, the evictions, and the forced emigration of many people which had followed. They feared any shadow of a recurrence of these events.

Given the economic and social conditions and the presence of political and religious differences between the landlords of the Protestant Ascendancy and their tenants, the small cultivator's reaction to distress easily became violent. Rent difficulties, eviction and the fear of it led to a revival of agrarian crime, never far away in nineteenth-century Ireland, at the end of the 1870's. From 1879 onwards, the discontented tenants, who had more resources than the starving peasants of forty years before, were organized in the National Land League, led by Michael Davitt and John Stewart Parnell. The land-war—an Irish landowner of those days, William Gregory, of Coole, in County Galway, wrote on 10 October 1881 'the landlord shooting season has set in with great briskness'—demanded the attention of the British government and the Irish land-question moved for two or three tremendous years to the centre of British politics. The Gladstone administration had already, in 1880, asked the

"Richmond Commission" to examine Irish agricultural distress as a matter of urgency. About the same time, another official body, the "Bessborough Commission", so named after its chairman, Lord Bessborough (1815–95), the Irish landowner and peer, was sitting to examine the working of the Irish Land Act of 1870. It recommended repeal of that act and the substitution of a simple uniform land law on the basis of fixity of tenure, fair rents, and free sale. These inquiries, together with the intense pressure exerted by the Land League, determined the shape which the policy of the British government took in 1881. By a new land act, that policy gave to the Irish tenant the right to have the rent of his land judicially fixed, on appeal, by a special court, the Land Commission. It also contained drastic provisions as regarded the tenant's security of tenure and his right to sell his tenancy, the so-called tenant-right, subject to his landlord's consent. So began a period of virtual dual ownership of the Irish land by landlord and tenant.

For the very special circumstances of Irish landholding and the development of British attitudes and policy, see for the period down to 1870 R. D. Collison Black, 'Economic Thought and the Irish Question' (Cambridge, 1960), more generally J. E. Pomfret, 'The Struggle for Land in Ireland, 1800–1923' (Princeton, N.J. 1930). M. J. Bonn, 'Modern Ireland and her Agrarian Problem' (Dublin, 1906) is a vigorous sketch by a well-informed German scholar. For the position in the early 1880's, James Hack Tuke, 'Irish Distress and its Remedies' (1880) gives a vivid personal impression of conditions in Donegal and Connaught, by an Englishman who had first known Ireland in the Famine. For an intelligent and civilized Irish landlord's point of view, Sir William Gregory's 'Autobiography' (1894), above quoted, is interesting. Conor Cruise O'Brien, 'Parnell and his Party' (Oxford, 1957) admirably describes the link between the Land League and Irish national politics. T. W. Grimshaw, 'Facts and Figures about Ireland' (1893), G. Shaw-Lefevre, 'Agrarian Tenures' (1893) and W. E. Montgomery, 'History of Land Tenure in Ireland' (1899) are useful contemporary studies.

IN common with the rest of the United Kingdom the agricultural depression of the years 1877, 1878 and 1879 has greatly affected Ireland, and has been to some extent increased in that country by the absence of manufacturing industries and other sources of employment. There is no doubt that the depression has fallen with extreme severity upon the smaller farmers.

We have, therefore, reason to fear that a very large proportion of these farmers are insolvent, and it is stated that the bountiful harvest of this year has alone prevented their entire collapse.

With respect to the very small holders in the western districts of Ireland we are satisfied that with the slightest failure of their crops they would be unable to exist upon the produce of their farms, even if they paid no rent. Many of them plant their potatoes, cut their turf, go to Great Britain to earn money, return home to dig their roots and to stack their fuel, and pass the winter, often without occupation, in most miserable hovels. Employment at a distance, always precarious, has largely failed them during the late calamitous season. [*The reference here is to the possibility of harvest work in England.*]

The causes of depression, seriously aggravated by unfavourable seasons, and especially by that of 1879, must be sought in the peculiar circumstances and conditions of the country, as well as in defects in the Land Laws, and they may be briefly stated as follows:

1. Inclemency of the seasons, and consequent failure of the potato crop.
2. Foreign competition.
3. An undue inflation of credit, partly produced by the security afforded by the Land Act of 1870, and partly by a series of prosperous seasons.
4. Excessive competition for land. The excessive competition is owing mainly to the fact that apart from the land there are few, if any, other means of subsistence for the population, and it has led to serious abuses, which have come before your Commissioners, in the evidence they have taken, such as—
   (a) Unreasonable payments for tenant right.
   (b) Arbitrary increase of rents.
   (c) Over-crowding of the population in certain districts.
   (d) Minute subdivision of farms.

To meet these the following remedies have been suggested:

Emigration and Migration

It is proved from the evidence that in some parts of Ireland agricultural depression arises from the population upon the soil being larger than can be profitably employed in the cultivation of the land, or than can be sustained by its produce. This has arisen from various causes, chiefly from the subdivision of holdings into lots too small to sustain the tenant and his family; and partly from the laying down of arable into pasture land, which renders less labour needful. The remedies which have been suggested are emigration and migration.

.   .   .   .

Your Commissioners are convinced that emigration under a properly organised scheme, and the voluntary act of the people, would materially tend to relieve the congestion of population wherever it now exists, and would conduce to the social, moral and material welfare of the emigrants and of the population remaining behind.

Migration, as it is proposed by some witnesses, assumed the existence of large tracts of land which could be profitably brought into cultivation; and it has been stated in evidence by competent witnesses that there are thousands of acres, irrespective of bog, that might under judicious management be made remunerative to the capital and labour needed for their development. Migration would involve the acquisition of such tracts, and the transfer to them of a part of the population from other districts....

That advantage has been derived from migration when voluntarily carried out may be admitted, and it is hardly to be doubted that similar advantages would arise from such a system if furthered by legislation; but it is open to serious question whether Parliament, even if the money were forthcoming from local sources, could be asked on behalf of the Irish peasant to confer upon the Crown, or its nominees, compulsory powers of purchase for this purpose.

Public Works

The employment of capital and labour upon the development of the country by arterial drainage, the construction of railways and other public works, and the encouragement of fisheries has also been urged upon us by witnesses as one of the best remedies for the present depression, and to prevent a recurrence of the existing distress. It will be seen in evidence that from want of regular and continuous employment the condition of this class, except on some large estates and well managed farms, is deplorable, and the sufferings and privations which they and their families have periodically to endure demand, we venture to think, the serious attention of Your Majesty's Government and of Parliament; and here we cannot forbear to express our opinion that the improvement of dwellings and farm buildings, and the extension of scientific agricultural teaching, with the view of an improved cultivation of the soil, are indispensable measures to secure general prosperity and an improved condition of the people.

Tenure

The tenure of land, using the term with the limited definition placed upon it by Your Majesty's former Commissioners viz., 'the interest which an occupying tenant has in his farm', has engaged a considerable portion of our attention....

Great stress has been laid upon the want of security felt by an improving tenant, which, it is alleged, limits not only the number of persons employed in agriculture, but also the quantity of food produced for the benefit of the general community.

Bearing in mind the system by which the improvements and equipments of a farm are very generally the work of the tenant, and the fact that a yearly tenant is at any time liable to have this rent raised in consequence of the increased value that has been given to his holding by the expenditure of his own capital and labour, the desire for legislative interference to protect him from an arbitrary increase of rent does not seem unnatural; and we are inclined to think that by the majority of landowners legislation, properly framed to accomplish this end, would not be objected to.

With a view of affording such security, 'fair rents', 'fixity of tenure', and 'free sale', popularly known as the 'three F's', have been strongly advocated by many witnesses, but none have been able to support these propositions in their integrity without admitting consequences that would, in our opinions, involve an injustice to the landlord.

It is only fair to add that the evidence which has been brought before us shows that there are very many estates which are well-managed, and upon which the tenants have no just ground of complaint.

18. THE CONGESTED DISTRICTS OF IRELAND

Source: 'Report of the Royal Commission on the Land Law (Ireland) Act, 1881, and the Purchase of Land (Ireland) Act, 1885, 1887', C. 4969, vol. XXVI, p. 11.

Tle continued fall of agricultural prices and further trouble between Irish landlords and tenants led to renewed inquiry by the 'Cowper

*Commission' of 1886–7. This body, presided over by Lord Cowper,
who had been Lord-Lieutenant of Ireland at the time when the Land
Act of 1881 was passed, reviewed the working of that act and recommended a reduction of Irish judicial rents, to meet the low prices of stock
and produce. They also picked out for special mention, as deserving
special treatment, the economic problems of the congested districts of
Western Ireland. These remarks appear to have been the origin of the
Congested Districts Board, established in 1891, with a small grant from
the British Treasury, to encourage in these very poor districts not only
the purchase of their holdings by tenants but also better farming, industries,
fisheries, communications and other works of economic development,
as well as schemes of migration and emigration. See W. L. Micks,
History of the Congested Districts Board (Dublin, 1925).*

NOTHING hitherto has been effectual in bringing any improvement
to the condition of the people inhabiting what are called 'congested districts'. It would, in our opinion, be a very grave mistake to
deal with this class of people as if they were 'farmers', i.e., people
understood to live altogether upon the produce of their holdings.
That is not their position; it would therefore be mischievous to attempt
to deal with them in this report, except as a class distinct and separate
from 'farmers' properly so called. The inhabitants of these districts
must be regarded as labourers, who occupy residences with portions of
land attached, which assist them in the support of themselves and of
their families. Regarding them as such, we have to consider the
conditions on which they occupy the holdings we have alluded to, and
the labour or employment upon which they must largely depend.

It is well to define what we understand by a 'congested district'.
We understand such a district as one where the land is of inferior
quality, not good enough for pasturage, and not naturally adapted for
profitable agriculture, occupied by a large number of poor people
holding at small rents, and where each separate holding is not of itself
capable of supporting the holder and a family....

We found that the occupiers of such holdings supplemented their
means of living by working as labourers during certain seasons of the
year in England and Scotland, or for farmers at home, or, when they
live near the coast, by fishing. In these congested districts a failure in
any year of the potato crop, and of labour, means utter destitution, or
public assistance. It is not their rent which reduces them to this

condition, any more than the payment of rent affects other labourers. The liability to pay for house and home is an incident to the existence of all tenants. The inhabitants of these districts have this advantage, that the law of the land steps in to fix a "fair rent" upon their holdings. Employment is the condition of their lives, but there is no field for it near their home. The relief of people living in such a precarious position seems to demand the careful consideration, and prompt action of the State.

The general introduction of mowing and reaping machines into England and Scotland has so greatly lessened the demand for Irish labour that these portions of the Kingdom can no longer be considered as offering a sufficient field for migratory labour of this kind. Under such circumstances, two remedies only have presented themselves; either employment must be found for these people at home, and we fear there is but little hope of this being practicable; or a considerable proportion of them must be enabled to move to some place where such employment exists.

19. LAND PURCHASE IN IRELAND

Source: 'Return of the Resolutions and Statement adopted by the Irish Landowners' Convention on the 10 October 1902' and 'Report of the Irish Land Conference, 3 January 1903, Parliamentary Papers, [89], 1903,' vol. LVII, pp. 6–7 and 9.

The land problem in Ireland entered upon a final phase about 1903. Experience since 1881 suggested that the system of dual ownership was not good for the tenant, or for the landlord, or for the land. Irish grazing interests were suffering temporarily from low stock prices, as well as from the tendency of Irish landed property to lose value. Irish landowners were increasingly disposed to sell out. Hence the conference between representatives of the tenants and of the landlords held at Dublin, in the first days of 1903. Agreement was reached on the terms under which estates might be transferred from owners to tenants, if the British Treasury could be persuaded to assist tenants to buy. This was the basis of the Irish Land Act, 1903, for which George Wyndham, the energetic Irish Secretary in the Balfour government, was responsible. Under this act, further amended in 1909, nearly 200,000 tenants were enabled to acquire their holdings and more than six million acres of agricultural land changed hands, at a cost of about £68,000,000, mostly lent by the State to the occupiers and carefully repaid by them. The Irish land question thus passed out of history. The issues between tenant and landlord had been

disposed of by substituting a wholly new system of owner-occupiers,
which is the basis of the Irish land system today. Important problems of
the proper management and cultivation of the soil remained unsolved by
the change of ownership, as a new generation of Irishmen, represented by
Sir Horace Plunkett (1854–1932) and 'A.E.' or George William
Russell (1867–1935) pointed out in the early years of the present century.

WHEREAS it is expedient that the Land Question in Ireland be settled so far as it is practicable and without delay;

And whereas the existing position of the Land Question is adverse to the improvement of the soil of Ireland, leads to unending controversies and lawsuits between owners and occupiers, retards progress in the country, and constitutes a grave danger to the State;

And whereas an opportunity of settling once for all the differences between owners and occupiers in Ireland is very desirable;

And whereas such settlement can only be effected upon the basis mutually satisfactory to the owners and occupiers of the land;

And whereas certain representatives of owners and occupiers have been desirous of endeavouring to find such basis and for that purpose have met in conference together;

And whereas certain particulars of agreement have been formulated, discussed, and passed at the Conference, and it is desirable that the same should be put into writing and submitted to His Majesty's Government.

After consideration and discussion of various schemes submitted to the Conference we are agreed:

    I. That the only satisfactory settlement of the Land Question is to be effected by the substitution of an occupying proprietary in lieu of the existing system of dual ownership.

    II. That the process of direct interference by the State in purchase and re-sale is, in general, tedious and unsatisfactory, and that therefore, except in cases where at least half the occupiers or the owner so desire, and except in districts included in the operations of the Congested Districts Board, the settlement should be made between owner and occupier, subject to the necessary investigation by the State as to title, rental and security.

    III. That it is desirable in the interests of Ireland, that the present owners of the land should not as a result of any settlement be expatriated, or having received payment for their land, should find no object for remaining in Ireland, and that, as the effect of a far-reaching settlement must necessarily be to cause the sale of tenancies throughout the whole of Ireland, inducements should, wherever practicable, be afforded to selling owners to continue to reside in that country.

IV. That for the purpose of obtaining such a result an equitable price ought to be paid to the owners, which should be based upon income....

V. That the purchase price should be based upon income as indicated above, and should be either the assurance by the State of such income or the payment of a capital sum producing such income at 3 per cent, or at 3¼ per cent, if guaranteed by the State....

Signed at the Mansion House, Dublin, this 3rd day of January 1903.

DUNRAVEN *Chairman*	JOHN REDMOND
MAYO	WILLIAM O'BRIEN
W. H. HUTCHESON POE	T. W. RUSSELL
NUGENT T. EVERARD	T. C. HARRINGTON

20. CROFTING TROUBLES IN THE SCOTTISH HIGHLANDS AND ISLANDS, 1884

Source: 'Report of Her Majesty's Commissioners of Inquiry into the Condition of the Crofters and Cottars in the Highlands and Islands of Scotland 1884', C. 3980, vol. XXXII, pp. 3, 7, 9–10, 16, 41, 108–10.

The revolution in the international market for grains and the tendency for agricultural prices to fall created a new situation for the crofters of Scotland as for many Irish farmers, in the 1880's. In the Highlands and the islands, a population which both fished and farmed lived out a hard life in a traditional way, in a land where the natural obstacles to economic development of any kind were great. Falling prices touched the crofters in a small but essential part of their income, the cash with which they paid the rent, for they were the tenants of great estates. At the same time, however, the importation of cheap grain and flour into Scotland seemed to abolish the need for the crofter to concentrate his attention upon a subsistence crop and to open the way for him to use his time and energies in other and more profitable activities, if only he could find them. Here, as in the West of Ireland and as in some other European countries, such as parts of Norway, an economic question easily became social and political. It involved the future of a society which found extreme difficulty both in keeping its old life intact and in adapting itself to changing conditions. This was perceived by the 1884 commission of inquiry, under the chairmanship of Lord Napier (1819–98) who brought to Scottish problems eyes trained in the East, as a former governor of Madras. The Crofters Act 1886 went, however, beyond the 'Napier report'. It gave to the crofter as tenant the protection of law and extended to him the system of security of tenure and a judicial rent, fixed by an independent tribunal, with power to wipe out arrears of rent, which had been given to the Irish tenant some years before. This was no solution to the problem of economic development in the Highlands, but it seemed to meet the immediate needs of the crofters and their families. On the special circumstances of the Highland economy, see Malcolm Gray, 'The Highland Economy, 1750–1850' (Edinburgh, 1957) and Adam Collier, 'The Crofting Problem' (Cambridge, 1953).

THE classes whose condition we have been directed to study are qualified as crofters and cottars. By the word crofter is usually understood a small tenant of land with or without a lease, who finds in the cultivation and produce of his holding a material portion of his occupation, earnings, and sustenance, and who pays rent directly to the proprietor. The term cottar commonly imports the occupier of a dwelling with or without some small portion of land, whose main subsistence is by wages of labour, and whose rent, if any, is paid to a tenant and not to the landlord. The crofter is a small farmer who may live partly by the wages of labour; the cottar is a labourer who may have some share in the soil....The distinction between the two classes is more easily felt and understood than delineated.

. . . .

The crofter of the present time has through past evictions been confined within narrow limits, sometimes on inferior and exhausted soil. He is subject to arbitrary augmentations of money rent, he is without security of tenure, and has only recently received the concession of compensation for improvements. His habitation is usually of a character which would almost imply physical and moral degradation in the eyes of those who do not know how much decency, courtesy, virtue, and even mental refinement, survive amidst the sordid surroundings of a Highland hovel. The crofter belongs to that class of tenants who have received the smallest share of proprietary favour or benefaction, and who are by virtue of power, position, or covenants, least protected against inconsiderate treatment.

. . . .

The population belonging to the class of crofters and cottars engaged in agricultural and pastoral pursuits, in addition to the evils attached to an unproductive soil, high elevations, and a variable and boisterous climate, suffer from several causes of indigence, discouragement, and irritation, which are subject to remedial treatment. These may be enumerated as follows: Undue contraction of the area of holdings; undue extension of the area of holdings; insecurity of tenure; want of compensation for improvements; high rents; defective communications; withdrawal of the soil in connection with the purposes of sport. To these we may add, as contributing in our opinion to the depressed condition of the people, defects in education, defects in the machinery of justice, and want of facilities for emigration. The fishing population, who are largely intermixed and identified with the farming class, share the same complaints, and have their own peculiar disabilities in the exercise of their hazardous calling, which may be summarised under the ensuing heads: Want of harbours, piers, boat shelters, and landing-places; inability to purchase boats and tackle adapted for distant and deep-sea fishing; difficulty of access to the great markets of consumption; defective postal and telegraphic intercourse.

In submitting suggestions for the diminution or removal of these numerous causes of depression and discontent, our proposals may be conveniently consigned to six sections of report, viz.;—(i) Land; (ii) Fisheries and Communications; (iii) Education; (iv) Justice; (v) Deer Forests and Game; (vi) Emigration.

[*The Commissioners set out their proposals. Briefly, they recommended public policies intended to strengthen and improve the agriculture of the area under the existing system of crofts, with enlarged holdings where necessary, some additional protection to the tenant, and, if possible, a reduced population on the land; to give state aid to land purchase, to the fishing industry and to emigration and to bring about some improvement in the public services, such as schooling.*]

. . . .

The limitation in the extent of tenancies belonging to the crofting class may be traced to several causes, some of which have ceased to operate, while one, at least, is still working in certain localities with destructive power. The chief incentives to multiplication of small tenancies in past times were the desire of the proprietor to unite large tracts in sheep farms, and to settle the mass of the population along the coast, either for the lucrative industry of making kelp or the prosecution of fishing, it being rashly deemed that a ready and reliable source of local prosperity and national wealth and strength would thus be opened. The processes by which the comminution of crofters' holdings and the displacement of the people were effected are too familiar to require detailed description. The reduction or withdrawal of common pasture, the diminution of arable ground, the obliteration of townships, and the transfer of the inhabitants to the moor, the shore, or the cultivated area of other communities, were the methods by which a revolution in the rural economy of the country was effected. Very different are now the definitive results from those which were expected. Foreign competition and scientific discovery have long since extinguished the returns from kelp which afforded for a season to the proprietor a dangerous opulence, and to the labourer a ready subsistence. The intended fisherman has remained an indigent cultivator with an exhausted croft, while the sheep farm, which long supplied a respectable rental, is passing in many cases from the condition of farm to the condition of forest. Eviction and repartition have done their lamented work and passed away for ever; the interests, the prudence, and the sentiments of the proprietor are alike enlisted for other views and purposes; but the dangers of subdivision are perpetuated by the tenacity of the tenant, who too often settles his offspring on the impoverished holding, in defiance of estate regulations and the dictates of self-preservation. In the Western Highlands and Islands something resembling an economical crisis has occurred in consequence of the surrender of large sheep farms, the failure of crops in recent seasons, and the prevalence of agitation in connection with the tenure of land. It may be that an occasion is approaching for a partial redistribution of occupancy, in which the extension of the crofting area will find a place. To us it seems that the moment is favourable for the intervention of legislation, by which an impulse may be given towards the consolidation and enlargement of small holdings. In assisting a movement in the direction indicated, it is apparent that a useful result can best be obtained by a temperate course of action, moving in harmony with the wishes of the people, and using them as willing and conscious instruments for their own good.

. . . .

It may at first sight appear strange to recommend the acquisition of small parcels of poor land at a high price by industrious and intelligent men who would be able to invest their savings or the surplus product of their daily toil with far greater advantage in the vacant tracts of America and Australia. Yet habit and local affection bear so great a sway in the actions of mankind, that Highlanders will be found who would rather be proprietors in the mountains of Skye, or the wastes of Lewis, than on the fertile plains of Manitoba, and for no other purpose would they be more likely to receive assistance....The possession of real property ought to be a powerful agent in forming habits of industry and self-respect, and in supplying sources of rational enjoyment. An opportunity of embracing this alternative condition of life and labour should be offered to the Highland people, and Government might lend its co-operation with manifest advantage and little risk.

. . . .

In concluding this Report, it is desirable to anticipate an objection to our recommendations, based upon general principles of public policy, which might be urged on the part of that school of economists, who, in dealing with social distresses, prefer to contemplate the operation of natural causes and tendencies, rather than the action of artificial remedies. It may be asked, on what grounds do we justify a complex system of interference on behalf of a class in the community which is not numerous, which does not contribute a preponderant share to the aggregate sum of national wealth, and which does, after all that has been said, possess, in ordinary times, conditions of welfare and happiness unknown to some other orders of people, for instance, to the poorer sort of rural day labourers in England, or to those who depend on casual employment in great cities? If the Highland crofter, it may be said, can maintain his footing under the laws affecting landed property, common to the whole country, and against the forces which contemporary science and commerce bring to bear upon his situation, let him do so; if not, do not prop up his position by curious expedients, which may merely prolong his decay, and prevent the timely transfer of his powers to more congenial scenes and means of labour and subsistence. The small tenancies of the Highlands would not be the only interest abandoned to irresistible innovations. The hand-loom of the cottage, the sailing craft along the shore, the yeoman's freehold, are gone, or doomed to disappear. It is perhaps in the same order of necessity that the crofter should be extinguished.

To these objections we would thus reply:

The crofters and cottars with whom we are here concerned are, in truth, of no great significance in respect to mere numbers. All told, they probably do not comprise more than 40,000 families or 200,000 souls, the population of a single manufacturing town of the first class. They do, however, possess in their occupations and capabilities certain distinctive features which, in the opinion of many, entitle them to such exceptional attention and protection as has been granted to other special interests. These people take a considerable part in the fishing industry, a branch of national production, not of the first magnitude, but still of material value, and which should not be allowed to pass into other hands.

[*This industry might be subjected to better organisation and extension for the breaking up of the fishing population would be an irreparable loss. The Commissioners continue:*]

It is not only in regard to fishing that the crofting and cottar population have a peculiar value. They constitute a natural basis for the naval defence of the country, a sort of defence which cannot be extemporised, and the value of which, in possible emergencies, can hardly be overrated.

[*The Commissioners note that over four thousand of these people serve in the Royal Naval Reserve, and they continue:*]

The severance of the labouring classes from the benefits and enjoyments of property (certainly one of the elements of civilisation, morality, and public order), and their precarious and dangerous condition as dependants on capital and mere recipients of wages, is a question which engages the reflections of those who reason and of those who govern. There is a general desire that the labouring man in every sphere of activity should be invested with a greater share of substantial possession, and be attached by deeper and more durable ties to the soil of his country. This great object is being partly realised in Scotland among the elite of those workmen who are engaged in urban industries by the regulated purchase of their habitations, but the mass of dwellers and labourers in the country have still no permanent interest in the land either as occupiers or owners. It is in the Highlands and Islands that a partial exception to this rule is chiefly found, in respect to occupancy; and it is here that occupancy may perhaps be most readily converted into property. The connection between the crofter and his holding is indeed of an unsubstantial character, but the kindly custom of the country in many cases gives a practical security of tenure, while the cultivator is endowed with some of the simpler objects and adjuncts of personal possession; furniture, such as it is; livestock; boats; the implements of two pursuits, husbandry and fishing; some knowledge of pastoral and agricultural processes; habits of trade, the practice of purchase and of sale. Men thus equipped are, in some degree, prepared to become substantial occupiers of small holdings under lease, or to be the managers of land belonging to themselves. While the people are in this way apt for a change of condition, there are, in the present division of agricultural areas in the north, greater facilities for bringing that change to pass than exist in other quarters. To suffer the crofting class to be obliterated, or to leave them in their present depressed circumstances, if by any justifiable contrivance their condition can be improved, would be to cast away the agencies and opportunities for a social experiment connected with the land of no common interest....

The claim of the crofter is, however, based not only on his qualities, but on his necessities. The crofter is not in his average condition poor compared with the profounder poverty that exists elsewhere, but he is exposed to unusual risks and vicissitudes. A good harvest or a good haul may make him comfortable for a season. A blight, an early frost, a wet autumn, a long winter, a gale of wind, a wayward movement of the herring, may deprive him of food for his family, funds for his rent, and seed for his ground. In such emergencies he has heretofore appealed to his fellow countrymen for relief, or others have made the appeal on his behalf. The relief has been granted, yet not always without anxiety and doubt. A transitory and humiliating assistance thus bestowed is but a poor substitute for permanent and honourable encouragements, which might eventually enable the crofter and cottar to support the strain of temporary misfortune.

The last argument which we shall adduce in support of our views on this subject, is the argument of public expediency. The Highlands and Islands have recently been at some points the scene of agitation, and even of disturbance. Acts of violence have occurred on the occasion of the delivery of legal summonses regarding the occupancy of land, and the enforcement of lawful claims on the part of the proprietors have [*sic*] been delayed or impeded by apprehensions of opposition. We do not palliate the dangers attached to this condition of affairs. There are circumstances under which it is the plain duty of Government to carry out the prescriptions of the law at all risks, and by every means at their disposal. But collisions between proprietary rights and popular demands are to be deprecated, for they leave behind them lasting traces of resentment and alienation. The mere vindication of authority and repression of resistance would not establish the relations of mutual confidence between landlord and tenant, in the absence of which the country would not be truly at peace, and all our inquiries and counsels would be expended in vain.

CHAPTER 3

OLD INDUSTRIES AND NEW

Industry, not agriculture, led the way and made the pace in the British economy of the late nineteenth century. It was not only that mining and manufacture employed by now far more people than farming, in the proportion of five to one in England and Scotland.[1] The state of business expectations in industry tended at any given time to decide the main movements of investments and income throughout the kingdom, including even the country districts. The age was past when, before 1850, the home harvest had been a powerful influence upon the level of prices and the condition of the economy as a whole.

In a country where the occupied population was steadily rising and where capital, in the shape of buildings, power and equipment, grew even faster, it was natural that the total value of the output of mining and manufacturing should increase. It grew substantially between 1870 and 1914, bringing the national income up with it. The rise of personal incomes did not, however, in these years always go on at the same rate. There were significant differences. British real income for each head of the population, it has been estimated,[2] grew in the last quarter of the nineteenth century at the rate of between 2 and 2½ per cent every year; in the years 1900 to 1914, at less than 1 per cent. Conditions in great markets overseas, the state of activity and the rate of change in manufacture and farming there, the terms of trade between industrial Britain and the countries supplying her with foodstuffs and raw materials, clearly must have had their influence. But the main factor was the growth of the British industrial system itself, its success in finding new products, new markets, new levels of costs and prices. Its achievement in these vital respects evidently encountered limits. Industrial production continued to rise between 1870 and 1895, even during years which contemporaries thought depressed. But it increased more slowly than in the heyday of expanding output and aggressive investment in the early and middle Victorian age. After 1895 it rose more slowly still. Perhaps even more striking, output per operative, on which the expansion of industrial production depended, seems to have stopped growing almost altogether between 1900 and 1913.[3]

[1] M. G. Mulhall, *The Industries and Wealth of Nations* (1896), p. 403.
[2] G. Maynard, *Economic Development and the Price Level* (1962), p. 177.
[3] For discussion and analysis of the statistics of the period, see E. H. Phelps

78

Old Industries and New

These years in the history of British industry contrast therefore with the rapid expansion of the first half of the nineteenth century. The new industrial system of the early and middle Victorian age had shown a high rate of increase, decade by decade, from the close of the Napoleonic wars onwards. Then in the 1870's and early 1880's, its rate of growth begins to slacken. In the early 1900's, it becomes noticeably low compared with what it had been thirty or forty years before or compared with the contemporary industrial development of Germany and the United States. It remained low, although it is still a rate of industrial expansion, through the period of European war which opened in 1914, through the doldrums of the 1920's and the early 1930's. Round about 1935 a prolonged period of rapid industrial growth returned,[1] lasting down to the present day.

What did this notable change of pace in industrial life imply? It is hard to clothe the bare bones of statistical fact with flesh and blood, in terms of the day-to-day management and arrangements of industry, without knowing a great deal more than we do about the internal development of particular industries and concerns. Business history, which no doubt should ideally be the record of the policies of firms and the decisions of businessmen, so far unfortunately throws little light upon these general matters. But it may be possible to suggest a number of considerations which appear to bear.

One powerful influence which had supported Britain's industrial expansion for more than a century ceased to play an appreciable role after 1900. This was the incessant movement of population from country to town, the willingness of people to give up poorly paid work on the land for slightly less poorly paid industrial occupations under urban conditions. Internal migration of this sort had been part of the driving power of Victorian industrialisation, but although still running strongly in the 1870's and 1880's, it was nearing the end. There have been movements, and important ones, of country people into industry since, but the main shifts of population within Great Britain after 1900 have been not from country to town, but from one industrial area to another.[2] The comparatively easy resort of industrial employers to rural labour, which has played so great a role in the industrialization of many lands in the present century, became a thing of the past for this country.

Brown and B. Weber, 'Accumulation, Productivity and Distribution in the British Economy, 1870–1938', *Economic Journal*, vol. LXIII (1953), and G. Maynard, *op. cit.* pp. 168–84.

[1] Phyllis Deane and W. A. Cole, *British Economic Growth, 1688–1959* (Cambridge, 1962), table 77, p. 297, using the Hoffmann and Lomax indices.

[2] A. K. Cairncross, *Home and Foreign Investment, 1870–1913* (Cambridge, 1953), p. 74. This is a cursory summary of Cairncross's extraordinarily interesting analysis of internal migration in Victorian England.

While this change was taking place, another of a different kind but equally momentous for British economic development was taking place abroad. A nation which had become thoroughly industrial by 1870 found itself facing an increasingly industrial Western world. The forward spring of mining and manufacturing output, which had been obvious both in Europe and North America since 1850, accelerated in the last quarter of the century. Both Germany and the United States, which had been important markets for British manufactured goods at the mid-century, began to emerge as highly industrial communities after 1880. The same thing was happening on a less remarkable scale in other countries. British industrial exporters felt the effect, as a vast redistribution of markets began, and it had its consequences in the field of British industrial production.

The drying up of the old source of country labour and the ineluctable advance of the industrial power of other nations were major changes in the condition of British industry. They do not of themselves explain why industrial expansion slackened after 1870, still more after 1900. Nor does the later quickening of growth, a generation later, seem to have had much to do with them. General conditions might even appear to have favoured a continuation of the extremely swift development of mid-Victorian times. It is true that country labour was no longer there for the asking, after 1900, but there was no lack of labour, generally speaking. On the contrary, it could be argued with justice that some industries, including some of the fastest growing at the beginning of this century, such as coalmining, found the labour they wanted just a little too easily. The new industrial nations competed strongly on world markets, but they also bought. Their purchases of foodstuffs and raw materials in primary producing countries put new income into the hands of people there and created new export markets for British goods. Nor was there, although this is matter for debate, any shortage of capital.[1] The London capital market was in many ways better suited to finance countries abroad and international trade than home investment. But provincial capital was always available to those who knew where to look for it. The failure of industrial productivity per head to rise, after 1900, occurred despite a rise in the amount of capital per head invested. Why then the appearance of industrial events having taken a new and significant turn about 1870?

The long secular boom of mid-Victorian times had depended upon

[1] The discussion between A. R. Hall, 'A note on the English Capital Market as a Source of Funds for Home Investment before 1914', *Economica* (February 1957) and the 'English Capital Market before 1914—a Reply', *Economica* (November 1958) and A. K. Cairncross, 'The English Capital Market before 1914', *Economica* (May 1958), does not seem to me to affect the general point which is being made here.

the coincidence of many things. They included an unheard of expansion of foreign trade and the beginnings of foreign investment on the grand scale; excited railway-building and other capital-construction rushes, together with an expansion of city-life which far outgrew all conveniences and amenities; plus the steady mechanization of trade after trade. Between 1870 and the First World War, there was never at any time a prolonged coming together of the three great economic activities of house-building, foreign loans with foreign market expansion, and home industrial investment, in a way which would have encouraged the return of a lengthy spell of economic growth of the mid-Victorian sort. The pull of all three activities was enough to keep the industrial system running and expanding, but not at the high rate of the previous fifty years. House building, a form of investment which carries much industrial demand with it, suffered after the housing boom of the late 1870's from prolonged spells of relative depression. This was to the marked detriment of the nation's physical and social health, as well as of its economic stability. Home industrial investment was extremely active from time to time, especially in particular industries and districts; but it lacked the astonishing drive of the railway booms. There was no electrification boom comparable with the railway buildings. In an age of much emigration from Great Britain and much nation-building in new countries, speculation and investment abroad were often more interesting than they were at home. Like all fashionable investment, foreign lending tended to be overdone. In the late 1880's and again after 1906, in some years, one half of the national savings seems to have been going abroad. Foreign loans helped to maintain and widen international markets for the goods of the established export industries and from time to time gave a lift to the industrial system as a whole. It seems unlikely that they took capital away from new industries at home. They certainly removed it from housing when the foreign investment booms were at their height. Foreign lending also encouraged industrial specialization, by export manufacturer and merchant, along lines which were becoming conventional. This conventionality had its dangers, as time was to show.

The industrial climate of the period after 1870 was therefore less continuously stimulating than that of early and mid-Victorian Britain. From some points of view, this was as well. Towns and cities needed time to catch up with the problems created for their community life by a half century of reckless mining and manufacturing expansion. Nor was it altogether a bad thing that the late Victorians had capital to spare for the economic development of younger countries such as Australia, even though they would have done well to spend some of it on industry and town redevelopment at home.

If late Victorian and Edwardian times lacked some of the opportunities of huge industrial growth of the Railway Age, neither could they show anything like its strong forcing down of industrial costs. This had been the product of steam, the railway and machinery when they were new and revolutionary. It is striking that some of the largest industries in the country, such as iron and steel and cotton, over large numbers of firms, seem to have failed to reach any significant overall reduction in their costs between 1880 and 1913.[1] One huge industry, coalmining, on which many others depended, saw its extraction costs begin to rise during those years, as the more easily got seams were exhausted.

It is partly in the constant, even rising costs, of a number of large established trades that we must seek one half of the explanation of the tendency of industrial productivity as a whole not to rise so fast as it had done or even to rise at all, at any rate so as to make a difference to costs. That this should have been so, in an age full of talk about foreign competition and technical change, may appear surprising. But it seems to have been in itself no more than a sign or symptom of something bigger and more deeply rooted. With all its activity, prosperity and self-assurance, late Victorian and Edwardian Britain was faced by an industrial problem, slow maturing but of formidable proportions. Some contemporaries saw certain sides of this very clearly. Its full extent and dangerousness did not reveal themselves until the 1920's and 1930's. Then it developed towards a crisis, in a situation already complicated by the war of 1914–18.

This was a problem of a kind which could arise only in a society which had already reached an advanced stage of industrialization. Like all economic problems, it was in its nature one of the correct use of resources, including the most important of all, labour. Britain was passing out of an era, characteristic of most of the nineteenth century, in which the nation stood to gain by every person transferred from the two old forms of employment, agriculture and domestic service, to industry, because the productivity of labour in industry, though low by modern standards, was still higher than it was in agriculture or domestic service. She was entering an age where the addition to the national income necessary to meet the needs of growing population and rising living standards could only be obtained by transferring people from established industries to new ones. The sole but important condition of the change was that the new industries should show a higher productivity, which was also a higher value for labour, than the established. Such a change could take place only and literally at the expense of the older industries.

For a country such as Great Britain, heavily dependent on international markets in a world industrializing fast, this was the course

[1] G. T. Jones, *Increasing Return* (Cambridge 1933), was the first to look into this question for the years 1880–1913.

marked out by the turn of events. As other nations, such as Japan in the early 1900's, moved from agriculture to the simpler machine trades, only in this way could an old industrial country hope to meet competition in the world's markets and raise its material standard of living. Anything else would be a waste of resources, human and material.

Change becomes the law of industrial life in a rapidly developing economic world. But this trite and painful fact is more easily grasped now, with many years of experience to support the argument, than it was then. Few at that time saw the need for fundamental change in the structure and pattern of industry or were prepared to concede it, until under the overwhelming pressure of the unemployed men and capital of the 1920's and 1930's.

The structure of British industry down to 1914 continued to be dominated by a comparatively few very large and well-developed industries, the overwhelming influence of which over the labour market had been justified in the nineteenth century by their growth and their profitability. They were the half dozen or so industries which in the hundred years before 1870 had taken the lead in the industrialization of Britain; coalmining, which had been a first-class employer of former agricultural labour; the iron and steel trades and their cutlery and hardware subsidiaries; the cotton and woollen textiles of Lancashire and Yorkshire; and the branches of mechanical engineering, including ship-building, which had developed out of the application of steam to manufacture and transport. These flourishing and until 1920 still expanding industries had created new industrial regions from Belfast to the North-East coast and from Somerset to the Clyde. The technique, the organization and the methods of British industry were largely due to them and to the leadership which they exercised. Sometimes, these industrial staples were depressed; at other times, as in the long export boom between 1906 and the First World War, active and prosperous. But they were always there, holding between them a large proportion of the available national resources. Their control was to remain unchallenged until the 1920's and their activity, although highly regional, influenced business expectations, employment and investment throughout the nation.

Important structural changes in industry were already on the way by the beginning of the present century. The interest of the years between 1870 and 1914 lies in their having been the time when the nineteenth-century structure of British industry reached its full height. Late Victorian and Edwardian opinion could hardly see beyond it. Too often the existing pattern of industrial investments and occupations appeared as fixed and inviolate, even something to be defended at all costs against competition and inevitable change. But this was also the time when new forms of industrial power, such as electricity, new industrial materials, such as plastics and rayon, and new industrial products, such as the aeroplane and the motor car, of high significance for the future, were coming into use. The foundations of whole new industries were being laid. Within the last sixty years, a new structure of British industry, very different from that of 1900, has been created. This retains the staple industries of the nineteenth century in modified form. But the lead in building it up has been taken by industries which were new or unknown at the turn of the century. The immense, often hurried, growth of these new industries has made the techniques, the organization and the industrial relations of modern industry very different from the Victorian and it has largely created the characteristic problems of modern society.

Considered from this point of view, the years before 1900 in British industrial history seem to belong to the nineteenth century, not only chronologically but in a more profound sense. They were a time when the nineteenth-century structure, depending as it did very much on the leadership of particular industries and on a prevailing order of technology, of the age of steam and iron, some of it, such as steel shipbuilding, relatively new, had still a substantial contribution to make towards the expansion of the national income. The years after 1900,[1] down to about 1935, seem to have had this in common that they formed a period in which economic circumstances were radically adverse to the growth of incomes. War after 1914 and deteriorating world trade conditions between the wars counted for much. But among the most important circumstances was one which was already operative before 1914. The range of staple industries which had done most to build up incomes in the nineteenth century began to reach the limits of their usefulness in that way, while no new group of leading industries had arisen to supplement and improve upon their efforts. Very slowly, an exchange of power and leadership in industry got under way. The transition which took place between 1887 and 1914 in the Midlands, in South Staffordshire and the Birmingham district, from coal and iron and the hardware trades to the newer industries, such as electrical manufacturing, cycles and motor cars, was prognostic of much that was to happen to the nation in the next thirty years.[2] How slow was the pace may be seen from the Census of Production of 1907, the first attempt in this country to determine how much in value each industry

---

[1] This view of Britain's economic development as having reached the end of one chapter and the opening of a new one towards the end of the nineteenth century was first advanced by E. H. Phelps Brown and S. J. Handfield Jones in their paper, 'The Climacteric of the 1890's: A Study in the Expanding Economy', *Oxford Economic Papers* (New Series), IV, no. 3 (October 1952), 266–307.

[2] G. C. Allen, *Industrial Development of Birmingham and the Black Country* (1929).

produced in the course of a year.[1] The output of the groups which a generation later were to be the industrial pace-makers, chemicals, motor vehicles, metals and engineering, including electrical manufactures, was still very modest. Their time was to come later.

Whether the necessary change of structure in industry, away from overmuch reliance on foreign markets towards home demand, away from the simpler and cheaper industrial products towards the more complex and expensive, could have been advanced in the years before the First World War by early action must remain a matter of opinion. It would certainly be a mis-reading of the mind of late Victorian and Edwardian Englishmen to suppose that this was possible as an act of public policy. According to conceptions which prevailed at that time, although strongly challenged from one quarter by the Tariff Reformers and from quite another by the Socialists, the employment of industrial resources was a matter for unaided private decision. The state had no part to play. There was no public sector in industry and there could be no public industrial policy.

The economic philosophy of the nineteenth century remained unchallenged, firmly based to all appearance in logic and experience. These were the policies of non-interference under which industrial Britain had grown great; the same policies which had built a power must maintain it. But there were contemporaries, drawn from many social and political camps, who pointed out that non-interference as it was practised in the Britain of their day was seriously inconsistent with itself at important points. One of these failures seems to have a bearing upon the problem of industrial growth. The argument for leaving all economic decisions to private initiative was logically also an argument for securing that private judgment got the best education that was available, so that it might take good decisions and not bad. This was all the more necessary in an age of rapid technical and economic change, when simple capital accumulation was far less of a recipe for success than technical ability, innovation and resourceful management. Some of the industries which held out the best hopes for the future, such as chemicals and electricity, were science-based, to use the jargon of a later age, in a way that few industries had been in the past. They stood in special need of science-trained managers and staff and of a science-trained public too, if they were to realize their full potentialities.

It was a serious matter that what was probably the greatest single contribution the State could make in that age towards economic development, the creation of an educated nation and the opening of careers to talent in industry, although it came well within the scope of the economic philosophy of the day, liberally understood, arrived

[1] B. R. Mitchell and Phyllis Deane, *Abstract of British Historical Statistics* (Cambridge, 1962), table at p. 270.

slowly and imperfectly between 1870 and 1914. The building up of a national primary education system had only just begun in the 1870's, under the Education Act, 1870, after much loss of valuable time. National secondary education had to wait for the act of 1902. Meanwhile, in the long interval between, the pressure of foreign competition forced Parliament in the 1880's to inquire at length into technical education and to pass the Technical Instruction Act of 1889. This made it possible for the first time for the industrial towns and cities to do what needed to be done and was long overdue, in the field of technical training. But logically and practically, primary and secondary education were the basis of technical education. They should have been established first. It cannot be said that the main issues of education in relation to science and industry, which were vital to Great Britain's industrial future, were ever squarely faced and properly settled in these years, despite a vast deal of discussion. Neither did they ever engage the attention of a statesman of the first rank, with the exception of Balfour.

British industrial growth met various limits during this period. Perhaps the limit of the education available was the most serious of all because its influence was pervading. The failure of education to change in an age of swift economic and social transition made itself felt in many directions and over a long series of years. Educational reformers in the nineteenth century could unfortunately always rely upon controversy between the Church of England and the Nonconformists whenever change was discussed. But the barrier to educational advance lay less in any particular institution than in the structure and the values of British society. Social and political attitudes changed too slowly. After 1900 they were beginning to alter fast. But it took the shock of war to extract from government in 1916 the final recognition of a special relationship between state, industry and science, with the formation of an Advisory Council for Scientific and Industrial Research, the beginnings of the later Department of that name.

There was perhaps only one other circumstance of the time which was as relevant as science to the long-term prospects of industry. This was the state of industrial relations. In a country which was on the eve of industrial developments of a far-ranging character, where new industries must be made out of old, with a consequent need to regroup and retrain large sections of the industrial population, a sound system of industrial relations, creating relative confidence between managements and men, was essential. But from this point of view, the outlook was not promising. Industrial relations in a number of great British industries were going through a period of heavy strain between 1890 and 1914, particularly in 1911. Relations tended to be stormy where the coming need for change was going to be greatest, in coalmining and on the railways. The consequences of this mutual want of confidence and understanding were to be deeply felt later.

While these were among the main issues of industrial development in the late Victorian and Edwardian time, the documents chosen can naturally illustrate only a few parts of this enormous field. They deal mainly with the great established industries of the day (nos. 22–36) and with the introduction of those newer manufactures which marked the beginning of the move away from the Victorian structure (nos. 37–56). The critical relations at this time between education and science and industry, little appreciated as they were by most men, seem also to deserve consideration (nos. 58–67).

Perhaps it is worth pointing out, although without intent to excuse shortcomings here, the intrinsic difficulty of documenting the processes of industrial growth. In the perspective of time, we see the results of those processes smoothed out, rather than the processes themselves. In their rough and untidy actuality, where the long period was merely the sum of many short and few men looked five years ahead, economic decisions were taken by particular persons in specific situations, accepting and rejecting alternatives under the influence of arguments or habits of mind which remain often obscure to us. To take only an *ex post* view of such decisions and of the consequent action taken is to be half way towards misunderstanding the processes by which industries and firms grow and decay. They need also and first to be seen *ex ante*, at the point of time when calculations were still being made and expectations formed, when error and contingency entered in without being recognized for what they were, when the future was uncertain and information was imperfect, before results were known, when the outcome was a matter of probability or possibility only, not disclosed fact. Such is the nature of economic decision[1] and it is precisely that nature which eludes us in much of the surviving documentation of industry and in a great deal of industrial history as it is written.

FURTHER READING

The volume of industrial production during this period was first examined by W. Hoffmann, *British Industry, 1700–1950* (English edition, 1955). His index has been critically viewed by J. F. Wright, *Journal of Economic History*, XVI (1956), 356–64 and W. A. Cole, *Economic History Review* 2nd series, XI (1958), 309–15. Measurements of output after 1900 are in K. S. Lomax, 'Production and Productivity

[1] See the highly abstract but illuminating discussion in G. L. S. Shackle, *Decision, Order and Time in Human Affairs* (1961).

Movements in the U.K. since 1900', *Journal of the Royal Statistical Society* (1959).

The great transformation of the structure of British industry in the last sixty years may be studied in G. C. Allen's *The Structure of Industry in Britain* (1961) and in the two volumes edited by D. L. Burn, *The Structure of British Industry* (1958). For the structure as it stood before the First World War, Alfred Marshall's *Industry and Trade* (1919) contains what was in its day a masterly analysis, based mainly upon the experience of the years before 1914. From the late Victorian age, J. S. Jeans's *England's Supremacy; its Sources, Economics and Dangers* (1885) is interesting. There was a large literature about particular industries and their problems before 1914, to which H. L. Beales, 'The "Basic" Industries of England 1850-1914', *Economic History Review*, v, no. 2 (April 1935) is an admirable bibliographical guide.

Regional economic histories for this period of the sort which throw some light on industrial growth and decay—more of this sort are needed—are G. C. Allen, *Industrial Development of Birmingham and the Black Country* (1929), J. D. Marshall, *Furness and the Industrial Revolution* (1958), E. D. Lewis, *The Rhonddha Valleys* (1959). See also the interesting contemporary description by Talbot Baines, *The Industrial North in the last Decade of the Nineteenth Century* (1928).

It is not easy to get near to the industrial entrepreneur of the period or to follow the conduct of business. The following business histories, out of the many good, bad and indifferent histories which exist, help one to do so. T. C. Barker, *Pilkington Brothers and the Glass Industry* (1960), R. D. Best, *Brass Chandelier* (1940), R. H. Mottram and C. Coote, *Through Five Generations: the History of the Butterley Company* (1950), J. D. Scott, *Siemens Bros.* (1958) and *Vickers, a History* (1963), R. E. Threlfall, *One Hundred Years of Phosphorus Making, 1851-1951* (1951), C. H. Wilson, *The History of Unilever* (1954).

21. THE DECLINE AND FALL OF THE SMALL WORKSHOP

Source: "A Black Country Resident" in 'The Ironmonger', March 20, 1897, pp. 491-2.

England's earliest industrial reputation had been made not by the factory but by the small craftsman, working with his family, possibly with apprentices, in his cottage-workshop, under pure country or half-countrified conditions, from the time of the first Queen Elizabeth onwards. Over a long period, to be measured by generations rather than decades, the movement towards large-scale output and factory organization brought to an end the age-old dominance of the small workshop. This was still marked in Victorian times in the metal-working Midlands. Not until the last quarter of the century was it clearly on the way out in many of its old quarters in Birmingham and South Staffordshire; a change which was associated with the decline of old industries and the gradual rise of new ones. See G. C. Allen, 'The Industrial Development of Birmingham and the Black Country, 1860–1927' (1929).

AN important and interesting feature in the industrial life of the Black Country is the steady but most decided diminution of the number of little domiciliary workshops which formerly overspread the district. For two centuries have these small hives of industry been handed down from father to son from generation to generation. Hard work during protracted hours, only broken by Sunday's rest and a drinking-bout at the holidays or the various local wakes, summed up the life of most of these 'little masters' in the olden days. Now and again would rise up one among them more thrifty than the rest, who would supplement the earnings of the anvil and the vice by setting up a retail shop or a beerhouse in the forefront of his dwelling, such as the 'missus' could manage. This is the type of 'little mester' [*sic*] who laid the foundations twenty or thirty or forty years ago of not a few factories which now rank among the best ordered and most flourishing in the district.

The conditions of life and labour in these small workshops, within the memory of people still living, have been so well described by Disraeli in the oft-quoted pages of *Sybil*[1] that we need not dwell upon them here. It may, however, reasonably be doubted whether in any part of the Black Country the social and general conditions of the workpeople were quite as deplorable as in the nail-making districts of Gornal, Netherton, Halesowen, Cradley, and Lye Waste. In the year 1830 it was computed that in these and neighbouring localities some 50,000 men, women, and children earned their bread—truly by the sweat of their brow—in the production of hand-made nails. In the year 1866 the number had dwindled to 20,000; and now it is doubtful if one-half of that number are so employed all the district through. The type of stalwart muscular lasses forging nails on the anvil, which old Hutton[2] so racily describes, has almost wholly disappeared, and the remnant who still cling to a doomed and decaying industry are

[1] [*Disraeli's novel was published in 1845.*]
[2] [*William Hutton (1723–1815). The reference is to his 'History of Birmingham' (2nd edition, 1783), p. 84.*]

mostly folk who know no other occupation and are too old to learn one, and who will leave few—if any—successors to take their place.

Of the 5000 locksmiths employed in the year 1866 in Wolverhampton and Willenhall it is doubtful if half that number were working in what may be properly described as factories. At Willenhall twenty years ago quite a large percentage of the smaller dwelling-houses had a little workshop as part of the back premises. The building of such houses to-day is quite unknown, and the number of such workshops now no longer used for the purpose may be counted in scores. Not, perhaps, with such rapidity as in the nailing district, but to a large and increasingly appreciable extent are the little workshops of Willenhall being absorbed by the larger factories.

Similar absorption is going on at Walsall and Bloxwich, where a large proportion of the saddlers' ironmongery required by the trade was formerly produced by the 'little mester'. At Darlaston and Wednesbury the old and once extensive domestic handicraft of 'gunlock filing' is practically extinct. And more or less throughout the Black Country the same experiences prevail, and ere long there will be a general silencing of the clinking of the little hammers which Elihu Burritt[1] aptly described as 'supplying the *aria* to the great concerts and oratorios of mechanical industry'.

No one who takes an all-round view of the subject can say that this evolution in local industry is a matter to be deplored. The fight between human flesh and muscle and mechanical power has for generations been increasingly unequal, even in the days when human muscle—including that of women and children—was surprisingly cheap. But now that mechanical appliances have made such marvellous advances, and the sanitary officer has a word to say about the arrangements of the little workshop, and the attendance officer drives the children to the Board schools, the struggle has become absolutely hopeless. The 'little mester' finds himself much better off as an artisan in a well-ordered factory, and his children emerge from the school standards with ideas far above the life of drudgery and ill-requited labour which fell to the lot of their forefathers. So much from the social aspect of the question. From a commercial and industrial point

[1] [*Elihu Burritt, 'Walks in the Black Country and its Green Border-land' (1869), p. 211.*]

of view the change is equally welcome. A consolidation of industrial forces of the district under conditions which secure not only economic production, but which afford a fuller guarantee of 'up-to-date' work, cannot fail to benefit the district and enhance its already great reputation as a manufacturing centre for all the markets of the world.

22. THE QUESTION OF COAL RESERVES

Source: W. S. Jevons, ' The Coal Question; an Inquiry concerning the Progress of the Nation and the Probable Exhaustion of our Coal Mines' (2nd ed.) (1866), pp. v–vii.

The fears expressed by the economist, Stanley Jevons (1835–82), that coal would prove, by the physical limits to its extent and the rising cost of extraction, the Achilles heel of the British economy and national income, continued to find an echo throughout the years 1870–1914, in more than one official inquiry into coal reserves. Extraction costs did rise. But they proved not inconsistent with an immense expansion of the industry and its working population. Between the time when Jevons wrote and the First World War, the growth of the coal industry was rapid. With the production of the mines doubling every twenty or thirty years, the long wave of expansion lasted down to 1913, when the outturn was 287 million tons, a figure never reached again. The coal industry at this time was supplying energy not only to an expanding British economy but also to growing economies abroad. Electricity, oil and natural gas were still relative newcomers to the field. Hence the rising costs foreseen by Jevons could be and were for the time being shouldered by consumers.

I AM desirous of prefixing to the second edition of the following work a few explanations which may tend to prevent misapprehension of its purpose and conclusions.

The expression 'exhaustion of our coal mines', states the subject in the briefest form, but is sure to convey erroneous notions to those who do not reflect upon the long series of changes in our industrial condition which must result from the gradual deepening of our coal mines and the increased price of fuel. Many persons perhaps entertain a vague notion that some day our coal seams will be found emptied to the bottom, and swept clean like a coal-cellar. Our fires and furnaces, they think, will then be suddenly extinguished, and cold and darkness will be left to reign over a depopulated country. It is almost needless to say, however, that our mines are literally inexhaustible. We cannot get to the bottom of them; and though we may some day have to pay dear for fuel, it will never be positively wanting....

Renewed reflection has convinced me that my main position is only too strong and true. It is simply that we cannot long progress as we are now doing. I give the usual scientific reasons for supposing that coal must confer mighty influence and advantages upon its rich possessor, and I show that we now use much more of this invaluable aid than all other countries put together. But it is impossible we should long maintain so singular a position; not only must we meet some limit within our own country, but we must witness the coal produce of other countries approximating to our own, and ultimately passing it.

At a future time, then, we shall have influences acting against us which are now acting strongly with us. We may even then retain no inconsiderable share of the world's trade, but it is impossible that we should go on expanding as we are now doing. Our motion must be reduced to rest, and it is to this change my attention is directed. How long we may exist in a stationary condition I, for one, should never attempt to conjecture. The question here treated regards the length of time that we may go on rising, and the height of prosperity and wealth to which we may attain. Few will doubt, I think, after examining the subject, that we cannot long rise as we are now doing.

23. EXPANSION IN COAL MINING BEFORE 1914

Source: 'Coal Mining: Report of the Technical Advisory Committee, 1944–5', Cmd. 6610, IV, 3–4.

This extract, from a report by Sir Charles Reid and other coal mine managers and engineers, examining the technical state of the coal industry at the end of the Second World War, is retrospective. It describes some general features of the organisation and methods of the industry during one of its most active periods of growth. There are questions about the coal industry and its methods at this time which are not asked here. They concern chiefly the tendency of its costs to rise and the extent to which counteracting measures were available and were used, in the way of new forms of power and illumination, machinery for coal-getting and conveying, mechanical transport, improved layout of the mine, development of new coalfields and so forth. On many of these things see A. J. Taylor, "Labour Productivity and Technological Innovation in the British Coal Industry 1850–1914", 'Economic History Review' (August 1961), pp. 48–70.

Old Industries and New

BEFORE the 1914–18 War the technical conduct of the British coal-mining industry seems to have been carried on without any radical changes in the practices long established in the various coalfields. Local customs, traditions and methods of mining often bore little or no relation to those prevailing in other coalfields, even where conditions were similar. The developments which did take place were not revolutionary, but evolved gradually on the initiative of the mining engineers of individual companies. There was, however, a good deal of interchange of experience by means of papers read to the Institution of Mining Engineers, and other professional or learned societies.

Within the coalfields ownership of the numerous separate undertakings was widely dispersed, and while there were a good many mines producing large outputs, the average output per mine was small. In 1900 there had been 3089 coalmines at work with an average annual output per mine of 73,000 tons, against 2734 mines with an average output per mine of 97,000 tons in 1914.

The individualism of a large number of self-contained units was unlikely to encourage major developments in the science of mining. Managers were not sufficiently encouraged to widen their experience by visits to other countries, for example, and fresh ideas and different techniques spread but slowly. It was considered sufficient to keep ahead of your neighbours, and the doctrine of the survival of the fittest was in full operation. The numerous small undertakings did not employ a technical staff outside those engaged on day-to-day supervision of mining operations, and thus development depended, almost entirely, upon the initiative and abilities of individual mining engineers. Concentration upon traditional practices, without analysis of the conditions which gave rise to them, was not conducive to the development of new techniques. It is not, therefore, surprising that progress was slow.

Nonetheless the years of which we write, and the years which came before were the days of the pioneer. The thriving industries of the biggest exporting country of the world needed coal, and yet more coal; and a large coal export trade was built up which contributed greatly to the national wealth and wellbeing.

The employers and the mining engineers who made this possible were hardworking, adventurous and self-reliant men. They set out to get cheap coal, and the country reaped the fruits of their efforts. If they were hard taskmasters, they worked hard themselves, and they depended on the work of men's hands rather than on machinery. They believed in competition and were prepared to meet it. Their capital resources were often limited, and, as soon as a mine was sunk, the cry was for output. Whatever planning was done was, for the most part, done on a short-term basis. In their work they met many difficulties, and they were not always successful in their ventures. The dangers of flooding, for example, with the crude pumping machines available, were often a nightmare.

Though they left the mining engineers with a legacy of mines not easy to reconstruct to fit the requirements of today, these men were the product of the days in which they lived, and the circumstances of the time dictated their actions.

The miners, generally speaking, lived in isolated communities with little access to towns or contact with those employed in other industries. The whole life of these communities was bound up with the colliery upon which the livelihood of the population was largely dependent. With few alternative openings for employment, the sons followed naturally in the footsteps of their fathers. As soon as they left school, they would enter the colliery and proceed to the working face, in some districts at once, and in others after a period on the haulage, there to be trained by their father, or another miner, in his working place and learn all the traditions and customs handed down from one generation to another. The miner took pride in his craftsmanship, and, through it, in his calling. The traditions and customs amongst which he lived, the gradualness with which the methods of work had changed, and the fear of unemployment (without the measure of security now provided by insurance) all combined to lead him to regard the introduction of machinery with misgivings, and sometimes with open hostility. He preferred to preserve his traditional methods of work and the customs with which he had grown up, unsuitable though they sometimes were, to the changing circumstances of the time.

We would pay tribute to the old miner too. He also worked hard and played his part in helping to build this great industry. Perhaps his skill and craftmanship were neither sufficiently remunerated nor recognized. We know, at least, that the grievances of these past days are still in the minds of many, and there has been a tendency to hand on the memory of them when their reality has largely disappeared.

And here we must remember also the manufacturers of mining machinery. They have provided the industry with coalcutters, conveyors and other machines, and they too pioneered and experimented, at their own cost, living strenuous lives and guiding the application of the machines they had designed and built.

When we come, therefore, as we must, to point out the mistakes which were made in these early years of the coalmining industry, let us beware of merely being wise after the event, or of withholding the meed of praise due to a great race of men, employers, mining engineers, workmen and machinery makers alike. For whatever their faults, they were fit to rank with the greatest of Britain's industrial pioneers.

24. COAL EXPORTS

Source: H. S. Jevons, 'The British Coal Trade' (1915), pp. 677 and 681–2.

Jevons, a son of Stanley Jevons (see no. 22, above), who had doubted the future of the coal industry in 1866, described in 1915 the great growth in British coal exports which had taken place since mid-Victorian times. This trade was very largely a result of the expansion of coal-using industries in countries abroad, especially in Europe, and the deficiencies of those countries in coal reserves and coal output. It was also, of course, due to the needs of steam-driven merchant fleets and the world bunkering trade which sprang up to supply them. The trade reached its peak in 1913 when, out of 287 million tons of coal raised, 98 million tons were exported.

THE outstanding feature of the trade of the great manufacturing countries of Germany, the United Kingdom and the United States during the past quarter of a century has been the remarkable growth in coal production. In Britain the rate of increase has not been so great as in America and Germany, but the development of the export trade has been far greater. In our foreign commerce coal now occupies an exceedingly important place, and the value of coal exported in 1913 was no less than $8\frac{1}{2}$ per cent of the total value of all goods produced in the United Kingdom which were exported....

...from 1855 to the present date the value of our exports of coal has risen from $2\frac{1}{2}$ to 10 per cent of the total value of the produce of the United Kingdom exported, whilst it has increased nearly twenty-two times in actual magnitude. At the same time the quantity of coal exported has also increased nearly twenty-fold, and has grown from about $7\frac{3}{4}$ per cent to 34 per cent of the total quantity raised in the country.

Coal Exporting Countries

At the present time the United Kingdom stands second (the United States being first) among the nations of the world in respect to the amount of coal produced; but our own country is easily first in respect of the amount of its exports....

...the British overseas trade in coal is more than twice that of the whole of the rest of the world put together. Our first formidable competitor is Germany, whilst the United States probably comes next, as she is making some shipments to the Mediterranean and South America, which compete with the British trade. On comparing the figures for 1912 with those of 1906, it is evident that Australia and Japan are both increasing their trade. Japan supplies the China Seas, the Pacific Islands and Australia; and besides these markets, sends large cargoes to the Pacific Coast of South America and even to ports on the Indian Ocean. With the development of distant coalfields, and the growth of shipping on all ocean routes, we are naturally losing the position of almost complete monopoly of the overseas trade in coal which we held in the nineteenth century. In 1900 our overseas trade was still about 85 per cent of the world's total. By 1906 it had fallen to 80 per cent, and in 1912 was 71 per cent. The year 1912 was, however, an unfortunate one for this country, owing to the miners' national strike, which reduced our own exports and deflected orders to our competitors. If I had the figures for 1913 complete, they would show a slight recovery; but the general tendency will continue to be a fall in our proportion of the whole world's sea-borne trade, at the same time that we continue to increase the total amount of our exports.

25. MIGRATION INTO THE COALFIELDS

Source: Jack Lawson, M.P., 'A Man's Life' (1932), pp. 56–8.

The rapid growth of the coalmining industry in these years was accompanied by an equally rapid migration of people into the coalfields, in search of work, and the absorption of a relatively high proportion of Great Britain's population by the industry. Just after the 1914–18 war, it was reckoned that one-twelfth of the British population depended on this markedly labour intensive industry.

BOLDON Colliery was at that time a typical example of the way in which the county of Durham had become a sort of social melting-pot owing to the rapid development of the coalfield during the nineteenth century. Its population consisted of people from every part of the British Isles, some of the first generation and some of the second, all boasting they were Durham men, though their parents spoke or had the accent of the distant place of their birth. Many of my Durham friends may not know it, but the fact is that, although we are all now Durham men and proud of it, not all of us by any means are native to the soil. Few can trace far back to a Durham lineage. True, the immigration slowed down, and then stopped in the early years of the twentieth century. Marriage and time now almost obliterated the old county and national landmarks, and made them one people. But at the time of which I write [*1890's*] there was a combination of Lancashire, Cumberland, Yorkshire, Staffordshire, Cornish, Irish, Scottish, Welsh, Northumbrian, and Durham accents, dialects, and languages. All these and more tongues were to be heard in a marked way; and not only that, but the families in each group gravitated together and formed a common bond. While we were all good neighbours, I have seen the clans come together in my boyhood days and fight it out in very rough and ready style. If anyone thinks the blood bond does not matter, let them live under such conditions and their theory will be strained, to say the least of it. While in my boyhood lines of division existed in Boldon, as in all the other growing collieries of the east of the county, it was different in the west of the county. There the process of amalgamation was farther advanced, because they were older collieries. The older collieries were more settled in their personnel, but among the great coast collieries there was constant ebb and flow of the population. A new colliery or a new seam meant bigger money, and there was always an emigration followed by the incoming of new people to take their place. Thus the great collieries were less settled in their personnel, and this fact, together with their large-scale operations, produced a different type of people from those of the west, and a different spirit as well. They had many problems which did not trouble the older collieries. Union and mining officials have a different and far more difficult job in these new collieries than in the older collieries.

26. STEEL: THE THOMAS PROCESS

Source: W. T. Jeans, 'Creators of the Age of Steel' (2nd ed. 1885), pp. 307–08.

A new metallurgical material was coming on to the industrial market in the 1850's and 1860's. This was steel made by the Bessemer and Siemens' processes. Sir Henry Bessemer (1813–98) announced his "converter" method of steelmaking at the Cheltenham meeting of the British Association for the Advancement of Science in 1856. The Siemens open-hearth furnace was first used for steel manufacture in 1866. For the gradual, firm-by-firm adoption of both processes, see Charlotte Erickson, 'British Industrialists: Steel and Hosiery, 1850–1950' (Cambridge, 1959), pp. 141–66.

These great innovations had been confined to the use of non-phosphoric or haematite ores, in which Great Britain was rich. The discovery of the Thomas process, described in the document which follows, in 1879, opened up the possibility of making relatively cheap steel of good quality in large quantities from phosphoric ores. Either the Bessemer or the Siemens process could be used, if suitably adapted. The adaptation consisted in lining the furnace or the converter with a basic material such as magnesian limestone which would combine with the phosphorus. The basic material and the phosphorus were removed later together, in the form of basic slag, leaving what came to be known as basic steel, as distinct from the acid steel made from haematite ores.

This invention was the work of a scientifically minded young man, Sidney Gilchrist Thomas, who was employed as a clerk in one of the London police courts, and his cousin, P. C. Gilchrist, an analytical chemist working in South Wales. These investigators were not the first to work on the problems of phosphoric ore, but with the help of Edward Windsor Richards, who was general manager of the Bolckow-Vaughan steelworks at Middlesborough in Yorkshire and author of this statement, they were the first to solve them and to do so on a commercial scale. The result was a new expansion of the British steel industry, especially in

Scotland and on the North-East coast, and a rapid growth of new steel industries abroad, especially in Germany and the United States, where vast reserves of suitable ore were available.

For the state of the iron and steel industry and its markets at the time, the impact of the new processes and an analysis of the economic problems which followed, see D. L. Burn, 'Economic History of Steelmaking, 1867–1939' (Cambridge, 1940). There is much useful information in J. C. Carr and W. Taplin, 'History of the British Steel Industry' (Oxford, 1962).

MESSRS Thomas and Gilchrist prepared a paper giving very fully the results of their experiments, with analyses. It was intended to be read at the autumn meeting of the Iron and Steel Institute in Paris in 1878; but so little importance was attached to it, and so little was it believed in, that the paper was scarcely noticed, and it was left unread till the spring meeting in London in 1879. Mr Sidney Thomas first drew my particular attention to the subject at Creusot, and we had a meeting a few days later in Paris to discuss it, when I resolved to take the matter up, provided I received the consent of my directors. That consent was given, and on the 2nd October, 1878, accompanied by Mr Stead of Middlesborough, I went with Mr Thomas to Blaenavon.[1] Arrived there, Mr Gilchrist and Mr Martin showed us three casts in a miniature cupola, and I saw sufficient to convince me that iron could be dephosphorised at high temperatures. I also visited the Dowlais Works, where Mr Menelaus informed me that the experiments in the large converters had failed, owing to the lining being washed out. We very quickly erected a pair of 30-cwt. converters at Middlesborough, but were unable for a long time to try the process, owing to the difficulties experienced in making basic bricks for lining the converters and making the basic bottom. The difficulties arose principally from the enormous shrinkage of the magnesian limestone when being burnt in a kiln with an up-draught, and of the failure of the ordinary bricks of the kiln to withstand the very high temperature necessary for efficient burning. The difficulties were, however, one by one surmounted, and at last we lined up the converters with basic bricks; then, after much labour, many failures, disappointments, and encouragements, we were able to show some of the leading gentlemen

[1] [*Where P. C. Gilchrist, who was employed at Blaenavon, had been testing his cousin's theories, at the latter's request. Ed.*]

of Middlesborough two successful operations, on Friday, April 4 1879. The news of this success spread rapidly far and wide, and Middlesborough was soon besieged by the combined forces of Belgium, France, Prussia, Austria, and America....

Our Continental friends were of an inquisitive turn of mind, and, like many other practical men who saw the process in operation, only believed in what they saw with their own eyes and felt with their own hands. And they were not quite sure even then, and some are not quite sure even now. We gave them samples of the metal out of the very nose of the converter.

27. THE END OF THE IRON AGE

Source: 'Second Report of the Royal Commission appointed to inquire into the Depression of Trade and Industry: Minutes of Evidence and Appendix Part I, 1886', C. 4715, XXI, 324–5.

In evidence submitted to the official body inquiring into the slump of the mid-1880's, Sir Lowthian Bell (1816–1904), an iron-master and pioneer in the development of the industrial resources of the North-East coast, describes the rapid changes then taking place in the iron and steel industry. Expansion in the output and use of steel, especially in shipbuilding, had much to do with the recovery of trade in the late 1880's. When Bell wrote, steel was coming in for the first time on a big scale as an industrial material. Malleable or wrought iron, made according to the processes of Henry Cort (1740–1800) and generally consumed by the iron-using trades, except where cast-iron was required, was the material which was going out. Its decline was slow, but in the 1870's and 1880's final, especially in certain fields of engineering, such as railway construction and shipbuilding, where the use of steel had marked advantages. Certain footnotes have been omitted.

THE effect of the large increase in the quantity of steel produced in the United Kingdom was of course followed by a diminution in the make of malleable iron, as is evidenced by only 5134 puddling-furnaces returned as being in existence in 1880, a number which was further reduced to 4577 in 1884. In further illustration of the distress which overtook this branch of the trade, it is stated by Mr Jeans in his report to the British Iron Trade Association, that malleable iron works, representing a million and a half of money, were lying idle in the year 1877 in the north-eastern district of England alone.

The quantity of puddled iron made during the last four years, according to the returns in the Report of the British Iron Trade Association, is as follows:

——	1881	1882	1883	1884
Tons	2,681,150	2,841,534	2,730,504	2,237,504

Largely as the make of haematite pig made from British ore has been supplemented by that smelted from imported mineral, the demand for this quality of iron, for home consumption and exportation, occasionally exceeded the supply to such an extent that the price rose considerably....Further on the consumption of iron for shipbuilding will be given, in which steel will be included. In the meantime the following figures will show how rapidly the latter is gaining ground for naval purposes:

Tonnage of Vessels built of Steel

——	1877	1878	1879	1880	1881	1882	1883	1884
Gross tonnage	1,118	9,516	21,222	38,164	71,533	135,086	125,841	151,339

In addition to the substitution of steel for iron in shipbuilding, the use of the former is extending in other directions, of which tin plates and wire afford striking examples. When it is considered that about 349,000 tons of the former were made in Great Britain in 1884, and that the latter is a rapidly increasing trade, it is clear that these two items alone present a considerable field for an increased application of steel.

As regards wire, for which steel is admirably adapted, the make for fencing and other purposes has greatly increased in late years. The Germans turned out 179,000 tons in 1878, which rose to 378,000 in 1882. Of this last quantity 145,000 tons were of steel. I have no account of the make in Great Britain, but it looks as if half a million tons a year at least is the total annual production of this one article. Not the least important advantage of Bessemer steel over iron lies in its greater economy of manufacture. To make railway bars of this material the waste of metal is about one half, while the wages and fuel for the conversion are only about one third, of what is required for iron.

This extended consumption of steel, not only in this country, but on the continent of Europe and in the United States, both of which latter also import Bilbao ore, might inspire some apprehension as to the supply of the pig iron required for its production. The basic process, incidentally mentioned on a previous page, relieves us from all difficulty on this score. By means of linings made of dolomitic limestone in the converters or open hearth furnaces, and by the use of lime in the operation itself to neutralise the silica produced in the process, pig iron containing any amount of phosphorus, usually found in the metal, can be safely used. This mode of treatment is attended with some additional expense, but as this does not exceed the usual difference between the cost of producing haematite and Cleveland iron, the world need not fear that its demand for steel runs any danger of being limited by the want of the necessary raw material. In order to show the extent to which the basic system has been applied for the dephosphorisation of Cleveland and other iron, I have obtained from Mr Gilchrist, one of the patentees of the process, the following particulars of what has been done in England and other countries up to September 1885:

Table IV

	England	Other Countries	Total
1878 – – –	20	—	20
1879 – – –	1,150	50	1,200
1880 – – –	10,000	40,000	50,000
1881 – – –	46,120	289,880	336,000
1882 – – –	109,364	340,636	450,000
1883 – – –	122,380	511,993	634,373
1884 – – –	179,000	685,000	864,000
To September 1885	145,707	799,610	945,317
Total—Tons	613,741	2,667,169	3,280,910

Whether the basic process is capable of furnishing steel suitable for all the purposes to which this material is applied, experience alone can show. In the meantime it may be observed that by it a product has been obtained equal in purity to the best steel got by the ordinary Bessemer process from English or Spanish haematite ore; and, further, that for railway tyres and boiler plates the basic process has been largely and successfully used in Germany and elsewhere.

From what has preceded in reference to the production of pig iron, it may be inferred that not only has excessive competition between old and new seats of the iron trade been engendered by the discovery and speedy development of cheaply worked beds of ironstone, but that the change from wrought iron to steel has caused the partial or entire abandonment of one class of mineral and the adoption of another suitable for the Bessemer or Open-hearth processes. South Wales offers a remarkable instance of an almost complete revolution in the character of its iron industry. Twenty years ago or thereabouts, about one million tons of pig iron were annually converted into malleable iron—to-day the puddling process of Cort, after a reign of about a century, is almost a thing of the past. The old ironworks are now engaged in the manufacture of steel, and hence, in describing that of pig iron, I have been compelled to enter at some little length into its conversion into the secondary products.

28. IRON AND STEEL: COMPETITION ABROAD

Source: 'Report of the Tariff Commission' (1904), vol. I. 'The Iron and Steel Trades', paras. 46, 1014, 1019–20, 1024–6.

The calm tones of the British steel manufacturers in the mid-1880's were succeeded by deep alarm within a remarkably short space of time. This was the result of competition coming from many quarters but especially from Germany and the United States. Here steel industries had sprung up, mainly since the Thomas process was discovered, which were both very large and most ably managed. The products of these new industries began to appear on world markets, particularly in times of trade depression, when their own home markets fell off. As these times tended to be also periods of slack trade for the British industry and as the prices charged abroad for German and American steel were often different from those charged at home, the new rivals for custom were strongly resented.

A return of sluggish demand and keen international competition early in the 1900's, just after the boom which had marked the turn of the century, revived controversy about the future of the industry. The report of the Tariff Commission shows the extent of current concern. The commission had no official standing. It was an unofficial organization, set up to collect information in support of Joseph Chamberlain's Tariff Reform campaign following his resignation from the Balfour government in 1903. On its proceedings see W. A. S. Hewins, 'Apologia of an Imperialist' (1929), vol. I, chs. 3 and 4; Hewins was its organizer. The first industry to be examined, partly because of its association with national defence, was the iron and steel trade.

A wide-ranging inquiry, in which leading steelmasters took part, traced the lack of growth and lost leadership of the British industry in the world in the previous quarter century and concluded, superficially, that it was due not to a lack of efficiency but to the protection afforded to industries abroad by their governments and to differential price policies. A measure of protection from the British government was demanded in return. Critics of the industry and of the commission retorted to this that too little had been done by managements and men to alter their ways or to be other than defensive and that all would be well with a change of heart. The general arguments on both sides of the controversy tended to oversimplify a highly complex situation and to miss the mark in consequence. For a keen analysis of them, see D. L. Burn, op. cit. ch. XII.

A year or two after this report was issued, the tide of trade turned and the steel industry entered upon a relatively prosperous phase, which lasted, with some bad fluctuations, down to 1913. But its international competitive position did not improve. The alarms of the 1890's and early 1900's therefore marked the beginning of a crisis of confidence in the steel industry which was to be of long duration and much importance, for the industry itself and the nation.

Relative decline of the Iron and Steel Industry: Summary of Evidence

With all the Inquiry Forms and the evidence of Witnesses before us, we do not find there is any dispute as to the industrial and commercial conditions we have so far reviewed. British manufacturers had, in former times, a virtual monopoly of the home market for iron and steel; they had foreign countries, as yet undeveloped, as customers for their surplus products; and they had no competition in British Colonies and Dependencies. The methods of production, first established in the United Kingdom, have since 1870, in the ordinary course of economic development, which no power could check, extended to foreign countries; and these countries have made it the principal object of their policy to encourage national industries similar to those carried on here. Great areas, formerly divided by tariffs into many separate states, have been consolidated, and thus foreign manufacturers have obtained large and growing home markets, from which British products have been shut out by import duties, so high as to be practically prohibitive. These countries have adopted every means in their power to exclude foreign competition, to improve their methods of production and to secure absolute control of their home market. Having achieved these objects, in recent years their policy has been directed to the capture of the home, foreign and colonial trade of the United Kingdom. In the British home market, their competition, commencing at the lower stages of production, has rapidly advanced until it is now practically co-extensive with the Iron and Steel Industry. By thus attacking our home market, which is open to them without let or hindrance, they have diminished the competitive power of British manufacturers to push their trade in neutral markets, and they are now threatening our position in British Colonies.

The evidence shows that we are only at the beginning of the era of foreign competition, that that competition is certain to become more and more severe, and that to maintain the British Iron and Steel industry in a state of efficiency, strenuous efforts are absolutely necessary.

. . . .

One of the first questions that a steel manufacturer asks himself when putting down a new, and extending or modernising an old plant, is that of how far there is likely to be a market for the increased product? The answer appears to have been more encouraging to the Americans and Germans than to our own countrymen, judging from the enterprise with which they have both considerably more than doubled some product within six years, while we have advanced much more slowly. The problem remains to-day the same as in former periods. Will the world consume the vast increase of steel now being arranged for, or will that increase prove the undoing of those whose energy and enterprise have made it possible?

. . . .

In this country it is much more difficult to find constant employment for iron and steel works than in either America or Germany, partly because the home market is much less certain, and partly because it is necessary to export a larger proportion of our total output, in respect of which there is great irregularity.

The steel industry of this country has of late years passed through a difficult time. This remark more especially applies to the Bessemer process, which has been so largely displaced by the open-hearth. In no other country except our own and Austria has this been the case to the same extent. The difficulty of obtaining orders for Bessemer steel and of manufacturing at a profit, has led to the closing of a number of British Bessemer works. Open-hearth works have generally done much better, although the resources of production, as has already been stated, are probably at least twice as much as the actual demand. We may admit that larger outputs are obtained in American works, but that is due to causes which do not operate here, and not least to their having a more suitable quality of pig iron, and to their control of a very much larger market.

· · · · · · ·

Manufacturers in this country are blamed by outsiders, and often by their own countrymen, because they do not show greater enterprise in laying down large capacity plants, such as are common in the United States, and are now being laid down to some extent in Germany. Some American furnaces produce 200,000 to 220,000 tons of pig iron a year, whereas the average annual output of British furnaces is not more than 28,000 tons. Some American furnaces, with complete equipment, cost over £200,000 each, whereas the average cost of British furnaces is not probably over £25,000. The average annual production of a pair of Bessemer converters or of an up-to-date rolling mill in the States will generally exceed that of corresponding plants in this country in the ratio of 3 to 1. The truth is that the British manufacturer would not at present know what to do with such a vast product if he had it. Our own home market does not absorb more than 3 to 3½ million tons of steel a year, whereas the American market consumes nearly 15 million tons, and the German market finds an outlet at home for about five million tons.

This noteworthy fact in the steel industry of the world—the much greater output of a given plant in the United States than in any other country—is partly due to the more suitable composition of the iron used, partly to more speedy methods of charging furnaces, and partly to the use of molten iron. In Bessemer practice short blows and short intervals between them count for much. In this country short blows are not so easy, mainly because of the character of the iron used. Even when the plant employed is fully up to date, as it is in many English works, the quantity of steel produced is less than one-half, and sometimes less than one-third, the quantity produced in the best American practice. Most English engineers, on visiting American workshops, have been greatly surprised to see so few men about. Automatic machinery is much more largely used there than in this country.

The combination of up-to-date plants, economies, and improvements has enabled our American rivals, paying the highest wages known in the trade, to produce plates at a cost of only about 3s. 6d. per ton for labour, averaging some 225 tons of plates per shift. One mill of Homestead Works has produced 1,049 tons of sheared plates in 24 hours, which is at the rate of 315,000 tons in 300 working days. A 40 in. cogging mill at the Illinois Works at Chicago produces 200,000 to 250,000 tons per year. These results are not equalled in our own mills. And yet there is no reason to suppose that our plate mill practice is generally much behind that of other countries. It was until lately, if it is not now, in advance of that of any other country. If it has now fallen somewhat behind the best American practice, probably not much ground has been lost.

29. AN ENTERPRISING PARTNERSHIP IN SHIPBUILDING

Source: 'Memoirs of John Wigham Richardson': privately printed, Glasgow, 1911, pp. 142–44.

John Wigham Richardson (1837–1908), the son of a Newcastle business man, after an apprenticeship to iron shipbuilding and marine engineering, and brief periods of study at University College, London, and Tübingen, set up in business on his own in 1860 at the age of twenty-three as a shipbuilder on the Tyne. The first two years were disastrous, but he decided to go ahead with his offer of partnership to John Christie, a Scotsman. Christie was a fine ship designer and engineer. Wigham Richardson's talents seem to have been primarily financial and commercial. They made their firm famous as specialist ship constructors, building train-ferry ships, refrigerated vessels, cable-layers, ice-breakers and so forth. The company, Wigham Richardson and Company, amalgamated with their neighbours at Wallsend, Swan Hunter and Company, in 1903, as a financial preliminary to the launching of the Mauretania, in her day the largest and fastest vessel in the North Atlantic passenger trade, in 1907. See 'Launching Ways' (Swan Hunter and Wigham Richardson Ltd.: Wallsend-on-Tyne, 1953).

FOR forty years I carried on business with Christie [*Charles D. Christie, 1831–1905, W.R.'s manager from 1860, his partner from 1862 in Wigham Richardson and Company*], and I never ceased to differ from his as to the principles on which business ought to be conducted. The conservatism of Christie's nature was beyond belief. But whatever the road he was on, he was a magnificent worker. No labour was too great for him. There never was a man who had a pleasanter way of arranging the details of a contract, and every one, high or low, spoke of him with respect and esteem. Then he was a born naval architect, and his models of ships influenced every designer on the north-east coast.

One of our early contracts was for a small screw steamer called the *Beautiful Star*, built for the firm of Bloomfield and Whitaker of Sydney, N.S.W. She was chartered to take out salmon to Australia.[1] When she arrived out, Bloomfield wrote to his partner Whitaker in England—'She is a perfect gem! well may you call her the Beautiful Star, for beautiful indeed she is....'

Whatever the line of business, it is after all the main thing to please your customers, and this Christie did to perfection. But he was far too much a scientific naval architect to make his business a commercial success. In fact it is, however, a curious thing to remark that the men in my experience who have succeeded best from a business point of view as shipbuilders have been men with but little knowledge of ships. I might instance Sir William Gray, a draper, T. Y. Short, a timber merchant, Sir Christopher Furness and others. Over and over again during forty years I have demonstrated that our principal profits have been made from simple cargo steamers and from repetitions of them, but not the less, if an inquiry came for a passenger steamer, Christie's face would brighten up and he would set to work to estimate the cost with every bias to minimize it and to regard hopefully the outcome of guarantees of speed, and so forth.

It may be asked, why did I not insist upon building the steamer which would pay best; I might reply that it involved the changing of the man, and possibly from a strictly business point of view I ought to have done so even at the cost of dissolving partnership. Such a step as that, however, is a very serious one, and indeed almost impossible. If one partner has to be bought out, from what source are the funds for doing so to be obtained? Beyond all, however, was the sincere friendship between us....

---

[1] [*Live salmon to be turned out in the rivers of Victoria and Tasmania. Ed.*]

One result of Christie's special bent was that all the financing of the business fell to my share, and also all the travelling. In fact, I became a veritable *commis voyageur*, though at first I was much puzzled how to set to work.

30. STEEL IN SHIPS

Source: '*Lloyds Register of British Shipbuilding*', *1895, quoted Sir Henry Bessemer, 'An Autobiography' (1905), p. 254.*

Steel was first used for ships, as material that is for ship-plates, using Bessemer steel, in the 1860's. It began to drive out iron for shipbuilding in the 1880's and was closely connected with the expansion of the ship-building industry towards the end of the century. As material for the shipbuilder, steel had substantial advantages over iron, being lighter, with important effects on the speed, carrying capacity and earning power of the ship, and safer, with less risk of losing the vessel.

DURING 1895, exclusive of war ships, 579 vessels of 950,967 tons gross (viz. 526 steamers of 904,991 tons and 53 sailing vessels of 45,976 tons) have been launched in the United Kingdom. The war ships launched at both Government and private yards amount to 59 of 148,111 tons displacement. The total output of the United Kingdom for the year has, therefore, been 638 vessels of 1,099,078 tons.

As regards the material employed for the construction of the vessels included in the United Kingdom returns for 1895, it is found that, of the steam tonnage, nearly 98·8 per cent has been built of steel and 1·2 per cent of iron. The iron steam tonnage is practically made up of trawlers, and comprises no vessel of more than 425 tons. Of the sailing tonnage, 97·0 per cent has been built of steel, and 3·0 per cent of wood. No iron sailing vessel appears to have been launched during the year.

31. CHARLES PARSONS AND THE STEAM-TURBINE

Source: A. Richardson, ' The Evolution of the Parsons Steam Turbine' (1911), p. 9.

In 1894, a small company, the Marine Steam Turbine Company Ltd, was formed to develop the steam-turbine for marine purposes, against the hesitancy of ship-owners. Charles Parsons (1854–1931), one of the most distinguished inventors of his day, was its managing director. The result of the company's operations was the successful demonstration of the " Turbinia", a small vessel fitted with the first Parsons steam-turbine, at the Diamond Jubilee Naval Review at Spithead, in 1897.

The following was the company's prospectus. What the steam turbine did, at a time too when the innovatory effects of steam might appear to have been exhausted, was to revolutionize high-speed travel at sea. It was soon adopted for the warship and the passenger liner, but for marine use proved uneconomical in coal consumption at lower speeds than about twenty knots. This was, of course, though important for the shipbuilding industry, but one of the applications of the new style steam-engine; it found an immense field in electricity power station practice.

T HE object of the Company is to provide the necessary capital for efficiently and thoroughly testing the application of Mr Parson's well-known steam turbine to the propulsion of vessels. If successful, it is believed that the new system will revolutionize the present method of utilising steam as a motive power, and also that it will enable much higher rates of speed to be attained than has hitherto been possible with the fastest vessels.

Up to within the last five years it has been found impracticable to obtain economical results from a motor of the steam turbine class, though such motors, on account of their light weight, small size, and reduced initial cost present great advantages over ordinary engines for certain classes of work.

Recently—and more especially within the last two years—the steam turbine has been developed and improved. It has, further, been adapted for condensing, and results have been attained which place its performance as regards economy among the best recorded. Reports have been made upon it by the following well-known authorities: Professor J. A. Ewing, F.R.S., Professor A. B. W. Kennedy, F.R.S., and Professor George Forbes, F.R.S.

It is confidently anticipated that with turbines of, say, 1,000 horse-power and upwards, having a speed of revolution of about 2,000 per minute, the consumption of steam per effective horse-power will be less than with the best triple compound condensing engines.

The initial cost of a steam turbine will be very considerably less than that of an ordinary marine engine of the same power. To these advantages must be added the consideration that the space occupied by the turbines will be very much less than that occupied by ordinary engines, thus largely increasing the carrying capacity of the vessel. The reduction in the amount of vibration admits of a diminution in the weight of the hull, which under the present system must be built stronger and heavier than will be necessary under the new system, in order to resist the effects of the vibration of the present class of marine engines.

Another important feature is the reduced size and weight of the shaft and propeller. This will not only facilitate duplication and repair, and enable spare parts to be carried to an extent not hitherto practicable, but will also admit of screw-propelled vessels being used for navigating shallow waters, where at present only paddle steamers can be employed.

The merits of the proposed system may be summarized thus: Increased speed, increased carrying power of vessel, increased economy in steam consumption, reduced initial cost, reduced weight of machinary, reduced cost of attendance on machinery, diminished cost of upkeep of machinery, largely reduced vibration, and reducing size and weight of screw propeller and shafting.

The efficiency of the screw propeller, the arrangements incidental to the adoption of higher speeds, the best form and the proportions and mounting of the propeller, the material of which it should be made, and the other points, can only be decided by investigation and practical experiment; and it is to provide funds for the complete and exhaustive testing of the new system in these and other respects that the Company has been formed.

32. THE INDUSTRIALIZATION OF WAR: THE BATTLESHIP

The industrial changes of this period transformed material preparations for war. Innovation was especially swift at sea. Naval architects and engineers, working sometimes directly for governments but many of them for private firms, under the pressure of sharp naval competition, first with France and Russia, later with Germany, developed the ironclad of the middle nineteenth century into the battleship of the First World War. The evolution of the "all-big-gun" ship, steel-built and carrying an armament of unprecedented range and weight, took place in the twenty-five years before the launching in 1906 of the "Dreadnought", which temporarily threw all other battleships out of date. For the background of naval policy during these years see A. J. Marder, 'The Anatomy of British Sea Power: a History of British Naval Policy in the pre-Dreadnought Era' (New York, 1940) and E. L. Woodward, 'Great Britain and the German Navy' (Oxford, 1935). During these critical years, the increased power of the naval gun compelled the development of steel armour-plate and the growing resistance of armour forced on designs for the gun, in a technical dialectic which was only brought to an end by the submarine and the coming of air power. Commercial firms employing Admiralty contracts specialized in gun or plate. Thus John Brown and Company of Sheffield were armour-plate experts, while Thomas Firth and Sons of the same city became specialists in the gun and projectile. See Sir Allen Grant, 'Steel and Ships: the History of John Brown's' (1950) and for another armaments firm extremely active at this time, J. D. Scott, 'History of Vickers-Armstrong' (1963).

The extracts which follow are drawn from a variety of sources:

A. Sir William White, Presidential Address to the Institute of Civil Engineers, quoted in Frederic Manning, 'Life of Sir William White' (1923), p. 57. Sir William White (1845–1913) was from 1885 to 1902 Director of Naval Construction at the Admiralty.

B. C. M. Maclean, 'Mark Rutherford' (1955), p. 247. 'Mark Rutherford' otherwise William Hale White (1831–1913), the novelist, was Assistant Director of Contracts at the Admiralty, 1879–91. The guns of the "Inflexible", the largest warship in the Fleet at the time, were already out-of-date when they were tried, being muzzle-loaders. This was in 1880.

C. 'Under Five Flags: the Story of Kynoch Works, 1862–1962' (Birmingham, 1962), p. 32. The chairman of Kynoch Ltd, Arthur Chamberlain, reporting. Cordite, replacing gunpowder as propellant, made it possible to secure high velocity for the shell while lightening the gun.

D. Frederic Manning, op. cit. pp. 293–4: memorandum by Lord George Hamilton, First Lord of the Admiralty, writing in 1892.

E. Winston S. Churchill, 'The World Crisis, 1911–1914' (1923) pp. 129–31. Winston Churchill was First Lord of the Admiralty in the Asquith administration after 1911, when the decision was taken to create a Fast Division of the Royal Navy. One result of this was the acquisition by the British government of shares in the Anglo-Persian Oil Company, to secure oil supplies for these ships, a few months before war broke out in 1914.

A

THE French took the lead in the introduction of mild steel for shipbuilding; and an eminent naval architect, who was my friend of many years, the late M. de Bussy, had much to do with the matter from 1872 onwards. Mr Nathaniel Barnaby at once saw the possibilities of the material, and called on British manufacturers to furnish supplies. The response was prompt. Sir William Siemens undertook the contract at his Landore works, and in 1875 the first two vessels built of mild steel for the Royal Navy, the *Iris* and *Mercury*, were commenced.

B

The Isle of Wight had a suitable reminder of Advent and the message of peace on earth and goodwill towards men. The trial of the '*Inflexible's*' guns took place thirteen miles away from Ryde, but it shook the doors and windows.

C

In January (1895), after careful consideration of all other available localities, a site was chosen on the east coast of Ireland, abutting on the sea and extending to the pier and port of Arklow, and containing about 170 acres. All the necessary work for setting up and starting a new industry has since been increasingly pressed forward, and the place has been changed from barren sand hills into a completely equipped factory in the unprecedently short time of five months. The directors have every confidence in the future of cordite as the best all-round smokeless explosive on the market, and they have made arrangements to enable them to supply, in addition to Government requirements, the private gun and cartridge manufacturers in England, and foreign and colonial buyers. They believe cordite will lend itself to sporting purposes and are making experiments with a view to putting a satisfactory modification of it on the market.

D

The design for the new 12-inch gun has been under consideration for a considerable time past. An agreement has been reached with the War Office and the private firms competent to advise on the matter; and a specimen gun is now in hand which will, it is hoped, be ready for trial in June 1893....It has been decided that the two ships to be armed with these new 12-inch guns may be safely proceeded with in anticipation of the trial of the specimen gun, and that the guns for the armaments will be ready in time for the ships....This decision to adopt the new 12-inch gun has been arrived at after fully discussing the alternative of laying down at Chatham and by contract two more ships of the same type as the *Renown*. It has been considered, however, that while the *Renown* in speed, seaworthiness, secondary armament, and general defensive power compares very favourably with any battleship yet commenced for service in European waters, it is preferable to arm our largest battleship with 12-inch guns of an improved type.

E

The advantages conferred by liquid fuel were inestimable. First, speed. In equal ships oil gave a large excess of speed over coal. It enabled that speed to be attained with far greater rapidity. It gave forty per cent greater radius of action for the same weight of coal. It enabled a fleet to re-fuel at sea with great facility. An oil-burning fleet can, if need be and in calm weather, keep its station at sea, nourishing itself from tankers without having to send a quarter of its strength continually into harbour to coal, wasting fuel on the homeward and outward journey. The ordeal of coaling ship exhausted the whole ship's company. In wartime it robbed them of their brief period of rest; it subjected everyone to extreme discomfort. With oil, a few pipes were connected with the shore or with a tanker and the ship sucked in its fuel with hardly a man having to lift a finger. Less than half the number of stokers was needed to tend and clean the oil furnaces. Oil could be stowed in spare places in a ship from which it would be impossible to bring coal. As a coal ship used up her coal, increasingly large numbers of men had to be taken, if necessary from the guns, to shovel the coal from remote and inconvenient bunkers to bunkers nearer to the furnaces or to the furnaces themselves, thus weakening the fighting efficiency of the ship perhaps at the most critical moment in the battle. For instance, nearly a hundred men were continually occupied in the *Lion* shovelling coal from one steel chamber to another without ever seeing the light either of day or of the furnace fires. The use of oil made it possible in every type of vessel to have more gun-power and more speed for less size or less cost. It alone made it possible to realize the high speeds in certain types which were vital to their tactical purpose. All these advantages were obtained simply by burning oil instead of coal under the boilers. Should it at any time become possible to abolish boilers altogether and explode the oil in the cylinders of internal combustion engines, every advantage would be multiplied tenfold.

On my arrival at the Admiralty we had already built or were building 56 destroyers solely dependent on oil and 74 submarines which could only be driven by oil; and a proportion of oil was used to spray the coal furnaces of nearly all ships. We were not, however, dependent upon oil to such an extent as to make its supply a serious naval problem. To build any large additional number of oil-burning ships meant basing our naval supremacy upon oil. But oil was not found in appreciable quantities in our islands. If we required it, we must carry it by sea in peace or war from distant countries. We had, on the other hand, the finest supply of the best steam coal in the world, safe in our mines under our own hand....

The three programmes of 1912, 1913 and 1914 comprised the greatest additions in power and cost ever made to the Royal Navy. With the lamentable exception of the battleships of 1913—and these were afterwards corrected—they did not contain a coal-burning ship. Submarines, destroyers, light cruisers, fast battleships—all were based irrevocably on oil. The fateful plunge was taken when it was decided to create the Fast Division. Then, for the first time, the supreme ships of the Navy, on which our life depended, were fed by oil and could only be fed by oil. The decision to drive the smaller craft by oil followed naturally upon this. The camel once swallowed, the gnats went down easily enough.

33. LANCASHIRE COTTON

Source: S. J. Chapman, ' The Lancashire Cotton Industry. A Study in Economic Development' (Manchester, 1904), p. 148.

Towards the end of last century and the beginning of this, the cotton industry achieved a concentration in Lancashire higher than at any time before or since. This concentration made the cotton trade not only a great economic but also a great social and political power in the north-west counties.

It is difficult to realize the importance of the position in the British economy occupied by the Lancashire cotton industry at that time. In 1911 there were 620,000 people employed in the industry, the majority being women and girls. About three-quarters of the output of the industry was exported. Cotton yarns and manufactures represented one-quarter of the value of British exports.

THERE are some industries whose geographical centralisation becomes increasingly defined; there are others whose development appears to lie along the lines of decentralisation. The iron and steel industry is localised in a few places: engineering is less localised; the three leading textile industries are all concentrated almost entirely in one district each. Woollens have been pushed from Lancashire over to the main seat of the industry in the West Riding, and the manufacture of linen has been gradually forced from England and Scotland to Belfast and its neighbourhood. Years ago the cotton industry was more widespread in the British Isles than it is to-day; the process of concentration has been taking place: abroad, too, the same movement may be traced, but it has not yet proceeded so far. The geographical centralisation of the British industry is now remarkably complete. In 1899 Lancashire was the home of nearly 76 per cent of the cotton operatives in the United Kingdom and of more than 80 per cent of those in England and Wales, while Lancashire, Cheshire, Derbyshire, and the West Riding, contained together 91 per cent of the cotton-working population of the British Isles, and no less than 96 per cent of that of England.

34. COTTON TEXTILES: ORGANIZATION

Source: G. von Schulze-Gaevernitz, 'The Cotton Trade in England and on the Continent' (trans. O. S. Hall), 1895, pp. 67, 69–70, 73–5.

This description of the Lancashire cotton industry as it stood at the end of the nineteenth century is from the pen of a German. At the height of its success in world markets, the organization of the industry was described many times, both at home and abroad, by students of economic affairs. Compare Alfred Marshall's praise for the perfection of its standardization and specialization in 'Industry and Trade' (1919), on the eve of the industry's decline.

As Lancashire to-day is the seat of the industry, Liverpool is the world's market for cotton, Manchester that for yarns and woven goods.

.   .   .   .

The value of this concentration of the industry is best understood if one takes into account the division of labour made possible by it. The latter, first developed in the 'thirties' for the raw-cotton market, has since then taken hold of the whole cotton trade—the manipulation as well as the market for yarns and woven goods.

We will follow the cotton on its way from the importer to the export merchant. The cotton market in Liverpool, highly developed as early as the 'thirties', has entered since then under the influence of modern traffic facilities—i.e., the application of steam power to transport....

The first of these occurrences was the opening of the railway from Manchester to Liverpool. Up to this time the spinner chiefly bought from the dealer in Manchester, either from his warehouse or according to samples provided. From this time Liverpool and Manchester became practically one city. The spinner could go just as easily to the broker in Liverpool as to the dealer in Manchester, and choose there and then on the spot what he wanted. At the same time the paying capabilities of the spinners had increased sufficiently to dispense with the giving of credit on the part of the dealer. Since that time, therefore, the spinners began to buy direct from the brokers in Liverpool; the old dealer gradually disappeared altogether.

An event of far greater importance was the laying of the transatlantic cable (1866) and the consequent improvement of a network of telegraph wires encircling the whole world. Liverpool had now approached nearer to the American Continent than it had been before this time to the neighbouring city of Manchester. Therewith disappeared the necessity of a special class of business people, whose particular forte had been the knowledge of the raw-material market. In a similar direction tended the opening of the Suez Canal and the extension of Indian railways....

There are, therefore, only the importer and the spinner, and, between both, the buying broker left remaining as different types. The buying broker so far justifies his existence that he is superior to the spinner—a non-commercial man, even to-day—in his knowledge of the market. The existence of the broker makes it possible for the mill-owner to concentrate his attention on the progress within his factory, and to trouble himself as little as possible about commercial conditions.

⋅ ⋅ ⋅ ⋅ ⋅ ⋅

This far-extending linking of the market has been followed by a similar linking within the industry, whereof in the 'thirties', even, scarcely a trace was to be seen. In the first place, weaving and spinning have separated themselves. Only firms which date from the older period couple both together; new mills are devoted to the one or the other trade, and are arranged under the most favourable conditions for it. Herewith there comes at once the advantage of not needing any longer managers who are expert in both branches. Therewith weaving has also separated itself locally from spinning; whilst the latter clings to circles nearer Manchester, weaving describes a semicircle further north. The one seeks the declivities of the hills, with the level ground beyond, the other the valleys cutting through the hilly country. But division of labour has advanced further. Oldham is the chief seat of the great staple industry which produces the medium counts of yarn. There alone revolve 11 millions of spindles. The district of Oldham extends to Ashton, Middleton, and the factory places situated to the south of Manchester. Bolton, Chorley, and Preston, which border on the central point of commerce in the North, spin, on the other hand, fine counts, which, owing to climatic advantages, form a monopoly for England. The chief mass of weaving-mills seek the towns situated to the north of these, especially Blackburn and Burnley, in front of them, and extending to Todmorden and Rochdale. Burnley makes ordinary printings; Blackburn clothes India and China (so-called dhooties and T-cloths); Preston produces finer plain calicoes for the home and Continental markets. The factory places lying nearer to Manchester, and the first customers for spinning, have mostly their speciality in more complicated woven goods. Thus Oldham has cotton velvets, Bolton figured goods, Ashton and Glossop printing cloths of the first quality, the district of Colne, situated between these and the northern weaving district, makes ordinary coloured goods.

On the other hand, in Manchester, the central point of the industry, manufacturing is gradually disappearing. The mills there are mostly of an older date, but are still of historical interest as former cradles of the great industry. Manchester is constantly becoming more and more simply the seat of the export trade. Thiry years ago goods were packed in the northerly weaving districts for export. At the present time this takes place in Manchester—in many cases in the cellars underneath the high warehouses, which often go down several stories into the earth, and in which, by means of steam engines and hydraulic presses, the bales of yarn and woven goods are pressed into half their bulk, and even less. ...

The division of labour which exists between the industrial places extends to the single mills. One employer produces at the present time few specialities. The large spinning-mills of Oldham and Bolton spin, for instance, not more than one count, or at most but a few counts, and these from year to year. In the same way many weaving-mills of North Lancashire produce only one sort of current staple goods.

This far-reaching division of labour is only made possible by the certainty of sale which is guaranteed by the organisation of commerce in Manchester.

35. COTTON TEXTILE: COMPETITION FROM ASIA

Source: Thomas Ellison, ' The Cotton Trade of Great Britain' (1886), pp. 317, 320–1, 322–3.

Eastern markets had become very important to the cotton industry in mid-Victorian times, all the more worth having as mechanical cotton textile spinning and weaving spread in Western countries. Any sign of Eastern competition was therefore watched with concern.

BUT although Lancashire has not yet suffered severely from American or Continental competition in the outside markets of the world, the same cannot be said of the competition of the rapidly increasing cotton industry of India.... The most recent developments of this comparatively new branch of Indian enterprise are quite surprising. Fifteen years ago the consumption of cotton by the Bombay and other mills in India was only 87,000 bales of 400 lbs. per annum; eight years ago it was 231,000 bales; last year it was 585,000 bales! Part of this rapid development of cotton spinning by machinery imported from England is, no doubt, at the expense of the ancient domestic spinning and weaving industries of India; but, unquestionably, a large part is at the expense of Lancashire, whose trade with India and the East has been either retarded or diminished by the competition of the yard turned out by the new Indian mills.

. . . .

But the Indian mills, besides being dangerous competitors of Manchester in India itself, are even more active competitors in the outside markets of the East. In the following table we give particulars of the exports of yarn from Great Britain and India to China and Japan, in 1,000's of lbs.

| EXPORTS TO CHINA | | | | EXPORTS TO JAPAN | | |
| | From | | | | From | |
	England Lbs.	India Lbs.	Total Lbs.		England Lbs.	India Lbs.	Total Lbs.
1876–77	12,475	6,330	18,805	1876–77	17,323	261	17,584
1877–78	17,962	13,762	31,724	1877–78	15,125	81	15,206
1878–79	11,058	18,146	29,204	1878–79	25,409	1,194	26,603
1879–80	14,343	23,567	37,910	1879–80	24,608	1,814	26,422
1880–81	19,514	22,946	42,460	1880–81	26,912	2,143	29,055
1881–82	19,149	25,717	44,866	1881–82	28,330	2,921	31,251
1882–83	15,226	37,372	52,598	1882–83	19,144	5,600	24,744
1883–84	13,370	41,041	54,411	1883–84	20,129	6,247	26,376

At one time England monopolised the yarn trade with China and Japan. Even in 1877 she supplied 89·1 per cent of the imports, leaving only 10·9 per cent for India; but in 1883–4 England's proportion had fallen to 41½ per cent, while that of India had risen to 58½ per cent....

The exports of piece goods from India are much less important than the exports of yarn, but the business is rapidly increasing, the shipments having risen to 55,564,000 yards in 1883–4, against only 15,544,000 yards seven years previously. These goods go chiefly to the Eastern markets.

The severity of this Indian competition has only been felt within the past few years, and its serious significance is not yet adequately appreciated by those immediately concerned. In an interesting paper on 'The Cotton Trade of India', written by Mr Lewis Rushworth, formerly manager of the Hollinwood Spinning Co., Oldham; and now manager of the City of Bombay Manufacturing Co., the author concludes as follows:

'Having taken into consideration all the facts mentioned we are brought to the following results: First, that the cotton trade of India is at present in a fairly remunerative condition, and also that it is only in its infancy; and that it is in the centre of the consuming markets of the East, which are the largest in the world, and, as time goes on, there is every probability that the cotton manufacturing industry here will be very much increased; also that the workpeople will, year by year, become more efficient, consequently will individually produce more at a less cost to the spinner in consequence of this greater efficiency.

Secondly, that it is very probable American cotton will be imported here before long, and consequently more direct competition with Lancashire cotton mills, as the same kind of goods will be produced, and, in my opinion, at less cost. Thirdly, that there is every reason to believe that with increased railways the people will become richer in consequence of being able to sell the produce of their lands, and also will be enabled to grow cotton very similar to American cotton, as by becoming richer they can devise means for irrigating their lands. Fourthly, I am forced to the conclusion that there is a good future in store for the Indian cotton industry, and I shall not be surprised to see that in the next few years the industry will make very rapid strides indeed, and will become a very great competitor against Lancashire manufactured goods.'

36. EXPORT BOOM IN LANCASHIRE

Source: B. Bowker, 'Lancashire under the Hammer', 1928 (2nd impression), pp. 9, 12–16, 22–23.

These personal impressions, published after the First World War, ostensibly relate to the whole period 1900–14. But they are interesting chiefly as a description of the atmosphere in the cotton industry during the years of flourishing exports, 1906–14.

THE Lancashire I was brought up in was the heyday Lancashire; the Lancashire in which quite ordinary men could make a fortune in ten or fifteen years.

Looking backwards, I remember most vividly the opulent years from 1900 to the beginning of the World War. That was the gold-rush time....

There were several very good reasons to account for the coming of easy money to the cotton trade.

Lancashire's unheroically damp climate was an asset of which great pioneers had made full use. From early to late Victorian days the biggest minds in the trade had worked creatively and build tenaciously. No body of intelligent men can for years give energy, invention, and hard work to a trade without making it magnificently efficient, and for three generations before the Boer War the great Lancashire cotton trade pioneers had made the production of cotton cloths their life....

They had fine helpers. Not only had they an unromantically

admirable climate, they had a body of workpeople in whose lives spinning and weaving, bleaching and dyeing, were dominant forces. There may have been in Sheffield cutlers who loved their work as Lancashire men and women loved theirs. I do not know. But I doubt if any great industry had either the amount or the quality of affection spent on it by its workers that Lancashire had from 1840 to 1914.

They were cotton proud. They were cotton saturated. They were the source from which the industry drew its directive being. One generation of spinners and weavers produced the spinning and weaving masters for the next. In 1913 it is pretty certain that few governing families in any branch of the trade could not look back to clogs and an operative forbear inside three generations. It is true that the fortunate who rose were also few; that the many who remained as workers, generation after generation, were badly used; that operatives who became masters worked their fellows whom they had come to control unconscionably long hours, and left their organized welfare almost wholly unattended to.... What most filled the eye in the Lancashire of the nineties was the efficiency of both master and man and the reward that was coming to it: the first dawnings of a prosperity hitherto unexperienced on a big scale.

Lancashire's efficiency was not alone of the individual. In the building-up years the cotton area did more than evolve big masters and fine men. It developed a science of its industry. Through its best minds it brought to its beloved trade during this period an intensive and wholly exceptional technological study....

All over Lancashire, much further back than I can remember, evening institutes were beginning a close investigation of the textile possibilities of cotton. To them came established fabrics of the trade for examination. In them young weavers, who were to be manufacturers of the next phase, learnt the elements of design. They were teaching institutes. They were also institutes for learning and creation. In the bigger towns these old 'mechanics' became stepping-stones to day technological centres....

In all the world there was none so fit to produce cotton cloths as Lancashire. Before 1900, it is true, Germany, Italy, and the U.S.A. had begun to take their first textile lessons. Japan, too.... But in all these countries capacity to produce was as nothing to their own and their neighbours' needs. When the old century died Lancashire was astonishingly placed. It had a cotton-making machine—compact, efficient, established—without real rival; before it was a world demanding cotton piece goods to an extent no early pioneer of the trade could have imagined. The day of easy money was at hand.

The chance of easy money in any trade carries with it two quick consequences. It attracts the uncreative money-grabber. It produces in the trade itself an attitude of mind that makes for trouble. Between 1900 and 1913 the riches that flowed in on Lancashire from its unparalleled opportunity brought both these consequences intensively....

I recall another day in 1911. I then realised for the first time what it meant to commit sacrilege. Innocently I noted the growth of spindles in Japan, and the sharply dwindling British trade in cottons with Japan. Rashly I commented aloud on it in the presence of a manufacturer. He gave me an angry lecture about the iniquity of the tariffs to which Japan had taken. Then the majesty of Lancashire's unchallengeable greatness came upon him again, and he finished serenely: 'My lad, never again let anybody in Lancashire hear you talk this childish stuff about foreign competition. It's right enough for Londoners and such like, but it puts a born Lancashire man to shame as an ignoramus. It's just twaddle. In the first place, we've got the only climate in the world where cotton piece goods in any quantity can ever be produced. In the second place, no foreign Johnnies can ever be bred that can spin and weave like Lancashire lasses and lads. In the third place, there are more spindles in Oldham than in all the rest of the world put together. And last of all, if they had the climate and the men and the spindles—which they never can have—foreigners could never find the brains Lancashire cotton men have for the job. We've been making all the world's cotton cloth that matters for more years than I can tell, and we always shall.'

37. FOOTBALL BY ELECTRIC LIGHT IN THE 1870's

Source: 'The Electrician', 1 (19 October 1878), 253.

The theory and the phenomena of electric energy had been the subject in Europe of profound scientific study, much of it, as with Faraday, unconnected with practical purposes, for many years before the industries of electrical supply and manufacture emerged. After the appearance of the electric telegraph at the hands of Wheatstone and Cooke in the 1840's, practical applications of wide scope had to await the perfecting of the dynamo, which was the work of a number of men, including William Siemens (1823–83), late in the 1860's. This made possible for the first time the industrial generation of electricity on a large scale. Electric arc lamps using alternating current had been employed in lighthouses off the French and British coasts in the 1850's and 1860's; but in the late 1870's people began to experiment in electric public lighting in a way which brought it much nearer to general use. The Sheffield lamps would be arc lamps.

THE intense interest aroused by the application of the electric light to novel uses was strikingly apparent on Monday night in Sheffield, when nearly 30,000 people gathered at Bramall-lane Grounds to witness a football match played under that light. The match, which was played by two teams belonging to the Sheffield Football Association, commenced at half-past seven o'clock. The electric light was thrown from four lamps 30 ft. from the ground, and the rays, which were of great brilliancy, lighted nearly the whole of the ground, the players being seen almost as clearly as at noonday. The brilliancy of the light, however, dazzled the players, and sometimes caused strange blunders. The illuminating power was equal to 8,000 standard candles.

38. THE ORIGINS OF THE ELECTRIC LAMP INDUSTRY

Source: 'Nature', XXI (1 January 1880), 202.

The first electric lighting was by arc lamp, which was suitable for the illumination of large spaces such as football fields but not for room lighting. The growth of an electric light industry therefore depended on the invention of a suitable lamp. This arrived with the incandescent lamp, making use of a permanent carbon filament. Thomas Edison (1847–1931) in the United States and Joseph Swan (1828–1914) in Great Britain independently perfected this important invention late in the 1870's so preparing the way for the development of electric lighting and manufacturing in the next decade. Swan, who was in business in Newcastle as a prosperous chemist and druggist, pursued his scientific researches privately. He had been interested in the problem of the electric lamp for many years. His letter to the scientific periodical 'Nature', claiming the invention, was written from his home at Gateshead in county Durham.

I OBSERVE in Nature, vol. XXI, p. 187, a statement to the effect that Mr Edison has adopted the use of carbon in his new electric lamp, and that the carbon he uses is charred paper or card in the shape of a horse-shoe.

Fifteen years ago I used charred paper and card in the construction of an electric lamp on the incandescent principle. I used it, too, of the shape of a horse-shoe, precisely as, you say, Mr Edison is now using it. I did not then succeed in obtaining the durability which I was in search of, but I have since made many experiments on the subject, and within the last six months I have, I believe, completely conquered the difficulty which led to previous failure, and I am now able to produce a perfectly durable electric lamp by means of incandescent carbon.— *Underhill, Low Fell, December 29, 1879.*

39. A MEETING WITH JOSEPH SWAN

Source: M.E.S. [Mary E. Swan] and K.R.S. [Kenneth R. Swan]
' Sir Joseph Wilson Swan, F.R.S.: A Memoir' (1929), pp. 70–1.
   R. E. Crompton (1845–1940), who was later to play a distinguished part in the electric manufacturing industry, was at the time of his first meeting with Swan in the autumn of 1880 making arc lamps in London. C. H. Stearn (see also no. 48), here mentioned, was a young bank-clerk, stationed at Birkenhead, who was interested in science. He experimented with high vacua in his spare time. This work brought him into touch with Swan who needed his knowledge for the manufacture of the lamp. As a result of this meeting, a company was formed to exploit the Swan lamp.

A GENTLEMAN (Mr Morgan I think his name was) whom I believed to be one of the travellers of Messrs Manson & Swan, sent in his card to my office, 4, Queen Victoria Street, and said he had come with a request of such an urgent nature that I must take it as a mandate that I would accompany him that very evening to Newcastle to see Mr Swan. I was not allowed to go home to get any clothes or sleeping things, but was carried off to Newcastle, and was there and then taken to Mr Swann's laboratory, introduced to him, and shown a row of sealed glass bulbs containing carbon filaments which he informed me had been pumped by a form of Sprengel pump, invented by Mr C. H. Stearn, to a higher degree of vacuum than had hitherto been considered practically obtainable. The filaments, he explained, were mounted on platinum terminals and were formed of cotton which had been made into cellulose before carbonizing.

After explaining this, he had a gas-engine driving a Gramme machine started up, and lamps were switched on and glowed in a most satisfactory manner. He asked my opinion as to what could be done with it, and told me he was shortly afterwards to lecture to the Philosophical Society at Newcastle, and begged that I would be present to take part in the discussion, as he considered that I, as an apostle of the arc lamp, was to some extent in rivalry with him. He wished me to understand that there was a distinct place for the two kinds of illumination.

This was the first time I came in contact with him, and I was then struck with the extreme fairness and openness of his mind, and with his extraordinary modesty.

40. ELECTRICITY ATTRACTS CAPITAL

Source: ' The Electrician', v (8 January 1881), 90–1.

There was a small boom in electric lighting at the beginning of the 1880's. This marked the arrival of the electrical generation and manu-facturing industries. The boom failed to lead to a rapid growth of these industries within the next twenty years, as might perhaps have been expected. Compare the swift electrification of the United States; H. C. Passer, ' The Electrical Manufacturers' (Harvard University Press, 1953). Recent research (by Dr I. A. Byatt of Durham University) suggests that serious limits existed to the expansion of the British electrical industries and that these were to be found in a well-developed and highly com-petitive gas industry, in a dense railway network, leaving less room for electric transport than in the United States and in the relatively slower growth of British cities. Meanwhile, in the early 1880's, prospects appeared good.

1880

Electric Lighting

The year has been one of great progress in every stage of electric lighting; apparatus has been improved, extension has been great, and public opinion has been educated. The only company of importance existing at the commencement of the year was the British Electric Light Company. This company are [*sic*] the sole licensees of the Gramme machine, a machine which has hitherto held the first place, theoretically and practically, as an electric light machine. It would be superfluous to tabulate the whole of the work of the company during the year, it will be enough to state what is now in hand or to be completed in the immediate future. We may here say that this company does not pin itself to the use of any one particular kind of apparatus. It says, we exist for the purpose of supplying the electric light, and we will give you the best in the market. Hence, at one place you find the company using the André lamp, at another the Brockie lamp, at a third the Crompton lamp, and so on, considering the local conditions and acting accordingly....One noticeable feature in relation to the company is, that its work has been and is, successfully carried on with a comparatively small capital. It reflects great credit on the management that so much work should be performed, a dividend paid, and no fuss made.

The electric lamp that has found most favour with the British public is that designed by Mr Crompton. In 1878 this lamp was used in two places, in 1879 four more were added to the list, whilst in 1880 the makers have been unable to produce lamps fast enough....We understand that in order to meet these heavy demands Mr Crompton is building a large workshop for the purpose of manufacturing the Bürgin dynamo machine as well as his lamp, and on the completion of the works he hopes so to economise labour and time as to enable him to considerably reduce the first cost of electric light apparatus. A new pattern of lamp is to be made that will burn thirty hours without change of carbon. The energy with which Mr Crompton has pursued the subject, and the full belief he has in the ultimate success of the electric light have done much to improve the tone of public opinion. His constant efforts to reduce the cost have resulted in a considerable cheapening in the carbons. At the beginning of 1880 the cost of carbons in his lamp was 2*d*. per hour, at the end of 1880 the cost was reduced to 1·25*d*., and in some cases still more closely to the 1*d*., without interfering with the quantity or quality of the light....

Another lamp rapidly forcing its way into public favour is that invented by Mr Brockie. A number of these lamps are in use in Glasgow, in carpet factories, paper mills, ship-building yards, etc.; whilst here, again, the manufacturers are unable to turn out the apparatus fast enough. Special dynamo machines, we believe, of the Gramme type, have been built to supply the current to six or eight lamps per machine in series. The British Electric Light Company have supplied some fifteen of these lamps in Manchester, and, we understand, have adopted this lamp for use at the Cannon-street Station on the South Eastern Railway. This lamp has been specially designed for factory use, but the inventor is at present considering certain modifications necessary to adapt it to street lighting purposes. It will be remembered that the lamp is one of the type which adjust [*sic*] the carbons periodically.

Quite recently the Anglo-American Brush Light Corporation has been floated on a capital of £800,000, with a first issue of £400,000. The Brush system has been extensively tried in America. It has recently been used in Broadway, New York, and is spoken of as successful. For a new company its success in England has been wonderful. It remains, however, for the future to show that the 'income' is commensurate with the 'expenditure'. A company with such an enormous capital must necessarily transact a large amount of business to make both ends meet....

We regret that our review of electric lighting is incomplete, inasmuch as we have little authentic information of the work of Messrs Siemens. No doubt the incidental changes through the conversion of the 'house' into a 'limited', company have prevented the necessary details reaching us. Meanwhile, we have every reason to suppose that Messrs Siemens have been extremely busy in the supply of apparatus throughout the past year, not only in England, but over a far wider area—we might say the whole world. Among the most prominent and successful of their undertakings, however, we may mention the lighting of the Parade at Blackpool, the New Harbour at Holyhead, and the Royal Albert Docks, London. The light in the latter place is, we understand gaining more and more favour daily.

The Jablochkoff light seems to remain at rest, and is, we suppose, thankful.

Thus far we have referred to the more or less well known names before the public; there are others, perhaps not less well known, that we must briefly mention. Mr Edison, according to the newspaper reports, ought long since to have given public demonstrations of his success. As we anticipated, success in this direction is not to be achieved by Mr Edison without labour and knowledge. He has had to pay the penalty of trusting to the 'penny-a-liner,' or has been used by the keen-sighted speculator. We have reason to suspect that during his experiments he has done a large amount of good work that has not yet been published, and in a measure has been successful. Although we have been taken to task by our American contemporaries, we must state our conviction that Mr Swan of Newcastle, who twenty years ago experimented with incandescent strips of carbon, deserves and will receive the honour due to the successful experimentalist in this direction. We have so recently described Mr Swan's lamp that there is no need to mention it at length. The experience accumulating regarding its trials is so uniformly good that we may reasonably hope to see the commencement of a new era for the lighting of interiors.

41. FERRANTI AND CENTRAL STATION SUPPLY

Source: The Electrical Engineer, 26 October 1888, quoted Gertrude Z. de Ferranti and Richard Ince, Life and Letters of Sebastian Ziani de Ferranti (1934), pp. 58–60.

The "great Deptford installation" represented one of the first steps towards the supply of electricity commercially on the large scale. Ferranti (1864–1930), chief engineer to the London Electric Supply Corporation, then a young man in his twenties, conceived the plan of supplying electric light to all comers in London from a central power station, to be situated where land was cheap, where water was available and where cheap sea-borne coal supplies could be had. He designed the station at Deptford on the Thames, six and a half miles from the main centre of distribution, and astounded his contemporaries by proposing to transmit electricity at 10,000 volts by underground cable from generating units developing 10,000 horsepower apiece. His system of mains from Deptford to London remained in use until 1933. For further details, see R. H. Parsons, The Early Days of the Power Station Industry (Cambridge, 1940), pp. 27–41. Technically, Ferranti was a genius ahead of his time. Financially, the Deptford enterprise ran into early difficulties and was only pulled through by the tenacity of Lord Wantage and other large shareholders.

THE designer of the great Deptford installation was laughingly dubbed the Michael Angelo of that installation because from first to last, from foundation to top of highest turret, architecture, materials, foundations, and machines, all were specified or designed by one man, and the credit of the success of the really first central station in England will have to be given, without detracting one iota in favour of any other person, to Ferranti. As our readers well know, we have pretty consistently spoken of the perseverance and energy shown at the Grosvenor Gallery installation. Quietly and unostentatiously—too quietly from our point of view, for we could never obtain consent to say much about it—that installation has been carried to success. First undertaken as a private installation, it grew till it reached a plant designed for twenty thousand lamps, but that point has long been passed, and over thirty-three thousand lamps are lighted from this centre. Its capacity is reached. The promoters of the installation, however, confident in the possibilities of the electric light, confident in their business abilities, and supremely confident in their engineer, determined to erect what may really be termed a central station. It required some courage to jump from supplying tens to supplying hundreds of thousands of lamp, to put electric lighting upon the same footing as gas lighting, to supply an area as large as that supplied by the largest gas company. It required not only courage on the part of the engineer, but also a degree of confidence in himself that few men possess in the earlier days of industrial development. The question of distribution presented formidable difficulties; but it [*sic*] was met; experiments were made and a new design of main cables selected. A voltage unheard of in the previous history of the industry was determined upon, as were machines that even now frighten the cautious movers of infinitesimal steps.... At any rate it may safely be predicted that the work will either be a gigantic success or a gigantic failure. If the former, as seems most probable, the future of electric lighting will be assured, for when the light is supplied at 7¼*d*. or less per unit there can be no question of its power to compete successfully with the illuminant already in the field.

42. THOUGHTS IN WAR TIME UPON ELECTRICITY

Source: 'Report of the Committee appointed by the Board of Trade to consider the question of Electric Power Supply 1918', Cd. 9062, VIII, paras. 6–11, 13, 17.

From about 1895 the electric supply and manufacturing industries began to expand fairly rapidly. This was partly due to increasing efficiency, which enabled the electricity generating industry for the first time to compete strongly with gas, but also to the expansion of the industrial market. Industry began to require electric power upon a great scale. The rate of change varied, however, much between industries. Some, for example, ship building, with a vast need for power for many purposes adopted electricity early; others such as coalmining and textiles, two of the largest industrial groups in Great Britain, slowly and late. The electrification of homes, workshops and factories in the early 1900's was marked, but it was far less striking than the electrification of the German and American economies before 1914.

The demand for munitions in the First World War threw into strong relief the existing deficiencies in the supply and application of electricity. Public inquiry followed and the official report here quoted was a step on the way to legislation in the 1920's. The references in the document to the laws of 1882 and 1888, although they expressed a commonly held opinion, should be treated with scepticism. The structure of demand for electricity and the competition between the fuel and power industries for custom were more important in retarding the growth of electricity supply.

Past and Present conditions of Electricity Supply

A study of the legislative history of electric supply in this country during a period of over 35 years makes it clear that thorough revision is required of the whole situation if we are to avoid at the end of the war a continuance of conditions which are manifestly unsuitable for the full development of the application of electrical science to industrial production.

Electricity is at present generated and distributed mainly by authorised undertakers under the principal Electric Lighting Act, 1882, and the amending Act, 1888, which Acts were framed at a time when electricity was used principally for lighting, and its application for power purposes was almost unknown.

In 1898 a Joint Select Committee of the House of Lords and the House of Commons, presided over by Lord Cross, reported on proposals to supply electricity over wide areas, and, as a result, facilities more consistent with the development of the application of electric power to industry were granted in several private Acts, although these were restrictive and burdensome in many particulars, and have not been effectual in providing a comprehensive system of supply. These Acts usually did not admit of a general supply of electricity for lighting, and, in the area of an authorised distributor, a provisional veto, in practice amounting virtually to an absolute veto, was given to that distributor even in regard to a supply for power purposes. Other areas were in most cases unremunerative when dealt with by themselves, owing to the paucity of consumers or the long distances between them.

A general Act passed in 1909 gave somewhat wider facilities to electrical undertakers, but it may be said that the laws affecting the public supply of electricity are unsuited to the present times, and that legislation has hitherto been influenced by an insufficiently large and comprehensive outlook.

We may give without adopting in its entirety, the following extract from a letter written by the Electrical Trades Committee to the President of the Board of Trade on 19th January, 1917.

'Witnesses have been unanimous in showing how greatly the electricity supply industry is now handicapped by the following facts:

(a) Electrical legislation in the past has restricted the proper expansion of the supply industry—the electrical areas are too parochial and entirely discordant from the economic area of electrical supply. The result has been a great growth of small uneconomical stations, with resultant waste of coal and generally higher charges for energy than would have been the case from larger areas and greater concentration of plant in larger units, and more economically placed power stations.

(b) Past lack of foresight in the granting of authority for the supply of electricity has allowed even adjacent undertakings to establish works differing, not only in type of plant and mains, but also in pressures and frequencies, with the result that linking-up and interchange of power is now extraordinarily difficult and costly.

(c) At the present time all new or extension orders authorising electric supply must be sanctioned by the Board of Trade and afterwards confirmed by Parliament. All administrative matters affecting electrical undertakers generally are determined by the Board of Trade.

(d) In the case of Municipal Electrical Authorities, loans for extensions or for new projects have to be submitted to and sanctioned by the Local Government Board, or in the case of the County of London, by the London County Council. These authorities confine themselves mainly to a consideration of the financial position of the local authority, and the financial record of the undertaking, or to questions affecting lands, and have little regard to the efficiency or suitability of the projected expenditure.

There is no authority at the present time, nor is there any effective legislation which empowers any authority to ensure that the best system shall be adopted in the national interest in any district....

It has been conclusively proved that a Municipal or Local Government area is not necessarily, and in fact is rarely, the most economical area of electrical supply. The Electric Lighting Act, 1882, provides that powers may be granted thereunder in respect of any area and that a local authority may be authorised 'to supply electricity within any area although the same or some part thereof may not be included within their own district,' but in practice applications for Provisional Orders have been generally limited to the area of one local authority. This may be accounted for, in part, by the operation of provisions relating to local authority consent, and, in part, by the prospective operation of provisions relating to purchase.

The state of uncertainty as to whether or not action will be taken under the purchase provisions of the Electric Lighting Act, 1888, and as to their interpretation, has undoubtedly been adverse to the full and proper development of company undertakings subject to these provisions. As the time of purchase approaches, the effect of this uncertainty must be increasingly felt, and any substantial extension of generating plant by companies owning such undertakings, will become impossible by reason of the difficulty in raising the necessary capital....

Owing to the chaos of different systems, and the absence of any attempt to standardise pressures and frequencies, co-operation between neighbouring authorities is difficult and expensive. In London, for example, there are seven railway and tramway systems which generate electricity for the purposes of traction at differing frequencies—one at 50, two at $33\frac{1}{3}$, and four at 25—thus rendering exchange of electricity between them impracticable except at the great expense involved in converting it. Again, there are in the area of Greater London 70 authorities who supply electricity to the public, and own some 70 generating stations, with 50 different types of system, 10 different frequencies, and 24 different voltages....

To sum up as regards the present position, the evidence given before us was unanimous in declaring it to be unsatisfactory, and the opinion of practically every witness was that something must be done and as speedily as possible. Our investigation confirms fully the opinion of the Coal Conservation Sub-Committee and the Electrical Trades Committee regarding prevailing conditions, and leads us unanimously to the conclusion that the present state of affairs is contrary to the national interest, wasteful of fuel resources, deprives industries of the advantage which a well devised system of generation and distribution of electricity would give, and thereby handicaps them in competition with other countries.

43. MARCONI AND THE BEGINNINGS OF
WIRELESS TELEGRAPHY

Source: Sir Ambrose Fleming, "Guglielmo Marconi and the Develop-ment of Radio-Communication", 'Journal of the Royal Society of Arts', LXXXVI, (26 November 1937), 49–50, 52–5 and 62–3.

The theory of electromagnetic wave propagation was worked out mathematically by the physicist James Clerk Maxwell in the 1860's and confirmed by the experiments of Hughes and Hertz in the 1880's. But it was not until the 1890's that the possibility of long-distance com-munication implicit in these scientific investigations was turned to account for signalling between ships at sea. The commercial development of radio communications was the result of the enterprise and practical ability of the Italian-born and educated Marconi (1874–1937), a man of wealth and education, who came to this country towards the end of the nineteenth century to take out patents and organize the finance to exploit them. His Atlantic experiments were undertaken in order to prove that the earth's curvature was no bar to radio communication up to any distance which a transmitting station could reach. Fleming (1849–1945) was an electrical engineer and an inventor. Like many other things which were happening at the time, their work represented the beginnings of a technical revolu-tion of the utmost importance, but the immediate economic effects were negligible compared with its significance for the navigation and safety of ships and the swiftly developing art of naval war.

WHEN I made Mr Marconi's acquaintance at Bournemouth at Easter, 1898, he was working this apparatus [*an improved form of apparatus for wireless telegraphy by electric waves*] between Alum Bay, Isle of Wight and Bournemouth, a distance of fourteen miles over sea. I do not yet forget my surprise at seeing the paper tape run through the Morse inker with intelligible dot and dash signals printed upon it conveying a message to me....

In the early part of 1899 Marconi shifted his station to the South Foreland Lighthouse, near Dover, and set up another at Wimereux, near Boulogne, in France, and sent messages across the English Channel. This attracted great attention from the Press and public interest....

In 1899 the British Association met at Dover, Sir Michael Foster being President. I was asked to give the evening lecture, the subject being 'The Centenary of the Electric Current'. By arrangement with Marconi an aerial wire was erected on the Dover Town Hall and messages were exchanged by wireless with the President of the French Association, then meeting at Boulogne. At that time Mr Marconi had gone to the United States to demonstrate his system there, and on his return, having worked over a distance of seventy miles or so, he was fully determined to attempt the feat of transmitting message-bearing electric waves across the Atlantic Ocean.

It was clear, however, that to have any chance of success it would be necessary to replace the simple physical laboratory apparatus so far used by engineering plant of some considerable power. The directors of Marconi's Wireless Telegraph Company, formed in 1897 to operate his system, engaged me as adviser to specify the engineering plant which would be required. A rough guess suggested that 25 horse-power might be perhaps enough for a first experiment....

A site for the transmitting station was selected at Poldhu, a lonely place on the coast of Cornwall, and a plan for a first station building furnished also by me. In October, 1900, Mr R. N. Vyvyan, one of the Marconi Company's engineers, was sent to Poldhu to erect this plant, and the writer went down in January, 1901, to test it....

...Much work had to be done, both by the writer and by Mr Marconi before the above-mentioned plant was ready for a test. But when it was found capable of giving strong signals at Crookhaven, in the south of Ireland, Mr Marconi considered a transatlantic test might be made, and in December, 1901, he went over to Newfoundland, taking with him two assistants, Mr G. S. Kemp and Mr P. W. Paget, and some kites and balloons to elevate a temporary aerial wire.

After some trials he was able to hear by telephone placed in series with a self-restoring coherer, triple sounds which were the Morse code for the letter S which he had directed should be signalled from Poldhu at 3 to 6 p.m. on certain days. It was then clear that some small part of the electric-wave energy sent out from Poldhu had found its way across the Atlantic to St John's, in Newfoundland and it seemed demonstrated that with more energy intelligible messages could be sent....

The interest to us here present is perhaps particularly in the personal qualities which marked Marconi as a pioneer in wireless communication.

In the first place he was eminently utilitarian. His predominant interest was not in purely scientific knowledge *per se*, but in its practical application for useful purposes. He had a very keen appreciation of the subjects on which it was worth while to expend labour in the above respect.

In this work he had enormous perseverance and powers of work. He was not discouraged by adverse failures or adverse criticisms of his work. He had great powers of influencing others to assist him in the ends he had in view. He had remarkable gifts of invention and ready insight into the causes of failure and means of remedy. He was also of equable temperament and never seemed to give way to impatience or anger, but he did not suffer fools gladly or continue to employ incompetent men. He also owed a good deal to the loyal and efficient work of those who assisted him. Although born and brought up in Italy, and, I think, never in England before 20 years of age, he had the most perfect command of the English language, both in speaking and writing. The lectures and papers he gave here and elsewhere were models of lucid and accurate description. He complied in a high degree with the definition of an engineer given in the Charter of the Institution of Civil Engineers, as one who utilises and controls the energies of Nature for the assistance and benefit of mankind.

44. THE BRUNNER-MOND PARTNERSHIP IN CHEMICALS

Source: John I. Watts, 'The First Fifty Years of Brunner, Mond and Company, 1873-1923' (Brunner, Mond and Company, 1923), pp. 20-4.

Ludwig Mond (1839-1909), one of the most eminent industrialists of his time, was also a trained scientist. A German Jewish immigrant, he came to Great Britain in 1862 and joined a firm, John Hutchinson and Company, at Widnes, in Lancashire, to exploit a process which he paten-ted for the recovery of sulphur from Leblanc alkali waste. Some years later he became interested in a new Belgian process, discovered by Ernest Solvay (1838–1922), which was to drive out after lengthy competition the Leblanc method of making soda from salt. What hap-pened as a result of his interest is described in the words of his friend and partner, John Brunner (1842–1919), an accountant, in a memorandum written shortly before the latter's death. Brunner, Mond and Company, Ltd, which expanded vastly during the First World War, merged with other companies in 1926 in a new combine, Imperial Chemical Industries, Ltd. Certain footnotes to the original are here omitted. See also, Dr W. F. Hardie, 'A History of the Chemical Industry in Widnes' (Imperial Chemical Industries Ltd, 1950) and L. F. Haber, 'The Chemical Industry during the Nineteenth Century' (1958).

I WAS in the service of John Hutchinson & Co., and so was my elder brother Henry. He was technical manager of the works and I was head of the works office, having started there in my twentieth year, October 17th, 1861. I do not know any details of Mond's negotiations with Hutchinson, nor even what royalty was agreed on; but I understood that on the whole Hutchinson paid him about £10,000. I remember how Mond wrote very well-informed addresses to scientific societies (British Association, Norwich, 1868; 'Chem. News,' 1868) on the subject of his process, because I regularly helped him in their prepara-tion on account of his then deficiency in knowledge of English. . . .

Whilst Mond was an earnest worker, occupied in putting his process into shape at Hutchinson's works, he was a very jovial person-age, as we all were, and he enjoyed the cheery evenings we had together to the full. We talked, of course, on all manner of subjects, and we were, on the whole, a well educated lot of men, musical, well up in literature, and naturally, most of us, men of scientific training.

Carey and Mrs Carey had their musical evenings, and Mond was always ready with a song, as he had then a fairly large repertory. He had an exceedingly powerful bass voice. My brother sang tenor and played the zither.

After spending two years in Widnes, Mond went to Holland for three years, returning to England in 1867 with his wife. I had married in 1864.

Some time later, he and I, discussing our future, after many an intimate talk, came to the conclusion that we would try working together, and, naturally, as manufacturers. At one time the idea was so simple as to be merely the manufacture of soda crystals from soda ash bought for the purpose, and, of course, Mond had his ideas of cheapening the cost of manufacture. Another project that we discussed most intimately was the idea of taking a lease from Messrs Gamble, of St Helens, of their heaps of alkali waste, in order to recover sulphur from it.

Finally, Mond came to me one evening to say that he had heard of Ernest Solvay's success in working the ammonia process for the conversion of salt into carbonate of soda at his works at Couillet, near Charleroi, in Belgium. We both knew that Mr Henry Deacon, of Gaskell, Deacon & Co., of Widnes, had worked a similar process in 1854, and failed to make it pay. The process is based upon the following reactions:

$$1.\ NaCl + NH_3 + CO_2 + H_2O = NaHCO_3 + NH_4Cl$$
$$2.\ 2NH_4Cl + CaO = 2NH_3 + CaCl_2 + H_2O$$

It was agreed that Mond should see Solvay and ask to be shown the works with a view to taking a licence from him. This was done, and after spending several days going carefully through the works, Mond returned to England to tell me that he thought Solvay was at the beginning of a big success, and saying that he greatly admired Solvay's apparatus, his ability as an engineer, and his great mental power.

When we had decided to adopt the Solvay process, Mond and I went from Widnes to Hartford Station on May 4th, 1872, and thence walked up the Weaver valley as far as Winsford, to survey the ground with the idea of choosing a site upon which which to establish our works. Thereafter, Mond called on Mr Hermann Falk, the salt manufacturer at Winsford, and explained his ideas to him. Mr Falk strongly urged taking a lease of land from him, which he had on lease from Lord Delamere. Now I, on my part, was very loth indeed to put any money for which I was responsible on a leasehold plot, and I positively refused to do so then.

After further investigation of the salt field of Cheshire, we hit upon the land at Winnington as being far away the most suitable in the whole district for our purpose. It was freehold, it had a long frontage to the navigable River Weaver, and, therefore, easy access by water to the Liverpool docks, and it had railway connection with the Cheshire Lines at a convenient level. Mond said no doubt we could get brine there....

There were 130 acres of land, a considerable part covered by fine timber, and Mond emphatically declared that a purchase was beyond our hopes. I said on the contrary that we could easily borrow upon it after Hutchinson's fashion, who, as I knew, was an expert borrower....

My friend, Charles Menzies Holland, eldest son of Charles Holland, a Liverpool merchant, a friend of my boyhood, undertook to join us in the purchase. I carefully considered the best method of obtaining money and suggested a lease, which was duly created from the three of us, to Mond and myself, of the small area which was to be occupied by our works at the riverside, pointing out that we could borrow upon that area separately on account of its great commercial value, and we mortgaged it at Parr's Bank as a security for our varying overdraft.

We borrowed through Holland's friends, Messrs Parker, Rooke and Parker, solicitors, of Bedford Row, £12,000. Through them, we mortgaged all but the works land, and we paid them off on the formation of the limited company, in March, 1881. Mr Holland's money towards Brunner, Mond & Co,'s capital was paid to us between March 26th, 1873, and August 1st, and amounted in all to £5000; and on September 2nd, 1874, he lent us £1500 which we re-paid on January 1st, 1876. We raised £6000 by means of bills on Holland, and we paid these off in the first three months of 1875.

I borrowed from my father and my mother-in-law, and put into the business £4000, and Mond put £1000.

As a consideration for his £5000, we undertook to pay Holland one-third of our profits, to be limited to a maximum of 25 per cent per annum, on the money from time to time in our possession, including interest. Our agreement with him was framed at my suggestion under Bovill's Act, and he became a lender of money, and not a partner. Under Bovill's Act he was not liable for the firm's debts beyond the amount he had lent us, whilst Mond and I were fully so. Our bargain with him included the right to pay him off, if and when we became a limited company.

During 1874 we lost money, but in 1875 and 1876 we paid him his one-third share, being about 11¾ per cent and 19 per cent. We dealt with Parr's Banking Company, and their General Manager, Mr John Dun, was an exceedingly good friend to us. He had absolute faith in my honesty and frankness, and he allowed us to overdraw all through that time in very generous fashion.

45. LUDWIG MOND

Source: J. M. Cohen, 'The Life of Ludwig Mond' (1956), pp. 159–60.

Ludwig Mond, a German Jewish immigrant and university-trained scientist, in partnership with John Brunner, had in 1873 established a works to make soda by the new Belgian Solvay process at Winnington Park, Northwich, near the Cheshire salt mines. At the time of this description, written by one who applied to work with him, in 1886, he was forty-six. Henry Roscoe was the Professor of Chemistry at Owen's College, Manchester, now the University of Manchester.

HE was only some 5 feet 8 inches in height and stooped forward slightly, a rather fearsome figure, with magnificently developed chest and arms. He was just in from a tour of the works, and wearing a black shapeless hat with a broad brim, both hat and coat much covered with white dust. From under the brim of this hat a much tortured and disfigured left eye (damaged with caustic in a Dutch works) first met me, and then a heavily bearded face with a powerful racial nose. His moustache and beard were rough black hair, rather aggressive, and he was smoking a dark cigar. The right eye was very powerful and searching. The whole head seemed very powerful in proportion to the body.

He met me with a remarkably amiable smile, and took me into a small neighbouring office. He at once commented on my youthfulness and very short period of College training. He strongly recommended a further two years training in a German University. I replied that my father would sooner see me go to Hell than Germany. This amused and, I think, pleased him. He then questioned me as to how much I was taught at Owen's about the ammonia-soda process, and was decidedly pleased to learn how little was known about it. My repetition of Roscoe's remark to Watson Smith ('We really must pay some attention to this process at Northwich') amused him.

46. RARITY OF CHEMICAL ENGINEERS IN BRITAIN

Source: Ivan Levinstein, "Observations and Suggestions on the Present Position of the British Chemical Industries, with Special Reference to Coal-Tar Derivatives", 'Journal of the Society of Chemical Industry', v (1886), 351–3.

The failure of Great Britain to develop a strong aniline dyes industry, despite an abundance of the raw material, crude coal-tar derived from gas-works and coke-ovens, the early researches of such a man as William Henry Perkin (1838–1907) in the 1850's and 1860's and an initial growth of the industry in London and Manchester, was observed and commented upon at the time. The remarks of Ivan Levinstein (1845–1916), an immigrant like Mond from Germany, who was himself successful in the industry, go deeper than most, for he was thoroughly familiar with the German light chemical industry, which was extremely strong. See further, L. F. Haber, op. cit. pp. 162–8 and Alfred Marshall, 'Industry and Trade' (3rd ed. 1927), pp. 240–2, for the economic aspects of this type of massive treatment of industrial by-products.

IN the year 1878, Professor Bayer, the discoverer of artificial indigo, made the following remarks in a speech delivered on a special occasion:

'Germany, which, in comparison with England and France, possesses such great disadvantages with reference to natural resources (raw materials), has succeeded, by means of her intellectual activity, in wresting from both countries a source of national wealth. Germany no longer has to pay any tribute to foreign nations, but is now receiving such tribute from them, and the primary source from which this wealth originates has its home, not in Germany, but in England.

'It is one of the most singular phenomena in the domain of industrial chemistry, that the chief industrial nation, and the most practical people in the world, has [sic] been beaten in the endeavour to turn to profitable account the coal-tar which it possesses. The numerous German colour works purchase from England the greater portion of the products of the distillation of coal-tar, and they supply three-fourths of the world with the colours made from it. However, we must not rest on our laurels, for we may be sure that England, which at present looks on quietly while we purchase her tar and convert it into colours, selling them to foreign nations at high prices, will unhesitatingly cut off the source of supply as soon as all the technical

difficulties have been surmounted by the exertions of German manufacturers, etc.'

Eight years have elapsed since these remarks were uttered, and what
is our position in England to-day? We have not cut off from Germany
the source of supply; we still supply Germany with three-fourths of
the hydrocarbons which she requires; and we still allow Germany to
supply us with at least three-fourths of the colouring matters which we
use....

And there is only one sound way of stopping the supply to competitors of our raw materials, and that is by using them ourselves, and
thus turning them to profitable account. Only thus can we secure
to ourselves their full value, and benefit not only the industry more
directly concerned, but also other collateral industries....

The question then arises—if it is a fact that the natural advantages
are all on our side, and if it is also a fact that lower wages and superior
chemical knowledge in the manufacture of a large number of coal-tar
derivatives can no longer be pleaded—What are the reasons why far
greater progress has not been made in this country in the manufacture
of these products? or, Do *other obstacles* exist to prevent us from taking
full advantage of the lower cost of the primary materials? I, for one,
contend that there are no real difficulties in the way of getting hold of
the larger share of this business, if only the true position of this industry,
its constantly growing extension, its daily increasing importance, and
its important bearing on the development of other industries, were
fully understood and appreciated by the nation, and especially by its
enterprising capitalists. The development of industrial enterprise in
this country has for the last thirty years been practically confined to
cotton, wool, iron, and coal, to the lamentable neglect of other
industries of apparently minor importance, while the chemical
industries have been left in the hands of a few, who—often more by
good luck than through intelligent and economical management or
scientific attainments, but aided by the natural wealth of the country—
have carried on the business more or less successfully, whilst outside of
these few the general public was in profound ignorance of industrial
chemistry. Hence the total want of enterprise in this direction on the
part of the nation, owing to an insufficient appreciation of the importance of the chemical industries; the consequent apathy, and the

absence of any intimate connection or intercourse between our scientific men and our manufacturers; and, finally, the very great facility with which fortunes had been made in years gone by in what were then considered staple industries. All these combined were the primary and principal causes which fully account for our present position in regard not alone to the coal-tar industry, but to most other branches of chemical industry.

The position of Germany was quite different; in her case none of these adverse circumstances existed. There was no superabundance of accumulated wealth, nor the same easy opportunities of acquiring it, the great natural advantages did not exist, and a knowledge of chemistry was more diffused among the people, consequently new branches of chemical industry were eagerly sought for and energetically taken up by enterprising capitalists, supported by the people and the scientific men.

It is obvious that the unfortunate circumstances which have hitherto influenced and restricted our national industrial enterprise in certain directions must have exercised injurious effects not only on the development of the chemical industries, but also on that of other industries. This country possesses eminent engineers, whose names have a world-wide reputation, but we do not possess what may be termed chemical engineers, or at any rate they are very few indeed in number. For suggesting or discovering new chemical products or combinations we require chemists of talent, but for carrying out their suggestions to a successful issue, highly-trained chemists and chemical engineers capable of devising the necessary apparatus are also needed, and often the practical value of these suggestions depends largely on the skill of the chemical engineer. I apprehend that the expression, chemical engineering, by which I understand the conversion of laboratory processes into industrial ones, is by very few appreciated to the extent which it deserves, and the devising and constructing of plant and appliances in chemical and similar works is as a rule left either to engineers who are not conversant with the chemistry of the processes for which the apparatus is destined, or to the works mechanic, who simply proceeds by rule of thumb, or else it falls to an inexperienced chemist who understands nothing of engineering.

47. ARTIFICIAL SILK: THE CONTINENTAL LEAD

Source: W. P. Dreaper, "The Artificial Silk Industry", 'Journal of the Society of Chemical Industry', xxviii (1909), 1301.

The argument here referred to, justifying a certain slowness in taking up new processes compared with other nations, was used of other industries besides artificial silk. It represented perhaps rather an excusing mood than a serious argument.

I T is interesting in passing, to examine the position taken up by some authorities in this country, that there is an advantage in letting other nations work out new processes, and then establishing a position on the market with their early experience and failures before us. The manufacture of this material under the conditions reviewed starts here with a financial handicap, for the leading Continental firms have already written down their works, plant, and rights, to a nominal amount, out of the abnormal profits in the past; they have a trained staff and great experience at their disposal. So that this must be set against any security arising out of such an assured position. On the other hand, it is claimed that in the two processes working to-day in this country, at Coventry and Yarmouth, respectively, the details of manufacture have been more successfully worked out here than on the Continent. The Viscose process is working on a large scale at Coventry, and there are indications that the Yarmouth research works may lead to an equally important development in the production and marketing of finer counts. The Flint Works is not yet producing yarn.

48. FIRST DAYS IN ARTIFICIAL SILK

Source: C. H. Ward-Jackson, 'A History of Courtaulds' (privately printed, 1941), p. 100.

The early history of artificial silk in this country was connected with Joseph Wilson Swan and his search for a filament for the incandescent electric lamp. In the mid-1870's Charles Fred Topham, son of a glass blower, met Charles Henry Stearn, a scientifically minded cashier in the Liverpool branch of the Bank of England, for whom he did laboratory technical work. A year or two later Stearn began experimenting with Swan on the lamp. Topham made the bulbs for the first Swan lamps and remained in association with Stearn when the latter moved to London to manufacture lamps and artificial silk. Swan was himself one of the discoverers of artificial fibre. This he came across and patented in 1883 in the process of perfecting the carbon filament of his lamp. He squirted nitro-cellulose dissolved in acetic acid into a coagulating fluid, where it formed a continuous homogeneous thread. This thread was fine enough to be crocheted and was exhibited by Swan as "artificial silk" in 1885. One year before, in 1884, Chardonnet in France had patented a method of extruding a solution of nitro-cellulose through orifices, to make a filament suitable for textile use. But nitro-cellulose did not become the base of the artificial silk industry in Great Britain. Two industrial chemists, Charles F. Cross and Edward J. Bevan, who had met at Owen's College, Manchester (now Manchester University) as students and had both become professionally interested in cellulose and vegetable fibres, conceived the idea of producing a substance which they called viscose, by the action of caustic soda upon vegetable cellulose. It was viscose manufactured by them, under a patent taken out in 1892, which was after much experimentation spun by Stearn and Topham as a fibre on a scale which made possible the mass production of artificial silk. Topham's invention in 1900 of a centrifugal spinning box for this purpose is said to have been suggested to him by noticing, while cycling home from work, that the mud on the road was thrown out in a circular fashion by the wheels of his byke. The letter here printed is from an early American buyer of the new fibre, at that time called Stearnofil. Courtaulds, a highly successful and well-managed Coventry silk firm, engaged in the making of crape for fashionable mourning, bought out Stearn and his friends in 1904. For Swan's part in the early history of this invention, M.E.S. and K.R.S., 'Sir Joseph Wilson Swan: a Memoir' (1929), pp. 98–9; for the Stearn-Topham association and the Courtauld intervention, Ward-Jackson's book.

[Letter from D. C. Spruance, vice-president of the General Artificial Silk Company, Philadelphia, to C. H. Stearn, at 47 Victoria Street, London, 4 April 1903:]

Dear Mr Stearn,

The hanks of Stearnofil sent us, the one of 18 strands and the other of nine strands, each of 100 deniers, we sent to our largest silk manufacturers to weave up. Enclosed I hand you a sample of this cloth. They are so delighted with the results of the reeling, weaving and finishing that they report that they could not spare any more of the cloth than the enclosed sample. I have no criticisms to make on the fiber whatever, and they maintained that it weaves as good as any silk ever used and that the result is something wonderful. However, they say that the nine-strand fiber is somewhat stiffer than the 18 strand and that, in view of the fact that the 18 strand fiber worked perfectly, they really prefer the 18 strand. I wish you would give our superintendent, Mr Baldwin, when he arrives in Europe, full and complete working drawings of your apparatus and any samples of apparatus that he may require, also as much woven fabric as you can spare and also, in addition to this, 25 or 50 pounds of your yarn. Messrs Baldwin, Taylor and Fox will sail from New York on the *Oceanic* on the 8th inst. and should arrive in London on the 16th.

49. THE INVENTION OF THE PNEUMATIC TYRE

Source: J. B. Dunlop, 'The History of the Pneumatic Tyre' (Dublin, 1924), pp. 10–15.

John Boyd Dunlop (1840–1921) of Belfast, a veterinary surgeon, was inventor rather than business-man. It was William Harvey Du Cros (1846–1918), a Dublin business-man and athlete, interested in cycling as a sport, who acquired the patent of Dunlop's invention and floated a successful company to exploit it. Within the next five years, the pneumatic cycle tyre largely replaced the solid. This improvement marked a new stage in the popularity of the cycle and prepared the way for the cycle industry boom of the mid-1890's. It also set men thinking about and experimenting with the adaptation of the pneumatic tyre to the motor-car.

As long as I can remember I have taken an interest in locomotion by road, rail and sea. Like many others I entertained the idea that spring wheels with flexible rims would run lightly on the road....

For a period of twenty years or more, I occasionally thought of various forms of spring wheels. At one time I entertained the idea of a flexible band of steel running at each side of a horse drawn vehicle, with a number of wheels or rollers supporting the vehicle and bearing on the steel band underneath....

Having abandoned the idea of spring wheels, it occurred to me that the problem of obtaining speed or ease of propulsion of vehicles, might be solved by a peculiar mechanical arrangement of cloth, rubber and wood. At length, it dawned on me that the problem as to light vehicles, at any rate, might be solved by means of a triple tube of rubber, canvas and rubber distended with compressed air. These are some of the ideas, which after being considered from time to time led up, eventually, to the invention of the pneumatic tyre....

At the period when I invented the pneumatic tyre, I had the most extensive Veterinary practice in Ireland. I employed twelve horse-shoers and did a considerable business in the sale of specialities in medicines.

I had never ridden a cycle, and there were no cycle or rubber factories in Ireland. Everyone, who took any interest in cycling, knew that the small solid tyres then in use were impractical over square setts....

The problem which I set myself to solve, was to produce a large tyre, which would overcome vibration, and also be fast on all surfaces. About the end of October, 1887, I communicated my idea to my son, who, at the time rode a boy's tricycle, fitted with rather small solid rubber tyres....

After this, my son Johnnie often asked me to hurry and make the air tyres, as he wanted to beat his bigger companions, who he often met, after school hours, and sprinted with in the People's Park, Belfast....

Perhaps I should mention that I had gained experience in making rubber appliances which I had invented in connection with my veterinary work. This experience stood to me when I made the first air tubes out of thin sheet rubber.

50. THE CYCLING BOOM OF THE 1890's

Source: Blanche E. C. Dugdale, 'Arthur James Balfour' (1936), I, 194–5.

The bicycle had been introduced in the late 1860's, but it was not until the end of the century, after a long series of technical improvements, that it became popular. At the time this letter was written, Balfour was Leader of the House of Commons in the Salisbury administration. About this time, he appeared on the Treasury bench with his foot in a slipper and his arm in a sling.

House of Commons
March 20, 1895

My dear Lady Elcho,

You will be amused to hear that I went for my first bicycle expedition through the streets of London on Sunday afternoon. I chose Sunday of course because the traffic was small, and I hoped that I might escape being run over by hansom or omnibus, even though my skill should be somewhat in default. I got on pretty well; in fact the streets were so empty that I found no difficulty at all.... I won't tell you where I went, for you would not know the names of the streets!

51. CRISIS AMONG THE CYCLE MAKERS

Source: 'The Ironmonger' (26 November 1904), pp. 354–5.

Much of the business during the cycle-boom of the 1890's was done by local agents, assembling bicycles from component parts supplied to them by manufacturers. When the reaction came, the new conditions of trade, with prices and profit-margins falling, played into the hands of the big firm, mass-producing cycles from completely interchangeable parts and supplying agents throughout the country wholesale. The editor of the 'Ironmonger' was commenting on the annual London cycle show, where a £6 model was on exhibition.

THE cycle-makers of to-day move in sad times. One cannot but contrast the present with the heyday of cycledom, when the National Show covered the large floor and overflowed into the gallery of the Crystal Palace, when gas-barrel and solder realised in the auction-rooms as much as, or more, than the finest samples of cycle mechanism which Coventry can produce bring to-day in ordinary trade, when premiums were sometimes paid for delivery under six months, and when prophets scouted the commercial possibility of a ten-guinea cycle. The reasons for the remarkable changes are, of course, expansion of production, shrinkage of demand, the competition of the motor-car as a fashionable pastime, and good tyres being obtainable at about a third of the price ruling eight years ago. This last is a startling feature. ...The probable effect of the cycle-cut upon the trade in components is worthy of consideration...for there is no question but that the cheapening of cycles will make it more and more difficult for the assembler to make assembling pay.... There will always be a few cycles made by the local maker, as there are still boots made to measure, but the 'trade' will be in the Coventry and Birmingham article, built and finished in the workshops of these towns from the bracket to the transfer.

One result will be the centralisation of the trade. Birmingham and Coventry will benefit, as they will secure work hitherto done in repair shops throughout the provinces. The small man will be deprived of the fruits of his labour in assembling. He will find it harder to live, but he may find salvation in attention to the motor-car business, which will be not so essentially a season's trade....

52. CYCLES: AN ASSEMBLY INDUSTRY

Source: G. R. Carter, "The Cycle Industry, in Sydney Webb and Arnold Freeman", 'Seasonal Trades' (1912), pp. 109–16.

On the eve of the European war, the cycle industry, like motor-car manufacture, was well established. Both grew rapidly among the light engineering trades of the Midlands. The city of Coventry, which played a big part in the establishment of these industries, was an old centre of silk riband weaving and watch-making, which at this time was moving rapidly over to engineering. Birmingham, formerly the headquarters of the hardware trades, was making the same kind of transition.

THE all-important event in the development of the industry was the boom of 1895–7, and the subsequent depression from 1897–1900. The phenomenal increase of demand during the boom, and the critical period following, permanently affected the organisation of the industry. Two immediate results of the boom were the importation of foreign cycles—especially American—and the undue expansion of the home industry. Works and output were increased, and almost every firm received financial inflation. With the reaction of 1897–1900, enormous financial loss was sustained amounting to almost £15,000,000, but several peculiar consequences ensued:

1. The American cycles, so largely imported, proved quite unreliable, and have never since obtained any considerable market in England.

2. With the boom, a vast quantity of automatic machinery was introduced, and with the slump came a reliable bicycle at a low price—formerly an unknown combination. This gave a new impetus to the trade.

3. Inefficient makers were eliminated, and the surviving firms compelled to attain the utmost efficiency. The expansion of the industry since 1901 has been steady and sure.

4. The transference of the manufacture of cycles to the Midlands was completed. The London firms were unable to withstand the highly equipped Midland firms, and dropped out.

5. Some assert that the seasonal character of the industry has since become more pronounced, if it does not really date from this period. The adoption of automatic machinery during the boom enabled makers to produce vast quantities of cycles so rapidly, that the season's demand could be easily met by working the factories at full pressure during the season alone. When the season's demand fell off, slack work was immediately the result. Formerly, the manufacture of a cycle took a much longer period, and makers were engaged all the year in preparing machines to meet their rush of orders....

In all, the leading firms number about a dozen or so. The 'Cycle Manufacturers' do not make their own supplies of tyres, wheel rims, chains, accessories—bells, lamps, etc.

(i) The 'parts' and 'accessories' are purchased from firms who specialise in making certain of them, e.g., Dunlop Tyre Company for tyres, wheel rims, pumps, etc.; Lucas Ltd for lamps, bells, etc.; Perry and Company for cycle chains.

The specialisation is carried to a very high degree. Traders testify to the increasing specialisation of the industry, and its tendency to reduce the effect of seasonal variation in the trade. Considerable plant is necessary, and the large investment of fixed capital would not be profitable in this seasonal trade unless the producing firm can ensure a large and fairly constant output. The quantities required by individual 'cycle manufacturers' would not justify the outlay of capital for independent plants. It is more profitable to all concerned to purchase supplies of these parts, accessories, etc., from firms specialising in certain kinds of them. These firms are thus finding a larger demand and securing more constant employment for their works. The centre for the manufacture of accessories and parts is Birmingham.

(ii) The 'Cycle Manufacturers' purchase their supplies of steel tubes, bars, wire, accessories, etc., and thence produce the finished cycle. This branch of the industry is centred at Coventry. Here the leading works are situated, and here the industry can be seen at its best. Large quantities of cycles are produced at Birmingham, some few individual firms have their works at Redditch, Nottingham, Wolverhampton. All the leading cycle-makers produce motor cycles as well as cycles and carriers. The present tendency is to include the manufacture of automobiles also....

Regarded even in its most general aspect, the variation of trade in the cycle industry appears to be 'seasonal' in the strictest sense of the word. Without exception, those engaged in the various branches assert decisively that the condition of the trade, the volume of business, in any year, or period of the year, is fundamentally determined by the weather and the particular season. The industry is probably unique as regards the enormous influence of the weather in determining the volume of business at any time. The supply of raw materials is constant, trade conflicts are conspicuously absent, foreign competition is little felt in the home market and thoroughly matched abroad. The volume of trade is on the increase each year, and there is sometimes a scarcity rather than over-supply of some workers.

53. FOUNDATIONS OF THE MOTOR-CAR INDUSTRY

Source: Birmingham Post (newspaper) 5 November 1896.

The practical application of the principles of the internal-combustion engine to the needs of road transport were first worked out upon the Continent, in the 1880's, by Gottfried Daimler and Karl Benz. The mid-1890's saw the beginnings of motor-car manufacture in Great Britain. This was the result of a sudden boom in demand, the repeal of the so-called "red-flag" legislation, which had set a very low limit on the speed of all horseless vehicles on the road, in the interests of horses and their owners, and a series of company flotations, some of them highly speculative, in both the cycle and motor-car trades. Motor-car manufacture was already established in France and there was a French influence in the early British industry. The cycle-making cities of Birmingham and Coventry were very much interested in the new manufacture, which lent itself to many of the same technical processes and to methods of assembly from many component parts, produced by other industries.

The Auto-Car Industry: Local Preparations

On the 14th inst. the Act of Parliament comes into operation which opens our streets and roads to a form of traction of which at present we know very little. Hitherto, except under special conditions, no locomotive—for that was the general category under which motor-cars came—was permitted to travel at more than four miles an hour, and even then in most cases during the night. As a further safeguard—whether during the night or day—it was necessary that a flagman should precede all automatically-propelled vehicles. The new Act, however, abolishes all these limitations, and motor-cars may in future claim as much freedom in the streets as cabs or private horse-drawn vehicles.... Mechanically-driven vehicles on roads for the conveyance of passengers are no new things in this country. They take precedence in point of date of the railway system, but were starved out of existence by the railways and by the extraordinary restrictions placed upon them by the various local authorities. The unexpected removal of the restrictions has taken the country by surprise, and the roads will be free before there is any perfect motor ready to be placed upon them. Motor-cars, as we know them, are in their infancy in England. For some years they have been in use on the Continent, and most of the motors employed here are based upon foreign inventions. There are steam, oil, electric, and gas motors, but to almost all there is the same objection—an excessive amount of vibration. What is wanted is a noiseless and pulseless motor, with the driving-power separated from the carriage. It may be confidently anticipated that no pains will be spared to produce a perfect machine. The subject is one which is receiving unremitting attention in a large number of different quarters throughout Birmingham and the Midlands....

Whether the motor-car will ever displace horse-flesh remains to be seen. There are circumstances in which one can conceive that a ride upon an automatically-driven car at, say, ten miles an hour would be preferable to a seat in an omnibus or a 'growler,' but lovers of horses are not likely to sacrifice the pleasure of driving a fast-going and reliable animal without very considerable compensating advantages. The question of cost, too, will be another drawback to the use of horseless carriages. We have before us the price list of a local company, which shows the cost of a parcel delivery van to be £150, whilst a brougham would cost £300, a landau £260, a four-wheel dog-cart £240, and a char-a-banc capable of holding from twenty to twenty-four persons £340. The original outlay, however, is the only expense, barring accident and ordinary wear and tear. Unlike a horse, the cars will not 'eat their heads off' when there is no work for them to do. This is a fact which is likely to influence the great carrying firms and others who employ large numbers of horses, and with whom the cost of keep, especially in periods of stagnation, is a serious item. It is in this direction that the most rapid development of motor traffic is looked for. Already makers are inundated with enquiries for particulars as to the price and capabilities of light delivery vans....Electricity or oil appear to be the two agents upon which inventors rely, though, as will be seen below, a gas-motor has been invented, which may be brought into competition with the other forces. Steam seems to be almost out of the question, chiefly on account of the weight of water which would have to be carried, and the necessary boiler. But for the cost and trouble which is at present involved of getting secondary batteries recharged, electro-motors would no doubt take first place as the source of power for all light vehicles. There is, perhaps, amongst motor-car builders a preponderating leaning to oil, which can be more readily procured in the course of a journey than exhausted batteries could be recharged. If with the new Act of Parliament the flagman becomes extinct there must at the same time be called into existence in various towns, as well as country districts, a class of men capable of doing repairs to motors or motor-cars.

We cannot ascertain that any manufacturing of motor-cars is taking place in Birmingham at present, but preparations are being made in several directions for commencing operations....

Coventry, which is at the head of the cycle trade of the country, is also taking the lead in the matter of the manufacture of motor-cars. A very brisk business is already being done there, and employment is being found for some hundreds of hands. The British Motor Company are located in the old mills of the Coventry Cotton Spinning and Weaving Company. The leading spirit of the company is Mr E. J. Pennington, an American gentleman, who is the inventor of a motor which is small, compact, light in weight, and of high power.

54. A PIONEER IN MOTOR-CARS: F. W. LANCHESTER

Source: P. W. Kingsford, 'F. W. Lanchester' (1960), pp. 47–8, 49, 67.

The construction of motor cars was to begin with, like the making of bicycles, treated as a craft and only gradually handled by large-scale factory methods. Among the many small engineering firms engaged in the trade, that of F. W. Lanchester (1868–1946), a man of the highest attainments in this difficult technological field, was outstanding for the standards of design and workmanship which it set. He became general manager of the Lanchester Engine Company in 1899 and describes early difficulties. Rudyard Kipling was a friend as well as customer.

THE difficulties of management were very great, partly owing to the fact that no ancillary trades had then developed and we had to do *everything* ourselves, chassis, magnets, wheels, bodywork, etc., everything except the tyres, moreover for many purposes I had personally to train my labour, especially did this relate to the making of interchangeable bodywork. Those who have entered the field within the last twenty-five years have no conception of what the organization of even a small motor vehicle factory meant in these early days.

In those days, when a body builder was asked to work to drawings, gauges, or templates, he gave a sullen look such as one might expect from a Royal Academician if asked to colour an engineering drawing.

[*Telegram from Rudyard Kipling to F. W. Lanchester*]
Jane [*an experimental seven-seater sent to Kipling for trial*] is disembowelled on the village green. Please collect your disorderly experiment.

55. THE DEMAND FOR MOTOR-TRANSPORT

Source: C. S. Rolls, "Motor Vehicles", in 'Encyclopaedia Britannica'
(11th ed. 1911), XVIII, 916–17.
    Charles Stewart Rolls (1877–1910), who had been killed in one of
the first flying accidents a year before this article of his was published,
was like Lanchester a pioneer both of the motor-car and the aeroplane.
He founded Rolls-Royce Ltd in 1904 and here describes the rapid growth
in the demand for mechanical transport to which the establishment of the
firm was an answer. For the Napier Company see C. H. Wilson and
W. Reader, 'Men and Machines: a History of D. Napier and Son,
Engineers, Ltd. 1808–1958' (1958).

...But the great factor in the triumph of British motor engineering arose from the fact that, in England, there was a great wealth of knowledge concerning the properties of steels and steel alloys, and that knowledge, which was advancing all the time, was turned to such good use that it is safe to say that, in only the very best of French cars is the same strength and efficiency obtained from the same weight of metal as would be used in the construction of quite a number of British cars. Lightness of moving parts had led to increased engine efficiency and to economy of fuel, whilst the inert parts of the mechanism—the frame and other fixed details—by being lighter, call for a smaller expenditure of power to overcome their inertia. Apart from the employment of special steels for motor-car construction, in which England took a leading part many improvements in design and method have originated in Great Britain. For instance, the multiple-disk clutch, which permits a car to be started without shock, is an English invention, as are the detachable wheel, the spare wheel and the six-cylindered engine. The latter, introduced by the Napier Company and employed extensively by them, by Rolls-Royce and others, has exerted a great influence upon British tastes, because it created a growing dislike to noise, one of the consequences being the rapid development of the silent car....

Concurrently with its development into a reliable, silent, odourless and smokeless power-propelled vehicle, the motor-car gradually came into more general use. It no longer appealed only to a few but gained converts daily, and its final triumph came when it began seriously to displace the horsed vehicle, becoming the private carriage of the wealthier classes to be used on all occasions.

If the motor-car in the guise of a private carriage has developed at an astonishing rate, its adaptation to the needs of the community, as a public service vehicle, has been even more rapid. The first cabs placed on the streets of London in 1903 were by no means a success, but the cabs constructed by the French house of Renault and first introduced in London in 1906 rapidly effected a revolutionary change in the means of individual transport. Apart from the improved speed of the motor-cabs, they gained popularity because of the use, on each one of them, of the taxi-meter, showing at a glance the amount of the fare, thus preventing overcharge on the part of the driver. One effect of the employment of motor-cabs and motor-omnibuses has been to reduce slightly the total number of vehicles, and to quicken a large volume of the traffic; it is now being recognized that to increase the speed of the whole of the traffic of London by about 5m. an hour is practically equivalent to doubling the width of the whole of the main streets.

The Paths of Economic Change

56. THE ASSEMBLY LINE

Source: 'Internal Combustion Engineering, incorporating the Auto-mobile Engineer', III (1913), 350, 379–80.

By 1907, the year of the first Census of Production, the combined annual output of cycles, motor-cycles and motor-cars was valued at £12 millions—or between one-seventh and one-eighth of the value of British engineering production.[1] This was a substantially higher proportion of the total value of engineering output than the electrical manufacturing industry could show. The industry of motor-car manufacturing attracted men of high engineering achievement and was not short of capital. Its assembly methods, as this description shows, were already moving away from the craftsman's shop and were becoming modern. On the technical side, the foundations for new production and sales policies which would be essentially those of large-scale factory production had already been laid by 1913.

The expansion of the industry worked, however, within sharp limits. The manufacturers concentrated on the private car for upper-class use, rather than as a general necessity. Costs and prices were relatively high and the Ford works at Detroit, in the United States, supplied much of the demand for the cheap car in the United Kingdom. The industry as a whole seems to have lacked the will to attack the mass market for the popular car and to interest the machine-tool industry in doing so. The Morris-Oxford car, which was intended by W. R. Morris, an Oxford cycle and motor-cycle repair shop owner, to do this and to challenge the imports from America, was not announced at the Motor Show until 1912 and had hardly gone into production when war broke out, two years later. For the economics of the British motor industry at this time, see S. B. Saul, The "Motor Industry in Britain to 1914", 'Business History', V (1962), 22–44. Also P. W. S. Andrews and Elizabeth Brunner, 'Life of Lord Nuffield' (1955). The contrast with American conditions is interesting. See Allen Nevins, 'Ford the Times, the Man, the Company' (New York, 1954).

WHEN comparing the European with the American methods of production, great stress is always laid upon the different methods adopted when assembling the various parts of the chassis, and nearly all comparisons show the excellence of the American method without drawing sufficient attention to the underlying differences which govern the two trades, or the change which has come over European shops during the past few years. With the immense quantity

[1] *Committee on Industry and Trade, Survey of Metal Industries (1928), p. 134.*

156

which is produced by an American automobile manufacturing firm, it is possible to lay down dies and tools which turn out parts nearer to finished size than is possible with the limited output on this side of the water, and also it is necessary to do away with every possible operation in order to reduce the price of the chassis to the level which prevails in America. European manufacture, besides being limited in the quantity which it can produce economically, is also required to make a chassis which shall be better finished than the American article, and the price therefore is not such a tremendous consideration, albeit a great deal must yet be done to eliminate or reduce certain operations in the manufacturing process, so that unnecessary cost may be avoided. Everybody realises what a tremendous advance has taken place in the design of the automobile during the last five years, but very few understand exactly how the erecting shop methods have been altered by the new design of chassis, or how much time has been eliminated when the car is going through the works.

.　　.　　.　　.　　.　　.　　.

Turning now to the other case, that of the Sunbeam Motor Company, this firm is an excellent example of the manner in which assembling has been studied as a science, as here every possible care has been taken in order to eliminate the use of tools other than spanners during the erecting process. It will be remembered that the Sunbeam Motor Company have an especially elaborate jig and tool system, which was described and illustrated in the issue of THE AUTOMOBILE ENGINEER for October, 1911, and which is always being checked in operation, so that whenever possible an improvement may be thought out or the work done on any component simplified or reduced. The progress of the material through the machine shops is watched with extreme care, and in some cases the jigs are designed first and the car part afterwards, this being done only in cases where a certain amount of licence exists in the construction or formation of that particular part. Like the machine shop, the erecting shop is very carefully set out, the method adopted differing from the Daimler Company as regards the manner in which the men are divided up into groups. In the Daimler factory there are a number of gangs consisting of perhaps twenty or more men under a single charge-hand. All these men are fitters, with of course, the addition of labourers and gang boys, and they are sub-divided into small groups of three or four, to which groups a frame is given and the necessary components as they are turned out from the other shops; thus the material is delivered to the gang and assembled by each small group of men, while each individual out of those groups may be called upon to assemble or fit any part of the chassis. Benches are practically eliminated, but a small cast-iron table, having a vice securely affixed to it is used, this being on castors, so that it can be dragged to the particular job for which it is needed. From the delivery of the frame until the time that the finished chassis is wheeled away the parts remain in the hands of the men to whom they were delivered originally.

Another system is exemplified by the Sunbeam Company, as here each frame is sent in from the frame makers with all holes drilled, and the smaller fittings, together with the cross-members rivetted into position. The erecting shop is then divided up into a great number of small gangs of which each is responsible for one particular job and is never called upon to do any other; thus the frame is delivered to the first of these gangs at one end of the erecting shop, and this gang does nothing but reamer out the eyes of the springs and fit them to the chassis together with certain other small brackets which must of necessity be fitted in the erecting shop and not by the frame makers. As soon as this job has been concluded a small hoist is run along the girder tramway which is suspended from the roof beams and the frame is hoisted up and taken away one step further along the shop. At this point the sub-frame and engine are fitted, the gearbox being slung on a three point suspension of a type which has been often illustrated and which allows the box to swivel in any direction. The usual setting bar is employed, this being secured to the front of the driving shaft and the pointer adjusted to the flywheel until it shows a certain setting or clearance which varies with the length of chassis under test. In the longer chassis as much as 3mm. clearance is allowed at the top with the pointer just touching the bottom of the flywheel, but it is less, of course, with the shorter frames. Owing to the fact that the sub-frame is three point suspended by means of two rigid brackets at the top and a ball joint at the front, it is possible to fit this frame to the engine and to make a very compact job of the whole, it being only necessary to clamp the engine in position, ascertain that the alignment is as it should be, then an electric drill is used for the holding down bolt holes, which in this case are placed through the web and not through the flange of the frame. Every possible effort is made to eliminate any fitting as the shop is supposed to be an assembling shop and, although the file and similar tools have not been eliminated altogether, their use is, as far as possible, followed by an enquiry into the particular jig or tool which has necessitated any fitting. . . .

Each particular operation, such as the assembly of the axles, and aligning of the engine and frame and the erection of the back axle is accomplished by a separate gang in the Sunbeam works, and each fresh operation causes the frame, with those components which are already on it, to be shifted in the shop.

The result is that there are always fresh frames at one end which are having the springs and smaller brackets fitted, while at the other end the complete car is receiving its coat of "shop" paint preparatory to being delivered to the testing department. The whole system is very methodical and seems to work admirably in practice, especially as the men must naturally become expert at the particular job allocated to them, seeing that they do nothing else to each chassis as it comes into their hands. Generally speaking, the Sunbeam job impresses one with the fact that every effort has been made to arrange for a methodical progression of the components. Certainly there is less work put upon the chassis than is the case with the Daimler and even there the amount of fitting which is done cannot under any circumstances be called great. . . .

It must be remembered that the duty of a designer does not end even when a car has been designed which is perfectly satisfactory in the hands of the ordinary user, but the parts of this car must also be drawn out in such a way that they will be both easy and economical to machine, and presuming that the jig designing is all that it should be, they should be practically untouched after delivery to the erecting shop. Obviously the presence of files and other tools in the erecting shop is really a proof of an error in the machining methods of that company, and although there is bound to be a certain amount of fitting this should not be of a serious nature nor need any elaborate equipment. With a great number of models it is obviously more difficult to bring down those operations which the chassis must undergo in the erecting shop to the minimum, as it very frequently happens that one casting, such as the steering box, is used for each different length of frame, although the rake of the steering column may alter. Even then, it is possible to overcome the difficulty by fitting a steering column which is adjustable and therefore need only be unlocked and reset whatever the angle required by the customer. As a whole, however, the improvement in this particular part of European works is quite as marked as that which has taken place in design, and despite the comparatively small number of chassis which are produced, assembly as a manufacturing process compares very favourably with the American system.

57. TRADITION AND INNOVATION BEFORE 1914

Source: 'Final Report of the Committee on Commercial and Industrial Policy after the War, 1918', Cd. 9035, XIII, paras. 93–4, 96–9.

This rapid sketch shows the pre-1914 position of British industry in its international setting, as it appeared to men who had lived through the period. It formed part of a document primarily concerned with the reconstruction problems which were expected to arise when the war came to an end and with future government policy.

FROM the preceding sketch, and from the examination into the position in respect of a number of essential industries which is contained in our Interim Report of the 16th March, 1917, it is possible to draw certain conclusions as to the condition of British industry and trade, and the nature of the competition to which it was exposed, immediately before the War.

Whilst British industry on the whole had shown in the preceding decade great vitality and power of extension, its strength and development had been mainly in a certain number of long established manufactures, of which coal, cotton and the textile trades generally, shipbuilding and some branches of the engineering trades (such as textile machinery) are the most conspicuous examples. One important exception must be made from this general proposition; the iron and steel trades had made comparatively little progress, and had come to be entirely overshadowed by their great competitors in Germany and the United States. In the rise and expansion of the more modern branches of industrial production the United Kingdom had taken a very limited share, as is evidenced by our relative weakness in respect of the electrical, chemical and chemico-metallurgical industries; and it is admitted that in a number of smaller trades foreign manufacturers had shown greater enterprise and originality....

In overseas trade it appears from the Reports of the Departmental Committees and from the merchant evidence which we have received that British merchants and manufacturers were encountering energetic and successful competition, which is ascribed in part to the increasing efforts made by foreign countries to promote their own industrial development, in part to cheaper cost of production in certain countries (of which Japan is the most notable example, but which was also characteristic of certain European countries), and in part to the adoption by foreign merchants and manufacturers of methods of organisation and distribution different from, and in some cases markedly more effective than, those hitherto pursued by British traders.

This position was due to a number of causes. Undoubtedly one of the most important was the influence of history and tradition—the long start which the United Kingdom had enjoyed in the world's trade and the great achievements of her manufacturers and merchants had engendered a feeling of confidence in the maintenance of our position and in the methods hitherto pursued, with the result that there was until recently but little recognition of the necessity for constant vigilance and constant effort to meet the changing conditions and requirements of world trade. The strength of British industry in respect of the old staple lines of production had forced the new industrial nations to devote their efforts to the search for new branches of production, to the creation of new economic needs, and to the discovery and development of new methods of trade organisation and marketing. The admitted success in many directions of the competition of Germany with the United Kingdom was due in part to the comparatively late entry of German industry into the field, with the consequence that, as already stated, in order to make headway at all, it had in the first instance to devote its efforts to those branches of trade in which economic conditions in Germany made very cheap production possible, and to seek new branches of production in which it would not have to encounter the competition of old-established and powerful British industries. Further, in these and in the older branches of industry, Germany started with all the advantage of completely modern equipment and without the handicap of a traditional organisation. From the first there was in Germany complete recognition of the great value of the application of science to industry and the close co-operation of the two; this, though most strikingly exemplified in the chemical trades, may fairly be said to be characteristic of German industry as a whole. Amongst British manufacturers, though there were some marked exceptions, there was, speaking generally, no such recognition. Moreover the very success of individual enterprise in the United Kingdom had had the result that British industries were carried on in the main by great numbers of small concerns operating on a limited scale and suffering from all the resultant disadvantages, but nevertheless, as a rule (though there were some very important exceptions) reluctant to merge their individuality into larger concerns, or even to enter into any effective scheme of co-operation for common purposes....

The competition of the United States has not been hitherto a very serious factor, though the great scale of the industries and the methods of production and organisation which prevail in that country may make its competition at least in certain lines of production (notably the iron and steel and engineering trades) very potent in the future, particularly in the great markets of South and Central America, where it will be in some measure aided by political influences.

With regard to Eastern markets British cotton manufacturers and our witnesses have expressed great apprehension in regard to Japan, which derives marked advantages from its geographical situation and the cheapness of its labour. Japanese competition is already very pronounced in common quality goods in China and India, and is extending in range with some rapidity....

58. INDUSTRY AND THE EDUCATION ACT, 1870

Source: Rachel E. Waterhouse, 'A Hundred Years of Engineering Craftsmanship (a short history of Tangyes Ltd.)' (Birmingham, 1957), p. 72.

Richard Tangye relating, in 1883, his firm's experience since the Education Act of 1870 was passed. No national system of primary education existed before that date and many employers would have said it was not necessary.

SINCE the passing of the Education Act more than one thousand Board School Boys have found employment in the Cornwall Works, and universal testimony concerning them is, that as compared with those of the era previous to the existence of the Board Schools, there is a most marked improvement in every way. The lads are more orderly, more amenable to discipline, and much more intelligent; they show a great eagerness to learn the business of their lives, and as a natural consequence they master it much more thoroughly and in considerably less time.

59. THE INFLUENCE OF WAR, 1870–1

Source: W. C. Aitken, Senior Vice-President of the Birmingham and Midland Institute, at the Annual General Meeting of the Institute, January 1872. Quoted R. E. Waterhouse, 'The Birmingham and Midland Institute 1854–1954' (1954), p. 76.

The emergence of Germany as the leading power in continental Europe, which was the result of the defeat of France in the Franco-German war, 1870–1, faced British public opinion with a puzzle. Englishmen were used to military powers, such as Russia, which were industrially backward or relatively so compared with Britain. But Bismarckian Germany was both militarily powerful and industrially progressive; she made intensive practical use of the powerful intellectual influence of science. This was a new sort of challenge between nations and was noted as such by some men. W. C. Aitken was an industrial designer.[1] The Institute he was addressing was characteristic of Victorian England; it existed largely to promote the teaching of science and art, on a part-time and voluntary basis, to artisans and clerks, many of whom had had no regular education.

WHENCE the success which crowned the Prussian arms? From science training; from masses of steel produced by the metallurgical knowledge of Krupp of Essen—converted into ordnance by industrially-educated engineers and workmen—served on the battlefield by artillerists trained to a perfect knowledge of the laws which guide projectiles in their course.

60. SCIENCE AND THE STATE

Source: C. T. Kingzett, 'The History, Products, and Processes of the Alkali Trade' (1877), pp. v, 5.

IN the following pages I have endeavoured to give a concise but comprehensive account of the largest branch of chemical industry of this country.

[1] H. R. G. Whates, *The Birmingham Post, 1857–1957*, p. 91.

Importance has been attached in this attempt, to matters of history, interesting as they are in showing how gradually knowledge is perfected. It will, for instance, be seen that at no time in the history of the Alkali Trade has an inventor brought into use a totally new process; so-called new processes are but the perfected forms of old ones, and are based upon previously known facts. Moreover, the greatest commercial successes have been achieved, not by the practical application of new ideas, but in the development of old ones. Taken as a whole, this trade well exemplifies the truth that scientific investigations necessarily precede industry.

...even now, in these days of boasted civilisation, no fact is more striking than that science is not sufficiently recognised by the Government of this country. It is and must be admitted on all sides that scientific research necessarily precedes the application of science to industry, and yet, even now, the pay of the chemist is little or no better than the recompense of an unskilled labourer. True it is that the patent laws afford some protection to those who are in a position to patent, but many even of our best chemists are not possessed of the means, while for the most part chemical inventions and discoveries do not admit of protection in this way....

We can only hope that the time is near at hand when we shall have a Government sufficiently enlightened to appreciate that it is to its best interests to foster and encourage science in all its multiplicities, for by so doing alone, can England maintain that supremacy over all other nations which it now possesses in its varied industries.

61. THE WORLD ECONOMY AND SCIENCE

Source: Lyon Playfair, 'Subjects of Social Welfare' (1889), pp. 108–9, quoted Wemyss Reid, 'Memoirs and Correspondence of Lyon Playfair' (1900), p. 438.

The transforming influence of science upon the economic world was not limited to wartime or to select industries; it was pervasive and continuous. Lyon Playfair (1818–98), who was both a trained scientist and public man, and at the time of this speech M.P. for South Leeds, played a considerable part in educating Victorian opinion in the importance of scientific and technical education (see below, no. 63). Of the three men mentioned here, Charles Wheatstone (1802–75) patented in 1837, jointly with William Fothergill Cooke, a workable electric telegraph,

Old Industries and New

*Henry Bessemer (1813–98) announced (see no. 26 above) in 1856 his
new process for making steel, and James Prescott Joule (1818–89) the
physicist, of Manchester, a pupil of John Dalton, was a profound student
of, among other things, the mechanical value of heat.*

...The economical applications of science in the vast improvements of
the telegraph, the railroads, and the steamships have changed the whole
system of commerce. The effect of this has been to destroy local
markets, and to consolidate all into one market—the world. If our
landlords and farmers want to know the names of the three persons
who have knocked out the bottom of our old agricultural system, I
can tell them. Their names are Wheatstone, Sir Henry Bessemer, and
Dr Joule. The first, by telegraphy, has changed the whole system by
which exchanges are made; the second, by his improvements in steel,
has altered profoundly the transportation of commodities by sea and
by land; and the third, by his discoveries of the mechanical equivalent
of heat, has led to great economy of coal in compound engines. By
these changes the United States, Canada, India, and Russia have their
corn crops brought to our doors. The effect of these discoveries upon
the transport of corn will be realised when I state that a small cube of
coal which would pass through a ring the size of a shilling, when
burned in the compound engine of a modern steamboat, would drive
a ton of food and its proportion of the ship two miles on its way from
a foreign port. This economy of coal has altered the whole situation.
Not long since a steamer of 3000 tons going on a long voyage might
require 2200 tons of coal, and carry only a limited cargo of 800 tons.
Now, a modern steamer will take the same voyage with 800 tons of
coal, and carry a freight of 2200 tons. While coal has thus been econo-
mised, human labour has been lessened. In 1870 it required 47 hands
on board our steamships for every 1000 tons capacity. Now [1887]
only 28 are necessary.

...Four men in the United States, working for one year in the
growing, milling, and transportation of wheat could produce flour for
a year's consumption of 1000 other men, allowing one barrel of flour
to each adult...you will all see how this has acted upon agriculture.
It has made one grain market all over the world.

62. NECESSITY THE MOTHER OF INVENTION?

Sources: Ludwig Mond, inaugural session of the Society, 29 June 1881,
'Society of Chemical Industry, Proceedings of First Meeting, 1881',
p. 128. The same, Presidential Address before the Society, 10 July
1889: 'Journal of the Society of Chemical Industry', VIII (1889),
510.
    The Society of Chemical Industry was a national society of academic
and industrial chemists formed in 1881. Ludwig Mond (for whom see
no. 44 above) was one of its distinguished founders. At the time of his
second address, Ludwig Mond had been describing to the Society his
work on nitrogen, which was aimed at obtaining industrially fertilizers
for European agriculture of a type which previously had to be imported
from South America, in the form of guano and Chilean nitrates.

A

IN our present state of civilization, and of generally and widely diffused knowledge, any invention for which a need exists—and necessity has always been the mother of invention—is sure to be supplied from more than one quarter within a reasonable time. Science tells us how very far we are from obtaining our industrial aims with anything approaching the theoretical expenditure of force; science also tells us in what direction we may look forward to arriving at improvements. I might say that we are on the eve of creating a science of invention, that is of developing scientific methods for solving new industrial problems.

B

The statement is frequently made that 'Necessity is the mother of invention'. If this has been the case in the past I think it is no longer so in our days, since science has made us acquainted with the correlation of forces, teaching us what amount of energy we utilise and how much we waste in our various methods for attaining certain objects, and indicating to us where and in what direction and how far, improvement is possible; and since the increase in our knowledge of the properties of matter enables us to form an opinion beforehand as to the substances we have available for obtaining a desired result. We can now foresee, in most cases, in what direction progress in technology will move, and, in consequence, the inventor is now frequently in advance of the wants of his time. He may even create new wants, to my mind a distinct step in the development of human culture. It can then no longer be stated that 'Necessity is the mother of invention'; but I think it may truly be said that the steady methodical investigation of natural phenomena is the father of industrial progress.

63. TECHNICAL EDUCATION: THE EUROPEAN EXAMPLE

Source: 'Schools Inquiry Commission: Report relative to Technical Education, 1867' [3898], XXVI, pp. 6–7.

This letter by Lyon Playfair, of 15 May 1867, was described by the Royal Commissioners on Technical Instruction, writing in 1884, as "the first impulse to an inquiry into the subject of technical instruction". Playfair, who was professor of chemistry at Edinburgh University, addressed his letter to Lord Taunton, who was the chairman of a royal commission appointed in 1864 to inquire into the state of secondary education, outside the public schools. Playfair's scientific eminence and his long experience of international industrial exhibitions—he had been one of the organizers of the Great Exhibition of 1851—gave him much influence. Public opinion was in any case disturbed both by foreign competition and by the sense of educational inadequacies. The Taunton commission, in publishing his letter and extensive correspondence expressing agreement with it, suggested an inquiry into technical education in Europe, particularly in France, Germany and Switzerland. This was done and it confirmed Playfair's impressions about the superiority of education for industry on the Continent, where this had been an important instrument in catching up with and overtaking England's manufacturing lead. It was not until 1881, however, that this question was taken up again by a royal commission on Technical Instruction. This reported in 1882 and 1884. It was 1889 before the Technical Instruction Act was passed, under which the big cities and county councils could organize technical education. Even so, financial help from the central government came as the result of a political windfall in 1890, when funds collected from an increased duty on spirits—the so-called whisky money—to compensate licence-holders for the extinction of liquor licences were directed at the last moment towards the county councils and their educational projects. A fairly rapid expansion of technical education followed in the next fifteen years. See A. Abbott, 'Education for Industry and Commerce in England' (1933) and Stephen Cotgrove, 'Technical Education and Social Change' (1958). For Playfair, T. Wemyss Reid, 'Lord Playfair' (1899).

The Paths of Economic Change

[*Letter from Dr Lyon Playfair to Lord Taunton, Chairman of the Schools Inquiry Commission.*]

London, May 15, 1867

My Lord,

As you desire that I should put in writing the substance of the conversation which I had the honour of having with your Lordship this morning, I willingly comply with your request.

I have just returned from Paris, where I acted as a Juror in one of the classes of the Exhibition. In this capacity I had no other opportunities than any other Juror of forming a judgment in regard to it; but having had the charge of the working of the Juries in the Exhibitions of 1851 and 1862 I naturally made the acquaintance of many eminent men of different nations, and meeting with a large number of them congregated on the International Juries in Paris, I endeavoured to gather their opinions as to the position which England occupied in this great industrial competition.

I am sorry to say that, with very few exceptions, a singular accordance of opinion prevailed that our country had shown little inventiveness and made but little progress in the peaceful arts of industry since 1862. Deficient representation in some of the industries might have accounted for this judgment against us, but when we find that out of 90 classes there are scarcely a dozen in which preeminence is unhesitatingly awarded to us, this plea must be abandoned....I naturally devoted attention to elicit their views as to the causes. So far as I could gather them by conversation, the one cause upon which there was most unanimity of conviction is that France, Prussia, Austria, Belgium, and Switzerland possess good systems of industrial education for the masters and managers of factories and workshops, and that England possesses none. A second cause was also generally, though not so universally, admitted, that we had suffered from the want of cordiality between the employers of labour and workmen, engendered by the numerous strikes, and more particularly by that rule of many Trades' Unions that men shall work upon an average ability, without giving free scope to the skill and ability which they may individually possess.

Dumas, well known as a *savant*, and who, from his position as a Senator of France, and President of the Municipal Council, has many opportunities of forming a correct judgment, assured me that technical

168

education had given a great impulse to the industry of France. In going through the Exhibition, whenever anything excellent in French manufacture strikes his attention, his invariable question is, 'Was the manager of this establishment a pupil of the *Ecole Centrale des Arts et Manufactures?*' and in the great majority of cases he received a reply in the affirmative....

In 1853 I published a little work on 'Industrial Education on the Continent,' in which I pointed out that as an inevitable result of the attention given to it abroad, and its neglect in England, other nations must advance in industry at a much greater rate than our own country. I fear that this result is already attained for many of our staple industries. But as my opinion is only that of an individual, I trust that it may accord with the objects of the Commission over which your Lordship presides, to take the evidence of some of the leading jurors, many of whom had as good opportunities as myself of judging of the position which our country has taken in this great international competition.

Permit me also to make another suggestion. My inquiry of 1853 into Industrial Education on the Continent was a private one, and had neither official aid nor sanction, and is now antiquated. It would be important that the Government, either through your Commission, or through the Committee of Council on Education, should hold an official inquiry on this subject, and should tell the people of England authoritatively what are the means by which the great states are attaining an intellectual preeminence among the industrial classes, and how they are making this to bear on the rapid progress of their national industries.

My Lord, I have, etc.

LYON PLAYFAIR

The Right Hon.
Lord Taunton

64. QUINTIN HOGG AND THE POLYTECHNIC

Source: '*The Times*' *newspaper, quoted Ethel M. Hogg,* '*Quintin Hogg a biography*' (*2nd ed., 1904*), *pp. 215–20.*

While the State was slowly making up its mind to do something about technical education, private enterprise stepped in, as it so often did in Victorian England, and tried to fill to some extent the educational gap.

Quintin Hogg (1845–1903) was a wealthy London merchant, well educated and religious, who in the 1860's, when the lack of a national system of primary education was acute, entered education, as other men did too, as a form of philanthropy. He became a founder of "ragged schools" in London. After the Education Act of 1870, the public discussion of education moved over from primary to secondary and technical education. Hogg's interests moved with it. His Regent Street Polytechnic, the building of which was acquired by him in 1882, was aimed at the rank and file of London industry, rather than its managers. He organized sound technical training and some general education for artisans and mechanics between the ages of sixteen and twenty-five. He did this as others had done before him, but with far more energy and success. He spent £100,000 on his working men's college, before he was forced to look for financial help in order to continue. A public subscription and a grant from the Charity Commissioners allowed this. The Regent Street Polytechnic became the model for similar institutions in other parts of London. These benefited in the 1890's like other technical schools from the whisky-money.

A T a time when the demand for higher education is heard on all sides, when it is being taken up by parliament, and when the London County Council are announcing their intention of devoting large sums of money to it, the public will be glad to learn something of one of the most remarkable social experiments that has ever been made with higher education for its principal, though not its exclusive object. This is the Polytechnic Institute in Regent Street; it owes its existence and its maintenance to the energy, devotion, and munificence of one man, Mr Quintin Hogg.... The classes are of two kinds, science and art classes, which are held in connexion with the Department at South Kensington; and industrial classes, which are independent, but which are more or less informally related to the City and Guilds of London Institute of Technical Instruction, and also to the London Trades' Council. The industrial classes are again subdivided into classes of mechanics and into 'practical trade classes' for apprentices and young workmen, and it is these last which are the special feature of the Institute.... The wonder is that young men can be found who care to spend the evenings in doing much the same work as that they have been employed upon all day; but such unquestionably is the case; the class-rooms are well filled with lads making engines, carving wood, shaping bricks, or learning the best method of cutting out cloth. These are led partly by the genuine desire of learning, and partly by the wish to better themselves; for example, a young plasterer, who as yet knows only the plainer elements of his craft, comes to the Polytechnic to learn modelling and cornice moulding, and when he has learnt his lesson, he perhaps emigrates to America, and finds himself able to earn something like four times the wages that he had been earning as single plasterer in London. In the engineering room, where there is a certain amount of machinery worked by a central gas-engine, a dozen young men may be seen profoundly interesting themselves in the joining of a screw, or in adapting some rough-cast bolt to the required purpose; the room is full of iron lathes and other small machines, every detail of which has been made and finished on the spot by the boys....

There still remains, however, about £17,000 to be raised. Mr Hogg's own friends are exhausted; he feels constrained to appeal to the public to save this flourishing and most useful Institute.... We trust he will have little difficulty in raising the amount. As we said at the outset, the need for higher education is one which is every day becoming more present to the public mind. Our commercial prosperity is being threatened by competition all over the world; assuredly it will be impossible for us to keep our markets unless our workmen succeed in putting themselves on a level with the best workmen in Paris, Berlin or Philadelphia.

65. TECHNICAL EDUCATION: THE CASE AGAINST

Source: 'Memoirs of John Wigham Richardson'; privately printed, Glasgow, 1911, pp. 300–1.

Many business men, including some who were among the most resourceful and enterprising, were sceptical of what schools and universities could do for industry. John Wigham Richardson (for whom, see no. 29 above) was addressing on 13 October 1890, the North-East Coast Institution of Engineers and Shipbuilders.

MUCH has been said in recent years about technical education. The expression has been much abused, for technical education can surely only mean the teaching of an art. In our own arts I can conceive of no better school than the workshop. You have there the experience and skill of the best artisans, you have the feeling of being engaged in serious constructions, you are in the very atmosphere of your craft.

More than this, you are learning by doing. There is the learning by committing to memory, and there is the learning by doing, and of the two perhaps the latter is the better education. Some of the most successful men whom I know in other walks of life have been educated in the workshop. The workshop will develop some faculties in a way that Cambridge or Oxford cannot touch. But when your years of apprenticeship are over, or during them, you will do well to add to your practical knowledge all that you can cull from the schools of science. Nor should you neglect the study of modern languages, which are not difficult to acquire if you have a hearty will to do so, and if you learn by the ear rather than, or as well as by, the eye.

66. BRITAIN'S LACK OF SCIENCE-BASED INDUSTRY

Source: Mary E. Swan and Kenneth R. Swan, 'Sir Joseph Wilson Swan F.R.S.: a Memoir' (1929), pp. 154, 134-5.

The chorus of criticism about the nation's indifference to science and general education, which had been heard from the 1860's onward, continued into the new century. Among the critics was the inventor and manufacturer, Joseph Swan, himself largely self-taught, who had played a large part in the foundation of the electric lamp industry (see above no. 38). In the first of these extracts, he was recording his impression of the Paris Exhibition of 1900; in the second, he was addressing some general remarks, in October 1903, to the students of the School of Pharmacy in London.

A

I DID, in addition, see the wonderful Creusot exhibit, that of the firm where all the Boer guns, or most of them, were made—the 'Long Toms', etc. It is a wonderful example of the extensive—the *immensely* extensive and complete organization of the engineering factory methods of our day—where one proprietor gives employment to tens of thousands of men, and produces not only a great variety of engineering products, but some of them of gigantic size; bridges, cannon, shot, engines, dynamos, and the metals from which these are all made. I have not seen the Krupp exhibit, but I expect it is something like the Creusot one in its scope and the scale of the work it represents. America is not behindhand in this kind of elaborate and widespread factory organization, as several exhibits representative of its great works show; and Germany also. Beside Krupps, England presents a sorry spectacle. Here and there you see something English; but one is struck by the fewness of English exhibits and the general want of 'go' they indicate. If the light exists with us, it is hidden somewhere. I walked through the French department, devoted to the illustration of the educational and research work done by the Government in further-ance of scientific knowledge bearing on agriculture and its improve-ment.

B

There is, no doubt, a considerable change for the better, but it did not come till long after it was an urgent necessity, and it has not yet gone nearly far enough. We see one of the evil consequences of our educational deficiencies in the much less rapid progress that we, as a nation, have made, comparatively with our industrial rivals, more especially in those branches of industry which are the outcome of the scientific discoveries of recent times, and which largely depend for their evolution and successful practical application on original research and on the intelligent appreciation, by the capitalist and commercial class, of the resources of science and the advantages of high scientific training and scientific work as auxiliary forces in promoting industrial development and progress.

We are still desperately in need of more thorough general education and of the means of larger and better organized exploration of new fields of knowledge. While we are slowly learning by the painful process of ruinous loss the lesson of our want in this respect, our competitors abroad have long been reaping the benefits of their recognition of the value of knowledge and of the means of acquiring knowledge as a basis of industrial prosperity.

67. THE WARTIME SCARCITY OF INDUSTRIAL SCIENTISTS

Source: General Sir Frederick Maurice, 'The Life of Viscount Haldane of Cloan' (1939), II, 30–2.

Between the earlier comments of Sir Joseph Swan and the speech by Lord Haldane here reproduced, an important event intervened. This was the Education Act of 1902. During the arguments about technical educa-tion in the 1880's and 1890's, men who knew European conditions of education and industry had often pointed out that Great Britain suffered economically not only from want of schemes of industrial training and technological education but also from the lack of good general education. With no national system of secondary schools, she possessed nothing comparable with the lycées of France or the gymnasia of Germany. Highly educated men worked in the top ranks of British industry but there were too few of them and the middle ranks suffered from a deficiency of general intellectual training, valuable both for its own sake and as a foundation for advanced work. A nation willing to terminate so much of its schooling at thirteen and fourteen years of age was handicapping itself severely in the full and intelligent use of its resources. Many purposes, both idealistic and practical, lay behind the Education Act 1902. Its general intention was to raise national efficiency all round, by men who had become acutely conscious of the political and economic dangers of the world they lived in. Perhaps the unintended results were no less important than the intended.[1] But on any showing it was a significant economic event. One cannot measure its economic consequences. But if we are looking for any one force capable, over the next thirty years, together with the advance of knowledge, the economies of large-scale output and other changing conditions, of pushing back the limits to British industrial productivity which made themselves so painfully evident in the early 1900's and preparing the way for the sharp increases in productivity which began to take place after 1935, it was perhaps this.

Meanwhile, the inability of average public opinion to take education and science seriously in the generation before 1902 had to be paid for. The bills were still coming in when the First World War broke out, as Haldane's speech shows. Haldane (1856–1928), one of the ablest lawyers and public men of his day, was addressing the House of Lords on 12 July 1916, on a motion "calling attention to the training of the nation and to the necessity of preparing for the future". The war in the West was at its height and its economic and human cost extremely severe.

...We suffer in this country from want of experts. Instead of experts being diffused, as they are in Switzerland, which has a most admirable system of training them, and as they are becoming diffused in the United States, where that very practical people are waking to it, we have taken too few steps to produce experts. It is no use saying to the manufacturers, 'Employ more chemists'. There are no properly trained chemists to employ. Our training machine is not adequate to produce the supply we require. At the beginning of the war I was

[1] A. J. Balfour (1848–1930), the statesman chiefly responsible for the act, was a believer in the general educational value of science, not for the few only but also for the many. See his comments on the relation between pure science and industry in his Henry Sidgwick Memorial Lecture on *Decadence* (1908), pp. 48–57.

chairman of a technical committee which had to go into one of the great chemical industries, and I found, rather to my horror, that we had become dependent upon Germany to an alarming degree; in fact to such an alarming degree that in regard even to great discoveries that we had made in this country it had been left to the Germans to produce what we wanted. I asked why it was, and I was told "We cannot get chemists. The Germans organize so well and made the product in such a way that it is our best course to buy from them." When the war came, one result of this was that we were almost without aniline colours, and your lordships will remember the acute distress that was caused in the dye trade owing to that want. It was entirely due to our not training men who were required for an industry which was originally a British industry, but which we had allowed to languish.

The other day I had occasion to inquire how many trained chemists there were available for the hundreds of chemical industries that there are in this country, because I had been struck by the fact that many of the chemical works were without chemists. On inquiry at a source on which reliance could be placed I found that there were only 1500 trained chemists in this country altogether, and the reason was that we had not the means of encouragement to produce the business kind that was wanted. Our public schools do not aim at preparing an aptitude in the boys' mind for the study of chemistry; nor do our secondary schools; nor have we any trade continuation schools which stimulate the working man's son of exceptional talent to go on with this. Nor are our Universities equipped to produce these men in large numbers. But we have made progress in that direction, as I shall point out later. We have only 1500 trained chemists in this country. On the other hand four large German chemical firms, which have played havoc with certain departments of our trade, employ 1000 highly trained chemists between them. Those men were trained and produced by the great schools which exist there for that purpose. I will take another illustration of what we suffer because of the want of experts. I had the honour of knowing the late Lord Kelvin, who used to talk to me about energy, and I used to ask him about the possibility of using the energy of the sun and the tides in case of the giving out of our supplies of coal. Lord Kelvin would smile and say, 'A pound of coal is worth far more than anything that you can hope to get from the sun or the tides or anything else; there is plenty of it for a long time to come, if you will only use it economically.' And I got to know this the other day from a well-known expert, that whereas the ideal capacity of a pound of coal—what you could get if you had the power of proper scientific appliance—would be one-horse-power per hour, as a matter of fact and in practice it requires five pounds of coal to produce one horse-power per hour, which one pound would produce if properly used. Another great chemical expert has calculated that we could, by the use of expert knowledge, which exists, produce the whole of the motive power which we use in this country from one-third of the coal which we actually consume in doing so. My noble friend who sits near me (Lord Joicey) knows what I mean when I speak of the wonderful transformation of coal into electrical energy in the north, and the splendid scientific way in which it has been done by certain engineers.

Then take another case. It has been calculated by high experts that every year in the various stages of consumption and of the making of bye-products, and so on, we waste as much coal as would pay the interest on £500,000,000 of War Debt after the war. That is a compassable figure, and it is only a question of applying the requisite expert knowledge and the requisite methods. But we have not got the experts although the expert knowledge exists. It is a great mistake to suppose that in this country we have not got the very highest science. We have the very highest science and knowledge, but we have not enough individuals possessing that high science and knowledge to go round. The result is that we suffer....

CHAPTER 4

INCOMES EARNED ABROAD

In the nineteenth century, the British people became the most travelling, colonizing, trading and investing of all European nations, the most thoroughly at home in the world beyond Europe. But they preserved also a deep insularity. This they owed to a naval ascendancy which they enjoyed throughout almost the whole of the century, combined with a marked abstention, most unlike their eighteenth-century behaviour, from European alliances and wars. Their cosmopolitan concern came partly from the incessant rivalry between the European powers, in which, despite their guarded attitude, they were thoroughly involved. It was owing above all, however, to an immense extension of their economic activities.

The world trading position of Great Britain during the nineteenth century has long ago become a thing of the past. It depended upon the coming together of many influences to create a situation without parallel in earlier times. The first set of these new influences were internal to Great Britain herself. Her population more than trebled itself between the first census of 1801 and the outbreak of the First World War, while the massive industrialization of her economic life went far beyond anything that early or middle Victorian opinion had ever expected. The second set of influences were external. They came from the rapid spread of new communication systems in the world, especially after 1850, with the building of railways and steamships and the laying of telegraph lines and cables. World resources opened up on a vast scale.

Between these processes at home and abroad, there was a special relation. Great Britain was too small a country to industrialize alone. Without the help at every step of the foodstuffs and raw materials of other lands and without their inhabitants' labour and willingness to exchange, she could not grow. The primary producing areas of the world needed a market for their raw produce. They found it in the demand of the new industrial state of Great Britain. They supplied the products, Britain came forward with the capital and population required for their development.

Much of the economic history of Britain in the Victorian age is the record of the increase of her dependence upon the foodstuffs and industrial raw materials provided by new European settlers, many of them British, in the temperate zones. The United States became first

177

the world's largest seller of raw produce, then its largest manufacturer. Australia, New Zealand, Canada and South Africa within the Empire, Uruguay and the Argentine outside its borders, all belonged to the circle of countries exporting largely to the British market. Britain's consumption demand, represented by a twenty-fold growth of her imports, and the process of European capital investment and settlement in a relatively small number of newly opened and developing countries of great potential wealth, dominated the pattern of world trade and economic growth. A situation which was passing away by 1914 assigned a leading role to the British people. World trade became the medium through which the high rate of growth of their fast-moving economy communicated its drive to other lands. Great Britain for a short but vital period was the centre of the economic development of the earth.

The building up of this exceptional position came in the first three quarters of the century. It did not arrive without difficulty. An antiquated financial and commercial policy at home stood in the way. It had to be removed by the Free Trade legislation. Abroad, down to the coming of the railway and the steamship, transport and communications were too deficient for easy mobilization of the economic resources of the continents. But from the early 1840's onwards, British foreign trade began to increase fast. Between 1841 and 1870 exports grew by nearly 5 per cent per annum, well ahead of the rate of expansion of national output. From 1854 to 1880 exports more than doubled, while net imports trebled.[1] Trade expansion of this order altered the character of the national economy and it affected the outlook even of the man in the street. By 1880 he was aware as never before that his bread and employment depended upon overseas markets.

The balance of payments, the balance of what was owing to Britons from abroad as compared with what they owed, was extremely strong. Year by year, there was a substantial surplus of money available for lending abroad, first and always to governments, later and on a huge scale, to commercial, industrial, transport and public utility enterprises of every kind. This capital investment was directed particularly towards the countries whence Great Britain bought foodstuffs and raw materials.

By 1875 foreign securities had become familiar to well-to-do Britons and represented a large sum, about £1,200,000,000, in the values of those times, mostly in government stocks or railway shares. They were the means by which other lands drew wisely or unwisely

[1] P. Deane and W. A. Cole, *British Economic Growth, 1688–1959* (1962), table 83, p. 311. B. R. Mitchell and P. Deane, *Abstract of British Historical Statistics* (1962), p. 328.

on the British national income for their own development. The loans were made by private persons, as part of their personal investment, and they were organized and floated by the merchant bankers and issue-houses of the City of London.

After 1870 large changes took place in the relation of exports and imports. The most immediate and most obvious cause was a falling away in the rate of expansion of exports. These continued to grow down to 1914 but more slowly. The crisis of 1873 marked the break in the trend. The bad trading years of the 1870's and the return of depression in 1886 made it clear that the change towards a slower growth of exports might be lasting. Its origins were fundamental. They were connected with the increasing speed of industrialization in other lands, especially in Western Europe and North America, and with the spread of protective policies abroad designed to exclude imports in the interests of new home industries. These influences dominated much of international trade from 1870 down to the First World War.

World trade was expanding fast throughout most of these years and it was the good fortune of British exports to grow with it. But whereas between 1841 and 1870 they had grown at the rate of nearly 5 per cent per annum, from 1881 to 1911 they grew by no more than 2·7 per cent per annum.[1] This latter period included the years of booming exports between 1906 and 1913. The years of heavy foreign investment and extensive export business based upon them, concealed the unsatisfactory nature of the trend from contemporary eyes. The total volume of exports, being between 20 and 30 per cent by value of all that the country produced, was of course at all times impressive.

The falling off in the rate of growth of exports would have been less significant but for the trend of imports. This was steadily upwards. The increase was in keeping with the growing volume of manufacturing, with its need for raw materials, and with the purchase by city populations of food, much of which could be obtained more cheaply abroad than at home. The mid-Victorian rise of exports reached its peak in the early 1870's. They equalled in value 22 per cent of the national income. Imports went on rising fast for some years after that date. In the 1880's they were annually equal to about 36 per cent of the national income.[2] This huge disparity between exports and imports of commodities was much discussed at the time, especially when trade was bad. So too was the dependence on foreign foodstuffs.[3]

[1] P. Deane and W. A. Cole, *op. cit.* table 83, p. 311.
[2] P. Deane and W. A. Cole, *op. cit.* p. 310.
[3] See, e.g. Stephen Bourne's *Trade, Population and Food* (1880).

This came to equal about one half the food consumed. The reliance on raw materials imported was always great.

On the whole, the nation stood to gain greatly by these extended foreign connexions. An easy and enviable command over the world's foodstuffs and raw materials, which affected the national standards of life at every point, was what the Victorians acquired. But they possessed this command only on the condition that they could provide by way of payment what the world wanted.

The most fundamental of the advantages which Great Britain possessed in world exchange was a high rate of industrial innovation and a lowness of industrial costs. On a long view, it was extremely important that after 1870 she ceased to be marked out by her rate of industrial innovation from such countries as Germany and the United States. Many of her industrial costs in large trades remained relatively constant. Too much British export trade between 1870 and 1914 was done in products already established in world markets, for which the demand grew slowly, as compared with products which were new, for which the demand grew fast. With the help of large loans to developing countries exports still continued to make an impressive show, especially in sales to primary producing countries. But it was a continuation of a nineteenth-century pattern and it was growing out of date.

There was no vast growth of new manufacturing industries and new lines of export trade in the later years of the nineteenth century such as had taken place earlier on. What did occur was a great redistribution of markets forced on by the growth of industries and of tariffs abroad. Many firms and industries and many parts of Great Britain, varying with the swing of the trade-cycle and the rough impact of protective policies, felt the blasts of the new competition. The middle 1880's, for example, still more the early 1890's, were uncomfortable times for many people engaged in overseas trade. The disturbance to established interests was not the only cause of complaint, although this was continuously present. International trade was by its nature bound up with international rivalry between nations. Englishmen took the passing of their mid-century supremacy in the field of trade badly. In terms of national economic gain and loss, the decline was largely relative, in many ways of little real moment. But it was not to be expected that public opinion would see it in that way. A revolution began in economic and political thinking, directed against Free Trade policies and in favour of markets within the empire.

Meanwhile, whatever fears men might have for the future of British trade, and every trade depression revived the talk of decline in some quarter or other, commerce remained active. The balance of payments continued to be most satisfactory. In the prosaic business of meeting the nation's bills abroad, British hands held cards both numerous and of a high total value, outside of export manufacture.

The disparity between goods imported and those exported, although it became wider between 1870 and 1914 than before, was not new. Other forms of income besides industrial exports had for many years been called in to meet the balance. The profits of merchants and ship-owners, bankers and insurance underwriters, often with offices and branches abroad, played a decisive role. It is inconceivable how many opportunities for profit were opened up by wandering Englishmen and Scotsmen, sometimes as representatives, sometimes representing only themselves, everywhere from Shanghai to Buenos Aires, often in quarters comfortably unknown except to the few. Business of this kind increased immensely with the spread of railways and steamships and the ocean cable. Much of it created income in Great Britain, without the commercial operations being British-based.

The generation before 1914 saw great developments in shipowning and ship management. The technical basis of this was the advance of marine engineering, following the invention of the steel hull and the compound engine. But the constant expansion of import and export business and the growing up of distant communities sharing European tastes, were incentives just as important. With a third of the world's ocean-going tonnage in his hands and carrying something like a half of the world's seaborne trade, the English-cum-Scottish shipowner enjoyed a dominating position in ocean freights and fares. Shipping earnings made an important contribution, round about 5 per cent of the whole,[1] towards the national income.

Foreign investment was the other grand source of foreign payments. The sending of capital abroad, like the earnings of ships, was not new. But as in shipping, so in foreign investment, there was an unprecedented growth of this type of business. The late 1880's and the early 1900's, between 1906 and 1913, saw two foreign investment booms of the utmost importance. Following the many investments before 1870, these booms built up the capital invested abroad to about £4,000,000,000. Capital held in foreign securities had increased far faster than capital invested at home. One tenth of the entire national income was earned in the form of interest on savings which had been exported. Out of these interest payments came much of the income available for further investment, on the part of the well-to-do people and institutions who were chiefly interested. These were the habits of a nation and a generation unique both in its international confidence and in its social arrangements.

The position of Great Britain was then this. In a century in which

---

[1] P. Deane and W. A. Cole, *op. cit.* p. 236.

economic growth depended very much on international commerce, no country's development had benefited more from world trade or had contributed more towards its expansion. But as Britain ceased to be the workshop of the world and had to meet the competition of industries in other lands, the question before her was coming to be, how to find in the home market, in her own resources of technique and demand, the stimulus to further industrial development which she had found so often in the past in markets abroad. She had at the same time to hold on to what she needed in export markets for the sake of her purchases of foodstuffs and raw materials. The Indian summer of Edwardian foreign investment only postponed the challenge of this formidable problem to her industry and society, in the days before the war.

The documents which follow are intended to illustrate in the first place (nos. 68–71) some general aspects of the foreign trade of Great Britain at this period—the dependence of the standard of living upon it, the over-plus of imports compared with exports, the method of finance. They then turn (nos. 72–75) to particular markets and products. The tariffs and the stiffer competition which faced the export merchant and manufacturer then come in for notice (nos. 76–8). But in this period, when overseas lending played such a part in prolonging the exceptional position which the Victorians had built up in world markets, it is necessary also to consider where these loans went and how they came to be made (nos. 79–87).

FURTHER READING

For the many-sided character of British trade at this period, see principally S. B. Saul, *Studies in British Overseas Trade 1870–1914* (1960). Also, W. Schlote, *British Overseas Trade* (1952), translated from the German by W. O. Henderson and W. H. Chaloner. A. H. Imlah's *Economic Elements in the Pax Britannica* (1958) contains valuable statistical series. There is an interesting although rather one-sided analysis of fundamental trends by K. Zweig, 'Strukturwandlungen und Konjunkurschwingungen in Englischen Aussenhandel der Vorkriegs-zeit' in *Weltwirtschaftliches Archiv*, xxx (1929), Chronik und Archi-valien, 54–104 and 317–51.

The world trading system and its international payments after 1870 within which Great Britain functioned, were the subject of penetrating studies by the Economic Intelligence Service of the League of Nations, *The Network of World Trade* (1942) and *Industrialization and Foreign Trade* (1945). See also the comment on the special character of world trade in the nineteenth century in R. Nurkse, *Patterns of Trade and*

Development (1962) and the discussion of the British position in W. A. Lewis, *Economic Survey, 1919–1939* (1949).

The study of the structuring of the world market for particular commodities towards Great Britain in the nineteenth century, made possible by marine technology and telegraphic communication, has scarcely begun. It belongs as much to the economic history of other countries as to ours and does not fit easily into the period '1870–1914'. E. F. Söderlund's *Swedish Timber Exports, 1850–1950* (Stockholm, 1952), using primary sources, including business records, to tell the story in a proper economic setting, is a model of the kind of work that needs to be done.

For the trend of shipping freights at this time, L. Isserlis, 'Tramp Shipping Cargoes and Freights', *Journal of the Royal Statistical Society*, CI (1938), 53–154, gives a wonderful statistical picture not only of general trends but also of freights on a multitude of routes and in a vast variety of cargoes. For the economics of shipbuilding, S. Pollard, 'British and World Shipbuilding, 1890–1914', *Journal of Economic History*, XVII (1957), 426–44. For a discussion of the economics of the ship and some of the effects of changes in the shipping business on economic development, D. North, 'Ocean Freight Rates and Economic Development, 1750–1813', and M. E. Fletcher, 'The Suez Canal and World Shipping, 1869–1914', both in *Journal of Economic History*, XVIII (1958), 537–73.

For the study of foreign investment, A. K. Cairncross, *Home and Foreign Investment 1870–1913* (1953) is indispensable. See also, H. Feis, *Europe the World's Banker 1870–1914* (1930). The contemporary investor's manual, *Fenn on the Funds: a Handbook of Public Debts*, which went through many editions, is worth looking at. London was the centre of the financial world at this time, but the city has been largely indifferent to its own history. Full-length histories of city institutions, written with full access to private papers, are few. The Edwardian foreign investment boom is still without an historian. Some hints of how things were managed can be gathered from R. S. Sayers, *Lloyds Bank in the History of English Banking* (1957) and a view of what the financial world looked like from one great institution from Sir John Clapham's *The Bank of England: a History* (1944). S. G. Checkland, 'The Mind of the City, 1870–1914', *Oxford Economic Papers*, new series, vol. IX (1957) is worth reading. The other end, so to speak, of foreign investment history is the receiving end. It belongs to the economic history of many countries. One might do worse than begin with the 'land boom' and 'bank crash' chapters in an old but still vivid book, Edward Shann's *Economic History of Australia* (1930). But H. S. Ferns's *Britain and Argentina in the Nineteenth Century* (1960) or G. A. Simpkin's study of New Zealand, *The Instability of a Dependent*

Economy (1951) or J. Viner's *Canada's Balance of International Indebtedness, 1900–1913* (Cambridge, Mass.) are all illuminating on what British capital meant for the 'new' countries of the nineteenth century, when they were new.

The movement of capital from Great Britain is not intelligible without some knowledge of the movement of people, not only British, but of many nationalities. The history of emigration, too big a subject to be documented here, is part and parcel of the history of capital movements. So far as British emigration is concerned, there is a contemporary study of it in S. C. Johnson, *A History of Emigration from the United Kingdom to North America* (1913). See also W. A. Carrothers, *Emigration from the British Isles* (1929). But R. E. Foerster, *The Italian Emigration of our Times* (Cambridge, Mass. 1924), would be equally relevant to the expansion of British investments and trade in non-British countries. See in a more general way, Brinley Thomas, *Migration and Economic Growth* (1954) and F. Thistlethwaite, 'Atlantic Partnership', *Economic History Review* (1954), pp. 2–17.

68. THE DEPENDENCE OF THE STANDARD OF LIVING ON FOREIGN TRADE

Source: A. L. Bowley, 'A Short Account of England's Foreign Trade in the Nineteenth Century' (1893), pp. 131–2.

Arthur Bowley, who was to become one of the leading statisticians of the next generation, published in 1893 what was substantially his winning Cobden Prize Essay in the previous year at the University of Cambridge. In its sensitiveness to the importance of the great expansion of overseas trade which had taken place in the middle decades of the century, it was characteristic of much of the economic writing of the time.

OUR foreign trade is to a great extent an elaborate machinery for supplying us with food. Of the £410 millions'-worth of goods which come to our share, [*sic*] at least £155 millions'-worth is food; while £105 millions'-worth is of raw materials, which can be definitely reckoned, and of the remaining £150 millions, if it was possible to distinguish materials for manufacture from materials for sale, part would be found to be materials for our factories, rather than goods for consumption.

Let us consider how this enormous annual bill for food is paid, regarding the whole nation as a single family. Tabulating imports and exports thus:

	Imports	
Food	£155 million	
Raw textiles	85 ,,	
Other Raw Materials (Chiefly Metals and Ores)	20 ,,	
Miscellaneous (Manufactured Articles, Raw Materials for consumption, and Miscellaneous Raw Materials)	150 ,,	
Total	£410 million	
Interest on Capital	75 ,,	(approximately)
	£335 million	(to be paid by exports and shipping)

	Exports	
Textile Manufactures	£110 million	
Hardware and Machinery	75 ,,	
Miscellaneous	80 ,,	
Earnings of Shipping	70 ,,	(approximately)
	£335 million	

In the manufacture of textiles, so great is the increase of value, that after the home market has been supplied the exports of yarn and cloth are worth £35 millions more than the raw materials. The cotton workers thus pay for the raw cotton we use at home, and have this surplus towards our food supply.

Workers in mines, iron foundries and the like, add to the value of the ores extracted and the ores and metals imported to such an extent that we are supplied, and a surplus of £55 millions is ready to pay for imports.

These sums added to the earnings of our ships make up the £160 million sufficient to cover our bill for provisions.

This done, we may reckon that half the miscellaneous goods imported are in return for miscellaneous exports, while the other half are the interest due on our foreign investments.

69. THE CAUSES OF AN EXCESS OF IMPORTS OVER EXPORTS

Source: 'Memoranda, Statistical Tables and Charts prepared in the Board of Trade with reference to various matters bearing on British and Foreign Trade and Industrial Conditions 1903', Cd. 1761, LXVII second series, 99–103.

This blue-book was published in the very early stages of the 'Fiscal

Controversy'. Joseph Chamberlain launched in May 1903 his political campaign for a return to a protective tariff. The Board of Trade compiled its statistics in the two and a half months which followed, under the direction of Gerald Balfour, then President of the Board, by way of official comment on the issues involved. Official opinion was strongly Free Trade. The memorandum from which extracts are given constituted an optimistic although well-founded analysis of the recent and current state of the balance of payments.

O F the whole of the commercial and financial transactions between any country and the outside world, which over a period of years, though not necessarily within the limits of any single year, must balance one another, only a portion are embodied in the commodities which pass outward and inward as exports and imports. There is thus no necessary equality between the values of imports and exports of commodities. As a matter of fact, for many years imports into the United Kingdom have always exceeded exports. An inquiry into the causes of this excess of imports is, therefore, an inquiry into the nature and value of the unrecorded transactions and services rendered and received which, one year with another, will balance the account.

It may be said at once that any answer of a statistical nature to the inquiry can only be of the roughest kind.

The Excess of Value of our Imports over our Exports as recorded in the official Trade Accounts in each year, 1893–1902, was as follows:

Year	Merchandise £ (million)	Bullion and Specie £ (million)	Total £ (million)
1893	128	4	132
1894	135	11	146
1895	131	15	146
1896	145	−6	139
1897	157	−1	156
1898	177	6	183
1899	155	10	165
1900	169	8	177
1901	174	6	180
1902	179	5	184
Decennial average	155	6	161

We have, therefore, to account for an annual excess averaging 161 millions over the past 10 years, and varying in individual years during that period from a minimum of £132,000,000 to a maximum of £184,000,000.

The excess on the whole has tended to increase....

(1) There are in the first place some minor adjustments of the recorded figures in order to make them complete e.g. by including items such as diamonds....

(2) The first great item which is omitted in our trade returns, and which has to be added to our exports, is on account of the earnings of our carrying trade—both ship-owners and underwriters—not only on the carriage of our own imports and exports, but also in carrying goods between foreign countries or between British Colonies.

We have in fact to add to our exports the whole gross earnings of our merchant fleet engaged in the foreign trade *less* any amount which is expended abroad....

Thus in the last year for which figures are available the statistics of entrances and clearances seem to indicate that about half the carrying trade of the world was done by British vessels. If the earnings were in proportion, we have about 112 million pounds for the gross annual earnings of British vessels (including underwriters' profits)....

[*Concludes that, deducting that part of earnings which is spent abroad and never reaches British shores, about 90 million pounds represents the net annual earnings of shipping.*]

(3) The second great item to be considered is the effect of our foreign investments on the balance of imports and exports. It is necessary to distinguish between the results of the actual transference of capital and of the annual return received on the aggregate sum invested....

In considering, therefore, the average amount to be allowed annually on account of income from foreign investments, we are justified in concluding that 62½ millions is a *minimum* figure, which is probably largely exceeded, though we are unable to say by how much.

...Whatever the actual total may be, it is evident that when added to the 90 millions to be allowed for the carrying trade it is sufficient, and probably more than sufficient, to account for the average excess of imports, viz., 160 millions.

70. OVERSEAS SUPPLIES OF FOODSTUFFS AND RAW MATERIALS

Source: 'Report of the Royal Commission on Supply of Food and Raw Materials in Time of War, 1905' (Cd. 2643), paras. 12, 22, 27, 28, 35, 36–40; and 'Minutes of Evidence' (Cd. 2644), questions 4280, 5036, 5092, 5093–5.

The world trading position of Great Britain as it emerged at the end of the nineteenth century has been described as one of 'maximum profits derived from maximum risks'.[1] The more distant risk, that the economy might fail to adapt itself to changes in world production and exchange, did not materialize until after the First World War was over. The more immediate, of war and its effects, was anxiously discussed in the early 1900's. It was clear then that increased dependence on imported food and raw materials had been accompanied by a technical revolution in sea warfare (see above no. 32) which made effective blockade of the island for the first time a practical possibility and a desirable aim to any enemy possessing strength at sea. Moreover, Great Britain's isolation in international politics and the depth of continental antagonism towards her had been painfully exposed by the Boer War, 1899–1901. The official body of inquiry here quoted accepted the new dependence on overseas supplies: 'We look mainly for security to the strength of our Navy; but we rely in only less degree upon...our mercantile fleet and its power to carry on our trade and reach all possible sources of supply.' In saying this, the Commission badly overestimated the protection which might be afforded to the food trade by international law during war and they failed to foresee the two main war-time problems of food and raw material import, the scarcity of shipping space and the difficulty of finding foreign exchange. In 1905, all these things were matter for hypothesis and conjecture. The risk of the economy's reliance on overseas' supply, and consequently on overseas' markets was, on the contrary, a matter of daily fact.

[Cotton]

Mr Wright, representing the Liverpool Cotton Association, informed us that the consumption of raw cotton in the United Kingdom has increased steadily from 588 million lbs. in 1850 to 1649 million lbs. in 1902, though this great quantity is less than the present consumption either in the United States or on the Continent of Europe. Of these imports about three-fourths come from the United States, which is about the proportion that the United States crop bears to the world's crop.

[1] A. Loveday, *Britain and World Trade* (1931), p. 180.

As regards the risk likely to arise from this large dependence on one source of supply, Mr Helm, Secretary of the Manchester Chamber of Commerce, pointed out that during the Civil War in the United States our supplies of cotton from that source were practically stopped. The other sources of supply were drawn upon to the uttermost to meet the deficiency, but our total imports which were 1257 million lbs. in 1861, fell in 1862 to 524 million lbs., and though from this point there was a gradual recovery, yet even in 1868 the quantity imported only reached 1297 million lbs.

[*Petroleum*]

The quantity of petroleum produced in our islands is very small, amounting in 1901 to less than 2000 gallons, while the imports have increased from 77 million gallons in 1887 to 250 million gallons at the present time. Of this quantity nearly the whole comes from two sources; the cheaper kind from Russia and the better class from the United States, a result which follows inevitably from the fact that of the whole world's supply the United States furnishes 42 per cent and Russia 51 per cent.

[*Meat Supplies*]

Meat and animals for food. We have obtained detailed information as to the supply of meat in this country from Mr Rew, who was reporter to the Special Committee appointed by the Royal Statistical Society to inquire into the production and consumption of meat and milk in the United Kingdom. The Committee arrived at the conclusion that approximately 45 per cent of the meat consumed in the United Kingdom was imported, the rest being produced at home.

The following table shows for the period 1898 to 1902 the results obtained by the Committee with regard to the average amount of the various kinds of meat annually consumed in this country, and the percentage of imports to total consumption: [*shown overleaf*]

As regards London, however, the proportion of imported meat entering into consumption is probably higher than the average given in the above table. Mr Cooper, Chairman of the Meat and Cattle Trade Section of the London Chamber of Commerce, gave it as his opinion that two-thirds of the meat eaten in London is imported from abroad.

*Average annual production, imports and consumption of meat in the
quinquennial period 1898 to 1902*

	Home Production	Imported*	Total	Percentage of Imports to Total
	Tons	Tons	Tons	Per Cent
Beef and Veal	662,520	386,400	1,048,920	37
Mutton and Lamb	313,822	193,150	506,972	38
Bacon and Pork	269,578	410,394	679,972	60
TOTAL	1,245,920	1,001,171†	2,247,091†	44½

* Including the weight of dead meat derived from animals imported alive.
† Less total of imported meat re-exported.

A small proportion of our imported supply is fresh killed meat,
which consequently cannot be stored for a long period, coming chiefly
from Holland, Denmark, and other European countries. But the
great bulk is in the form of either live cattle from Canada and the
United States or frozen carcases from Australasia and Argentina. It is
impossible for large stocks of the former to be held, for the Board of
Agriculture's regulations, issued under Diseases of Animals Act, 1896,
compel imported cattle to be slaughtered within 10 days of landing,
and as a matter of practice they are rarely kept for even that length of
time....

[*Wheat and Flour*]

...We are of opinion that the consumption per head per year
[*of wheat, including flour expressed as wheat*] will not normally exceed
350 lbs., which would give a present annual consumption in the
United Kingdom of about 31,000,000 qtrs., equivalent to an average
weekly requirement of approximately 600,000 qtrs.

Of this total it appears from the information furnished by Mr Rew,
in his capacity as Head of the Statistical Branch of the Board of
Agriculture, that rather less than six million quarters, or approximately
20 per cent of the whole are home grown; for though the total crop
of the United Kingdom at the present time amounts on an average to
about 7 million quarters, a deduction of 15 to 20 per cent has to be

made for grain unfit for milling or required for seed and other farming purposes.

We note that there has been a great decline in the quantity of wheat grown in this country during the later decades of the last century, and this tendency has gone so far that the acreage under wheat in the United Kingdom has decreased by more than one-half in the last 30 years. This diminution has been brought about by a variety of causes, chief amongst them being probably the large decline in price. It would be unsafe to say that the production of wheat has reached its lowest point; the amount of the harvest declined again considerably both in 1903 and 1904: but this latter decrease appears to be largely attributable to the special climatic conditions of those years, and whether the tendency will continue must depend, as in the past, on the course of prices and other considerations which we discuss below in paragraphs 65 and 66.

On the other hand, the imports of wheat and flour have not merely increased in proportion to the decrease in the home-crop during the 34 years from 1870–1904, but have risen, with the increase in consumption, from 8·61 million qrs. in 1870 to 27·72 million qrs. in 1904, i.e. over 300 per cent, and while our imports in 1870 were about 40 per cent of the total consumption, they now amount to the high figure of over 80 per cent.

In view of this unprecedented growth of imports it was necessary for us to examine the sources from which these immense quantities are derived, and to find out what are the countries on which we are so dependent, and to what proportionate extent in each case. The situation has, in appearance at any rate, been rendered additionally serious by the fact that during the past 30 years the tendency has been to draw them preponderantly from a single source, the United States of America; but we should add that in 1903, and in a still more marked degree in 1904, a large reduction has taken place in the quantities received from the United States. So marked has been that tendency that that country, which for 30 years has held the pre-eminent position as a source of supply, has, for the present at any rate, declined to the fourth rank as an exporter to the United Kingdom.

Comparing the quinquennial period 1871–5 with 1898–1902, to which, for purposes of further comparison, we have added the single year 1904, we find that our supplies were drawn from the different groups of countries in the following percentage proportions, respectively:

Sources of Supply to the United Kingdom of wheat and flour (in equivalent weight of grain) in the quinquennial periods 1871–5 and 1898–1902 and in the year 1904

	Percentage Proportion		
	1871–5	1898–1902	1904
British Colonies and Possessions	10·9	19·0	39·1
Europe (including Turkey)	41·4	8·8	25·4
United States of America	39·9	62·2	15·9
South America	2·9	9·7	19·2
Other countries	4·9	0·3	0·4
	100	100	100

[*Iron Ore*] [*Evidence of J. S. Jeans, Secretary of the British Iron Trade Association*]

...the British iron trade consumes annually from 18 to 20 million tons of ore, of which about 7 millions are imported....The importation of iron ores into this country has been going on for many years on an increasing scale. Spain began to furnish supplies about 1865; Italy about 1870; Algeria about 1866; Norway about 1864, and other countries at later dates. In 1870 our total imports of iron ore were about 208,000 tons, or 1·4 per cent of our total consumption. In 1880 our imports rose to about 8 per cent of our total consumption; and for the last few years they have been about 25 per cent of our total consumption. But their importance as sources of supply for our iron industry is not accurately measured by their percentage proportions. Imported iron ores are considerably richer than the average of British ores; so much so, indeed, that while it may be said that of home ores three tons are used per ton of pig iron, foreign ores would only be consumed to the extent of two tons per ton of that metal. Hence, when our imports of foreign ores reach 7 million tons, which they have recently done, it may be taken that they will provide some 3½ million tons of pig iron, which would be about 41 per cent of our total pig iron in 1902. If in the event of war this supply were interfered with, it is obvious that much inconvenience and anxiety, not to speak of possible panic, would be caused to our iron industry. That industry, however, could still be kept going to a large extent from British sources of supply. Probably there would not be much difficulty in raising at home from 15 million to 16 million tons of ore. The leading district has hitherto been that of Cleveland, in North Yorkshire, which produces an average of about 5½ million tons a year, or over one-third of our total home output. This district has produced in a single year about 6½ million tons, and no doubt that figure could be reached again under pressure. Probably also, a considerable increase of production could without much trouble be got in Northamptonshire, Lincolnshire, Derbyshire, Leicestershire, and other Midland centres; but the difficulty is that those districts produce phosphoric ores which are not so much the urgent desideratum of the trade to-day as the non-phosphoric ores imported from abroad. Four-fifths of the total output of British steel is produced from non-phosphoric ores, while our home output of such ores does not exceed one-fourth of our total consumption of the same variety. In most engineering specifications drawn up in this country, non-phosphoric ores are specified; in other words, British engineers prefer what is known as acid, or non-phosphoric steel, to basic steel, which is produced from phosphoric ores, although basic steel is the leading product in Germany and some other foreign countries, and promises to become so in the United States, in the not far distant future. If the engineers of this country were as ready to accept basic steel as those of the Continent, it would be possible greatly to diminish our dependence on imported ores....It will be seen, therefore, that under existing conditions the discontinuance of British iron ore imports would practically close some two-thirds of the iron works in Scotland, all the iron works in South Wales, nearly one-half of the iron works in Cleveland, and nearly one-half of the blast furnaces in West Cumberland, and North-West Lancashire, which includes the Barrow district. It would mean the reduction of annual output of haematite iron in this country by about 3½ million tons, and would withdraw pig iron to that extent from the service of our great acid steel industry, which in its turn would seriously react on the British supplies of steel specially suited and applied to the building of ships and the manufacture of tyres, axles, wheels, and other important railway requirements. As far as the foreign sources of supply are concerned, the principal country of origin is Spain, which in 1902 shipped to this country 5,310,000 tons of ore, or over 70 per cent of the total quantity imported from all countries. Other 15 foreign countries and 10 British colonies contributed supplies of iron ore.... In addition to the iron ores supplied by foreign countries, considerable quantities of manganese ores are also imported. The largest quantity of such ores imported in any recent year was 265,757 tons in 1900. The principal countries of origin in this case are Russia, Brazil, India, and Chile. This ore is indispensable to the manufacture of ferro-manganese, which is employed in modern processes of steel manufacture, to replace the carbon which gives its essential character to that metal. As practically no such ore exists in this country, and as, in the event of war, our supplies of the metal would be as liable to be interfered with as our supplies of the ore, the question is in some respects of the highest importance. The actual quantity used is, of course, relatively small, but it is indispensable....

[*Wool*]

The raw material comes from a great many countries. The largest quantity of wool used is colonial. 637 million lbs. of raw wool were imported into this country last year;[1] 525 million lbs. came from British Possessions (Australia chiefly), and only 112 million lbs. from all other countries. Of the latter amount 24 million lbs. came from the Argentine Republic. This is but a very small portion of the supply available in that country, and in future possibly very much larger quantities will be imported. I might add that the clip of the Argentine this year is about 500 million lbs.; therefore 24 million lbs. is a very small proportion of their production. In the United Kingdom about 135 million lbs. of raw wool and probably 80 million lbs. of shoddy are produced. The world's production of raw wool is estimated at 3000 million lbs....

According to your Table A we export 269 million lbs. of wool; where do we send it?—It is chiefly colonial wool re-exported.

Do we export wool raw?—Yes, of foreign and colonial wool we send 85 million lbs. to Germany, 22 million lbs. to Holland, 36 million

[1] 1902.

194

lbs. to Belgium, 79 million lbs. to France, and 54 million lbs. to the
United States, as well as 27 million lbs. of home-grown wool to the
United States.

Is the greater part of that wool that is exported wool that had been
imported first from our Colonies and other countries?—Yes.

I think you have said that we do export about 35 million lbs. of
our own wool?—Last year we exported about 35 million lbs. of home-
grown wool, which is quite exceptional; we have hitherto not exported
so much as that.

71. THE FINANCE OF OVERSEAS TRADE

*Source: George Clare, 'The ABC of the Foreign Exchanges' (1893),
pp. 11–12, 37–40.*

*As the largest buyer of foodstuffs and raw materials and the greatest
seller of manufactured goods, Great Britain was at this time the centre of
the world's trade. The trade was also largely financed in London, through
the purchase and sale of bills of exchange. The bill might be described as
a kind of cheque, carrying interest until it was paid, and internationally
acceptable. The bill on London, i.e. drawn for settlement in London,
was the chief means of payment in world trade. With its help, accounts
were balanced between many different parts of the world, through London.
The demand for and sale of bills determined the current exchange of other
currencies in terms of sterling. Bills of exchange were not only a means
of payment, but also a much sought-after short-term investment for idle
money.*

IT has been shown that, if two countries buy of each other to the
same amount, their transactions need not give rise to two separate
sets of bills [*of exchange*], but that on the contrary, if the foreigner
draws on us to the full value of his exports, the bills so created will be
sent as remittances to the exporter on this side and will pay him for his
sales. Conversely, if the British exporter draws, there is no necessity
for the other side to do so.

What then are the facts? Does the United Kingdom, generally
speaking, draw on abroad, or does the foreigner take the initiative by
drawing on London?

As a matter of fact, both sides draw; but, as all who are acquainted
with the customs of trade are well aware, the bills drawn by Great

Britain on abroad are vastly outnumbered by those drawn from abroad on London.

Owing chiefly to the magnitude of our trade, but also to several contributory causes—such as the stability of our currency; the certainty that a bill on London means gold and nothing but gold; the facility with which those who deserve credit can obtain it here; our freedom from invasion, or any chance of invasion etc.—London has become to a great extent the settling place of Europe and the world and the seller, wherever he may be, of a good bill in London can always be sure of finding a buyer, and of realizing a fair price. As the sale of a bill, moreover, carries the valuable advantage of ready money and a speedy turnover of capital, it is invariably preferred by the foreign exporter, who has consigned or sold produce to us, to the alternative plan of awaiting remittances from this side....

There is perhaps no public edifice in the City which is better known or less understood than the Royal Exchange....The Royal Exchange was intended as a meeting-place for merchants, and up to a quarter of a century ago London merchants actually did meet there, each separate branch of trade collecting in its own corner or round its own particular pillar. But, as the various sections grew in numbers, it became more convenient to make homes for themselves in the localities they specially affect, and the coal, wool, corn, produce, and other interests now possess their own separate Exchanges.

One important group still remains true to its allegiance. Twice a week, on Tuesdays and Thursdays, the Royal Exchange wakes up for a brief space. Immediately after luncheon-time those who have business to transact in foreign bills begin to gather at the eastern end of the courtyard, and for about an hour 'Change is held. The assemblage, which is never a very large one—not more perhaps than five or six score at the outside—consists of a small number of brokers and of the chiefs of all the great foreign banking-houses. Of bankers, in the ordinary acceptation of the term, scarcely one is to be seen, except on rare occasions: London being perhaps the only great capital in the world of which the home-banking interest is not regularly represented on 'Change. There is an entire absence of noise and excitement. So quietly is the business transacted that it is difficult for an onlooker to believe that anything is going on. Now and again one observes a broker draw a likely buyer aside, covertly exhibit a contract-note, and suggest a price in a whisper. A simple nod of the head, almost imperceptible to a bystander, signifies acceptance; the broker scribbles down the rate, passes over the contract, which the banker thrusts unconcernedly into his pocket, and the bargain is complete. In an hour or so all is over; and the broker hurries back to his office to write out his course of exchange, or list of current prices, a copy of which appears in the newspapers the next morning.

72. STEAM AND THE CANAL IN THE EASTERN TRADE

Source: W. S. Lindsay, 'History of Merchant Shipping and Ancient Commerce', IV (1876), 434–7, 438–9, 444.

William Shaw Lindsay (1816–77), a merchant and shipowner, was writing when the Suez Canal had only recently been opened, in 1869. He describes the impact made upon the Eastern trade by two great events, the opening of the Canal and the introduction into the steamship of the compound engine, with its very considerable economies of fuel and carrying space. Sailing vessels, at this date, still carried by far the largest proportion of the goods traffic in the Indian and Australian trades. Lindsay's doubts whether the iron sailing ship would be immediately displaced proved to be well founded. On the Australia run, the passenger sailing vessels continued to be well filled all through the 1880's; the iron wool clippers were in great use down to the 1890's.

AMONG the instances where anything like success has attended steam voyages direct to Australia, may be mentioned the services performed by Messrs Gibbs, Bright, and Company, in their steamship *Great Britain* from Liverpool, and in the steamers belonging to Messrs Money Wigram and Sons, of London, which now trade to these colonies. Occasionally other steamers are despatched to Australia and also to New Zealand, and recently a company was formed—the Australian Direct Steam Navigation Company—with the intention of maintaining a regular monthly line from London to Melbourne, calling at Falmouth, the Projectors anticipating the performances of the passage in 'under forty-five days.' But though this undertaking failed at the outset, and experience can alone test the realization of the sanguine expectations of its promoters, it may be said in favour of their views, that the difficulties previous pioneers of steam-vessels on long oversea voyages have had to encounter are being rapidly surmounted by the new compound engines, where the consumption of coals required to attain a given speed is not one-half of what it was twenty years ago.

So far as regards the trade with India and China by way of the Cape of Good Hope, the steam-line started by Mr Alfred Holt of Liverpool in 1865 is the only one within my recollection, which has hitherto proved successful. Though the steamers of this line now proceed to China by the Suez Canal, their performances were remarkable when engaged in the former route. Starting from Liverpool they *never stopped till they reached Mauritius, a distance of 8500 miles*, being under steam the whole way, a feat hitherto considered impossible; thence they proceeded to Penang, Singapore, Hong Kong, and Shanghai, and, though unaided by any government grants, performed these distant voyages with extraordinary regularity.

In forwarding the particulars of his first three vessels, Mr Holt[1] remarks: 'Since the Suez Canal was opened I have found that the square sails of the *Agememnon*, *Ajax*, and *Achilles*[2] were of little use, and, therefore, I have converted these three ships into what the Americans call "barquentine rig" (i.e. no square yards on mainmast), and have constructed all my new ships with poll-masts only.'

These three vessels are each 2270 tons gross or 1550 net register, with engines of 300 nominal horse-power.[3] Messrs Holt have also eleven other steamers, similar in size and power, at present engaged in trade

[1] Mr Alfred Holt is the third son of my old friend, the late Mr George Holt of Liverpool. He is an engineer by profession, having served his apprenticeship to Mr Edward Woods, the engineer of the Liverpool and Manchester Railway.... Though he has no claim to be considered the inventor of the compound engine, for that is almost as old, in one form or another, as the present century; he was the first to apply the principle on *long oversea voyages*. The ships of the Pacific Company had, it is true, that description of engine in use before him, but only in those of their ships engaged in the coasting trade of the Pacific. Mr Holt's steamers were consequently the first to show the advantages to be derived from the compound principle on such voyages as those from England to Mauritius, a distance of 8500 miles without stopping, then a marvellous performance; and it was, only, from the time he thus *practically* demonstrated the great value of such engines, that they have been generally adopted.

[2] The Achilles left Foochow, July 16th, 1869, and arrived at London round the Cape of Good Hope, September 16th, having been fifty-eight days nine hours under steam—13,552 miles.

[3] Their dimensions are as follows: 309 feet in length, 38½ feet beam, and 28½ depth of hold to upper or spar deck.

with the East, and three more in course of construction, besides a tug-steamer of 350 tons to attend on them in their passage through the Suez Canal. They carry goods right through to Penang, Singapore, Hong Kong, and Shanghai, calling at Galle and Amoy, or other ports in the Eastern seas when required; and one is struck with the low rates at which goods are now conveyed[1] to India and China compared with the freights charged by the sailing-vessels of the old East India Company, together with the wonderful regularity and expedition[2] with which they are delivered.

Although the fleet of this spirited undertaking is known as the Ocean Steam-ship Company, it is neither a public nor a limited company, the vessels being owned in shares under the old law by a few individuals (like many others of a similar description in this country), but chiefly by the managing owners, Mr Alfred and his brother Mr Philip H. Holt, whose thorough business habits have materially promoted the success of the company.

It would be impossible to notice within the limits of this work the different lines of steam-ships now trading to the East by way of the Suez Canal. Among the most conspicuous, however, may be mentioned those of Messrs Gellatly, Hankey, Sewell, and Company, London, which, from the order and regularity of their despatch, bid fair to rival the subsidized companies. Many of the vessels under their agency belong to Messrs Thomas Wilson, Sons and Company, of Hull, long known as large owners of vessels trading from that place to various ports in the Baltic, but who, since the opening of the Suez Canal, have established a line of very fine steam-ships from London to India.

Their *Hindoo* for instance, of 3257 tons gross register, has capacity for about 3500 tons weight, 'including coals in bunkers, and from 80 to 120 passengers,' for whom accommodation is provided 'amidships, a method which has apparently given great satisfaction to those who have been travellers by them'....

[1] [*Details are given in this footnote of the freight charges on goods to places in the Near and Far East.*]

[2] The *Agamemnon* left Hankow, 604 miles above Shanghai, on May 25th, 1873, and arrived (by way of the Suez Canal and Gibraltar) at London, July 12th. The mails, which left Shanghai June 1st, arrived in London *via* Brindisi, July 21st, and the passage of the *Agamemnon* is not an exceptional one.

As a specimen of the ordinary first-class merchant steamers now trading between Liverpool and Calcutta, I may instance one of the vessels belonging to Messrs Rathbone Brothers, of that place. She is of 2610 tons gross and 1682 tons net register, and has capacity for 2200 tons of cargo, besides 450 tons of coal.[1] She is rigged merely with poles (a mode of rig now becoming very general in all steam-vessels), on which, with the exception of one fore-square sail, a few fore and aft sails alone can be set. The owners remark the "best passages of our ships as yet are as follows: Liverpool to Calcutta (via Gibraltar) to Saugar (near Calcutta), thirty-one days, including all stoppages; Calcutta to London (via Galle and of course Suez Canal) to *Nore* light-ship, thirty-four days thirteen hours, steaming time on the whole voyage (exclusive of Suez Canal and stoppages) sixty-one days twelve hours. The best homeward passage hitherto made by any of our ships, landing cargo at Colombo and Port Said, occupied thirty-three days seventeen hours, inclusive of all stoppages."

From these and previous figures, my readers will more fully understand the progress that has been made in our ordinary trading communications with India and China, since the days of the East India Company, and ascertain what has been gained, since then in the speed, capacity, and current expenses of our merchant-ships.

Such are the vessels now carrying on the more valuable portion of our trade with India, through that great maritime highway, which the genius and industry of De Lesseps has so recently opened to our vast commerce with the Far East, three-fourths of which, however, is still conducted by the way of the Cape of Good Hope.[2]

[1] The dimensions of this vessel are 350 feet in length, 37 feet in breadth, and 27 feet 5 inches extreme depth of hold. She has three decks, her engines are 300 nominal horse-power, and her crew consists of fifty persons all told.

[2] I may here state that the bulkiest articles of Indian produce, consisting as they do of cotton, jute, rice, sugar, saltpetre, cutch, and such like, as also woods of various kinds, cannot, as a rule, afford to pay the rates necessary to remunerate a steam-ship for their conveyance; hence, such articles will most likely continue to be sent to Europe by the Cape route, except when in special demand. That such will most probably continue to be the case is apparent from the fact that, though, during the last two years, the competition between the steamers passing through the Suez Canal has been so great as to reduce their rates of freight almost to a level with those paid to sailing-vessels, the latter will continue to secure full

73. SHIP MANAGEMENT ON THE INDIAN OCEAN

Source: Hector Bolitho, 'James Lyle Mackay First Earl of Inchcape'
(1936), pp. 34–5.

James Mackay went out from Scotland to India in 1874, as one of
the assistants of Mackinnon, Mackenzie and Company, a firm interested
in shipping in Indian waters. From 1878 he managed on their behalf
the ships of the British India Steam Navigation Company. Mackay
arrived in India at a time when the opening of the Suez Canal and the
invention of the fuel-saving compound marine engine were beginning to
reshape the prospects of commerce on the Indian Ocean. His career was
symbolic of the expansion which followed, for he became chairman of the
Peninsular and Oriental Steam Navigation Company, the largest of
the British shipping companies engaged in the trade to India and
Australia. This description of early days comes from the reminiscences of
Shivram Ramchandra. It is worth noticing how much of the business
done by British-owned shipping companies was done by ships which
never touched British shores, but which traded wherever prospects were
good.

MR MACKAY employed me as a clerk under him in 1880....
I was credited with having more than average intelligence and
being active. I was fortunate in coming under the direct control of
Mr Mackay and so came into closer contact with him than many of the
other Indian employees.

Mr Mackay was residing in the office premises converted into a
chummery with Mr William Bell of Messrs Wm. Bell and Co. and
Mr Curwen, editor of the *Times in India* as his companions. He rode
much on his favourite chestnut horse and occasionally rode up the
stairs into the office to frighten us. After dismounting he would give
the horse a biscuit or so to eat and order it to get down, which it
obeyed.

The British India services then were from Bombay to Calcutta, via
coast ports and also from Calcutta and the Coromandel Coast to

cargoes. This may, in some measure, be accounted for by many, indeed, the bulk
of those cargoes being sold 'to arrive' hence, merchants frequently prefer sailing-
vessels, especially for the shipment of jute, rice, and other articles of comparatively
low value, as thus they have a longer time at their disposal, and thus frequently
avoid the expense of warehousing, to which, in the case of goods by steamers,
they are often obliged to resort, from the short time allowed in all contracts, for
the discharge of such vessels.

Rangoon and Moulmein regularly; from Bombay to Africa and to the Persian Gulf via Karachi, and Kathiawar Coast ports; and from Bombay and Calcutta to London. A lot of canvassing had to be done for cargo in those days and Mr Mackay worked very hard, meeting merchants and gaining them over to ship by the company's steamers....

His eye for business was keen and every pilgrim season when the number of pilgrims awaiting transport were [*sic*] sufficiently large, he would charter ships for Jeddah and personally go to the Musafarkhana at Bhendy Bazaar with me to book the pilgrims. He encouraged the Madras and Southern Mahratta Railway authorities to negotiate with the Portuguese Government for extension of their Line to Marmagoa and took the agency for the supply and transport of materials for the construction of the Line.

74. BARTER IN WEST AFRICA

Source: John Harford, "A Voyage to the African Oil Rivers Twenty-five Years Ago", in Mary Kingsley, 'West African Studies' (1899), pp. 574–5, 577–8.

Late in the nineteenth century, important branches of world trade could be and were carried on by barter. Of this type was the trade on the West African oil rivers. The oil rivers were so called because the Africans who lived around them sold palm-oil, which was valuable in Europe for lighting, soap and lubricants. Barter formed the foundation of the trade for many years after the 1870's. But few parts of the world changed their trading methods faster than West Africa, with the growth of world demand for African products, steamship communication, silver currency and banking facilities. The 1914 position was very different, as the history of Lagos shows.

W E took a few passengers on board [*at Santa Isabel, in the island of Fernando Po*], and then set sail for the Cameroon River. This being only fifty miles distant, we were not long before we came to anchor off what is called the Dog's Heads....Now we come in sight of the then noted King Bell's Town, called after a king of that name. Here our ship is moored with two anchors, and here she has to remain until the whole of her cargo has been purchased. This was done, and is even today, by barter, that is exchanging the goods our ship has brought out for the products of the country, which at that time consisted only of palm oil, ivory, and cocoa-nuts....

The trading would be carried on in this way. The after end of the ship was partitioned off and made to resemble a shop as nearly as possible, in this were displayed goods of all kinds and descriptions too numerous to mention here. In front of this shop, at a small table, the captain sat, while an assistant would be in the shop ready to pass any goods that were required out to the purchasers, who first had to take their produce, whatever it might be, to the mate, who would be on the main deck to examine the oil and see that it was clean and free from dirt of any kind; he would also measure whatever was brought by the natives, then give them a receipt, or what was commonly called a book. This book was taken to the captain, who would ask what they required. All that could be paid for from the shop was handed over, while for the heavy goods another receipt or book was given which had to be handed to the man in charge of the store on the beach, who gave the native his requirements there. So the work would go on from day to day, and month to month, until the whole of the ship's cargo had been bought, then the mat roof was taken off, masts and spars rigged up, sails bent and the ship made ready to sail for Old England. This, I must tell you, was a happy time for all on board, after lying, as we often did, some fourteen or fifteen months in the manner I have described. During the long months many changes took place; some of our crew fell ill with fever, and worst of all dysentery, one of the most terrible diseases that had to be contended with at that time.

75. HOW TO SUCCEED IN THE SKIN AND LEATHER BUSINESS

Source: A. H. John, 'A Liverpool Merchant House being the History of Alfred Booth and Company, 1863–1958' (1959), pp. 69, 84–5.

The operations of Alfred Booth and Company may perhaps serve as an illustration of much other British commercial enterprise in the late Victorian age. Their particular sort of business could hardly have existed in any other country or time. A commission house in Liverpool formed in 1863 by two young brothers, Alfred and Charles Booth, they supplied the American market, through New York, with sheepskins suitable for making boots and shoes and other purposes of the leather trade. When the first of these memoranda was written, in 1883, they were a merchant house and a shipping line operating on both sides of the Atlantic. Twenty years later, when the second was put on paper, they had added manufacturing to their other interests. They supplied their own highly successful leather factory, the Surpass Leather Company at Philadelphia, with skins, by this time mostly goatskins, drawn from all parts of the world, but mainly from South America (Brazil), India and China. These reflections on stocks and sales were prompted by events in 1906, when the rapid rise of prices in the American boom forced Booth and Company in New York to abandon their usual policy, which was to avoid large stocks so far as possible, and invest heavily in skins and leather, to the value of more than three million dollars. These had to be sold off at a substantial loss next year, when the American economy was shaken by a violent crisis of confidence. The writer of both these memoranda was Charles Booth (1840–1916), better known as a social investigator and a writer on social questions (see below, no. 99). Between 1890 and 1914, he was in active control of the Booth interests in Liverpool, in the United States and in Brazil.

A

I WANT the business to be so organized here as well as in America that under superintendence and direction it goes of itself. This in order to have no more partners—and to give the excellent men who serve us a good future and to solidify the whole structure. Further I want the American side to be so perfect that it will run of itself with a yearly visit from this side. The immediate need for this is made by Romilly's illness.[1] In England I should like it to be so that one of us, whether at Liverpool or London, could safely and without strain run the whole thing as I am doing by way of experiment at this moment. The active work of a second partner here, would then turn towards the working up of new business, which is essential to the life of any concern such as ours. Similarly the back and forth going of one or other of us between England and America would tend to keep breath in the body corporate and strengthen us where we are now weakest as compared with our opponents.

B

1. The smaller the capital employed in conducting a business of fixed volume, the larger the possible ratio of profit.

2. The more rapidly raw stock, once purchased, is converted into cash, the smaller will the capital involved be.

3. From these two principles it is evident that prompt sales increase the possibility of profit.

[1] [*Henry Romilly, the fourth partner in Alfred Booth and Company. He died in 1886. Ed.*]

4. One of the most important parts of the leather business is the lowest price to pay for raw material. To know this it is necessary to make an experiment in raw material and to understand thoroughly the raw material you have purchased. The material must be manufactured and sold and complete confidence given to the skill in both departments. After this it is justifiable to make further purchases in accordance with the result of your experiment. Practically speaking, the general course of your business must, to some extent, follow the stricter course indicated above for fresh experiment, that is to say, no permanent buying methods can be satisfactory unless your purchases are intended to replace the material which was used to make the finished product you have just been selling. Of all manufacturing business, that dealing with skins most requires to be a constant stream and no theoretic or speculative ventures have any right to exist.

5. As a maxim on selling, it can be truly said that no one needs more experience or more constant training. To Americanize, it is essential for buyer and seller to get the habit of dealing with each other. Fine offices and highly-paid salesmen make it necessary to get higher prices for our leather, but do not of themselves sell it, and it may here also be added that insensate over-capitalization hampers still further the work of a salesman by increasing the price he has to try to get. The only possible way of standing the expenses of an expensive sales organization is to spread that expense over an enormous volume of sales. Let it be understood that the margin of possible profit is very limited. A very little carelessness in buying, or in manufacturing, will eliminate it, and strictest economy in the finance department and a wide sense of proportion between selling expenses are essential to the discovery of any profit margin at all at the close of the year's trading.

76. BRITISH EXPORTS AND FOREIGN TARIFFS, 1886

Source: 'Final Report of the Royal Commission on the Depression of Industry and Trade 1886', C. 4893, XXIII, paras. 73–6.

For the official commission of inquiry into the state of trade which sat in the mid-1880's, see above, no. 3. The inquiry took place at a particular point in the trade-cycle, when the recovery and minor boom of the early 1880's failed and when trade and industrial activity temporarily fell back to the low levels of 1879. But the commissioners considered the long-term influences at work as well as the short. Among these influences, they picked out the raising of foreign tariffs for particular comment. The reference to German competition is interesting. Germany was appearing upon world markets during these years both as a great purchaser of food and raw materials for her rapidly advancing population and as an active exporter of manufactured goods. The result was an extensive and keen competition with British exporters, which led to much bad feeling in the 1880's and 1890's. For this, see R. J. Hoffmann, 'The Anglo-German Trade Rivalry' (1933) which, however, a little overdraws the picture. The protectionist recommendations of the minority of the commissioners showed the strength of contemporary feeling.

Diminution of demand for our goods at home and abroad

There can also, we think, be little doubt that the demand for commodities has fallen off in quarters where formerly our goods found a certain and remunerative market.

First, as regards our home market. We have...suffered a serious loss in our purchasing power by reason of the deficient or unremunerative character of the produce of the soil. Sir James Caird estimates the loss in the purchasing power of the classes engaged in or connected with agriculture at 42,800,000L. during the year 1885, and the loss in several of the preceding years must, no doubt, have been equal to or even greater than this. This amount has been lost to the markets in which it was formerly spent, and cannot fail to have had an important influence upon the demand for manufactured goods.

An effect of a similar kind, though less in degree, has been produced by the increased competition in our own market of foreign manufactured or partly manufactured goods, the importation of which appears to grow at a slightly more rapid rate than the population, having been 1·97 *l.* per head in the period 1870–4 and 2·35 *l.* per head in the period 1880–4.

To this may be added the falling off in our 'entrepôt' trade owing to the increasing tendency of foreign countries to supply themselves directly instead of through our markets.

Secondly, our trade with foreign countries is becoming less profitable in proportion as their markets are becoming more difficult of access owing to restrictive tariffs. It will be observed...that the value of our exports to the principal protectionist countries was larger, in proportion to our population, in the years 1880–84 than in any of the four quinquennial periods under review,[1] with the exception of the five years 1870–74, during which, as is well known, our export trade was abnormally inflated; while, if due allowance is made for the high range of prices which prevailed in the two earlier of the four periods, it will probably be found that the volume of exports in the years 1880–84 was larger than in any preceding period. But, notwithstanding this increase there can be little doubt that the obstruction to our trade caused by the growing stringency of the commercial policy of those countries tends to make it far less profitable.

Further, in neutral markets, such as our own colonies and dependencies, and especially in the East, we are beginning to feel the effects of foreign competition in quarters where our trade formerly enjoyed a practical monopoly.

German Competition

The increasing severity of this competition both in our home and in neutral markets is especially noticeable in the case of Germany. A reference to the reports from abroad will show that in every quarter of the world the perseverance and enterprise of the Germans are making themselves felt. In the actual production of commodities we have now few, if any, advantages over them; and in a knowledge of the markets of the world, a desire to accommodate themselves to local tastes or idiosyncracies, a determination to obtain a footing wherever they can, and a tenacity in maintaining it, they appear to be gaining ground upon us.

We cannot avoid stating here the impression which has been made upon us during the course of our inquiry that in these respects there is some falling off among the trading classes of this country from the more energetic practice of former periods.

Less trouble appears to be taken to discover new markets for our produce, and to maintain a hold upon those which we already possess; and we feel confident that, if our commercial position is to be maintained in the face of the severe competition to which it is now exposed, much more attention to these points must be given by our mercantile classes.

[1] [*The quinquennial periods under review were 1865–9; 1870–4; 1875–9; and 1880–4.*]

77. THE 'AMERICAN INVASION'

Source: 'American Engineering Competition: articles reprinted from the Times' (1901), pp. 67, 69–71, 109–11.

There was nothing unnatural in the American "invasion" of world markets at the end of the nineteenth century, although this was of small dimensions compared with American exports today. The industrial growth of the United States since the Civil War had been on an immense scale. American technical skill and American engineering competition had made themselves felt from the 1850's onwards. The United States was at last rising to her rightful place as the largest industrial state of that time, incomparably greater in resources than any European state. The change was, however, resented by many British industrialists and journalists, as 'The Times' articles of the spring and summer of 1900 show. The inference drawn by many contemporaries that American competition was wholly bad should have been resisted. On the contrary, American ideas and rivalry had a stimulating effect on a wide range of British industries during these years. See S. B. Saul, "The American Impact on British Industry 1895–1914", 'Business History', III, no. 1 (1960), 19–38.

A

FEW incidents have caused more excitement in the industrial world than the purchase last year of American locomotives for the Midland Railway. The circumstances which led to this transaction were exceptional, no doubt, but whatever allowances are made the matter remains not of a satisfactory nature for British engineering industry.

Discussions innumerable have taken place in the engineering Press and elsewhere on the respective merits of British and American locomotives, and the question is far too thorny to be broached with safety in these articles....

From what has been said it will be gathered that, in competing with British-made locomotives in neutral markets, the American system gives the maker a considerable advantage in the matter of price. So far as Great Britain and the United States are concerned, it may be said that each type is well suited for its respective field, but when we come to those neutral markets where locomotives are most likely to be imported we see that the British maker, who sticks with British pertinacity to his own home ideals, is likely to go to the wall. New countries, our colonies for instance, have railways more approximating to the earlier roads of America than to the solid constructions of our own land. It has been more than whispered that, in the past, British makers have shown what might be described as obstinacy rather than pertinacity. They have been apt to think themselves masters of the situation and tell their customers exactly what they proposed to supply rather than consult their wishes. 'We make only good engines; turn out nothing but high-class work,' they have said. 'That is what we consider a good, substantial locomotive, and if you want anything else you had better go elsewhere.' Foreign customers have taken this advice, getting, perhaps, an engine not so bright, not so good looking, not so economical in fuel, but one which may have cost less and which undoubtedly hauled big loads over roads that were as different from our splendidly laid and tunnelled lines as a New York street is to a Parisian boulevard.

The extent of the 'going elsewhere' on the part of the foreign purchasers of locomotives is given in the official import and export tables of England and America respectively. In 1889 the United States exported 144 locomotives, and in 1898 the number had risen to 468, and this in spite of a home demand that has lately been surprising in its magnitude. In our own returns numbers are not taken into account, so we must have recourse to values. In 1889 we exported nearly a million and a half pounds' worth of locomotives (£1,443,615), and in 1898 approximately the same quantity. Probably our total for 1899 will turn out a little less. The American values for these two years respectively were about a quarter of a million sterling and considerably over three-quarters of a million. It will be seen, therefore, that, whilst the value of our foreign trade in locomotives has not advanced during 10 years, that of America has increased threefold. It may be stated that the American return for 1898 exceeded our figure for 1894 and almost equalled that of 1895. In 1898 the United States sent more locomotives, or rather the value thereof, than we did to the following countries— to Russia (four times as much), to Canada (which took none from us), to Mexico, to Brazil, and to Japan. The Japanese have been great buyers of locomotives of late, being the best customers both to us and to the United States respectively; British makers have exported to the extent of £206,488, and American makers £260,000. On the other hand, we sent during the same year locomotives to the value of £138,570 to the Argentine Republic, the United States not exporting to that country a single engine. Our possessions in the East, however, contribute chiefly to the excess of our total exports over those of the United States, for we supplied the Indian Empire with locomotives to the value of £452,279, whilst the Americans sent less than £3000 worth.

Still, at the present time, Great Britain leads the world in its foreign trade in locomotives; but it will be seen that we do not hold our supremacy on a very certain footing, for one of our annual totals has already been exceeded by an American total, though not in the same year. It is, however, somewhat remarkable and, in some respects, not a little creditable to the British makers that they hold their own as well as they have done, for they have not the same advantages as the makers in the United States. As is well known, the chief British railway companies have extensive shops for the manufacture of railway engines, thus doing a large part of their own work. In the United States the same conditions do not prevail, the railroad companies as a whole more largely depending for their supply on the locomotive firms. The most notable exception is that of the Pennsylvania Railroad Company, which has most admirably arranged shops at Altoona. The American private firms do, therefore, an enormous trade, and, what is of even more importance, the demand is fairly constant. Our own export trade is of a fluctuating character, as will be seen by the figures already quoted, and, unfortunately for our locomotive makers, the home demand is apt to ebb and flow in unison with the foreign trade. The year 1899 is an example, for, while the foreign demand has been comparatively high, the home railways have been asking contractors for more locomotives than they could supply. The consequence has been importation of American-built engines into England, whilst we are sending large numbers of British-built engines abroad. The position is unfortunate.

B

In the manufacture of agricultural implements the Americans have always held a prominent position, and many—I do not know whether I ought to say most—of the ingenious devices by which human labour has been supplanted by mechanism in this field have been the character-istic product of American inventive genius. The subject is a big one, but only a few words can be devoted to it here. On my way to Columbus I visited the works of the Warder Bushnell and Glessner Company at Springfield, Ohio. They make only three kinds of machine —namely, binders, mowers, and reapers—thus carrying out the prominent American characteristic of concentration of effort to the end of doing one thing well. The works are well laid out with special automatic machine tools—extremely interesting to an engineer to see, but, mercifully, quite impossible to describe. One department, however, is not beyond a word picture; it is the painting shop. They do not use brushes, or even the more modern 'painting pump'. The large floor of the shop is fitted up with a series of tanks having the appearance of small swimming baths. Overhead there are the lines of a suspension railway. The tanks are filled with paint, the articles to be treated are run in on the railway, are lowered automatically into the bath, and are then carried off to drip. In this way a large and compli-cated agricultural machine can be painted in a few seconds.

This firm has doubled its output during the last four years, and they are extending their export trade in Australia, South Africa, South America, Russia, and in Great Britain. The methods of manufacture have been altering of late years, wood as a material fast giving place to iron, the difficulty of getting good timber increasing rapidly. This is interesting, as the encroachments of Americans on our foreign markets in this field used to be attributed to their better supplies of different woods. The management of these works attributes their success chiefly to their better practice in the malleable iron foundry. The McCormick Harvesting Machine Company have enormous works near Chicago. How vast is their establishment may perhaps be best told by saying they produce 1200 machines every ten hours. They work from 7 o'clock to 12, then take half an hour for dinner, and close at 5.30 p.m. I was informed here that all the English makers combined do not make one-tenth of the number of the machines they produce; and about one-fifth of their output was sent abroad during the previous year (1898). They had received an order from one firm in Paris, Messrs R. Wallut and Co., for 12,000 machines. I asked the reason why they had been able to do a much larger foreign trade than the British makers, and will give the reply I received, approximately in my informant's words:

You cannot compete with us in this trade, first, because your system of agriculture is entirely different to ours; it is so much smaller. I have seen a man in England leading a front horse and another man driving the horse in the shafts on a land roller; and nothing else happening. In America one man would be driving a team drawing a seeder and leading another team behind with a drag (or harrow) and another team with a roller behind that; all managed by one man. Besides this, the width would be probably 12 ft. instead of six. You have not room for a full-sized procession in your little fields.

You have been sitting in that chair ten minutes, and during that time we have finished and put into warehouse 20 reaping machines or field mowers, weighing from 700 lb. to 1500 lb. each. You English are our strongest competitors in foreign markets; but the Swedes and Germans are creeping up every day. They copy everything, but copying will never get more than the dregs of a trade. The country that originates will always be ahead. Moreover, it is no good copying patterns unless you copy methods too. If a German buys one of our machines and tries to make it he is met by difficulties at every turn. He wants our special tools, our organization, our materials; and then he must produce on the same scale we do to get the same economy.

This gentleman also made reference to the use of malleable iron castings, of which the firm probably work up a greater quantity than any other works in the country, the consumption for 1898 being over 18,000 tons. It was subsequently pointed out to me elsewhere that, even if there were no difficulty in other respects, it would not be possible to reproduce the American machines in Europe because the practice of annealing iron castings is not sufficiently advanced. The McCormick Company were building a new foundry 1487 ft. long and 88 ft. wide, in which they would cast 250 tons of grey iron daily. They have such a well-organized system of moulding by special apparatus that only five skilled moulders will be needed for all this immense number of castings. Ordinary moulding, by the old-fashioned hand tools, is one of the most highly-skilled operations in engineering practice; and perhaps for that reason the moulder's department is, in some works in this country, the most difficult to manage. The gentleman who gave me the above facts had been with the firm for 13 years and had seen the business multiplied fivefold in that time, whilst it has doubled during the last five years.

78. BRITAIN'S COMPETITIVE SITUATION, 1903

Source: W. J. Ashley, 'The Tariff Problem' (1903), pp. 75–9.

In the depressed years which followed the boom at the turn of the century, created partly by the war in South Africa but also a general and temporary revival of home investment, the constant spread of industrial production in other countries and their protective policies were again the subject of anxious discussion and speculation as they had been in the 1880's and 1890's. W. J. Ashley (1860–1927) was one of the best-informed economists of his day. He had lived for some time in the United States and was familiar with German conditions. He leaned towards the protectionist side in discussion and later became one of Joseph Chamberlain's advisers in his Tariff Reform campaign (see chapter 9 below). He is quoted here, however, as representative of the "literature of anxiety", highly typical of the years before the Edwardian investment boom, 1905–13.

THE diffusion of manufacturing industry over the world has been greatly assisted in the past, and is likely to be assisted far more in the future, by two sets of forces which deserve more attention than they have as yet received. The first [*Ashley's second influence was the increasing use of automatic machinery requiring a smaller skilled and much larger unskilled labour force, thus destroying Britain's advantage of large resources of inherited skill*] is the profit-seeking tendency of capital, which pursues an immediate gain without any regard to the ultimate effect on national prosperity. In several different ways has the business enterprise of England—in a less degree and more recently that of other manufacturing countries also—assisted the foreign customers to dispense with foreign imports. This assistance at first took the form of the exportation of machinery for the manufacture of the same sort of goods, and this process is still going on. With the machinery has frequently been exported the skill necessary to manage it at first and to instruct the foreigner in its use.[1] The significance of this educational service to backward countries has been pointed out by two observers, who—

[1] In one case, that of Park, Brother & Co., of Pittsburg, in 1862, 'several hundred English workmen were imported to insure success.'

poles asunder as they are in their social attitude—resemble one another in their large acquaintance with economic fact and in their freedom from conventional judgments. 'Japan and China', says Mr Carnegie, 'are building factories of the latest and most approved character, always with British machinery and generally under British direction. The jute and cotton mills of India are numerous and increasing. It is stated that one British manufacturing concern sends abroad the complete machinery for a new mill every week.'[1] 'English and German capitalists, English engineers and firemen,' says Prince Krapotkin, 'have planted within Russia the improved cotton manufactures of their mother countries; they are busy now in improving the woollen industries and the production of machinery; while Belgians are rapidly improving the iron trades in South Russia.'[2] And, as the last-named observer points out, the new producers start with advantages in the possession of the latest and best machinery, which only the most up-to-date plants in the older manufacturing countries possess.

In proportion as the wave of industrial production penetrates into younger countries, it implants there all the improvements due to a century of mechanical and chemical inventions; it borrows from science all the help that science can give to industry. The new manufactures of Germany began where Manchester arrived after a century of experiments and gropings; and Russia begins where Manchester and Saxony have now reached.

Equally important with the exportation of machinery and skill has been the investment of capital abroad; and it is this which has been most noteworthy in recent years. There has long been a good deal of investment of British capital in foreign works—thus the development of the railway system of the United States, which has done so much to stimulate manufactures in that country and in particular has reacted on the British agricultural interests by the cheapening of the transportation of grain, has been to a considerable degree encouraged by British capital. But in more recent years, with the heightening of the tariff walls of other countries, there has been a movement of capital of a still more ominous kind—viz., the establishment by English manufacturers of factories within the protected area. Anyone who is acquainted with

---

[1] Carnegie, 'Empire of Business', p. 317.
[2] Krapotkin, 'Fields, Factories and Workshops', p. 10.

an English staple industry can at once furnish the names of several firms which have adopted this policy. I understand that this is the case, for instance, in the woollen industries, with the firms of J. F. Firth & Sons, of Heckmondwike (carpet making), and Sir Titus Salt, Bart., Sons & Co., Limited, of Saltaire (dress goods, &c.), in the United States; of Isaac Holden & Sons, Limited, of Bradford (wool combing), in France; and of W. and J. Whitehead, of Bradford (worsted spinning), in Spain. In the cotton industry the Fine Cotton Spinners' Association have two or three mills in France; and Coats' is said to have a thread mill in Russia. In order to benefit by the fact that the German duty on yarn is considerably lower than that on thread, a Belfast linen firm has established thread works in Germany, where it twists, bleaches, dyes and finishes the yarn which it imports. In the metal and machinery trades the names occur to one of J. J. Savile & Co., of Sheffield (steel), with their works in Russia, and of Messrs Weir, of Glasgow (ships' pumps), with their works in Germany.[1]

It must be readily granted that American capital and German science have also to some extent imported themselves into England; but viewing the process as a whole it cannot but be regarded as an important factor in the destruction of England's earlier monopoly. It must be granted, again, that there is often some force in the argument of the concerns engaged that in any case the foreign market is lost to English goods. But by educating the foreign nation to higher standards of excellence in manufacture they assist the infant industry in its struggle towards maturity. And it should be observed that they furnish the protectionist with some additional theoretic arguments which are well worth weighing. Adam Smith argued that protection could only divert capital from one industry to another; the protectionists can reply that in many instances it has attracted fresh capital into the country. Adam Smith, again, relying on the transferability of capital, expected that the lessening prosperity of one particular home industry owing to foreign competition would result in the transference of capital to another home industry. But, as we have seen, it may lead to the transference of capital to the same industry in another country.

[1] On this as a contribution towards the development of the shipbuilding industry in Germany, see Schwarz and Von Halle, 'Schiffbau-Industrie', ii. 219.

79. THE SHADY SIDE OF FOREIGN LOANS

Source: 'Report from the Select Committee on Loans to Foreign States 1875' (367), XI, xliv–xlv, xlix–l.

The late 1860's and early 1870's saw an immense growth in the practice of floating foreign loans in London. A spurt of lending to governments abroad, in Turkey, Egypt, Portugal, Russia, Sweden, Peru, Brazil, the seceding states in North America, and other parts of the world, came to an end in May 1866 owing to the financial panic caused by the bankruptcy of the bill-broking house of Overend, Gurney and Company. One effect of the panic was to make investment in joint-stock finance companies look very risky. Men with money to lend returned to foreign stocks. Meanwhile, city men between 1867 and 1870 had got into a habit of marketing foreign loans through syndicates of houses, which made big operations possible. The years immediately after the Franco–German war, between 1871 and 1875, saw the greatest loans of the century, as well as much speculation and fraud. The select committee of the House of Commons here reporting was appointed to go into the frauds. The foreign investment boom was followed by a revulsion of opinion and a marked abstention from foreign loans in the late 1870's. For a well-informed contemporary account of the mania see 'The Bankers Magazine', XXXVI (1876), 424–30 and 517–22.

IN respect of all these loans, those who introduced them to the public seem to have been regardless of the financial resources of the borrowing State; such resources, if inquired into, would have been found to have been totally inadequate to meet the liabilities incurred. In no case before your Committee, with one unimportant exception, has the borrowing Government repaid any portion of its indebtedness incurred in respect of these loans, except from the proceeds of the loans themselves.

By means of exaggerated statements in the prospectus the public have been induced to believe that the material wealth of the contracting State formed a sufficient security for the repayment of the money borrowed. Even if such were the case, the several Governments have taken no steps to apply the revenues of the State, or the other subjects of special hypothecation in discharge of their liabilities.

The whole of these loans were ostensibly raised for purposes of a similar character. An undertaking was given that the proceeds were to be spent on works calculated to develope [*sic*] the industrial resources of the different countries, and from such works a large return was promised. Your Committee have shown how small a proportion of each loan was applied to the above-mentioned purposes.

In order to induce the public to lend money upon a totally insufficient security, means have been resorted to which, in their nature and object, were flagrantly deceptive....

Your Committee have carefully considered the Bill for the compulsory registration of Foreign Loans, and have examined two Members of the House whose names are on the back of it. They do not think that it will be expedient to proceed further with the measure. Registered documents are seldom inspected until the mischief against which they might have guarded is done, and are more useful in furnishing weapons for litigation than safeguards against loss. To declare unregistered documents to be null and void, would be certain to produce much confusion and injustice; and yet without such a provision, persons entering into questionable contracts and combinations, would run the risk of actions or penalties, rather than disclose matters which they have the greatest interest to conceal. It is, besides, easy for such persons to transport themselves beyond the jurisdiction of English Courts, as the evidence taken before your Committee proves. Your Committee prefer to trust to the plan of requiring certain matters to be stated in the prospectus, which appears to afford the best security for full disclosure which the case admits of....

Your Committee have been much impressed, in the course of their inquiry, with the great importance of the functions exercised by the agent or contractor for a foreign loan. Considering that in several of the cases which they have examined there has been something closely resembling repudiation, based upon the alleged misconduct of the agents in this country, they cannot escape the conviction that the proper discharge of these duties is a matter of importance, not only to the subscribers, but to the nation at large. They submit to the wisdom of Parliament, whether it is proper that an office, on the due exercise of which depends in no small degree our good understanding with the borrowing country, and our reputation for honesty and good faith, should be exercised by any person who may choose to undertake it, or, worse still, to whom the representative of some petty or insolvent state may choose to intrust it.

In conclusion, your Committee feel bound to express their conviction that the best security against the recurrence of such evils as they have above described will be found, not so much in legislative enactments as in the enlightenment of the public as to their real nature and origin. Your Committee hope that the history of the foreign loans embodied in this report will tend to enlighten the public, and to render it more difficult for unscrupulous persons to carry out schemes such as those which, in the cases on which it has been the duty of your Committee to report, have ended in so much discredit and disaster.

80. FLOATING A FOREIGN LOAN IN THE 1870'S

Source: Sir Henry Drummond Wolff, 'Rambling Recollections' (1908),
II, *63–6.*

Sir H. Drummond Wolff (1830–1908), member of parliament and diplomat, in his later years British ambassador at Madrid, was a man with much experience of international and financial circles. In the article from which the extract is taken, written at the time but never published, he endeavoured to describe the background of the speculation in foreign securities which was inquired into by the select committee of the House of Commons in 1875 and "the real nature of the acts of which complaints were made".

THE mammoths of finance are content with the dribblings of constant contributory streams, which perhaps bring an average ten per cent per annum to an enormous capital. Fortunate, perhaps, that such is the case. Otherwise nothing would be left for the smaller capitalists, struggling for a name, perhaps for a local habitation.

A loan, however, is required by a foreign Government, and one financier hears of it through his agent, or he is informed of it by one of the smaller intermediaries who troop about offices near the Bank. The foreign Government, perhaps, has sent an agent to England, or a friend of the Finance Minister is known to be lodging at Morley's Hotel, and to have left Baring's office the day before with a heavy countenance. The financier, of course, knows everything concerning the country. The duty on cinnamon is still unmortgaged, or the revenues of two provinces are paid direct into the Treasury. A tax on land is about to pass the Chambers. The traffic returns on the Government railway have paid a pound a mile a week additional.

'If', says the intermediary, 'you only carry out this loan, you will have the whole country at your feet.'

The financier cares little for the future.

'I think it can be done at 52', he soliloquises, and sends for two confidential brokers.

'Can't be done', says one. 'It was offered Baring's at 53, and they refused.'

'Yes, but they volunteered to take it firm at 49', rejoins the other.

'That was last year', breaks in the first.

'And they have paid off the old cinnamon loan since', continues No. 2.

'I think it can be done at 52', again soliloquises the financier, and, putting on his hat, he makes for Morley's Hotel.

The contract once signed, the financier proceeds to bring out the loan. A prospectus is drawn up, announcing that he himself, or some firm charged by him, will receive subscriptions. In this prospectus, a solicitor must naturally intervene, as well as a professional manufacturer of prospectuses with a command of epithets, the attractive traits of which do not exceed the strict limits of legal veracity.

Before the issue of a loan, a dinner is often given in the name of the financier, but at the cost of the Syndicate. It fairly comes within the item 'market expenses'. Here our financier presides, the diplomatic representative of the country on his right, a relative of the Finance Minister on his left. Near them are some retired Indian and Colonial officials be-ribboned, a few Admirals, a member of a late Government —all anxious to become Directors of Companies, all counting on selling the new loan at a premium. Near them are capitalists, leading stockbrokers, some newspaper-writers, a politician who has perhaps made a hobby in Parliament of the country in question, and a clergyman whose face is well known to most of the guests as a dabbler in Turks and Lombards, and as an eager though silent attendant at meetings of discontented bondholders. Dinner over, and the speculative divine having said grace, speeches are made by the M.P. and the financier, who look forward to this loan as a new pledge of alliance between the two countries. The prospectus-maker airs the adjectives cut out of his prospectus by the solicitor. The diplomatic representative makes speeches in a language utterly unknown to his fellow-guests.

The financier, not the better for his dinner, confides in English equally unintelligible to the Finance Minister's relative that the loan, if successful, will be entirely owing to his—the financier's—abilities; that if unsuccessful, failure will only be attributable to the rotten and bankrupt state of the borrowing country. The relative and the diplomatic representative retire home perfectly satisfied with their relations with British finance, and calculating how many loans the Finance Minister can bring out before the unhallowed cabals of his opponents have forced His Excellency into resignation or exile.

81. BRITISH MONEY IN AUSTRALIAN WOOL

Source: S. J. Butlin, 'Australia and New Zealand Bank: the Bank of Australasia and the Union Bank of Australia Ltd. 1828–1951' (1961), pp. 222–3, 217–18, 250, 251, 307–8.

In the last quarter of last century, the Australian colonies became one of the favoured fields for lending by Britons with money to spare. Among other forms of investment, considerable sums found their way into the Australian pastoral industry and the expansion of sheep stations, primarily in New South Wales and Victoria. Much of this money was borrowed by the Australian banks in London, where interest rates during many of these years ruled low, and lent by them to the squatters against the security of land and flocks. Both individual accounts and the total sum involved became large, before the long boom in Australian land, both urban and country, came to an end in 1893. In the early spring of that year, the Union Bank of Australia, a British-registered joint stock bank with headquarters in London, but deeply interested in squatter business, was operating with nearly two and a half million pounds worth of London deposits as well as its Australian money. Both the banks mentioned, the Bank of Australasia and the Union Bank of Australia, being well managed as well as fortunate, survived the banking crash which marked the boom's end in April and May of that year.

[*To the Board of the Union Bank of Australia Ltd in London from their General Manager in Australia, John McMullen, 1867*]

As the Board have to some extent recognised the expediency of borrowing money at moderate rates in England in preference to paying an excessive price for it here, I feel less hesitation in advocating it now as a matter of the utmost importance to our future interests than when I urged it upon their attention several years ago, although I then saw very clearly that we could not otherwise compete successfully with colonial institutions....This is really what we have to contend against. The colonial banks are gradually absorbing the local deposits, and with an undiscerning community we cannot prevent it. But in this colony [*Victoria*] especially we suffer from it in another way for the principal local banks profess not to care for high dividends and are therefore the better able to annoy us by paying excessively for deposit money...we must obtain cheaper money in England.

.   .   .   .

[*Court of the Bank of Australasia Ltd in London to their Superintendent in Australia, D. C. McArthur, 1871*]

The improvement in the wool market, noticed in my letters No. 1751 and 1755, is still maintained as you will see from the broker's circulars; and as the clip of this year promises to be excellent both in quantity and quality, it may be safely anticipated that a great advance will take place in the value of stock and station properties, while a stimulus will be imparted to trade and business generally throughout the Colonies.

Under these circumstances the Directors feel that a period has arrived when it is proper that the position and policy of the Bank should be reconsidered with the view of modifying in some degree the restrictive actions enjoined by them of late years in respect to station accounts and otherwise.

Influenced by these views, but at the same time warned by experience, the Directors feel, that although some relaxation may now be sanctioned, it should be circumspect and gradual, and arise only out of a healthy and legitimate demand for banking accommodation. It is for you to judge of the practical conditions which should regulate any extension of Branch operations, but it is the desire of the Directors that they should not be extended by any general circulars, but only through cautious instructions to special Managers.

In stating these views, however, I am to explain that the Directors do not contemplate any alteration of the existing policy in respect to New Zealand business, nor, I need scarcely add, in the regularity of the securities to be required for advances at all Branches. The general limit of the London office Cash Account is well known to you. At present there is a surplus in London available for Colonial requirements; but after this is absorbed, a further increase of means can be obtained only from a reduction of such accounts as are at present in excess, from the realisation of old property or secured accounts, and from obtaining a larger share of Colonial deposits.

. . . .

[*E. S. Parkes, of the Bank of Australasia Ltd, in evidence to the Victorian Royal Commission on Banking Laws, 1884*]

351. Your charter then absolutely prohibits direct advances on real property in the first place does it not?

It does; but I need not say from the way in which this is drawn that it is easily—I do not like to use the word evaded—but an advance can be made on the same indirectly.... For instance, we can advance the money today, and take the security tomorrow.

[*The same, to the Court of the Bank of Australasia Ltd, 1886*]

We can, of course, lessen the anxiety, [*i.e. the Court's anxiety about the high proportion of the Bank's assets in Australia held in the form of pastoral advances, then about 42 per cent of the whole*] and make our position more secure, by determining to reduce our squatting advances, but it must be remembered that there is nothing to fill their places, and that such a policy means reduction in profits and dividends....It is a question for the directors' decision whether the policy of the Bank shall be to do a smaller business and be content with reduced profits.

. . . .

[*John Sawers, Superintendent in Australia of the Bank of Australasia Ltd to officers of the Bank, May 1893*]

The severity of the present crisis and the probability of its increase render it imperative that the Superintendent should place before the responsible Officers of the Bank his views as to the course of action which they ought to pursue.

The Bank has scarcely ever before been so strong in coin as it is at this moment, but it is threatened, especially in Victoria, with heavy withdrawals of deposits in consequence of the prevailing public belief that all Banks, however sound, must sooner or later reconstruct....

This erroneous belief is fraught with grave danger to the Bank, and despite the large reserve of coin and the shipment of half a million of sovereigns on its way from England, the Superintendent very strongly feels that, in view of the probability of the crisis increasing in intensity, no money should be allowed to go out which can be retained and that a policy conducive to getting in coin should be followed for the present.

The loss of connection weighs as nothing in the balance as compared with the Bank's safety. At the same time the action of Managers must be conducted with great tact and discretion, as much more harm than good might easily be done by a display of too great eagerness to get in money.

The obvious courses to be pursued are: 1. To refuse all fresh advances on the grounds that they do not suit the Bank at present. 2. To charge all customers, not under special agreement, a higher rate of interest on their advances, on the perfectly true plea that money is much more valuable at present than it has been for a long time past....

The Superintendent is glad to think that he can rely upon the cordial cooperation of the Bank's officers even at the risk of injury to their business. There is no occasion to feel panic-stricken—as already explained, the Bank's position is strong, but the coming drain may be severe and, with so much at stake, the duty of wise men is to prepare for all eventualities....

82. BRITISH CAPITAL IN AUSTRALIAN CITIES

Source: Geoffrey Blainey, 'Gold and Paper, A history of the National Bank of Australasia Limited' (Melbourne, 1958), pp. 135, 137, 139, 145–6, 148, 156, 158–9.

These extracts, from the correspondence of Francis Grey Smith, general manager of a Melbourne bank, the National Bank of Australasia, give a view of the Australian land boom of the late 1880's and early 1890's, as it was seen by one of the most prominent of Melbourne bankers. The boom rested on a sound basis—the rapid expansion of the Australian economy both in town and country—but it was soon driven to extreme lengths. The building of much of the modern city of Melbourne was one of the results. Capital borrowed from Great Britain by the Australian colonial governments and municipalities, by land-banks and building societies, played a great part. Much money was also borrowed from Englishmen and Scots in the form of bank deposits. The National Bank did less of this sort of business than many Australian banks, raising less than 16 per cent of its deposits in Great Britain compared, say, with the 60 per cent of the City of Melbourne Bank, but it went down to be reconstituted later, along with far less conservative institutions, in 1893 when the investment boom broke. *The financial crisis of April-May in that year, in the absence of a central bank and a federal government to control the situation, was the worst in Australian banking history.*

[November 1887]

The speculation in City and Suburban property just now exceeds anything of the kind ever known in Australia. We are keeping well out of it! not so our neighbours on either side and westwards.... Still an end must come to all this, and woe unto him who is left last on the field.

[1888 (*Australia's centennial year, commemorating the first settlement*)]

It was well dubbed 'centennial' for I doubt if we shall see its like again, or rather if its like again will be seen for a century....

[October 1890]

How ever the dividend and the bonus are to be maintained I dread to think! The whole pressure is on Victoria—London helping fairly—and the strain is enormous.

[Early in 1892]

The public [*give*] us credit now for having abjured a class of business —Building and Finance Land Societies—they at one time ridiculed us for not acquiring!

[March 1892]

In these critical times, one cannot tell in what quarter suspicion may next show itself, and unfortunately there are a class of irresponsible chatterers parading about, who have no hesitation in naming the next of the Institutions who are, in their opinion, bound to come to grief.

[January 1893]

Financial affairs here are more intensely critical at this moment than they have been for the last eighteen months, and that is saying a good deal; the fact is the Federal Bank [*Federal Bank of Australia*] is dying by inches through the continuous withdrawal of deposits both in the Colonies and in London!

[*April 1893*]

It does seem hard that the banks which have conducted their affairs unostentatiously, and on conservative lines, should now be mistrusted, arising out of proceedings of others!

[*25 April 1893*]

We are as strong as usual in coin at this moment, but then the times are not as usual.

[*29 April 1893*]

The Board of Directors of the National Bank of Australasia announce with the deepest regret and concern that, in the exercise of their discretion, they have resolved that it is advisable for the bank to suspend payment on Monday morning, and that step will accordingly be taken.

The directors are thoroughly satisfied as regards the solvency of the institution, and the present course has been forced on them solely through the persistent continuous withdrawal of deposits during the past fortnight, and especially within the last few days, at the head office and the principal branches of the bank throughout Australia....

83. THE WESTERN RANGE-CATTLE INDUSTRY IN THE UNITED STATES

Source: ' *The Economist*' (*3 February 1883*), *p. 131.*

This rather cool notice in the leading city journal scarcely does justice to the excitement of the boom in cattle business in the American West between the late 1870's and the disastrous winter of 1885–6 or to the consequent activity among English and Scottish investors. These were drawn from a very broad section of British life, with an interesting and significant sprinkling of the peerage and landed gentry. British capital also contributed towards the development of railways, mines and agriculture in the American West; but the range-cattle industry established in Texas and on the Great Plains, involving heavy losses as well as high dividends, had a flavour impossible to find at any other time or place. See H. O. Brayer, " The Influence of British Capital on the Western Range-Cattle Industry", 'The Tasks of Economic History, Supplement to the Journal of Economic History' (1949), pp. 85–98.

The Irishman, Sir Horace Plunkett, later famous for his work on behalf of Irish agricultural co-operation, managed Western Ranches Ltd, in Wyoming and Dakota in its early days.

...Every Land Company now brought forward must be a 'Cattle Company' as well, in the same way that seven or eight months ago every Electric Light Company was also bound to be a 'Power' Company, because the market was just then hearing a good deal about the Faure Accumulator. The keynote of the present excitement in Scotland over the Cattle Companies is certainly to be found in the name of the first undertaking furnished in the list below: [*see facing page*]

The great Bulk of these have been introduced in the past three or four months, and the prospectuses of nearly all of them have dwelt upon the success of the Prairie Cattle Company, doubtless with the object of conveying the impression that they had but to transplant their shareholders' capital into the wilderness to realise like results. Had the Prairie Cattle Company been a London instead of an Edinburgh concern, we should have had the nucleus of the speculation here; but, as it is, Edinburgh and Dundee, and the other Scottish markets, are more largely interested in the success or failure of these undertakings than are the markets further South. It will be seen that the 'Texas', the 'Cattle Ranche', and the 'Western' Companies have also announced first dividends at high rates, and it is to be remarked that the four which have thus far paid dividends are all of them Texas companies.

Now, we are very far from decrying the value of Texas as a cattle-raising country. Indeed, it is well known that there are vast tracts in that immense State—nearly two and a-half times the area of the United Kingdom—excellently well adapted for breeding purposes....

...But as in all other businesses, competition will end by checking excessive profits in the Texan cattle trade; and though some of these Land and Cattle Companies may have a fair opening before them, it would give a mistaken idea of their profitableness to suppose that the present inflated prices realised by cattle in that State will continue indefinitely.

Incomes Earned Abroad

Some Recent Cattle and Ranche Companies

Name	Capital £	Per Share Paid up	Per Share Market Price	Dividend %
Prairie Cattle Company,				
Limited —1st Issue	125,000	5	9¾	27⅝
Do —2nd Issue	250,000	5	9¾	27⅝
Do —3rd Issue	125,000	2	6½	...
Arkansas Valley Land & Cattle, Limited	225,000	5	4¾	15
Buenos Ayres Land & Cattle, Limited	110,000	10	...	...
Cattle Ranche & Land, Limited—Pref.	100,000	5	5½	...
Colorado Ranche, Limited	20,000	100	...	...
Deer Trail, Land & Cattle, Limited	250,000	1	...	...
Freehold Ranche & Cattle, Limited—Pref.	170,000	1½	...	...
Hansford Land & Cattle, Limited	210,000	3	2¾	...
Matador Land & Cattle, Limited	400,000	3	3⅜	...
Maxwell Cattle—8% Mortgage	200,000	100	...	...
Powder River Cattle, Limited —Ordinary	200,000	2½	2⅝	...
Do —Preference	100,000	10	11	...
Scottish Mexican Freehold Land & Cattle Limited	300,000	1	...	...
Texas Land & Cattle, Limited	240,000	5	7	15
Do New	240,000	3	4⅛	...
Union Land & Cattle, Limited —Preference	175,000	4	...	...
Do —Ordinary	175,000	4	...	...
United States Cattle Ranche —Preferred	125,000	1½	...	...
Western American Cattle —Preferred	160,000	1	...	...
Western Land & Cattle, Limited	113,000	5	7¼	20
Do —Preference	113,000	5	7⅜	5
	4,126,000			

84. BORROWING FOR PUBLIC WORKS

Source: 'Fenn on the Funds', ed. S. F. Van Oss (16th ed. 1898), Introduction p. ix.

'Fenn on the Funds' was one of the works of reference mostly commonly used by those interested in the business of investment abroad. A handbook of international public finance, it gave details of the debts, budget and foreign trade of every country or at least of every country which in 1898 shared the £6,120,991,258 of the world's outstanding public debts.

...It has already been shown that war is the most fertile source of National Debts; but in recent times there has come a fresh agency which promises to add materially to national obligations, even when the lion has lain down with the lamb. We mean the tendency to borrow freely for public works. In an age of ever-extending State socialism there will not be, and there cannot be, reasonable objection to the contraction of debts for public works which yield revenue, and often profit. If applied wisely, this principle can be productive of much good. In Germany—a country which should receive full credit for its provident and frugal financing—the various States have more than their full debts represented by railways which give not only astonishingly cheap transportation to the people, but also yield enough profit to lessen taxation. Russia, Belgium, Austria, and Switzerland also own many railways which produce a good revenue. Virtually all Governments own the telegraph lines and work the post offices. There is no reason why, if sensibly conducted, Government should not borrow freely for reproductive public works, like railways, canals, river-improvements or harbours. But the trouble with borrowing for public works is that the restraint necessary to keep it within healthy limits is often absent; and thus we behold the deplorable 'over-development' which has wrought such havoc in our Australian Colonies, in South America, and to a certain extent also in South Africa.

85. THE EDWARDIAN FOREIGN INVESTMENT BOOM

Source: C. K. Hobson, 'The Export of Capital' (1914), pp. 156-9.

Foreign investment, its economic rationale, its political and moral significance, were subjects much debated in the early years of the present century. C. K. Hobson, later a statistician at the Board of Trade, but at the time fresh from Cambridge and the London School of Economics, analysed in a book published on the eve of the First World War the immense boom in loans to governments and undertakings abroad which gave rise to the discussion.

...When the Boer War broke out the amount of floating capital available for investment elsewhere was severely curtailed by the gigantic demands of the British Government. A powerful stimulus, it is true, was given to certain industries, notably the coal, iron, and shipbuilding industries, but the effect of the war was seen in an almost complete cessation of foreign Government loan issues in London, a heavy reduction in colonial issues, and an all-round decline in the demands of joint-stock enterprises....

The recovery of British foreign investments began late in 1904, when trade was reviving from the depression which followed the Boer War. In 1903 the success which attended the issue of a Transvaal loan for 30 millions had encouraged various colonial Governments to try their luck on the London market, but the result was not encouraging. The demands of Japan during the war with Russia in 1904, however, were freely met, and the amount of capital exported began to increase steadily. Large issues were made on behalf of Canadian and Argentine railways, and a current of foreign investment was started, which rapidly swelled in volume. Canada and Argentine, together with the United States, were destined in the following years to receive a greater share of attention than any other countries. Subsidiary and more or less irregular streams, however, flowed elsewhere. British capital spread itself geographically over a wider area than ever in the past.... Political conditions in the chief investment fields, excepting possibly Australia and India, were felt to be satisfactory, and the security of investors seemed to be well protected.

The chief streams of British capital, as has been said, flowed into Canada, the United States, and Argentina. Mexico, Brazil, Chile, and other countries in South America also benefited by more or less large British investments. A small flood of British capital poured into South Africa, while Egypt and the colonies on the east and west coasts of Africa were not neglected. India and the Far East vied with Russia and Australia in their endeavours to obtain British capital. Russia, it may be observed, began to regain the popularity in the eyes of British investors which she had lost a generation before, but Australia was far less attractive than she had been during the 'eighties. In quantity the efflux of British capital increased rapidly during the years 1904-7. During 1907, as we shall see later, the outflow reached the enormous total of about £140,000,000, a sum which far exceeds the amount invested at the summit of the great boom in 1872. In 1908 and 1909 the actual outflow of capital—as distinguished from capital issues— showed some decline, but even in these years the amount exported appears to have reached and exceeded £100,000,000 per annum. In the three following years the outflow grew again, and appears to have reached further new records.

The main purpose for which these gigantic sums are required is still railway construction in almost every part of the world. Docks, water and gas works, electric lighting, telegraphs and tramways, form another important group of enterprises which are constantly demanding fresh capital. All of these activities are conducted both by Governmental authorities—central or local—and by joint-stock companies. In addition there are mining concerns and plantations, land mortgage companies, banks, trust, insurance, and trading companies, all of which figured prominently during earlier periods of foreign investment. There is, however, a new characteristic visible in the course of foreign investment during the past few years, namely, a tendency to invest in manufacturing and industrial concerns. The movement is particularly noteworthy in North America, in India, and in Russia.

86. BRITISH INVESTORS IN CANADA

Source: F. Williams Taylor, "Canadian Loans in London", in 'United Empire: the Journal of the Royal Colonial Institute', III (new series) (1912), 985-7, 993-4.

In the early 1900's, Canada began to occupy the position which Australia had held a generation before, as a field for investment by people living in Great Britain. By this time, the difficulties of transport, climate, farming practice, wheat milling and marketing, and so forth which had long held back the settlement and development of western Canada were being successfully overcome. This was a time of rapid agricultural expansion in the Prairie Provinces of Alberta, Manitoba and Saskatchewan. But the greater part of the money from Britain—amounting to one quarter

*of the entire capital export of the British Isles, between 1907 and the out-
break of the First World War—went into new railways, government and
municipal bonds, and industrial and mining concerns. It helped to sustain
the prolonged boom in real estate in the Canadian cities, as Canada was
drawn more and more into the stream of world trade. See R. H. Coats,
'The Rise in Prices and the Cost of Living in Canada 1900–1914',
Statistical Branch, Department of Labour (Ottawa, 1915), pp. 29, 31.
Frederick Williams Taylor was at the time manager of the Bank of
Montreal in London. He was addressing the influential Royal Colonial
Institute, with the Canadian financier, Lord Strathcona, in the chair.*

THE statement has been made that Canada is over-borrowing in the
London market, the cry has been taken up, and now both the
Press and the public generally are expressing their views on the subject.
…It is gratifying to Canadians to know that there has been little, if
any, ill-natured comment, but harm has been done nevertheless, and
more will follow unless we are able to refute the charge....

It is common knowledge that Canada has been a large and popular
borrower in London during the past few years. For instance, the
Federal Government of the Dominion has been able to renew its
maturing obligations and finance its fresh requirements on terms more
favourable than any other Colony or Empire borrower, with the sole
exception of the Imperial Government itself. The credit of our provinces and large cities has become so well established that they have been
able to float loans on highly favourable terms, as good, for example, as
many favoured European governments and other high-class borrowers.
Secondary Canadian towns of comparatively limited population have
borrowed on a 4½ per cent basis to the envy of cities twenty times their
size in the United States, South America, and elsewhere. Our railways
generally have borrowed on terms equal to the best American roads.
It is an interesting and historic fact that the Canadian Pacific Railway
sold a million pounds of its Four per cent. Debenture Stock in London
at over par in the midst of the panic of 1907, when high class American
railway securities were unsaleable within reasonable distance of the
same basis. As for general investment, public and private, in public
utilities, in land and industrials, money has been freely forthcoming....

May I be permitted to add that no section of the community views
more regretfully some of the Canadian public issues made in London

or appreciates more keenly the necessity of preserving our credit in this market than Canadian bankers. American money will be forthcoming as in the past for the development of private enterprise, and English money for such purposes will doubtless follow in increasing volume, but the Federal Government, the provincial governments, important municipalities, and the great transportation companies, must be mainly financed in London. That is one reason why the safeguarding of the national credit of Canada in this, the greatest of all money markets, has been, is today, and will continue to be, one of the most important accepted duties and responsibilities of the Canadian banks with branch offices in London....

According to the most reliable English records, Great Britain and Ireland have invested more money in Canada than in any other country—excepting only the United States—the total being approximately £430,449,000, made up as follows:

	£
Dominion Government	50,484,000
Provinces	16,700,000
Municipals	32,327,000
Railways	236,129,000
Miscellaneous	74,809,000
	410,449,000
Sundries not publicly recorded (estimated)	20,000,000
	430,449,000

In ten years Canada has borrowed in this market, through the medium of public issues, about £205,043,900, plus probably £20,000,000 invested privately of which there is no published record.

. . . .

I am a comparatively young man, but I have seen our population increase from 3,200,000 to nearly 8,000,000. I can easily go back to the inception of the Canadian Pacific Railway. Less than twenty years ago the Canadian Northern Railway, Great Trunk Pacific, and National Transcontinental Railways were undreamt of.

I have seen our north-west territory converted from waste, un-populated land into a district producing crops which this year will approximate forty million pounds in value, although only an inconsiderable portion, say 10 per cent, of the arable acreage is under cultivation. If 50 per cent of this sum is deducted for cost of production, £20,000,000 profit remains from our North-West Provinces alone, or more than the amount required to pay 4 per cent interest on our total London indebtedness....

In conclusion let me say that there are two principal criticisms directed at Canada by embryo political economists, one with regard to the Dominion's adverse balance of trade, the other the debt *per capita*. Respecting the former, it is true our imports exceed our exports by a large amount, and if this condition were to last indefinitely there would naturally be room for dissatisfaction, but Canada to-day may be compared to a mighty industrial enterprise. We have had foundations to lay, superstructure to erect, plant to instal, mines to develop, inland and water transportations to create, even labour to import, all of which has entailed enormous expenditure....

...In other words our imports have been largely for constructional purposes, our exports are mainly in food supplies; the ratio of the former will diminish in time, the volume of the latter must steadily increase.

Statisticians should not forget to give us credit for another source of wealth in the uninterrupted stream of immigration which has been pouring into Canada at the rate of 250,000 per annum for the last five years, immigration of a superior class, appraisable at, say, one thousand dollars per individual....

As for our debt *per capita*, I am reminded of an incident which occurred in an Ontario town not long ago. There was a run on the branch of a secondary Canadian bank in a certain city west of Toronto. The manager, an Irish Canadian, was in his outside office endeavouring to allay the fears of his depositors, among whom was a farmer laboriously inscribing his name on the back of a deposit receipt for $10,000 prior to its withdrawal. The manager said: 'Caleb, what are you going to do with this money?' 'Oh', said the farmer, 'I am taking it across the road to the Bank of Montreal; they tell me it's all right.' 'What!' said the manager, 'the Bank of Montreal? Haven't you seen their figures?' 'No', said the farmer, 'what about them?' The manager hastily secured a copy of the Bank of Montreal balance sheet, and triumphantly pointing to its liabilities said: 'There, what do you think of that? Total liabilities aggregating $240,000,000, while our total liabilities are only $20,000,000.' 'Good heavens!' said the farmer, 'I had no idea of this—I had better leave the money where it is!' And he did.

87. INVESTMENT IN MEXICAN OIL

Source: J. A. Spender, 'Weetman Pearson First Viscount Cowdray' (1930), pp. 25–7, 149–50, 152–3, 154–5.

The firm of S. Pearson and Son began as a small building and contracting firm at Huddersfield, in Yorkshire. Under the grandson of the founder, Weetman Pearson (1856–1927), the firm moved to London and began to bid for contracts abroad. Pearson undertook the railway tunnel under the Hudson river at New York (until the Baring crisis in 1890 stopped construction), the Pennsylvania Railroad Company's tunnels in the same city, the Blackwall tunnel beneath the Thames, and other constructions of great note in their day. From 1895 onwards, his firm built up extensive interests in Mexico, first in railways and harbours, then in oil. He began to acquire oil-fields in Mexico in 1901 after a brief visit to Texas, where oil had just been drilled at Spindle Top, and invested over the years five million pounds in them. This was the origin of the Mexican Eagle Oil Co., which at the height of its operations and at a cost of five million pounds, owned 1,600,000 acres of Mexican soil, freehold property throughout Mexico for tankage and installations, 175 miles of pipe-line, and a crude oil capacity of 200,000 barrels a day. The Company was taken over by the Royal Dutch-Shell group in 1919. Pearson also became the owner of electrical undertakings in Mexico and Chile.

[*Memorandum by W. D. Pearson for the Capital and Counties Bank, 30 January 1900*]

S. Pearson & Son was founded in 1856.

W. D. Pearson a Partner in 1879 and the sole partner in December, 1894.

Owing to W. D. Pearson being a Member of Parliament, the Firm were [*sic*] precluded from carrying out Government Contracts; to get over this difficulty the Firm, at the suggestion of the Admiralty, was converted into a Limited Company in October, 1897, and the contract for the Admiralty Harbour at Dover secured.

The new Company took over the whole business of the old Firm.

The capital of the Company is £500,000 of Preference shares all issued and fully paid and £1,000,000 of Ordinary shares all issued but only 50 per cent paid. There is no Debenture issue. The capital of the

Company is owned by W. D. Pearson and family and the Directors. The Directors are:

W. D. PEARSON — President of the Company

CLARENDON G. HYDE — Barrister, who has been working with the firm for some 12 or 13 years

E. E. PEARSON
E. W. MOIR — These are active Managers of various Contracts, and joined the Board this month.
B. C. CASS

The assets of the Company on December 31, 1898, were £869,000.

These net assets are, of course, exclusive of goodwill or any value on the Contracts other than the actual profits realized.

The value of all assets is believed to be its realizable value and not its value as a going concern.

The profits of the Company for the year 1898 were £130,000. For the year 1899 we expect they will be equally good.

All the Contracts we have in hand, with the one exception of the Great Western Railway Contract on which a 5 per cent loss is anticipated, are turning out as expected.

We have every confidence in stating that we see as bright a prospect in the future as the Firm has enjoyed for the last 25 years, during each year of which the Firm has increased in prosperity.

The Firm has never had a Contract that it did not complete.

Up to 1879 the Firm's operations were confined to the North of England. In 1884 it opened offices in London. To-day it is perhaps the leading Firm of Contractors; the only Firm of similar standing being John Aird & Sons.

The Firm's Bankers are the Yorkshire Banking Co. Ltd., Leeds, and Williams Deacons Co. Ltd. The former we have banked with since 1857 and the latter for some 15 years. We have overdrafts at each Bank to the amount of £150,000. As our business grows we must increase our Banking facilities.

The Firm pays all accounts monthly, has no acceptances and no creditors except its Bankers.

The Contracts we have in hand exceed some £9,000,000. Our turnover exceeds £1,500,000 a year. Our business has grown from one with some £30,000 of capital in 1875 to its present position; not by any fluke but by hard work, enterprise and care; each year, as we have said before, being an improvement on the preceding one.

We have large interests in Mexico, where for the last ten years we have been actively and profitably engaged.

The Tehuantepec Railway, 190 miles long, belongs to the Government. As Contractors we are building two harbours, one at each end, for this railway on account of the Government for cash. We have a partnership agreement with the Mexican Government for the working of such railway and harbours. Although they will have cost the Government some £6,000,000, we pay no rent of any kind. We merely have to manage the property and pay half the losses if we make any, but get one-third of any profit we make.

To consolidate some of our interests and prevent competition, we have just acquired the Railway from Vera Cruz to Alvarado, 41 miles, and the trams at Vera Cruz. We pay for them on Thursday the first proximo.

We now require a credit for £100,000 against the deposit of some £55/60,000 of Stock Exchange or dividend bearing shares and debentures and the deposit of the Deeds of the Wouldham Cement Works....

[*W. D. Pearson to J. B. Body, April 1901*]

You will see that oil deposits frequently extend over big areas, so the oil rights must extend over a large district to be really valuable. Ten, twenty, or forty thousand acres appears [*sic*] to be no uncommon size—so in getting the option [*on oil-bearing land in the neighbourhood of San Cristobal on the Isthmus of Tehuantepec, Mexico*], get it over as big a country as possible. A short option is no good. We must have it for a year at least—preferably two, as it would take time to put down an oil well or otherwise prove it.

[*Memorandum by W. D. Pearson, dated 1 March 1906*]

Our oil-fields are situated in the States of Vera Cruz, Tabasco and Campeche, Mexico.

We own about 600,000 acres of land in the oil country and have royalty leases for 200,000 or 300,000 acres, which we have been four or five years in securing.

We are drilling four distinct fields. Our field forty miles from Coatzacoalcos produces first-class oil, as will be seen from the analysis and report of the fractional distillates. Our Refinery Manager is drawing up details of the first instalment of the Refinery we intend putting up with all speed. His first instalment will have a capacity of 4000 barrels of crude oil per day, or say 500 tons a day, of which 300 tons, or say 2000 tons per week, will be benzines and kerosenes.[1] We are hoping to get this Refinery at work before the end of the year, and after working it for three months, we intend increasing it with all speed to 12,000 barrels a day; thus, by the end of the next year, we expect 6000 tons a week of napthas and illuminating oils to sell. As the total consumption in Mexico at the present time is under 50,000 tons a year, this means that we should have a minimum of 250,000 tons of such oils a year to dispose of outside of Mexico.

We have acquired extensive river frontages and some 800 acres of land at Minatitlan for the Refinery. The climate is better there than at Coatzacoalcos, although only twenty miles from the coast, and the river is navigable, or if not will be made so, for vessels drawing 23 ft. or 24 ft. The load could be completed at Coatzacoalcos whenever necessary.

A 6-in. pipe-line is now being delivered to connect the oil-field with Minatitlan, and storage tanks are now being shipped for erection there.

We expect before July 1st to be in a position to deliver crude oil to steamers. This oil on account of the great quantity of benzine it contains is not suitable for fuel.

[*W. D. Pearson to his son, March 1908 (letter written but not sent)*]

I find things about as I expected; not much better (except on the Railway), nor much worse. The Refinery is going to be lighted up this week; not of course in full blast for the one-third unit, but still by still. It looks an immense place. Minatitlan market rivals Tehuantepec now. San Cristobal oil-field is in first-class shape. All the tanks are full of oil, and of course the pipe-line is in working order. I am afraid the area of

---

[1] This estimate proved to be unduly sanguine. The proportion of benzines and kerosenes to crude turned out to be 40 per cent instead of the 60 per cent which seems to be suggested here.

the field has been determined, as we have got a complete ring of dry wells around it except for say one eighth of its circumference....

As you know, we hedged by agreeing to purchase from Furbero a minimum of 2000 and a maximum of 6000 barrels a day for twelve years. So if we do fail to find more oil (which is an almost impossible assumption) than we have we avoid a failure. All this you know already, but it is cheering to put it down on paper when disappointments are all round me.

The oil business is not all beer and skittles....I entered lightly into the enterprise, not realizing its many problems, but only feeling that oil meant a fortune and that hard work and application would bring satisfactory results. Now I know that it would have been wise to surround myself with proved oil men who could give advice that their past life showed could be relied on, and not, as I did, relied upon commercial knowledge and hard work coupled with a superficial knowledge of the trade. However, all's well that ends well....

CHAPTER 5

COMPETITION AND MONOPOLY

Perhaps the economy of the Victorians was never so perfectly competitive as they supposed or chose to profess. Certainly the model of it which practical men and economists carried in their heads was competitive. They liked to think of competition, or as it was put, the laws of supply and demand, as ruling the roost. Competition was the rule, it was widely believed, monopoly was the rare exception. No man gave or could give a law to the market. The market had its own competitive rules. The laws of supply and demand ground out, through the price mechanism, what was wanted. They distributed the product in accordance with the same rules. This situation, where the individual will never could dominate, ensured that, as between the multitude of wills which must be satisfied, impartial justice would be done, both in the making of the social product and in its distribution.

Men had increasingly believed this to be the character of the economy which they ran, ever since Adam Smith in the eighteenth century first analysed in a way to carry general conviction the workings of market-competition. The belief had grown stronger with time, especially as the result of two great events of the early Victorian age, the one economic, the other social. The first of these was the building of the railways. This reconstructed markets both local and national and made many of them competitive for the first time. The other was the challenge presented about the same time by the middle classes to the political power of the landed aristocracy over the Reform Bill and the Corn Laws. It then became fashionable to contrast, in a deceptively simple fashion and in a way to flatter the self-esteem of the commercial classes, the land monopoly and the idle corruption of aristocratic life with the stern competition of business, equally without fear and without favour. The competitive model of the economy, as it was expounded by many men in mid-Victorian times, owed a great deal to memories of these happenings, still vivid in the 1870's and early 1880's.

Whether an economic model which had served in its day important economic and political purposes and could show practical benefits from its application was ever strictly in accordance with the facts is another matter. Men must simplify, if they are to think of anything so complicated as the society they live in. This was a theoretical pattern, of the economy of railway-and-steamship-and-steam-power Britain, formed by the men who ran it and by the economists of the day. There did not exist the measurements to prove whether it fitted or did not fit exactly all the countless Victorian markets for particular products. If they could now be measured it would not be surprising to find that the model did not fit at any time the economy with exactness and that belief in its accuracy included a substantial degree of self-deception. It represented nevertheless a keenly observed and logically argued view about dominant trends in the nation's economy, about the sources and direction of these trends, as these had been experienced by practical men over many years.

This makes it all the more interesting that the belief in competition as the dominant theory of the industrial system suffered a check and a weakening in the last quarter of the nineteenth century. The origins of this change of opinion were as diverse as those which in an earlier age had brought the competitive doctrine to the fore. To an important extent, the belief in the necessary supremacy of market forces was being undermined by changes which were political and social rather than economic. New classes and interests were making their way to the front in society and the state. The working man, for good reasons of his own, did not believe in the business man's competition. These things belong to the political sociology of the time. But they were also the consequence of a significant accession of new economic experience. This seemed to suggest that the trend towards competition, which had prevailed for so long, had at last found a counter-weight. It became possible to argue that there was a gathering move towards concentration of control in industry, even towards monopoly.

Concentration was to some extent called out and provoked by competition. The pace of competition during the long downswing of prices, accompanied by much technical change, at the end of the century, was found altogether too hot by some business men. During these years it became their aim in some industries to control the market. Trade associations, restrictive selling practices, such as resale price maintenance, and the amalgamation of concerns were the agents by which this was attempted. Many of these plans among business men miscarried. Many of those which succeeded were local rather than national. Some were not exactly new, for price agreements had not been unknown even at the height of the mid-Victorian market competition. The principle of the trade association, of varying degrees of formality, took root, however, and became increasingly used to fix or to try to fix prices. This was partly because there were other good reasons besides prices to bring business men together. Among the most important were industrial and commercial legislation and active collective bargaining. Even after prices started to rise in the early 1900's, the trade association continued to grow. Between 1880 and 1914 it became a characteristic, although reticent, part of the British industrial scene.

The tendency of transport industries towards amalgamation and monopolistic competition, for reasons inherent in their operating conditions, was of course old. On the railways, it had been obvious long before 1870 and continued to trouble public opinion, especially that of traders, down to 1914.[1] Then mechanical road transport began to offer a means to break the railway grip on inland communication. At sea, the fall of ocean freights in the last quarter of the nineteenth century and the spread of cargo-liner services brought the conference system and the shipping ring, with all that could be said both for and against such rate-associations. But the last years of the nineteenth century also saw a new and interesting move towards manufacturing amalgamations.

The tendency for industrial firms to increase in size was an old one. This was natural and to be expected given the increasing size of the market to be served and the growing elaboration of power and equipment. Now the giant firm began to emerge—the firm which looked very large even to men accustomed to think habitually in terms of the economies of scale and used to working with big typical firms. There were, again, sound reasons for this in the business world of the late nineteenth century and the early 1900's, quite apart from the speculative financial gains which entered into company promotions. Important economies could be gained—they were not necessarily obtained—by the very large concern. They were to be found both in buying and selling and in the processes of manufacture. The limitations on the expansion of the manufacturing concern were to be found elsewhere—in the preoccupation, more marked in those days than now, with exports and foreign markets, often small and specialized, and in an English consumer who did not take kindly to the standardized article, although he was learning fast. The free import policy and those technical and commercial factors of the age which made Great Britain a bargain counter for the rest of the world's surplus goods, to the benefit of the same English consumer, worked also to hinder the building up of the wide uniform market where the giant firms would have the greatest advantages. Competition remained real and keen, but in some markets it became increasingly monopolistic competition.

If it was not possible for firms to grow 'into the sky' the emergence of the very large concern, with varying powers of price-leadership in the market, was nonetheless a striking development. Never rapid nor attracting so much political debate as the American trust or the

---

[1] For some of the late Victorian discussions of the 'railway problem', see W. H. G. Armytage, 'The Railway Rates Question and the Fall of the Third Gladstone Ministry', *English Historical Review*, LXV (1950) and P. M. Williams, 'Public Opinion and the Railway Rates Question in 1886', *English Historical Review*, LXVII (1952).

German cartel of the same years, the trend towards concentration of control in certain branches of British industry was presumably rooted in the same general tendencies of an industrial civilization. It was much stronger in some industries than in others. Combinations of existing firms into big units for management and production and for price-setting were most successful in the smaller industries and in highly specialized branches of the staple trades of the day. Large combines, responsible for a high proportion of total output and sales, grew up before 1914, in soap, chemicals, explosives, salt, tobacco, whisky and cement. Some of these concerns had interests outside the United Kingdom—in a few trades there were producers who were parties to international cartels—but on the whole international agreement was rare.

The staple trades, on the other hand, by definition the largest industries in Great Britain, tended to be fiercely competitive. There many producers struggled for sales on the market. Coal, iron and steel, cotton and woollen textiles, shipbuilding, much engineering, were all carried on in this intensely competitive way. The tendency to organize in order to restrict competition, where it appeared in these industries, arrived in particular sections which lent themselves to close organization; in anthracite coal, textile-finishing, sewing-thread, some kinds of finished metal goods.

This move towards amalgamation and association was over a long period of years to modify the structure and the operating climate of British industry. The widespread character of the combination movement was reported on to the government at the end of the 1914–18 war (no. 97) as something affecting the public interest and requiring close study, possibly legislation. This was the first official recognition of its importance, although there had been much discussion by publicists and economists since the beginning of the century. The combination movement continued throughout the 1920's and 1930's. It produced in time the position which prevailed in 1951, when two economists found that in 219 industries a small proportion, about 10 per cent, of those employed worked in trades which could properly be called mono-polistic, a larger proportion, about 25 per cent, worked in industries which were indisputably competitive in structure and behaviour, and a much larger number, about three-fifths of the whole, were employed by industries which were neither monopolistic nor competitive but best described as imperfectly competitive.[1] The latter phrase did not come in until the 1930's.

This change towards an industrial world which exhibits some of the essential characteristics both of monopoly and of competition as part of

---

[1] R. Evely and I. M. D. Little, *Concentration in British Industry* (1960), pp. 81–2.

its normal condition was in the late Victorian and Edwardian period still in its early stages. This accounts for public opinion having given it far less attention at the time than its importance would now seem to warrant. Perhaps there was some willingness to turn a blind eye to developments which current opinion could not easily approve of. Certainly combinations never roused in this country the strong hostility which led to anti-trust legislation in the United States, in the Sherman Act of 1890. There was nothing in this country corresponding to the political pressure of the great American farm-group with its innate distrust of the cities and big business, which lay behind that act. British courts, left to themselves by the politicians, gave a surprisingly liberal interpretation to the common law doctrine of contracts in restraint of trade, although this might conceivably have been used against the new concentrations of power. The decision on appeal in the Mogul Steamship Company case in 1892 showed this toleration of combination (no. 95). In practice, the line between combination and monopoly might prove hard to draw. There was little sign, either in the legal or in other discussions, of any realization that the movement away from the fierce, crude, striving competition of a remarkable age of industrial growth, such as had prevailed in the middle nineteenth century, and its gradual replacement by a new industrial structure, with its own code of competition, modified and controlled, perhaps more suitable in its own way to a period of slackening industrial expansion and limited innovation, must sooner or later raise public issues of great importance in relation both to the use of resources and to the distribution of incomes.

FURTHER READING

For present-day business arrangements and legislation, G. C. Allen, *The Structure of Industry in Britain* (1961). Many problems of industrial combination and of public policy arising out of it have become common to all large industrial communities. See, for example, *Monopoly and Competition and their Regulation: Papers and Proceedings of a Conference held by the International Economic Association*, edited by E. H. Chamberlin (1954) and E. S. Mason, *Economic Concentration and the Monopoly Problem* (Cambridge, Mass. 1957).

German and American discussion of the cartel and the trust began in the 1880's 2, under the influence of powerful industrial development in those countries. In this country, the public debate came in the early 1900's, with the international movement in mind but largely as a result of events at home. Down to 1900 the best account of British industrial combination is to be found in a by-product of American inquiry, in the *Reports of the United States Industrial Commission*, XVIII (1901), *Industrial*

Combination in Europe by J.W. Jenks. F.W. Hirst's *Monopolies, Trusts and Kartells* (1905) was written by a convinced believer in the classical doctrine of competition. He did not see that, in the words of Marshall later, 'some of the most injurious uses of monopoly, being themselves extreme forms of competition, are not to be restrained by the advocacy of free competition' (*Industry and Trade*, 3rd ed. p. 512). H.W. Macrosty, *The Trust Movement in British Industry* (1907) was a valuable collection of information, which has been borrowed from ever since. Herman Levy's *Monopoly and Competition* (1911) was a translation from a book previously published in German as *Monopole, Kartelle und Trusts* (Jena, 1909). Levy was a German who knew England well, perceptive and explicit in his general views. G. R. Carter's *The Tendency towards Industrial Combination* (1913) added little. For the later history of many of the amalgamations and combinations of this period, see P. Fitzgerald, *Industrial Combination in England* (1927).

Two British economists before the First World War devoted much of their time to the forms of business enterprise and the economic meaning of combination. One of these was D. H. Macgregor, whose *Industrial Combination* (1906) was an acute and fair-minded essay. He was later responsible for introducing to English readers R. Liefmann's *Cartels, Concerns and Trusts* (1932—originally *Kartelle, Konzerne und Trusts*, 8th ed. 1930), still useful not only for comparison with German conditions but also for the whole Western background of industrial combination from 1890 on. The other man was Alfred Marshall, whose *Industry and Trade*, published in 1919, contained a handling of monopolistic tendencies, largely based on his knowledge of the years 1890–1914. This stood in a class by itself for range and sagacity.

Without a familiarity with the inner history of firms and industries it is impossible to discuss monopoly and competition with exactness or to move out of the sphere of generalization. Business histories which throw light are rare and the weakness of British historical writing when it touches modern industry is nowhere more apparent. C. H. Wilson's *History of Unilever*, 2 vols. (1954) is an exceptionally good description of the emergence of a giant firm. Two great chemical concerns, later merged into another giant combine, Imperial Chemical Industries Ltd, have been the subject of house histories not altogether empty: *The First Fifty Years of Brunner, Mond and Company* (1923) and *United Alkali Company: the Struggle for Supremacy* (1907).

88. THE SALT UNION

Source: '*The Times*', *13 October 1888, 1 February 1889,*

In the mid-1880's, prices of common salt were low. This was the result partly of the adoption of the Solvay process by the alkali industry, which reduced the important industrial demand for salt, partly of the general trade depression. Hence the emergence of the Salt Union in 1888, a combine controlling most of the salt output of the United Kingdom. This was one of the earliest of the great industrial amalgamations of the late nineteenth century and also one of the least successful. Over-capitalized from the start, the Salt Union succeeded in raising prices, only to call out in doing so new production both at home and abroad. It was compelled to write off a large part of the value of its capital. The Salt Union became a stock example for contemporaries of the evils and unwisdom of industrial combination.

A

The Great Salt Combination

The acquisition by a syndicate of capitalists of the chief salt mines and workings in Great Britain, with a view to controlling production and raising the price of salt, is the latest and, on the whole, perhaps most objectionable phase of a tendency that has been showing itself during the last few years. The avowed object of this, as of all other similar syndicates, is to regulate production, and thereby create a relative scarcity of the commodity 'syndicated', instead of permitting the existence of the glut that from time to time arises under a system of free competition among producers. The expedient is by no means a new one. It has been resorted to again and again when trade was generally depressed, or when there appeared to be a probability of securing a monopoly in a commodity of every-day use, in order to force prices up to a point which they would not be likely to reach under the or-dinary conditions of supply and demand.

This combination of salt producers, like every other movement of the kind, presents itself under two separate aspects, according as it is regarded as affecting the general public or the salt industry.

It may at once be conceded that the influence which the proposed artificial increase of the price of salt would be likely to exercise on the public, as consumers of salt for domestic purposes, will be almost inappreciable....

So far as the new combination is likely to affect the salt industry as such, it is perhaps too early to speak as yet. One thing, however, is tolerably certain. The syndicate has not acquired the control of all the mines or works at which salt is produced, and unless and until they do this they will not have an absolute monopoly. The firms that keep clear of the combination will thus be enabled to undersell the syndicate by a sufficient margin of price to enable them to get a leading place in the market, so far as price can give that position. The large firms, bound by the rules under which the combination is administered, will have their production curtailed in certain fixed proportions, while the firms that are independent will be in a position to produce to the fullest extent of their capacity. Again, unless the syndicate obtains absolute possession of or control over every inch of ground where salt can be got, the almost certain result of the combination will be to bring into existence a number of 'small fry' which would not otherwise come into being, and the resources of production will thereby, in all probability, be increased far beyond what they are now, thus defeating one of the primary objects of the movement, which is that of curtailing supply and creating an artificial scarcity. The fact that in all combinations of this kind the stronger and more important firms who are parties to the agreement have to carry the weaker and less capable firms òn their back is another manifest difficulty in the way of the new syndicate. These, however, are matters for the syndicate, as such, to deal with. What it concerns the public to know is that, even if the syndicate succeeds, the increase in the price of salt for domestic purposes is likely to be inappreciable; but that there is a grave danger threatened to the industries that depend upon salt as a raw material. Of the important question of public policy involved in this and similar movements we are likely to hear more by and by.

B

Since the Salt Union came into existence the prices of all descriptions of salt have been steadily raised, until common salt, which was selling at 3s. to 5s. per ton, is now quoted as 7s. to 10s. 6d. per ton. The quotations for lump and other qualities have also been increased by about 100 per cent, while some of the finer qualities have been raised 125 per cent

The Salt Union has drawn an imaginary line from Cardigan Bay to the Wash in Lincolnshire, and below that line the trade has been handed over to Mr Corbett, of Stoke Prior Works, Worcestershire, while Cheshire dealers will be confined to the country north of the line. This arrangement has given rise to some complaints.

89. RETAIL PRICE MAINTENANCE IN THE 1890's

Source: ' The Ironmonger' (7 December 1895), p. 399, (11 November 1899), p. 248, (7 May 1904), p. 217.

Partly because of the long fall of wholesale and retail prices and partly because of the constant growth of national as against local markets, the importance of keeping up a fixed retail price and the iniquities of the discount system became constant subjects of discussion among businessmen. Out of their talks something like a system of retail price maintenance began to emerge, commonplace now, but novel then. The extracts given show the progress of these ideas within the ironmongery trades, very broadly defined. But the Net Book Agreement among publishers, which ended the system of discounts on book sales, or the maintenance of prices on pharmaceutical products as sold in the chemist's shop, both of which were coming into force in the early 1900's, would be equally good examples.

A

Cutting prices in accessories

Joseph Lucas and Son, the well-known Birmingham cycle-accessory makers, have again given their careful attention to the subject of preventing ruinous cutting of prices in the handling of their goods. During the past season they have made a determined and, as they state, successful attempt to prevent profit on their goods from being cut down to the vanishing-point by excessive competition, and in some cases they have positively closed accounts with agents who refuse to maintain the minimum retail prices which the firm found it necessary to fix. In a circular which has been issued they state 'it is neither advisable nor even possible for us to say that every retailer of our goods shall sell at certain prices, but in the interests of us all it is necessary that we shall say the lowest prices at which our goods shall be sold, leaving agents to obtain higher prices wherever they can and think it advisable to do so. Our list, therefore, does not mean that an agent shall not obtain higher than our "lowest fixed prices", but merely that these prices are really the lowest he may sell at'. It is fully recognised by Joseph Lucas and Son that such profits as were formerly to be obtained are not to be had now, and they have therefore considered it advisable to reduce prices in their retail catalogue to such figures as an agent may have a chance of obtaining. The circular is worded in a judicial and temperate tone, and the matter is of so much importance that we cannot but commend its contents to the trade.

B

Ironmongers and Manufacturers

Direct trading seems to be the question of the hour with iron-mongers, and offending manufacturers are being constantly taken to task by aggrieved retailers through the medium of their newly-established associations. We do not object to this, but we think that the retail trade would also do well to consider at this juncture whether they on their side fully recognise their own duties and obligations towards "fair" manufacturers. While some manufacturers—unfortunately, an increasing number—carry on both a wholesale and a direct-supply business, others strictly confine their dealings to shop-keepers. On receipt of an order from an outsider these firms invariably refer the would-be purchaser to their nearest customer, or execute the order themselves and credit the ironmonger with the amount of profit he would have received had the transaction passed through his hands. But is such loyalty meeting with the recognition, encouragement, and reward which it deserves?...We are frequently told that the average ironmonger is ungrateful, that he takes loyalty on the part of a manufacturer as a matter of course, but that for the sake of a trifling advantage in discounts, or in some other direction, he will place an order with an unfair-trading firm....

C

Ironmongers' Federated Association meeting in Birmingham, May 1904; paper given by R. E. Leech on 'The Cultivation of Price Maintenance'.

He said that they would probably all agree that price-maintenance deserved their support beyond all other things in their trade. It was impossible to estimate the money lost to the retail trader through

concessions he had given to customers who came to him with circumstantial statements about prices that were accepted elsewhere...
his own self-respect and influence on his customer had been improved by the reflection that he was standing on sure ground when explaining to the customer that it really was not true that his quotations were being undercut.

Price maintenance promised to bring to the retailer—

(*a*) A satisfactory profit on the investment he makes in stock and trading facilities.

(*b*) Freedom to make his profit without fear of being undercut.

(*c*) A longer life for articles in which he has invested interest and energy, and which heretofore had commonly been molested by the jealousy of his neighbour.

(*d*) A better share of the trade which now goes to the unfairly cheap concerns, and thus an expanded business for himself proportionate to the energy he displays.

(*e*) More safety from the offended opinion of a public which can buy cheaper from the retailer's opponents where price-maintenance is not in force.

(*f*) The contentment which naturally arises from the knowledge that he can 'do the trade' as well as anybody else, and thus more encouragement to set out earnestly in the doing of it.

...It lay in their own hands to make price-maintenance not merely popular among manufacturers, but indispensable....

But they must be consistent. If manufacturers gave them a guaranteed profit they must support them. Where one manufacturer gave them fair play and another was pandering to their opponents they must encourage the one who was doing the fair thing....

90. NATIONAL PLAN FOR COAL

Source: 'The Times', 20 September 1893.

The coal industry, being 'the industry without which no other industry could exist', was hard hit by the severe and world-wide industrial depression of the early 1890's. One consequence was to plunge it into a most serious wage dispute. Another was to set some colliery owners wondering whether there was anything to be said for a change of organization, to limit competition. It was while the long war between the colliery

*managements and their workers about wages was still on that Sir George
Elliot, a well-known colliery proprietor, put forward publicly a scheme
for the amalgamation of the whole of the coal industry. One purpose of
his plan was to obtain an approximately uniform scale of wages throughout
the country and to provide for an insurance scheme for the miners and their
families in old age and sickness. The proposed trust was to control an
annual output of 145,000,000 tons of coal and a capital of £110 millions.
A central council and about thirty district committees were to administer
the trust. But opinion in the industry was generally adverse to his scheme
and perhaps the views of the general public were no more favourable.
Nothing came of the proposal.*

THE definite proposal which the scheme embodies may be summed
up in set terms as follows:

The coal lessees of the United Kingdom shall amalgamate their
existing interests in a co-operative company, charged with the entire
working of the coal deposits of the country, taking payment in the
form of one-third debentures and two-thirds stock. All stock shall be
interminable. A reserve fund shall be formed for opening further
collieries to take the place of those annually exhausted and to provide
for extensions and sinkings; an insurance fund for workmen shall be
set aside, and a sinking fund for the redemption of capital shall also
provide the means for rendering the consolidated property permanent.
All further earnings will be applied, first, in paying interest on the
debentures at 5 per cent; secondly, in paying a *minimum* dividend of
10 per cent upon the stock. In view of the exceptional nature of the
property concerned, it is believed that the dividend upon the stock
need never be less than 10 per cent, but the profits shall not exceed
5 per cent more without the approval of the Board of Trade, and such
5 per cent, if paid, shall be divided equally between the lessee and the
workman. In the event of the Board of Trade sanctioning an advance
in price sufficient to yield any interest beyond 15 per cent, the whole
further profit will then be divided equally in thirds between the workmen, the coal lessees and the purchaser. As in such an arrangement the
purchaser pays the whole difference and only receives back a third in
the form of discount, the interest of the workmen and the coal lessees
will manifestly be to bring pressure to bear upon the Board of Trade to
sanction an advance in price. The interest of the public will be to bring
pressure to resist an advance. Between these two fires the Board of

Trade is called upon by the terms of the scheme to protect the several interests of all parties concerned. If upon consideration it should be found that the political composition of the Board of Trade would render it inexpedient to invest it with ultimate powers of control, it is proposed to substitute referees, who shall be appointed by high judicial authority, say the Lord Chief Justice. The principle of limiting the interest on capital is, it is submitted, one that has long been recognized in this country in the supply of gas and water, and there need be no difficulty in the application of the same principle to coal.

If the calculations on which this proposal is based are correct, the coalowners, it is believed, would gain a security for their dividend which would be scarcely less than that of Government stocks. The public would gain the advantage of a steady, moderate price, which would be safeguarded from the fluctuations caused by strikes and other accidental circumstances, and would not be altered without the sanction of the Government. The workmen would gain better conditions of labour, better wages, and a share in the profits. The nation would gain in the more economical, and at the same time more thorough and systematic, development of the coal deposits.

All this is a great deal to promise, and to submit proposals for a scheme of this magnitude is manifestly a very different thing from carrying it to a successful issue. The first and most practical question for consideration is whether the coal lessees of Great Britain will be disposed as a body to consider that they serve their own interests by exchanging their present chances of a higher rate of profit for the practical certainty of 10 per cent which the new scheme claims to offer. A majority of two-thirds of the coal lessess of the country would be required in order to insure the success of the working of the scheme. Many of them have already been consulted, and, as it is believed that one effect of the better security would be to increase the capital value of coal property from the present figure of five or seven years' purchase to something like 20 years' purchase, little doubt is entertained that the requisite number would be found willing to join the enterprise. The amount of existing obligations, such as mortgages, etc., to which coal properties may be subject is also, by the necessarily private nature of many such obligations, difficult to estimate beforehand. It is believed by the supporters of the scheme that the readiness with which debentures could be disposed of would meet all requirements likely to arise on this head, and it is, in general terms, presumable that an increase in the security of a property can hardly be regarded as an injury to the interests of a mortgagee. But in its financial aspect the scheme must be regarded as an immense conversion scheme, and experience with the conversion of many public debts has shown that arguments in general terms are not always received as absolutely satisfactory in individual application. For all these reasons it is clear that many obstacles remain to be disposed of before it can become possible for the proposals embodied in the scheme to be carried into effect. Should these be removed and the full practicability of the measure be established, it will still be for the various parties involved to watch with care over the maintenance of the economic theory of the balance of interests upon which it takes its stand. Without attempting to predict its fate, it may be safely said that the conception and publication of the scheme will in any case have submitted for consideration one of the most interesting possibilities of industrial development which has been witnessed in this generation.

91. THE BRADFORD DYERS' ASSOCIATION

Source: 'Reports of the U.S. Industrial Commission', xvIII (1901): 'Industrial Combination in Europe', 48–53.

The Bradford Dyers' Association was one of the most successful combinations formed in its time. There was often a strong element of locality and neighbourhood about successful combinations. This was marked in the Yorkshire textile dyeing trade. The Bradford Dyers dominated from 1898, although not without considerable competition, the worsted piece-dyeing industry based on the city of Bradford. They were not much interested in the dyeing of ordinary woollens. The dyeing of woollen yarns was appropriated by another combine, in its beginnings much less successful, The British Cotton and Wool Dyers. Cotton piece-dyeing, the most important at that date of all dyeing trades, remained at the start outside, although that too came later under the control of a trade association of which these two combines were members. Textile dyeing was done on commission, the cloth remaining the property of the merchant concerned. Technically, it was related to the chemical rather than to the textile industries. See J. H. Clapham, 'The Woollen and Worsted Industries' (1907) for the general setting.

PROSPECTUS OF THE BRADFORD DYER'S ASSOCIATION,
LIMITED

Objects

This company has been formed primarily for the purpose of acquiring the businesses of the various companies and firms engaged in what is commonly known as the Bradford piece dyeing trade.

The following have entered into contracts with this association for the sale of their businesses:

Established	Names and addresses of vendors
1842	George Armitage, Limited, Bradford.
1835	William Aykroyd & Sons, Bradford.
1892	Bradford & District Dyeing Co., Limited, Halifax
1875	George Briggs & Sons, Cleckheaton.
1896	Craven Pearson & Co., Limited, Brighouse.
1862	Fountain Finishing Co., Limited, Bradford.
1863	W. Grandage & Co., Limited,[1] Bradford.
1893	Harry H. Hall & Co., Guiseley.
1892	Hunsworth Dyeing Co., Limited, Cleckheaton.
1846	Samuel Kirk & Sons, Leeds.
1889	John Mitchell & Co., Keighley.
1827	James Reffitt & Sons, Leeds.
1809	Edward Ripley & Son, Bradford.
1862	James & M. S. Sharp & Co., Limited, Low Moor, Heckmondwike.
1869	Shaw & Co., Shipley.
1891	John Shaw & Co., Limited, Bradford.
1893	Sam Shepherd & Co., Yeadon.
1828	Samuel Smith & Co., Limited, Bradford.
1887	John H. Stott & Co., Bradford.
1892	Thornton, Hannam & Marshall, Brighouse.
1880	Ward & Sons, Limited, Halifax.
1877	Whitaker Bros. & Co., Dyers, Limited, Newlay.

[1] This purchase does not include the company's slubbing works at Brighouse.

Extent of Business

The businesses to be acquired comprise about 90 per cent of the Bradford piece dyeing trade, two of the firms have also extensive warp dyeing departments. These works are situated in the midst of the great textile industrial district of which Bradford is the center [*sic*], and thus the goods pass from the manufacturers to the dyers and from them to the merchants with the greatest convenience and despatch, and with the least amount of carriage. As the value of the goods dyed annually by the associated firms amounts to some £12,000,000 to £15,000,000 this constitutes an important factor.

The industry is one of great importance and magnitude, the number of persons (mostly men) employed by the association being about 7500, and the consumption of coal alone about a quarter of a million tons per annum.

Goods Treated and Mode of Trading

The goods treated are in use in almost every household in the United Kingdom, besides being shipped to all parts of the world, and are of a very varied character, embracing the finest silk, mohair, and wool fabrics, as well as the lowest cottons. The business of the association is thus not dependent on any particular market or branch of trade. At the same time the commercial risks attached to the business are reduced to a minimum, as the dyers do not trade in the goods, the work being all done on commission and on cash terms, there is thus no risk or loss by falling markets and the bad debts are inappreciable.

Trade-marks

The trade-marks of many of the firms and companies in the association representing a very large percentage of the work done are known all the world over, and goods dyed under such trade-marks are demanded by the users and distributors.

Advantages of the Amalgamation

Amongst the advantages to be gained by means of this amalgamation of interests the following may be enumerated:

First. The avoidance of loss through undue competition and cutting of prices below cost.

Whilst it is apparent that the inclusion of about 90 per cent of the entire trade within this association amounts to what is practically a monopoly, the directors recognize that the interests of the company are largely identical with those of the manufacturers and merchants of the district, and though there are no doubt cases in which some readjustment and regulation of rates are at once reasonable and desirable to enable all the firms to produce their proper proportionate share of profit, it is no part of the present scheme to inaugurate an era of inflated price.

Second. The economies and improvements in production arising from the combined practical knowledge of the members forming the board of directors (who are all men of great experience in the dyeing trade) as a consulting and advisory body available for each branch.

Third. The economies due to centralisation of office work and of buying, distributing, and financial arrangements.

The directors are very fully alive to the desirability of conserving the individuality and initiative of the various businesses, and will not allow centralization to act detrimentally in these matters; but there are many obvious advantages to be gained, as, for example, in combined buying, in the supply of ample capital, and in relieving, where desirable, technical managers from the burden of many subsidiary duties and allowing them to concentrate their attention on their special department.

Management

It is intended, as far as possible, that the control of each firm shall remain in the hands of those who have been responsible for its conduct in the past, and in order that such management may have an inducement to continue to give their best efforts to the business, the directors are empowered under the articles to pay commissions on the profits of each individual branch, thus safeguarding the principle of individual effort to which so much of the success in the past has been due. It is felt that this policy will be as much in the interests of the general trade as that of the company, seeing that thereby healthy competition and rivalry between the associated firms for excellence and quality of work will be maintained and encouraged.

Managing Directors' and Directors' Remuneration

The managing directors will retire from their present firms and companies and devote themselves solely to the business of the association, their remuneration being entirely dependent on profits, and payable only out of the surplus remaining after providing for the interest on the debenture stock and the dividend on the preference shares. The remuneration of the board other than the managing directors will be fixed by the shareholders in general meeting.

Competition

As regards competition at a distance, the position of the company is almost unassailable for the following reasons:

(*a*) The cost of cartage or carriage and the extra time required in conveying to and fro.

(*b*) The trade is of so detailed and technical a character that it is of the utmost importance that the dyer should be in daily touch with his customers whose goods he is treating.

(*c*) The supply and the nature and quality of the water obtainable is undoubtedly of great importance, and appears to be essential in the treatment of certain articles.

(*d*) The location in the district of a large number of trained and experienced workmen, due to the fact that the trade has been so long established there, and to the highly technical nature of the processes.

Additional Profits

Offers have already been received which would give the association the benefit of manufacturing its own chemicals and dye wares. This would undoubtedly enable large sums annually to be saved, but it has not been thought advisable to include any such works in the combination at this stage. At the same time the directors are confident that they will be able with the funds at their disposal in many directions to largely increase the profits, and to this end they hold the unissued capital in reserve.

The valuation of the property and plant made by the well-known firm of valuers, Messrs Edward Rushton, Son & Kenyon, of which a copy will be found below, shows £1,943,218, in addition to which the association acquires under the contracts of sale, stocks in trade, and book debts guaranteed by the vendors and cash in hand, £246,034, giving a total sum of assets to be acquired of £2,189,252. This sum provides security to an amount more than double the proposed issue of debenture stock.

This issue also provides additional capital to the amount of, say, £129,360.

Working Capital

The businesses are purchased free of all liabilities, and fully equipped with working stock in trade. The whole of the book debts (excepting those of one vendor company), together with a considerable sum in cash, are also included in the sale; with this, and the £129,360 mentioned above, the company will start with a working capital which the directors consider ample....

[*The certificate of valuation follows.*]

The books of the various firms have been examined by a leading firm of chartered accountants, Messrs Jones, Crewdson & Youatt, of Manchester and London, who have a special knowledge of industrial amalgamations, and their certificate is as follows:

7 NORFOLK STREET, MANCHESTER
December 8 1898

To the Chairman and Directors of the Bradford Dyers' Association, Limited

Gentlemen: We have examined the accounts of the firms who have entered into contracts for the sale of their businesses to your association, and thereon we beg to report as follows:

In arriving at the combined average profits we have in the main taken the figures for a period of three years, but owing to the varying dates of stocktaking, and to the fact that one firm has only been recently established, this period is not in every case uniform; the commencing date, however, has in no case been taken prior to January 1, 1895. The periods, while varying inter se, are in all cases consecutive, and are brought down to the most recent available date. The figures have also in some cases been adjusted by us on the advice of your valuers in respect to the allocation of new machinery and plant as between capital and revenue, and do not include income tax and interest upon partners' capital and loans.

We find that the aggregate average profit thus arrived at has been the annual average sum of £225,656 16s. 6d.

A proper and adequate provision for the management of each of the various works and for the remuneration of the managing directors, as provided for by the articles, must be deducted from this sum, and we consider that, although the various firms point out that an amount of over £50,000 a year has been expended out of income on the maintenance and renewal of the buildings, plant, and machinery, a further sum should be provided as a depreciation fund.

In our opinion the sum of £63,000 would be a sufficient annual provision for management, salaries, and for a depreciation fund.

JONES, CREWDSON & YOUATT
Chartered Accountants

Estimate of Dividend

It will be seen that the above rate of profit is more than sufficient to provide for the following:

4 per cent on £1,000,000 debenture stock..........		£40,000
5 per cent on 1,000,000 preference shares.........		50,000
7 per cent on 1,000,000 ordinary shares		70,000
	3,000,000	160,000

but the directors believe that, owing to the economies resulting from the amalgamation, from the proportionately larger working capital, owing to the various businesses being worked as a whole, and from the employment of the additional sum of £129,360 above mentioned, they will be able to pay handsome dividends, besides putting a substantial sum to reserve.

Purchase Price

The purchase prices of the firms enumerated above, including £681,388 for good will, amount to the sum of £2,870,640, of which £333,330 is payable in debenture stock, £666,666 in equal proportions of preference and ordinary shares, and the balance in cash or as provided for in the agreements for sale in shares or debenture stock taken at par.

In the majority of cases the contracts for purchase provide that the association shall in addition to the above purchase money pay for any expenditure on additional property and machinery acquired since the date of Messrs Edward Rushton, Son & Kenyon's valuation.

Date of Taking Over Businesses

The association will take over the trading of all the firms with the exception of Messrs James & M. S. Sharp & Co., Limited, and Harry H. Hall & Co., as from the 30th of September last, and in the case of the firms excepted the profits will begin to accrue to the company from the 31st of October last.

The Company Buys Direct

The company buys in each case direct from the original owners of the business, no promoter's profit or underwriting commission being payable, and the vendors will bear the expenses of and incidental to the formation and establishment of the company up to allotment.

Contracts

The following contracts have been entered into, all of which are dated December 13, 1898, and are made between the association of the one part and the following persons, firms, and companies of the other part, being the contracts for sale to the company, viz:

[*The names of contracting firms follow.*]

Copies of the prospectus, with forms of application for shares or for debenture stock, can be obtained at the offices of the company or from the bankers, brokers, auditors, or solicitors.

Bradford, December 14, 1898.

92. PORTLAND CEMENT

Source: 'The Times', 14 July 1900.

The cement industry seemed well fitted for combination, for its organisation was based upon the local monopoly of raw materials and markets. The Association formed in 1900 had, however, considerable difficulties to face. It was launched at a time when the war in South Africa and the attendant industrial activity had depressed the London money market and driven up the price of fuel, an important element in the industry's costs. The Association also experienced trouble with the merchants and with foreign competitors. Unable to keep prices up as they would have liked, the Association were forced, during the years of depression which followed the war, to seek their profit by evening out the very considerable variations in production costs between the plants forming the combine. See H. W. Macrosty, 'The Trust Movement in British Industry' (1907), pp. 108–16. In view of the growing importance of cement in the building and construction trades, the formation of this combine was an important move.

ASSOCIATED PORTLAND CEMENT MANUFACTURERS (1900)
LIMITED

Abridged Prospectus

This Association has been formed for the purpose of purchasing the undertakings of the undermentioned firms and companies engaged in the manufacture of Portland Cement. With the exception of three, all the works are situated on the Thames and Medway, and possess such advantages in the quantity and quality of raw material, that the neighbourhood of these two rivers, from being the cradle of the Portland Cement industry, has now become the chief seat of the manufacture. It is believed that upwards of 80 per cent of the entire output of Portland Cement in the United Kingdom is produced on the Thames and Medway, where the supplies of chalk and clay are of the finest quality for the manufacture. The total production of cement on these rivers in 1899 has been estimated at 1,700,000 tons, whereas the estimate of production in 1895 was only 1,350,000 tons. This difference is due to the largely increasing demand for Portland Cement....

Many of the firms whose undertakings are acquired are old-established, and possess Brands and 'Trade Marks' of the highest reputation throughout the world. The certified production of the firms taken over by this Association was in—

1897	1,222,240 tons
1898	1,337,268 „
1899	1,404,569 „

and owing to improvements and additions the capacity of the combined works is now about 1,570,000 tons.

Although the demand for Cement is steadily increasing, there have been times when the supply has exceeded the demand, leading necessarily to fluctuations in profits. To avoid this in the future the present Association is formed.

Another object of the Association is to effect reduction in the cost, as well as improvements in the manufacture, by bringing all the businesses under one control. The Association will also aim at lessening the expenses of distribution, and at steadying prices without unduly raising them; while the tendency to cut prices in the winter, when storage is difficult at some of the Works, will be avoided. The Directors will have at their disposal a large amount of extra Working Capital to enable them to continue the policy already begun at some of the Works—of introducing new and improved methods of manufacture, which will effect savings, and consequent increase of profits.

The Directors of the largest undertaking acquired, having expended considerable time in investigating various methods for the manufacture of Portland Cement upon the Rotary Kiln principle, selected the Hurry and Seamen's as the best, and acquired a licence to work that system on royalty. A sum of over £120,000 is being expended on new plant in their works, for the yearly production of about 160,000 tons of Portland Cement on that principle, which only necessitates a substitution of different burning plant. It is proposed to manufacture another 70,000 tons a year on the same principle. An option has been obtained by the promoters for an exclusive licence to the Association in this country of this system, which the Directors will be in a position to use extensively.

Contracts have been entered into by the Vendor Company for the acquisition of, amongst other properties, the undermentioned businesses:

[*11 companies situated on River Medway; 16 cement companies on Thames; and 3 companies outside Thames and Medway.*]

In addition to the above, the Association will have, on terms which have been agreed, working arrangements for three years or over with the following firms:

> Martin Earle and Company, Limited, Wickham, Medway.
> William Lee, Son, and Co.
> Wouldham Cement Co. (1900) Ltd, West Thurrock.
> Queenborough Portland Cement Company, Medway.

The undertakings which the Association acquires, and others with whom they will have working arrangements, are estimated to produce about 89 per cent of the total capacity of production of Cement on the Thames and Medway.

An agreement has been entered into with George E. Wragge on behalf of the principal London Cement Merchants, which provides inter alia for all merchants joining them taking their whole requirements of Cement from this Association for the term of seven years.

93. CIGARETTES AND THE TOBACCO COMBINE

Source: 'Report of the United States Commissioner of Corporations on the Tobacco Industry' (Washington, 1909), Part I. 'Position of the Tobacco Combination in the Industry', pp. 166–9.

By 1901 the American Tobacco Company was a leading concern in the cigarette and tobacco trade of the United States. But it had also become interested in the export of cigarettes to Great Britain. Becoming dissatisfied with sales, it took steps to begin manufacture there by acquiring an important British firm. This led to the 'tobacco war'. Thirteen firms combined to hold the British market against the Americans. The Imperial Tobacco Company (Great Britain and Ireland) Ltd proved a very successful combination although it was not able to create a thoroughgoing monopoly, because of the survival of small firms which possessed popular brands of cigarette. The British-American Tobacco Company was established in 1902 by agreement between the American and the British combines to deal with markets outside Great Britain and the United States. It was so organized that the American Tobacco Company acquired two thirds of the stock, the Imperial Tobacco Company one third. Both combines turned over their export factories, their subsidiary companies in foreign countries and their foreign trade generally to the British-American Company. The latter extended its range by purchasing other tobacco manufacturing and marketing concerns in third markets. In this way, the 'tobacco war' led to a genuinely international type of combine.

...companies and agencies which operated simply as selling or distributing concerns (of the American Tobacco Company) were established in various countries. One of the most important of these was the London depot of the American Tobacco Company. In 1898 the sales of this depot amounted to $916,729.93, but as the total expenses of the depot, including cost of goods, were $916,732.07 the enterprise was by no means as satisfactory as might have been desired. From that year the sales of the depot declined in amount, and by 1900, the last full year of its operation, they were only $591,897.36. The cost of goods and the expenditures of the agency had not declined in like proportion, for they amounted to $646,835.99, showing a loss on the year's business of over $50,000. The American Tobacco Company ascribed this unsatisfactory condition of its English business to the duties on leaf and manufactured tobacco going into England, which were so arranged as to give a considerable degree of protection to the domestic manufacturer. In view of this condition the officers and managers of the American Tobacco Company decided that it was necessary to acquire or establish a manufacturing plant or plants in England if their business was to meet with success in that country...

...They (the officials of the American Tobacco Company who went to England in 1901) at once began negotiations for the purchase of Ogden's (Limited), one of the most important tobacco manufacturing concerns in Great Britain. Before the end of September, 1901, they had acquired substantially the whole outstanding stock of the company.... The total cost of the shares acquired was $5,347,888.87....

The purchase of Ogden's (Limited) caused immediate alarm among the British manufacturers of cigarettes and tobaccos. They feared the power of the American Tobacco Company, with its enormous business and resources. The American scarcely had time to show its policy in the management of the Ogden's concern before the other leading manufacturers of tobacco in Great Britain had formed a combination to resist this dangerous rival.

Thirteen of the largest manufacturers in Great Britain combined to form the Imperial Tobacco Company (of Great Britain and Ireland), Limited. This company, which was registered 10 December, 1901, amalgamated the tobacco businesses of the following firms: W. D. & H. O. Wills, Edwards, Ringer & Bigg, and Franklyn, Davey & Co., of Bristol; Lambert & Butler, Hignett's Tobacco Company, and Adkin & Sons, of London; John Player & Sons, Nottingham; Hignett Bros & Co., William Clarke & Son, and Richmond Cavendish Company, of Liverpool, and Stephen Mitchell & Son, F. & J. Smith, and D. & J. MacDonald of Glasgow. Preliminary agreements for the formation of this combination, which had been made on October 3 and 10, 1901, were ratified by the company on February 3, 1902.

.   .   .   .

An agreement was made by the Imperial Tobacco Company early in its career (January, 1902), with Salmon & Gluckstein (Limited), a corporation manufacturing tobacco and also controlling a number of retail stores in England. Under this agreement the existing £450,000 of the ordinary shares in the latter company were to be converted into 10 per cent preference shares, the dividend to be guaranteed by the Imperial Tobacco Company, and £100,000 in ordinary shares were to be created and issued and to be subscribed for by the Imperial Tobacco Company. This step assured the Imperial Tobacco Company the cooperation of the largest English retail house in its campaign against the American interests.

The Imperial Tobacco Company immediately began a campaign of active competition to check and frustrate the plans of the American Tobacco Company for strengthening its foothold in Great Britain. In March, 1902, the Imperial offered large bonuses to customers who would undertake not to sell American goods for a term of years. The American Tobacco Company, through the Ogden's Company, met this by offering to its British customers, for the next four years, its whole net profits on British business, and £200,000 a year besides. The offer was as follows:

Commencing April 2, 1902, we will for the next four years distribute to such of our customers in the United Kingdom as purchase direct from us our entire net profits on the goods sold by us in the United Kingdom. In addition to the above, we will, commencing April 2, 1902, for the next four years, distribute to such of our customers in the United Kingdom as purchase direct from us the sum of £200,000 per year. The distribution of net profits will be made as soon after April 2, 1903, and annually thereafter, as the accounts can be audited, and will be in proportion to the purchases made during the year. The distribution as to the £200,000 per year will be made every three months, the first distribution to take place as soon after July 2, 1902, as accounts can be audited, and will be in proportion to the purchases during the three-months period. To participate in this offer we do not ask you to boycott the goods of any other manufacturer.

This offer had a marked effect in opening the British trade to American competition. As a countermove the Imperial Tobacco Company threatened to invade the American market, and in the summer of 1902 it was reported to be selecting sites for factories in this country [*i.e. America*]. Before any definite steps were taken, however, to carry out this plan, an agreement was arrived at between the two great rival corporations which completely changed their position toward each other.

The agreement between the American Tobacco Company interests and the Imperial Tobacco Company was made on September 27, 1902, about a year after the purchase of Ogden's by the American and about seven months after the complete establishment of the Imperial. The agreement was embodied in two documents. The first related to the trade in the United Kingdom and the United States, providing for the transfer of Ogden's to the Imperial and for division of territory between the Imperial and the American. The second provided for the establishment of a new corporation (the British-American Tobacco Company), to be jointly controlled by the American and the Imperial, which was to do business in countries outside of the United Kingdom and the United States.

94. SHIPPING: THE CONFERENCE SYSTEM

Source: 'Royal Commission on Shipping Rings: Reports, 1909', Cd. 4668, XLVII, 75–76.

What trade associations with their organized price and discount systems were becoming for manufacturing industry, the "conference system" had already become for the owners of deep-sea ships, meaning the liner companies. It was the sharp competition among the owners of liners during the period of falling ocean freights, in the last quarter of the nineteenth century, which produced a new form of combination. Through their regular conferences, the shipping lines interested in particular routes and regions of the world operated systematic and regular rate agreements among themselves and enforced the shippers' loyalty to the members of the ring by granting or withholding deferred rebates as the price of enjoying their services. During the early 1900's, when competition in world markets for manufactured goods was stiff, British exporters complained that this system deprived them of the advantages of competition and low freights and favoured their foreign competitors. A royal commission set up by the Liberal government in 1906 reported in 1909. A majority of the commissioners accepted the argument of the liner companies that the kind of services, with heavy costs attached, which they provided could not be maintained without a degree of monopolistic control. A strong minority disagreed. No action followed. The commissioners here describe how the system grew up under the conditions of maritime competition prevailing in the late nineteenth century.

Growth of Organization in Shipping

In the days of the sailing ship, there was little variety in the methods of transport, and consequently little, if any, difference made in the treatment of different cargoes. The date on which a ship was likely to arrive could not be predicted with any certainty, nor was there any certainty as to the date at which she would sail. She would not in fact usually sail until her cargo spaces were filled. The substitution of steam for sail concurrently with the increase in postal and telegraphic facilities brought with it far-reaching changes in the methods by which merchants conducted their business.

The immediate effect was to render possible the supply of organized services of vessels sailing and arriving at fixed dates, and the advantages which such services conferred upon trade may be measured by the rapidity of the growth of regular lines. But it is not every cargo which requires regular sailings. Commodities of a rough kind exported in large quantities, especially those sent in bulk, are usually despatched in ships chartered for the purpose as occasion arises.

With the development of the steamship, therefore, there arose a marked variety in the methods of ocean transportation. On the one hand, the establishment of services of regular lines enabled the general merchant to ship comparatively small parcels of goods in execution of definite orders from importers abroad, instead of shipping them in large quantities in speculative anticipation of the requirements of the market. On the other hand, the tramp ship, a vessel of comparatively low class and speed, came to be used chiefly for the carriage of goods of a rough character shipped in bulk. The cleavage between these two classes of vessel was a gradual one and has never been absolute. Tramps are often temporarily employed as liners, and liners may also be employed as tramps.

Broadly speaking, the two classes of vessels are different both in their nature and in the sort of work on which they are employed. They differ as to functions. It is the function of the liner to sail as a member of a fleet, or an association of fleets, providing a continuous and organized service on a particular route—a service, that is to say, which is so arranged as to avoid duplication of sailings, and to ensure that the tonnage shall be despatched at regular dates advertised beforehand, and in sufficient quantity to meet the requirements of the trade. The tramp, on the other hand, is a self-contained unit of transport. It is not attached continuously to any given trade route; it does not conduct its operations in concert with others; its sailings are determined by no fixed plan. The function of the tramp, in short, is to fluctuate from one route to another, according to the shifting requirements of the various trades. Its movements are determined by the law of supply and demand; it goes where its voyage will yield the greatest profit; and it undertakes no obligation beyond that involved in each particular venture.

The two classes of vessel differ further as to the cost necessarily entailed and consequently as to the rates charged. Not only is the liner generally a much more costly vessel to build; not only are its working expenses on any particular voyage considerably greater than those of the tramp because of the higher speed required and the greater expense involved in the loading, stowage, and discharge of valuable cargo. It is also to be borne in mind that, in determining the cost of any sailing given by a liner, the expenditure involved in the maintenance throughout the year of a regular and speedy service confined to a particular trade route and usually embracing a large number of ports has to be taken into account. In the case of the tramp this consideration forms no part of the element of cost. But it is important to note that, notwithstanding this distinction between the functions and characters of the two classes of vessel, competition between them still exists. The tramp and the unemployed liner from another route do not compete with the vessels regularly employed on a particular route by offering a continuous service of a similar or comparable kind; but they do compete so far as particular sailings and particular kinds of goods are concerned.

The distinction between the tramp and the liner became very sharply marked about the period immediately prior to and succeeding the opening of the Suez Canal. Moreover, the competition between the regular lines themselves, owing to the obligations which the new demands of trade placed upon them, became so keen that after serious loss they found it necessary to draw together with a view to mitigating and regulating the severity of their competition with one another, and to staving off the opposition of new lines which might be started to challenge them.

The first of these objects, as we have shown, was attained by the establishment of Shipping Conferences or alliances of existing companies agreeing to charge the same rates and to regulate competition with one another by the apportionment of the trade in various ways.

The second object was attained at first by means which had been used in earlier and even in sailing ship days. The Shipping Companies made contracts with the individual merchant firms under which the latter agreed to send all their shipments by the contracting Shipping Companies. These contracts were of various kinds, but in all of them two features were apparent. The shipper who contracted got more favourable terms than the shipper who did not, and the shipper who had many and large consignments to make got better terms than the shipper whose cargoes were few and small.

This system, however, in the new conditions of trade was found to have disadvantages. In a large and general trade where different rates had to be placed on different articles, and where the shippers were many in number, it was a drawback either to have rates fixed by contracts over long periods or to have to enter into a large number of single and separate contracts. A 'tie' was therefore devised which is automatically applicable to all shippers in a given trade and which places all shippers on the same footing. The cardinal principle of this 'tie' known as the system of deferred rebates, is that a shipper who, during a particular period, ceases to confine his shipments exclusively to the Conference Lines, loses his right to the rebate not only in respect of goods shipped during that period but also in respect of goods shipped during the previous period; the aim and object of the system being to deter shippers from making shipments by any vessel outside the Conference.

Such was the origin of the system of Shipping Conferences and deferred rebates. It was first instituted in the trade to Calcutta in the years 1875–7, and in the succeeding 20 years was applied to practically all the chief outward trades from the United Kingdom in which the character of the trade is such as to demand an organized and regular service of high-class steamers. On the other hand it is absent from many of the homeward trades, and in those in which it exists it is restricted in its operation. It is absent also from the North Atlantic and Coasting trades. A careful examination of the peculiar circumstances of these exceptional trades strengthens the conclusion already stated that the presence or absence of the Conference system in a particular trade depends on the presence or absence of the need for an organized service.

95. THE JUDGMENT IN THE MOGUL STEAMSHIP CASE

Source: 'Law Reports, Queens Bench Division', XXIII (1889), 609–10, 614–16, 620.

The early days of the conference system produced a celebrated law case. This is interesting as showing the attitude of common lawyers towards combinations of this kind. The Mogul Steamship Company, a British concern interested in trade to the Far East, brought an action in 1888 against McGregor, Gow and Company, the Peninsular and Oriental Steam Navigation Company, Skinner and Company, the Ocean Steamship Company, William Thompson and Company, Alfred Holt and Company, John Samuel Swire and others, charging that in May 1884 the companies named had formed themselves into an association which had as its primary purpose to obtain the sole control of the carrying trade between China and Europe, excluding the Mediterranean and Black Sea ports. In order to secure this objective, they offered a 5 per cent rebate on freights to all shippers who made use of their vessels only. This agreement among themselves they renewed the following year. The Mogul Steamship Company in May 1885 sent two ships to Hankow to secure cargoes for the homeward voyage independently of the conference. The conference companies thereupon despatched vessels of their own to Hankow to exclude the intruders and, freight rates being deliberately pushed down against them, the ships of the Mogul Steamship line were only able to find cargo at unremunerative rates. The claim of the Mogul Steamship Company was for "damages for a conspiracy to prevent them from carrying on their trade between London and China, and an injunction against the continuance of the alleged wrongful acts".[1] When their plea was dismissed, they sought redress the next year in the Appeal Court (Queen's Bench Division). Coleridge's decision was upheld, although Lord Esher, Master of the Rolls, disagreed with the views of Lord Justices Fry and Bowen.

Our two extracts, taken from the speeches of the judges of the Appeal Court, demonstrate two diametrically opposed views as to what were the limitations which the law in the late 1880's and early 1890's placed upon combination for trade purposes. The sentiments of Lord Esher were, however, of little practical value when it came to the application of the law. In 1891 the case came before the Judical Committee of the Privy Council when all seven Law Lords upheld the decision of Lord Justices Fry and Bowen. See further on this: 'Law Reports, Queen's Bench Division', XXI (1888), 544–54 and 'Law Reports, House of Lords Judicial Committee of the Privy Council' (1892), pp. 25–60.

[1] *Law Reports, Queen's Bench Division*, XXI (1888), 544.

[*Lord Esher, Master of the Rolls:*]

The propositions applicable to the present case which are to be deduced from the above considerations are the following....

eighth, an agreement among two or more traders, who are not and do not intend to be partners, but where each is to carry on his trade according to his own will, except as regards the agreed act, that agreed act being one to be done for the purpose of interfering, i.e. with intent to interfere with the trade of another, is a thing done not in the due course of trade, and is therefore an act wrongful against that other trader, and is also wrongful against the right of the public to have free competition among traders, and is therefore a wrongful act against such trader, and, if it is carried out and injury ensue, is actionable; ninth, such an agreement, being a public wrong, is also of itself an illegal conspiracy, and is indictable.

It follows that in the present case the agreement of 1885 was within the rules (8) and (9) an indictable conspiracy, and that when it was carried out to its immediate and intended effect, which was an injury to the plantiffs' right to a free course of trade, the plaintiffs had a good cause of action against the defendants.

It follows that the acts of the defendants in lowering their freights far beyond a lowering for any purpose of trade—that is to say, so low that if they continued it they themselves could not carry on trade—was not an act done in the exercise of their own free right of trade, but was an act done evidently for the purpose of interfering with, i.e. with intent to interfere with, the plaintiffs' right to a free course of trade, and was therefore a wrongful act as against the plaintiffs' right; and as injury ensued to the plaintiffs, they had also in respect of such act a right of action against the defendants. The plaintiffs, in respect of that act, would have had a right of action if it had been done by one defendant only; they have it still more clearly when that act was done by several defendants combined for that purpose. For these reasons I come to the conclusion that the plaintiffs were entitled to judgment.

[*Lord Justice Bowen:*]

What, then, are the limitations which the law imposes on a trader in the conduct of his business as between himself and other traders? There seem to be no burdens or restrictions in law upon a trader which arise merely from the fact that he is a trader, and which are not equally laid on all other subjects of the Crown. His right to trade freely is a right which the law recognises and encourages, but it is one which places him at no special disadvantage as compared with others. No man, whether trader or not, can, however, justify damaging another in his commercial business by fraud or misrepresentation. Intimidation, obstruction, and molestation are forbidden; so is the intentional procurement of a violation of individual rights, contractual or other, assuming always that there is no just cause for it.... But the defendants have been guilty of none of these acts (i.e. acts of intimidation, obstruction, etc.). They have done nothing more against the plaintiffs than pursue to the bitter end a war of competition waged in the interest of their own trade.... To say that a man is to trade freely, but that he is to stop short at any act which is calculated to harm other tradesmen, and which is designed to attract business to his own shop, would be a strange and impossible counsel of perfection. But we were told that competition ceases to be the lawful exercise of trade, and so to be a lawful excuse for what will harm another, if carried to a length which is not fair or reasonable. The offering of reduced rates by the defendants in the present case is said to have been 'unfair'. This seems to assume that, apart from fraud, intimidation, molestation, or obstruction, of some other personal right in rem or in personam, there is some natural standard of 'fairness' or 'reasonableness' (to be determined by the internal consciousness of judges and juries) beyond which competition ought not in law to go. There seems to be no authority, and I think, with submission, that there is no sufficient reason for such a proposition. It would impose a novel fetter upon trade. The defendants, we are told by the plaintiffs' counsel, might lawfully lower rates provided they did not lower them beyond a 'fair freight', whatever that might mean. But where is it established that there is any such restriction upon commerce? And what is to be the definition of a 'fair freight'? It is said that it ought to be a normal rate of freight, such as is reasonably remunerative to the shipowner. But over what period of time is the average of this reasonable remunerativeness to be calculated? All commercial men with capital are acquainted with the ordinary expedient of sowing one year a crop of apparently unfruitful prices, in order by driving competition away to reap a fuller harvest of profit in the future; and until the present argument at the bar it may be doubted whether shipowners or merchants were ever deemed to be bound by law to conform to some imaginary 'normal' standard of freights or prices, or that the Law Courts had a right to say to them in respect of their competitive tariffs, 'Thus far shalt thou go and no further'. To attempt to limit English competition in this way would probably be as hopeless an endeavour as the experiment of King Canute....

If peaceable and honest combinations of capital for purposes of trade competition are to be struck at, it must, I think, be by legislation, for I do not see that they are under the ban of the common law.... The substance of my view is this, that competition, however severe and egotistical, if unattended by circumstances of dishonesty, intimidation, molestation, or such illegalities as I have above referred to, gives rise to no cause of action at common law. I should myself deem it to be a misfortune if we were to attempt to prescribe to the business world how honest and peaceable trade was to be carried on in a case where no such illegal elements as I have mentioned exist, or were to adopt some standard of judicial 'reasonableness', or of 'normal' prices, or 'fair freights', to which commercial adventurers, otherwise innocent, were bound to conform.

96. A FREE MARKET

Source: G. A. Auden [ed.], 'A Handbook for Birmingham and the Neighbourhood prepared for the 83rd Annual Meeting of the British Association for the Advancement of Science', (1913), pp. 401–3.

It would be a great mistake to underrate the persistence of individualism and free competition of the most complete sort in many industries. The Midland iron and steel industry was not a particularly distinguished branch either of the iron and steel industry or of British industry as a whole. Such as it was, however, and as it is described here, it was thoroughly representative of much manufacture, including many large industries.

THE district cannot boast of large progress, relatively, in the production of steel as has been the case in other parts of the country, but there are several works here, and some of them of more than local importance, such as those carried on by Alfred Hickman, Ltd, the

Earl of Dudley's Round Oak Works, and the Patent Shaft and Axle-tree Co., Ltd. These and others are highly-efficient, well-organized plants, and two of them at any rate are worked on what is known as the continuous process—the operations are carried through from the smelting of the iron ore to the finishing of the angle or joist without allowing the metal to become cold.

Organization

From the point of view of organization, the condition of the industry may perhaps be described without injustice as chaotic. There are, indeed, some fine examples of close 'integration'. In several instances firms own and get their own raw materials (coal and ore, for example), and carry on the manufacturing process to the end, even to the manufacture of steel railway trucks. These, however, are a small minority of the whole. The more common condition is for pig iron or finished iron manufacturers to own nothing but their plant, and to buy all their raw materials in the open market. From another point of view, that of trade associations, organization covers only a small part of the industry. There is an informal association of manufacturers of 'marked bars'. Marked bars are the survival of the original native product of the district. The 'mark' of the five firms who make this class of material has no striking singularity to distinguish it. It does not differ greatly from that of other firms. Every maker puts a mark of some kind on his best bars, often a crown with his initials, but bars other than those made by these five firms are never described as 'marked', even though they may be of specially good quality, approaching, if not equalling that of the marked bar. The marked bar, however, is an excellent product with a reputation based on a long history, and usually commands a price about 30s. in excess of that obtainable for an ordinary unmarked bar. The name 'marked bar' seems to be a quaint survival; and the association of manufacturers is about as great a survival in view of the development attained by modern trade associations. It is based on nothing more stringent than what has been called 'a gentlemen's agreement' to fix a price and adhere to it. The confidence which the firms have in each other, and the limited number of producers, combine to make such a method of price control successful. The only other organized industrial association in the iron trade proper is that of the makers of gas tube strips out of which gas pipes are made. In this case the association takes more the modern form, with assignment of production tonnages, a pool, and penalties. The steel makers are in association with each other, and with the similar combinations of their competitors in other parts of the country. Beyond these instances, there is no other association in the South Staffordshire iron and steel industry, and every manufacturer is a law unto himself.

97. COMBINATION IN INDUSTRY: A BACKWARD LOOK

Source: 'Ministry of Reconstruction: Report of the Committee on Trusts, 1918', Cd. 9236, XIII, 2, 11.

This official committee, one of the many which towards the end of the First World War were looking into the coming problems of peace, had as its terms of reference that it should inquire into any action that might be required by the public interest, in view of the probable extension of trade organizations and combinations. This appears to have been the first official investigation of manufacturing associations and combinations in Great Britain. There had been, of course, in the years before the war, when prices were rising rapidly, many complaints of price-fixing and monopoly, which led to inquiry at the time, chiefly in the field of transport. There was the report upon shipping rings in 1909, an investigation of agreements and amalgamations on the railways in 1911, and an examination of the anti-trust legislation in the Dominions in 1912–13. The new committee was able to go upon the experience of the Ministry of Munitions, which in the course of the war had had dealings with more than ninety trade associations. The committee felt that regular investigation and control, chiefly by the instrument of greater publicity, were necessary. No action followed.

THERE is at the present time in every important branch of industry in the United Kingdom an increasing tendency to the formation of Trade Associations and Combinations, having for their purpose the restriction of competition and the control of prices.

Many of the organizations which have been brought to our notice have been created in the last few years, and by far the greater part of them appear to have come into existence since the end of the nineteenth century.... There has been a great increase in the creation of trade associations during the period of the war....

We are satisfied that Trade Associations and Combines are rapidly increasing in this country, and may within no distant period exercise a paramount control over all important branches of the British trade.

We are satisfied that considerable mistrust with regard to their activities exists in the public mind, and that the effect of such mistrust may be equally hurtful to the political and social stability of the State, whether or not the public mistrust and resentment be in fact well-founded. We consider that it is desirable that means should be provided whereby the fullest information as to the activities of Trade Associations may be made available to the public.... We believe that it will be found necessary ultimately to establish further machinery for promptly and effectively dealing with such abuses as the Tribunal of Investigation may discover.

PART II

WHO GAINED BY CHANGE?

THE WELFARE OF THE PERSON AND
THE SAFETY OF THE STATE

CHAPTER 6

STUDIES IN POVERTY

Every structure of resources carries with it a given distribution of incomes. Most people, unless they belong to the technical and managing classes, care very little, and understandably so, about the structure of the national economy and the changes which go on in it. They do care about what they get in the way of a money-income and how hard they have to work for it. They are also capable of entertaining strong feelings about the distribution of incomes, according as they think wealth well or ill distributed.

So it was in Victorian Britain. A vast development of resources had taken place in the thirty years between the Great Industrial Exhibition of 1851, which marked Britain's industrial coming of age, and the early 1880's. The industrialization of the nation's life came a long step nearer to completion. There could be no going back on this. The immediate economic task of the next generation was set. From them was required a long series of acts and decisions, in the farm and on the estate, at the works, in the shipyard and the colliery, to maintain and develop and expand the industrial system which had been brought into being. These were economic decisions and acts of the strict type, determining the allocation of resources between one possible use and another, according to the opportunities of investment and of sale, of profit, interest and rent, which offered at the time. This process of continuous change in the use of the nation's resources, together with some of the questions of public policy to which it unavoidably gave rise, has formed the subject of the documents in the first part of this book.

But industrial growth on the grand Victorian scale could not take place without raising other issues too and making urgent decisions of a different kind. The mere fact that judgments touching the development of the nation's resources were being made year by year, almost hour by hour, raised inescapably a problem of ends. For whose good were these things being done? Whose welfare was at stake? This was not a question which Palmerston's Britain had been fond of asking. For one thing, the middle years of the century had been a period of abounding economic expansion. As such, they had been singularly free from the fundamental social criticism and controversy which had been common enough in the earlier years of the century, down at least to 1848 and the dying away of the Chartist agitation in the fifties. For another, the political and social arrangements of the country, following the compromise of the 1832 Reform Act, were for many years not such as to encourage public debate on the distribution of wealth. The landed gentry and the aristocracy retained much of their old grip on public affairs. They and the high middle-class had their own reasons for being satisfied with things as they were. The deferential phase of British politics, so perfectly described by Bagehot in his *English Constitution* (1867), was late to pass away. Even Disraeli's Reform Act of 1867 was slow to modify parliamentary life. The moral idealism also of the mid-Victorians was largely satisfied by a religious faith and an ethic of a highly personal character, content with works of charity within the existing order of things.

During the 1870's and the 1880's, these conditions gradually passed away. The pace of industrial growth slackened, the future looked less certain, the sense of a material progress which was as certain as fate diminished. Politically, the country was becoming a democracy. From 1884, every grown man had a vote. The newspaper press, that great potential organ of mass-communication, began to adapt itself to these new conditions. More profoundly, a crisis of faith and morals, from the 1860's onwards, spread down from the educated few to the uneducated many, with the decline of the force of organized Christianity. This had the result of directing much ardent thought and feeling from personal religion to public life. It had important effects upon politics.

These were the general circumstances under which the political element in the political economy of the mid-century, the economic teaching of Mill, Fawcett and Cairnes,[1] became transformed. In the last thirty years of the century a number of new and important questions moved to the forefront of the public consciousness. They turned upon what was coming to be known by 1914 as economic welfare. Economic welfare the economists of a new school defined as that part of the total good of society which depended more or less directly on income; and they were much concerned with the size, the stability and the distribution of incomes. In this concern, they were not so much dealing with matters of which the economists of the classical school had been ignorant, as reflecting, in a highly refined analysis, a changed balance of interests in the public mind.

Much water had flowed tumultuously under many social and political bridges by the time the thinkers of the universities began to expound the doctrines of economic welfare as part of their formal teaching in the years just before the First World War.[2] There were good

---

[1] These three men, the most eminent representatives in their age of the classical economic doctrines, died in 1873, 1884 and 1875 respectively.

[2] A. C. Pigou's *Wealth and Welfare*, published in 1912, represented the new trend in economic thinking. I. M. D. Little, *A Critique of Welfare Economics*, 2nd edition (Oxford University Paperback, 1960), argues that down to the end

practical reasons, close to the working of the economic system itself, why questions of economic welfare, which were only as to one half susceptible of analysis in terms of relatively scarce resources, and as to the other half clearly belonged to ethics and politics, should have become overwhelmingly important at this time. The industrialization of the half century before 1880, but above all the industrial investment of the 1850's and 1860's, had altered the structure of incomes. Equally important, it had begun the radical breaking down of conventional income expectations. Above all, it had raised the value of labour throughout Western countries in a way which no earlier generation could have believed possible. No country felt the impact of these changes more than Great Britain, the country farthest advanced on the road to full industrialization. It was not really surprising, although it surprised many people at the time very much, that a period of rapid economic advance in the middle of the century should have been followed, after 1880, by an era of violent controversy about incomes and their distribution. A conflict of wills was inevitable. This arose not only out of economic but also political and intellectual circumstances.

The aspirations of the individual, which lay at the bottom of the ferment, did not always express themselves in an individualistic way. Victorian Englishmen, living in a society strikingly differentiated according to function and class and sharply divided by gradations of income and status, were well aware of their position on the ladder. Social group tended to compare itself with social group and with the accepted standards of that group. This was true at all levels of society. Anthony Trollope's novel *The Way We Live Now*, published in 1875, just after the foreign investment boom and its scandals, expressed sharply enough what the old-established members of upper-class society thought of some of the newcomers into their ranks and the character of their social aspirations. But the transforming effect of massive industrialization upon incomes and through incomes upon human relations, was felt by individuals and groups, classes and sexes, throughout the nation, and to an astonishing degree. Nothing remained quite the same. The change was in no direction more marked or more charged with significance for the future than in the new attitude towards what the politicians of the early nineteenth century had called pauperism and what some people now were coming to speak of as the problem of poverty.

The altering use of words was itself remarkable. The men of the

of the nineteenth century economists talked about 'wealth' or if they were good Utilitarians, 'happiness'. He dates the introduction of 'welfare' language into formal economics from Pigou. There is something in this. But it would be a mistake to suppose that economists of an earlier generation than Pigou's, Marshall for instance, were not concerned with welfare because they did not use the word.

generation which passed the 1832 Reform Act had gone on to attack, in the Poor Law of 1834, pauperism. By this, they meant public assistance to the lowest incomes. They were firmly convinced that the mass of people receiving those incomes was so great as to threaten the standards of the nation as a whole. Whether the fears of 'pauperism' expressed at that time were altogether well founded or sincere is open to debate. About the depth of the fears then and for years afterwards there can be no doubt. It afforded the basis for political action. What is notable about the late Victorians is that they had lost this fear. A new generation had grown up among new conditions and had done their own thinking. For the old fear and the cruel, repressive attitude to which this gave rise, they had substituted a new belief. This was, that the kind of deep, hopeless poverty which created 'pauperism' and the need of public relief was not only an evil in itself, which most men had always been willing to grant, but a remediable evil. They suspected that it was no longer necessary in the state of society which they found themselves in or which they thought they were approaching. This astonishing reversal of attitudes, expressed by rational and cautious men, as well as by those on whose lips liberties in statement would have been natural, testifies to the magnitude of the economic changes since 1834, and to the revolution of expectations which they brought with them.[1]

The massive creation of work during the long mid-century boom, providing new jobs for new population and sweeping away much of the under-employment of the past, had bred a new optimism. This optimism persisted beyond the end of the great economic expansion, in 1873, and entered into the politics of the democratic age. But it encountered as time went on a new scepticism and a new despair. Too many of the optimists had forgotten or they had never fully faced the fact that the increase of population had been almost as massive as the growth of work and incomes. When the years of trade depression multiplied in the 1870's and early 1880's, many people pointed out very properly and forcibly that, let economic progress be what it may, their own situation was desperate. Others believed, on general grounds, and they went on publicly to state, that the industrial system as they knew it could only make the rich richer and the poor poorer.

---

[1] The evidence of Alfred Marshall the economist before the royal commission on the Poor Laws in 1893 is highly instructive. Marshall was cautious by nature and his own proposals for Poor Law reform were modest. But he emphasized again and again the extent of the change which had taken place since 1834. He refers to the possibility of poverty in the long run 'drying up' or 'shrivelling away'. Whatever he meant by these expressions and he probably intended no more than that the worst forms of poverty might disappear, they are remarkable. *Official Papers of Alfred Marshall* (1926), pp. 199, and especially 244-5.

Out of this clash of fundamental assertions and the attempt of anxious men to resolve it, there arose in the 1880's an economic and administrative innovation of great importance. This was the social survey, nowadays carried out by governments but in the late Victorian and Edwardian age the work of wealthy amateurs, inspired by two eminently Victorian things, science and philanthropy. The social survey became, inevitably under Victorian conditions, a study of the incomes of the largest social group in the country, the urban working class. Charles Booth's great survey of working-class incomes and occupations in London led the way from 1889 onwards. It formed the model for a whole family of such investigations before the First World War, covering town after town but also taking interesting glances at the agricultural workers. Thanks to these laborious inquiries, the distribution of incomes in Britain in these years is known in a sense that we do not know the division of the national product at any previous period in history.

These were empirical investigations, intended to discover the facts. They disclosed a mass of low incomes, far greater than the investigators had expected and a depth of poverty affecting about one third of the wage-earning classes. From this it was highly improbable that most of those who were born to it could ever escape, whatever they did.

The presence of a great volume of human destitution was one of the essential differences between Victorian society and our own. As it was explored and measured, it raised in men's minds questions of interpretation which went far beyond the simple collection of data. What was the economic meaning of the poverty which was being surveyed? If so many inadequate incomes, so much bitter destitution, still survived after so much increase of incomes over so many years, what was the implication of that? How far could groups and individuals trust to their bargaining power to wring out from the market an income equal to their demands on life or adequate for survival? How far would it be wise for local authorities or the State to supplement the incomes which people could earn for themselves with other forms of income or with services, in the way of education, medical care, pensions and so forth? Where was the financial basis for such a collective effort to be found? Even if it were granted that it would be right in principle for the State to raise and spend vast sums in the interests of its poorer citizens, how could that be reconciled with expenditure on the other form of welfare, which the Victorian or Edwardian mind accepted as naturally as it found the idea of social security strange, national defence? For this was the era of the armed peace and the quarrel with Germany. These were the questions which escaped from the studies of the social investigators, whether they wished it or not, into the streets, to mingle with the politics of an entire generation.

FURTHER READING

The late Victorians were not the first to take an interest in poverty and destitution, as distinct from the administration of the Poor Law, although they were the first to make these matters the object of scientific inquiry. Henry Mayhew (1812–87), a journalist and a founder of *Punch*, published in 1851 three volumes on *London Labour and the London Poor*, which made a great impression at the time and were reissued in 1861. They drew a vivid picture of the squalor of Charles Dickens's London. Good statisticians had also begun to make broad estimates of the national income and its distribution among the classes. R. Dudley Baxter's *National Income: the United Kingdom* (1868) is an example. He compared the national income in his day to the Peak of Teneriffe, 12,000 feet high in the Atlantic—'with its long low base of labouring population, with its uplands of the middle classes, and with the towering peaks and summits of those with princely incomes' (p. 61).

The work of men such as Charles Booth and of Arthur Bowley, the statistician, was to continue between 1880 and 1914 the line of these inquiries, with greater resources and in a more scientific spirit. For a late but good example of a social survey, see A. L. Bowley and A. R. Burnett-Hurst, *Livelihood and Poverty* (1915), containing studies of Reading, Warrington, Northampton and Stanley, in county Durham, made in 1912–13. This demonstrated that in these towns, representative of many others, a most serious degree of poverty existed and that the chief cause of it was the lowness of the wages of unskilled labour. The causes were, therefore, permanent, not temporary. They could not be expected soon to disappear.

There is a bibliography of Bowley's work in his *Wages and Income in the United Kingdom since 1860* (1937). This summarized many of his findings and those of others, including the official figures which began to pour out from the Board of Trade before 1914 on wages and earnings and cost of living. His *Division of the Product of Industry, an Analysis of National Income before the War*, published in 1919, has been republished in Bowley and Stamp, *Three Studies on the National Income* (1938). Sir Josiah Stamp's *British Incomes and Property* (1916) also refers mainly to the situation before 1914.

98. GIFFEN ON SOCIAL INCOME IN MID-VICTORIAN BRITAIN

Source: Robert Giffen, 'Essays in Finance: Second Series' (2nd ed. 1887), pp. 468–73.

The extract is from a paper read to the Royal Statistical Society, 19 January 1886. Sir Robert Giffen (1837–1910), who began life as a journalist, became head of the statistical department of the Board of Trade in 1876. He was for many years an active man in public life and a vigorous writer on economic questions. This statement of the progress of incomes in the previous fifty years was part of the optimistic national stocktaking of the first Jubilee of Queen Victoria in 1887.

THE contentions of my paper two years ago were that the working classes of the United Kingdom had enjoyed a great improvement in their money wages in the last fifty years, an improvement roughly estimated at 50 to 100 per cent; that the hours of labour had been shortened in the same period 20 per cent; that along with this improvement there had been a general fall, or at any rate no increase, in the prices of the principal articles of general consumption, with the exception of rent and meat, where the increase still left to the labourer a large margin for increased miscellaneous expenditure; that meat in particular was not an article of general consumption by the masses of the community fifty years ago as it has since become; that the condition of the masses had in fact improved vastly, as was shown by the diminished rate of mortality, the increased consumption per head of tea, sugar, and the like articles, the extension of popular education, the diminution of crime and pauperism, and the increase of savings bank deposits, as well as of other forms of saving among the masses; and that, finally, neither the amount of capital nor the return upon it, and especially not the return upon capital, had increased so much as the income of the workers of the country from their work.

In the present paper these conclusions have been additionally supported.

1. It has been shown, in opposition to various objections to the former paper, that the estimate of 50 to 100 per cent as the average improvement of the money wages of the working classes in fifty years, is not only not excessive but under the mark. Reasons have been urged for attaching special importance, in comparisons of money wages fifty years ago and at the present time, to the instances of maximum increase, where a given employment at a given place is compared with the same employment at an earlier period. It has farther been pointed out, on a broad survey of the facts, that the composition of the people of the United Kingdom is entirely changed from what it was fifty years ago; that whereas fifty years ago one-third of the working masses were

Irish peasants earning a doubtful 4*s*. a week on the average, and the agricultural population of Great Britain constituted another third of the total, this class likewise earning much smaller incomes than the third class, consisting of the non-agricultural workers of Great Britain, yet now the Irish labourers are less than one-eighth of the total, the British agricultural labourers are also one-eighth only, and the remaining three-fourths are artisans, and other non-agricultural workers in Great Britain, who constituted fifty years ago only about a third of the whole population. Even if the wages of the different classes had not increased, this change in the composition of the mass would itself imply an average improvement. An improvement of 50 per cent in the unit of each class would imply of itself, allowing for the change in the relative numbers of the classes, an average improvement of nearly 100 per cent.

2. The probability of a great average improvement is farther shown by the magnitude of the improvement in the case of the units of the worst paid labour, where there has been a diminution of numbers. In Ireland the improvement in the wages or earnings of small farmers and labourers is at least 100 per cent, the doubtful average 4*s*. of fifty years ago having been converted into a much less doubtful 8*s*., or its equivalent, at the present time. In Scotland and Wales the average improvement in agricultural labour has equally been about 100 per cent, from 9*s*. in the former case to 18*s*., and from 7*s*. 6*d*. in the latter case to 15*s*. In England the changes are not quite so extreme, but from 8*s*. to 13*s*., and from 10*s*. to 16*s*. are not uncommon figures, fully justifying Sir James Caird's conclusion, which I quoted in my former paper, as to there having been an improvement of 60 per cent.

3. The worst paid labour in Great Britain of a non-agricultural kind has equally undergone improvement. In the Metropolis, and the leading manufacturing towns, the rise ranges from 15*s*. to 25*s*., or about 70 per cent, but in other parts of the country, as in Glasgow, there are cases of an advance of 100 per cent, the improvement in wages generally appearing to be greater in places like Glasgow than in the leading towns of England.

4. There has also been a great increase in the number of income-tax assessments, implying an improvement of the artisan and other classes just below the income-tax limit.

5. There has been a simultaneous improvement in France, Germany, and other countries. The improvement in the United Kingdom is not an isolated fact.

6. There is accordingly nothing to be astonished at in an average improvement of the money wages of 'working classes' in the last fifty years amounting to 100 per cent. When the facts are considered, such an improvement is, in reality, antecedently probable.

7. The condition of the masses fifty years ago was in truth deplorable, as is shown by numerous extracts from the writings of Thomas Carlyle, Lord Beaconsfield, Mrs Gaskell, and Mr Thornton, and by references to numerous Blue-books. Even the manufacturing operatives of England, the most advanced class of all, were liable to frequent and great privations, through the complete suspension of work, and had at times to live on very 'short commons'.

8. With regard to the consumption of meat by the agricultural classes of England, as to which the statements made in my former paper were specially challenged, a farther inquiry has shown that the ground of the challenge was singularly erroneous. A table in Mr Porter's 'Progress of the Nation', which was quoted by an objector to prove that 50 per cent of the agricultural classes of England had meat as a regular portion of their diet half a century ago, is found to show, when the data are referred to, that much fewer than 50 per cent had 'bacon' as an *occasional* portion of their diet; and that there is hardly once mention of any other meat as a portion of the agricultural labourer's diet among the statements from which the table is compiled.

9. Finally it is shown, on a comparison of incomes in the aggregate, that while the total income of the country fifty years ago was about 500 millions only, of which two-fifths were [*sic*] derived from agriculture, the present income, on the authority of Mr Dudley Baxter and Mr Leone Levi, may be placed at about 1270 millions, of which only one-sixth is from agriculture. At the same time the agricultural labourer is better off, because, while his numbers have diminished, the net income from agriculture, and his share of that income, have both increased. Farther, the working masses of Great Britain have more than doubled their number in the interval, simultaneously with a vast diminution in Ireland, whose aggregate income remains much the same, though with a diminished number to share it. Hence the

increase of income in the fifty years has been mainly among the higher-paid classes, and the final result is that whereas fifty years ago the working masses of the United Kingdom, amounting to 9 millions, earned in all about 171 millions, or £19 per head, the working masses, now amounting to over 13 millions, earn about 550 millions, or nearly £42 per head, an increase of much more than 100 per cent.

10. When the increase of earnings from labour and capital is compared, it is found that the increase from capital is from 190 to 400 millions only, or about 100 per cent; the increase from the 'working' of the upper and middle classes is from 154 to 320 millions, or about 100 per cent; and the increase of the income of the manual labour classes is from 171 to 550 millions, or over 200 per cent. In amount the increase due to capital is about 210 millions; to labour of the upper and middle classes, 166 millions; and to labour of the manual-labour classes, 379 millions, a total increase of 755 millions.

The general conclusion from all the facts is, that what has happened to the working classes in the last fifty years is not so much what may properly be called an improvement, as a revolution of the most remarkable description. The new possibilities implied in changes which in fifty years have substituted for millions of people in the United Kingdom who were constantly on the brink of starvation, and who suffered untold privations, new millions of artisans and fairly well-paid labourers, ought indeed to excite the hopes of philanthropists and public men. From being a dependent class without future and hope, the masses of working men have in fact got into a position from which they may effectually advance to almost any degree of civilisation. Every agency, political and other, should be made use of by themselves and others to promote and extend the improvement. But the working men have the game in their own hands. Education and thrift, which they can achieve for themselves, will, if necessary, do all that remains to be done.

99. CHARLES BOOTH ON THE POVERTY OF LONDON

Source: Charles Booth, 'Labour and Life of the People' (3rd ed. 1891), I, East London. 6, 7, 26–7, 33, 37–8, 39, 42–3, 44, 55–6; 'Life and Labour of the People in London', 2nd Series: 'Industry' v (1903), pp. 327–8.

Studies in Poverty

Charles Booth, Liverpool merchant and shipowner (see above no. 75) was born in 1840; he died in 1916. He married Mary Macaulay, a niece of the Whig historian. Booth's interest in social questions seems to have been awakened in 1865, when he helped fight an election for the Liberals in one of the poorest parts of Liverpool. Rich and intellectually able, he became aware of a moral and personal dilemma in the division of rich and poor and as a Victorian agnostic, passionately interested in science, determined to resolve it by a scientific inquiry into the facts of poverty. The unemployment and the social unrest of 1885–6 made him embark upon a survey of incomes and occupations in London, where he was then living. Joseph Chamberlain seems to have suggested that he should ask the new School Board Visitors to assist him in house-to-house visiting. Booth's survey, which was carried out while he was still active and successful in business and ran ultimately into seventeen volumes, was a sociological inquiry of a broad kind. Isolated extracts do not do justice to its comprehensive character and its grasp of detail. His achievement was to show from a mass of data the existing relationships between social structure, social welfare and individual behaviour. But what most impressed contemporaries was his definition and measurement of poverty in what was then known as the largest and richest city in the world. Defining poverty as the inability to earn enough to maintain physical working efficiency, he was able to demonstrate that 30 per cent of London's population fell below this extremely low standard in their daily life. 'The Times' is said to have described 'Labour and Life' as "the grimmest book of our generation". Its effect on upper and middle class opinion was certainly profound. Booth's attitude towards social politics was that of a cautious reformer—he became an advocate of old-age pensions—but in economic affairs he remained an individualist. For a personal sketch by one who knew him well and worked with him on the survey, Beatrice Webb, 'My Apprenticeship' (1926). There is a discussion of his work in T. S. and M. B. Simey, 'Charles Booth Social Scientist' (1960).

A

THERE is struggling poverty, there is destitution, there is hunger, drunkenness, brutality, and crime; no one doubts that it is so. My object has been to attempt to show the numerical relation which poverty, misery, and depravity bear to regular earnings and comparative comfort, and to describe the general conditions under which each class lives.

Who Gained by Change?

B

The materials gathered together in this volume seem at first sight hardly sufficient for wide generalization or definite conclusions. But if what is shown to exist here may be taken as the most serious thing of the kind with us—if this district contains, as is supposed, the most destitute population in England—we may assume that to state the problem here is to state it everywhere, and to solve it here would be to solve it everywhere.

C

The special difficulty of making an accurate picture of so shifting a scene as the low-class streets in East London present is very evident, and may easily be exaggerated. As in photographing a crowd, the details of the picture change continually, but the general effect is much the same, whatever moment is chosen. I have attempted to produce an instantaneous picture, fixing the facts on my negative as they appear at a given moment, and the imagination of my readers must add the movement, the constant changes, the whirl and turmoil of life. In many districts the people are always on the move; they shift from one part of it to another like 'fish in a river'. The School Board visitors follow them as best they may, and the transfers from one visitor's book to another's are very numerous.[1] On the whole, however, the people usually do not go far, and often cling from generation to generation to one vicinity, almost as if the set of streets which lie there were an isolated country village.

D

The 8 classes into which I have divided these people are:

A. The lowest class of occasional labourers, loafers, and semi-criminals.
B. Casual earnings—'very poor'.
C. Intermittent earnings ⎱ together the 'poor'.
D. Small regular earnings ⎰
E. Regular standard earnings—above the line of poverty.
F. Higher class labour.
G. Lower middle class.
H. Upper middle class.

[1] A return prepared by one of the School Board visitors, who has a fairly representative district in Bethnal Green, shows that of 1204 families (with 2720 children) on his books, 530 (with 1450 children) removed in a single year.

The divisions indicated here by 'poor' and 'very poor' are necessarily arbitrary. By the word 'poor' I mean to describe those who have a sufficiently regular though bare income, such as 18s. to 21s. per week for a moderate family, and by 'very poor' those who from any cause fall much below this standard. The 'poor' are those whose means may be sufficient, but are barely sufficient, for decent independent life; the 'very poor' those whose means are insufficient for this according to the usual standard of life in this country. My 'poor' may be described as living under a struggle to obtain the necessaries of life and make both ends meet; while the 'very poor' live in a state of chronic want. It may be their own fault that this is so; that is another question; my first business is simply with the numbers who, from whatever cause, do live under conditions of poverty or destitution.

E

Class A—The lowest class, which consists of some occasional labourers, street-sellers, loafers, criminals and semi-criminals, I put at 11,000, or 1¼ per cent of the population, but this is no more than a very rough estimate, as these people are beyond enumeration, and only a small proportion of them are on the School Board visitors' books. If I had been content to build up the total of this class from those of them who are parents of children at school in the same proportions as has been done with the other classes, the number indicated would not have greatly exceeded 3000, but there is little regular family life among them, and the numbers given in my tables are obtained by adding in an estimated number from the inmates of common lodging houses, and from the lowest class of streets. With these ought to be counted the homeless outcasts who on any given night take shelter where they can, and so may be supposed to be in part outside of any census. Those I have attempted to count consist mostly of casual labourers of low character, and their families, together with those in a similar way of life who pick up a living without labour of any kind. Their life is the life of savages, with vicissitudes of extreme hardship and occasional excess. Their food is of the coarsest description, and their only luxury is drink. It is not easy to say how they live; the living is picked up, and what is got is frequently shared; when they cannot find 3d. for their night's lodging, unless favourably known to the deputy, they are turned out at night into the street, to return to the common kitchen in the morning. From these come the battered figures who slouch through the streets, and play the beggar or the bully, or help to foul the record of the unemployed; these are the worst class of corner men who hang round the doors of public-houses, the young men who spring forward on any chance to earn a copper, the ready materials for disorder when occasion serves. They render no useful service, they create no wealth: more often they destroy it.

F

Class B—Casual earnings—very poor—add up almost exactly to 100,000, or 11¼ per cent of the whole population.

G

In East London the largest field for casual labour is at the Docks; indeed, there is no other important field, for although a large number of men, in the aggregate, look out for work from day to day at the wharves and canals, or seek employment as porters in connection with the markets, there seems to be more regularity about the work, and perhaps less competition, or less chance of competition, between outsiders and those who, being always on the spot, are personally known to the employers and their foremen. Dock Labour is treated in a separate chapter. The number of those who are casually employed at the Docks does not seem large compared to the very great public concern which has been aroused, but as a test of the condition of other classes, the ebb and flow of this little sea is really important; it provides a test of the condition of trade generally, as well as of certain trades in particular—a sort of 'distress meter'—and connects itself very naturally with the question of the unemployed.

The labourers of class B do not, on the average, get as much as three days' work a week, but it is doubtful if many of them could or would work full time for long together if they had the opportunity. From whatever section Class B is drawn, except the sections of poor women, there will be found many of them who from shiftlessness, helplessness, idleness, or drink, are inevitably poor. The ideal of such persons is to work when they like and play when they like; these it is who are rightly called the 'leisure class' amongst the poor—leisure bounded very closely by the pressure of want, but habitual to the extent of second nature. They cannot stand the regularity and dullness of civilized existence, and find the excitement they need in the life of the streets, or at home as spectators of or participators in some highly coloured domestic scene. There is drunkenness amongst them, especially amongst the women; but drink is not their special luxury, as with the lowest class, nor is it their passion, as with a portion of those with higher wages and irregular but severe work. The earnings of the men vary with the state of trade, and drop to a few shillings a week or nothing at all in bad times; they are never high, nor does this class make the hauls which come at times in the more hazardous lives of the class below them; when, for instance, a sensational newspaper sells by thousands in the streets for 2*d*. to 6*d*. a copy.

H

Class C—Intermittent earnings—numbering nearly 75,000, or about 8 per cent of the population, are more than any others the victims of competition, and on them falls with particular severity the weight of recurrent depressions of trade.

I

The distinction we have drawn between Classes *C* and *D*, rests on the question of regularity or irregularity of earnings, and so carries with it some difference in standard of life. It would not be actually impossible for the family of a man who earned on the year's average 21*s*. a week, to live regularly at that rate, although he might make 35*s*. in some weeks and not more than 7*s*. in others. But such self-control is not to be expected, and consequently as a rule there is a great difference between the ways of life in Class *C*, where the work, though fairly well paid, is irregular and uncertain, and the habits of Class *D*, where the wages, though not high, are the same or nearly the same, week by week, all the year round.

In Class *D* there is never the consciousness of spare cash; the effect of any unwonted expenditure is felt at once in short commons at the week end. The result is that extravagances are avoided and the wife spends the regular sum she receives in much the same manner week after week. A good deal of bread is eaten and tea drunk, especially by the women and children, but the meals have a more attractive character than with Class *B*. Bacon, eggs, and fish appear regularly in the budgets. A piece of meat cooked on Sunday serves also for dinner on Monday and Tuesday, and puddings, rarely seen in Class *B*, are in Class *D* a regular institution, not every day, but sometimes in the week. On the whole these people have enough, and very seldom too much, to eat; and healthy though rather restricted lives are led. The clothes worn are sometimes second-hand, but if not new when bought they have at least been made to look new. More generally, however, these people buy new things of common though often sterling quality at cheap shops, and both men and women look creditably dressed. It is on the children that the passion for finery spends itself. In this class children play a great part, being at once the plague and pride of their parents' lives. But whether plague or pride, their influence in dragging families into poverty is seldom thought of at all. . . .

J

Thus it will be seen that Whitechapel is the dwelling place of the Jews—tailors, bootmakers and tobacco workers—and the centre of trading both small and large; Stepney and St George's the district of ordinary labour; Shoreditch and Bethnal Green of the artisan; in Poplar sub-officials reach their maximum proportion, while Mile End with a little of everything, very closely represents the average of the whole district; and finally Hackney stands apart with its well-to-do suburban population.

Each district has its character—its peculiar flavour. One seems to be conscious of it in the streets. It may be in the faces of the people, or in what they carry—perhaps a reflection is thrown in this way from the prevailing trades—or it may lie in the sounds one hears, or in the character of the buildings.

Of all the districts of that 'inner ring' which surrounds the City, St George's-in-the-East is the most desolate. The other districts have each some charm or other—a brightness not extinguished by, and even appertaining to, poverty and toil, to vice, and even to crime—a clash of contest, man against man, and men against fate—the absorbing interest of a battle-field—a rush of human life as fascinating to watch as the current of a river to which life is so often likened. But there is nothing of this in St George's which appears to stagnate with a squalor peculiar to itself.

100. THE WARWICKSHIRE LABOURER IN THE 1890'S

Source: Joseph Ashby and Bolton King, " Statistics of Some Midland Villages", 'Economic Journal', III (1893), 4–5, 8, 19–20, 193, 195–6.

Joseph Ashby, a labourer, later small farmer of Tysoe, in Warwickshire, and Bolton King, a landowner in the same part of the world (also a well-known historian of Italian unity) collaborated in the early 1890's in a social survey of some 56 villages in that county. This was a mainly agricultural district, going down to grass as wheat prices fell, with an extent of 127,697 acres and 27,186 inhabitants. Great towns—Birmingham, Coventry—were not far off. The authors were careful to say that they did not wish to generalize from the district to rural England or even the West Midlands. For Ashby, see Miss M. K. Ashby, 'Joseph Ashby of Tysoe 1859–1919' (Cambridge, 1961).

IT is difficult to speak with any certainty as to the rate of agricultural wages during the middle part of the century: they rose no doubt considerably after the passing of the new Poor Law Act, but there does not appear to have been any material change in the nominal wage between 1840 and 1870. In 1872 the Agricultural Labourers' Union raised wages to a tolerably uniform level of 15s.... The following tables gives the highest, lowest, and average wage at certain dates:

	Highest wage		Lowest wage		Average wage
	s.	*d.*	*s.*	*d.*	*s. d.*
1870	13	0	9	0	10·96
1873	16	0	12	6	14·98
1883	15	0	10	0	13·70
1888	15	0	10	0	13·10
1892	15	0	9	6	13·09

It need hardly be pointed out that, owing to the fall of prices, the above figures imply a rise in real wages at all events since 1883....

The hours of labour (exclusive of meal times) vary in summer from

8½ to 10½ hours, and average almost exactly 9½ hours. In winter the hours of work are necessarily limited by daylight, and average about 8½ hours. Great variations in the hours of labour occur in neighbouring villages. To a certain extent they vary with the rates of wages, and the reduction of wages since 1886 has led to a wide movement for shorter hours. The quantity of allotment land does not appear to affect the hours of work. There is no Saturday half holiday for agricultural labourers. In hay time it is generally the custom to pay either for overtime or at an increased rate of weekly wages. In harvest, wages, either paid by the piece or day, are increased from 40 per cent to 120 per cent....

The local variations in the rate of wages are often very remarkable. In one village the rate of wages has been throughout, from 1872 at least, 2s. below the rate in the surrounding villages. It is not at all uncommon to find a difference of 1s. 6d. to 2s. in adjacent villages. Two villages 25 miles distant, in both of which the demand and supply of labour seem to be about the same, show a difference of 4s. to 5s. in the weekly wage. Often different rates obtain in the same parish, in one case the variation amounting to 3s. On one farm the rate of wage has for 10 years been 3s. in excess of those of the neighbourhood without having any effect on the wage paid on adjacent farms...

...No doubt custom too is responsible largely for the small, if any, difference made in the wages of skilled and unskilled labourers. Skilled labourers, who can thatch and hedge and ditch and mend machinery, rarely get higher wages, though perhaps more regular employment. This want of distinction is strongly resented by the better labourers, and no doubt leads to a deterioration in agricultural skill.

There has been now for the past 10 or 20 years practically no agricultural work done by women, except to a slight extent in hay time and on allotments in harvest time. It is difficult to over-estimate the effect of this change on the conditions of home life and the welfare of the children. Gleaning by women and children is still prevalent, but tends to decrease....

The average income of a labourer's family, assuming that the man is in regular work (losing 3½ weeks from bad weather, work on allotments, and holidays), and that there is no other breadwinner, is as follows:

		£	s.	d.
40½ weeks' labour at 13s. 1½d.		26	11	6¾
4 " " " 16s.		3	4	0
4 " " " 24s.		4	16	0
Profit on allotment, garden, pigs		7	0	0
Charities, gleanings, etc.			18	0
Equals 16s. 4d. per week		42	9	6¾

The following is the yearly expenditure of a labourer with a wife and 4 young children:

	£	s.	d.
Rent (landlord pays rates, etc.)	3	18	0
Coal	2	12	0
Faggots		12	0
Bread and flour	7	16	0
Bacon	6	12	0
Light		9	0
Sugar	1	0	0
Ditto for preserving and fruit		15	0
Rice and tapioca		16	0
Tea	1	4	0
Butter	1	10	0
Lard and suet	1	6	0
Washing materials	1	6	0
Cheese	1	5	0
Blacking and blacklead		2	6
Salt, pepper, etc.		4	6
Vinegar for pickling		3	6
Sock benefit club	1	6	0
Clothing Club		13	0
Writing materials and stamps		13	0
Boots (mending not included)	2	5	0
	36	8	6

Assuming that this represents, as it approximately does, the normal expenditure of a total-abstaining labourer's family without grown-up children, it leaves £6.1.0d. to cover most of the clothing except boots, bed linen, sickness of mother and children, repairs to furniture and tools and utensils, butcher's meat, milk, weekly newspaper, or any luxury however modest. It is obvious that there is no margin left for savings for old age or want of work.

. . . .

Who Gained by Change?

It is doubtful whether there has been much improvement in the cottages of the district during the last twenty years. Certainly many of the worst sanitary abuses have been remedied, though much yet remains to be done, in the districts of some rural authorities much more than in those of others. The water-supply is now generally good, though in seven villages or hamlets it appears to be bad, and in four others indifferent or deficient in quantity. In many places the worst cottages are uninhabited....

The stationary numbers of the population in this district since 1841 show that migration must have been going on to a large extent for the last half century; a decreasing population is first noticeable in the districts touched by the trunk lines constructed about 1840; it began later in the more secluded districts. The depopulation has been increased, but not very greatly, during the last twenty years....Our enquiries show that in eight villages, where the population was almost stationary between 1881 and 1891, there is little or no migration now. There has been little emigration in the last ten years and practically none in the last six....

The direction of migration is largely a matter of custom. From the greater part of the district the stream sets mainly northwards to Birmingham and its neighbourhood; from another group of villages it is chiefly towards Coventry; from another to different railway works on the North-Western main line; from another to Burton-on-Trent.... A certain number go into the Metropolitan Police Force, but except for these there is practically no migration to London.

101. THE DIET OF THE WARWICKSHIRE LABOURER

Source: M. K. Ashby, 'Joseph Ashby of Tysoe' (Cambridge, 1961), pp. 36–7.

THE meagre diet of some years back [*i.e. a little before the early 1870's*] was mentioned often. Men used to start the day on a breakfast of bread soaked in hot water, salted and peppered. Bread and onions had been eaten in the fields at dinner-time. A man's wage would not buy bread for a family, let alone any meat....Someone told of an occasion when a family of parents and nine children had shared a single bloater at Sunday dinner. Cabbage had been a great standby.

The young children, they said, had lived on cabbage and lard. 'My old 'ooman', said one of them, 'says cabbage killed many a babby, but kept the next biggest alive'. Now in the seventies the men brought a bit of cheese as well as an onion. When they ate at home they might have suet pudding with scraps of bacon rolled in it and mushrooms, too, once or twice a year, and then it was the richest of dishes. Usually this talk was cheerful; times were not so bad as they had been, but sometimes a darker spirit ruled.

102. INCOMES IN A PROVINCIAL CITY: YORK

Source: B. Seebohm Rowntree, 'Poverty a Study of Town Life' (3rd ed., 1902), pp. viii–ix, 27–8, 32, 45–7, 132–4, 136–8, 300–1.

Seebohm Rowntree (1871–1954) was a York chocolate and cocoa manufacturer and a Quaker. He was led by a visit to the slums of New-castle-on-Tyne in 1895 and by reading Charles Booth to ask himself the question whether Booth's findings about the extent of poverty in London were exceptional or could be paralleled in other towns. He spent two years on a thoroughly organised inquiry into family incomes and expenditure in his native city of York. His results confirmed that primary poverty, i.e. want of elementary necessities of life existed among its population on a scale comparable with that revealed in London by Booth. Rowntree's inquiry became the model for many others by private investigators between 1901, when it was published, and 1914. He was one of the first to point out the significance of the cycle of poverty in the life of individuals, want being most sharply experienced on low incomes in childhood when the family was growing, after marriage when the children came and again in old age. Rowntree repeated his inquiry in the same city a generation later; see 'Poverty and Progress 1941'. By that time the "problem of problems" of Victorian and Edwardian society, the presence of primary poverty on a large scale, was in decline. Other aspects of a changing urban and industrial society were coming into view. Rowntree was an active industrialist and Liberal politician. For his life, Asa Briggs, 'Seebohm Rowntree' (1961).

A

HAVING satisfied myself that the conditions of life obtaining in my native city of York were not exceptional, and that they might be taken as fairly representative of the conditions existing in many, if not most, of our provincial towns, I decided to undertake a detailed investigation into the social and economic conditions of the wage-earning classes in that city.

Amongst other questions upon which I desired to obtain information were the following: What was the true measure of the poverty in the city, both in extent and depth? How much of it was due to insufficiency of income and how much to improvidence? How many families were sunk in a poverty so acute that their members suffered from a chronic insufficiency of food and clothing? If physical deterioration combined with a high death-rate ensued, was it possible to estimate such results with approximate accuracy?

It soon became evident that if these and groups of allied questions were to be answered with any fulness and accuracy, nothing short of a house-to-house inquiry extending to the whole of the working-class population of the city would suffice. I decided therefore to undertake this, and to try to obtain information regarding the housing, occupation, and earnings of every wage-earning family in York, together with the number and age of the children in each family. These particulars, obtained in the autumn of 1899, extended to 11,560 families living in 388 streets and comprising a population of 46,754. The present volume is the outcome of these inquiries....

B

Any classification of families according to income must be an arbitrary one. I have, in this chapter, adopted a method of classifying the population which is similar in some respects to that adopted by Mr Charles Booth in his *Life and Labour of the People in London*, but in other respects the differences of method employed are so important as to make a comparison of the two classifications misleading. But in Chapter IV, in which an estimate is made of the proportion of the population living above and below the Poverty Line, the comparatively small population to be dealt with in the city of York has enabled a more searching analysis to be made.

The population is divided into seven classes as follows:

Class

A   Total Family Income under 18s. for a moderate family.

B   Total Family Income 18s. and under 21s. for a moderate family.

C   Total Family Income 21s. and under 30s. for a moderate family.
D   Total Family Income over 30s. for a moderate family.
E   Domestic Servants.
F   Servant-keeping Class.
G   Persons in Public Institutions.

By a 'moderate' family is here intended a family consisting of father, mother, and from two to four children. In classifying, allowance has been made for families which were smaller or larger than such 'moderate' family....

C

Life in Class 'A'

Income under 18s. weekly for a moderate family

Total number of persons in Class	1957
Percentage of the working-class population	4·2
Percentage of the total population	2·6
Number of families	656
Average size of family	3
Average family earnings of those families who are earning anything	11s. 7d.
Average rent	2s. 9½d.

This class comprises the poorest people in the city....

It thus appears that in the case of 1295 persons, or almost exactly two-thirds of the whole, the immediate cause of poverty is the removal of the wage-earner by death or desertion, or the inability to earn wages through illness or old age. Economic causes, i.e. lack of work or lowness of wage, account for the poverty of 418 persons, or about 21 per cent of the whole class. The remainder of Class 'A' consists of casual labourers and families who would have been in Class 'B' had there not been more than four children.

It will be noticed that in the case of sixty-six families, comprising 247 persons, the wage-earner is in regular work, but earning less than 18s. per week. As the wages paid in York for unskilled labour are not as a rule under 18s., it may be presumed that these men are in some way 'unfit'. Such men have at all times to be content with the lowest paid work, and they are the first to lose their situations as soon as there is any slackness of trade. At the time when this inquiry was being made trade was good, and probably the proportion of 'unfit' workmen who were in work was above the average. The position of these workmen is one of peculiar hopelessness. Their unfitness means low wages, low wages means insufficient food, insufficient food unfitness for labour, so that the vicious circle is complete. The children of such parents have to share their privations, and even if healthy when born, the lack of sufficient food soon tells upon them. Thus they often grow up weak and diseased, and so tend to perpetuate the race of the 'unfit'.

Few people spend all their days in Class 'A'. It is nevertheless a class into which the poor are at any time liable to sink should misfortune overtake them, such as continued lack of work, or the death or illness of the chief wage-earner.

D

That so many wage-earners should be in a state of primary poverty will not be surprising to those who have read the preceding pages. Allowing for broken time, the average wage for a labourer in York is from 18s. to 21s.; whereas, according to the figures given earlier in this chapter, the minimum expenditure necessary to maintain in a state of physical efficiency a family of two adults and three children is 21s. 8d., or, if there are four children, the sum required would be 26s.

It is seen thus that *the wages paid for unskilled labour in York are insufficient to provide food, shelter, and clothing adequate to maintain a family of moderate size in a state of bare physical efficiency*. It will be remembered that the above estimates of necessary minimum expenditure are based upon the assumption that the diet is even less generous than that allowed to able-bodied paupers in the York Workhouse, and that *no allowance is made for any expenditure other than that absolutely required for the maintenance of merely physical efficiency*.

And let us clearly understand what 'merely physical efficiency' means. A family living upon the scale allowed for in this estimate must never spend a penny on railway fare or omnibus. They must never go into the country unless they walk. They must never purchase a half-penny newspaper or spend a penny to buy a ticket for a popular concert. They must write no letters to absent children, for they cannot afford to pay the postage. They must never contribute anything to their church or chapel, or give any help to a neighbour which costs them money. They cannot save, nor can they join sick club or Trade Union, because they cannot pay the necessary subscriptions. The children must have no pocket money for dolls, marbles, or sweets. The father must smoke no tobacco, and must drink no beer. The mother must never buy any pretty clothes for herself or for her children, the character of the family wardrobe as for the family diet being governed by the regulation, 'Nothing must be bought but that which is absolutely necessary for the maintenance of physical health, and what is bought must be of the plainest and most economical description'. Should a child fall ill, it must be attended by the parish doctor; should it die, it must be buried by the parish. Finally, the wage-earner must never be absent from his work for a single day.

If any of these conditions are broken, the extra expenditure is met, *and can only be met*, by limiting the diet; or in other words, by sacrificing physical efficiency.

E

The life of a labourer is marked by five alternating periods of want and comparative plenty. During early childhood, unless his father is a skilled worker, he probably will be in poverty; this will last until he, or some of his brothers or sisters, begin to earn money and thus augment their father's wage sufficiently to raise the family above the poverty line. Then follows the period during which he is earning money and living under his parents' roof; for some portion of this period he will be earning more money than is required for lodging, food, and clothes. This is his chance to save money. If he has saved enough to pay for furnishing a cottage, this period of comparative prosperity may continue after marriage until he has two or three children, when poverty will again overtake him. This period of poverty will last perhaps for ten years, i.e. until the first child is fourteen years old and begins to earn wages; but if there are more than three children it may last longer.[1] While the children are earning, and before they leave the home to marry, the man enjoys another period of prosperity— possibly, however, only to sink back again into poverty when his children have married and left him, and he himself is too old to work,

---

[1] It is to be noted that the family are in poverty, and consequently are underfed, during the first ten or more years of the children's lives. The effect of poverty upon the children is discussed in detail [*elsewhere in the book*].

for his income has never permitted his saving enough for him and his wife to live upon for more than a very short time....

We thus see that the 7230 persons shown by this inquiry to be in a state of 'primary' poverty, *represent merely that section who happened to be in one of these poverty periods at the time the inquiry was made.* Many of these will, in course of. time, pass on into a period of comparative prosperity; this will take place as soon as the children, now dependent, begin to earn. But their places below the poverty line will be taken by others who are at present living in that prosperous period previous to, or shortly after, marriage....The proportion of the community who at one period or other of their lives suffer from poverty to the point of physical privation is therefore much greater, and the injurious effects of such a condition are much more widespread than would appear from a consideration of the number who can be shown to be below the poverty line at any given moment.

F

We have been accustomed to look upon the poverty in London as exceptional, but when the result of careful investigation shows that the proportion of poverty in London is practically equalled in what may be regarded as a typical provincial town, we are faced by the startling probability that from 25 to 30 per cent of the town populations of the United Kingdom are living in poverty. If this be the fact, its grave significance may be realised when it is remembered that, in 1901, 77 per cent of the population of the United Kingdom is returned as 'urban' and only 23 percent as 'rural'.

103. HOW THE CASUAL LABOURER LIVED: LIVERPOOL

Source: 'How the Casual Labourer Lives: Report of the Liverpool Joint Committee on the Domestic Condition and Expenditure of the Families of Certain Liverpool Labourers read before and published by the Liverpool Economic and Statistical Society' (Liverpool, 1909), pp. v–vi, viii, xii–xiii, xiv, xv–xvi, xvii–xix, xx–xxi, xxvi–xxvii, 44–5.

The significance of casual employment as a cause of low earnings and the importance of docks and dock companies as casual employers on the large scale were subjects which attracted the notice of Charles Booth, when he first plunged into his study of London's East End. He asked Beatrice Potter, the later Mrs Sidney Webb, to write him a special report on dockside labour which was published in the first volume of 'Life and Labour'. But casual labour and its effects on personal income and expenditure in great ports were coming to be regarded as needing study elsewhere too, in the years before the 1914 war, when the cost of living began to mount. The report from which these extracts were taken was written by Eleanor Rathbone (1872–1946), member of a well-known Liverpool merchant family, and her helpers, at local request. It represented a study of family budgets among dockside workers, patterned on the work of Seebohm Rowntree at York but going well beyond him in the description of the 'sample' families and in the careful attention paid to the little-known subject of working-class debt. The family case-history here reproduced as part of her report, the sixteenth of her forty families, is that of a man getting beyond working age, but it shows what could happen when that point was reached. Family earnings in that particular household fluctuated between six and nineteen shillings a week. The money-lender made up the difference between income and expenditure. The main remedy proposed in the report for the low level of incomes it disclosed was a decasualization of dock labour through the new (1909) Labour Exchanges. For Eleanor Rathbone, later the chief exponent in this country of family allowances, Mary D. Stocks, 'Eleanor Rathbone' (1949).

A

Terms of Reference of the Inquiry

'The Research Committee [*a joint body formed by the Liverpool Branches of the Christian Social Union, of the Fabian Society and of the National Union of Women Workers; the Liverpool Economic and Statistical Society, the Liverpool Women's Industrial Council and the Victoria Settlement*] have decided to begin an investigation into the income and expenditure of Liverpool dock labourers.

The weekly earnings of the Liverpool dock labourers are known to be extremely irregular. The best man, in the prime of life, may earn 40s. or even 50s. in one week; 30s., 20s., or 15s. the next. Inferior or old and weakly men vary from 30s. to 4/6d. or nothing. A very large number are believed to average less than 15s. It is obvious that the task of adjusting the family expenditure to a violently fluctuating weekly income must be a very difficult one. The main object of this enquiry is to endeavour to find out how this difficulty is met. If the irregularity of earnings has an evil affect on the standard of living and on the whole conditions of family life, it is believed that this enquiry will do something to illustrate this evil and make it clear to the public. Secondary objects of the enquiry are:

(*a*) To obtain figures showing the actual earnings of individual dock labourers; such figures cannot be obtained from the study of employers' wage books, because most dock labourers' work sometimes at least for more than one firm.

(*b*) To supply for Liverpool a companion picture to Mr B. S. Rowntree's study of the diet of labourer families in York. Such a study may it is believed throw some light on practical problems such as the high infantile death rate in Liverpool, the underfeeding of school children, etc....'

B

In all, forty-one budgets [*i.e. budgets of family expenditure kept weekly by the labourer's wife, collected and checked by the investigator*] were kept, of which one has been rejected as untrustworthy. Of the forty, 29 were from dock labourers; 4 from other casual labourers; 2 from ships' firemen; 5 from labourers in regular work (platelayer, carter, cotton-porter, corporation labourer, ironworker's labourer).

The number of weeks for which the budgets were respectively kept were as follows:

1 for 62 weeks	1 for 16 weeks	1 for 5 weeks
1 for 45 ,,	2 for 11 ,,	4 for 4 ,,
1 for 42 ,,	2 for 9 ,,	2 for 3 ,,
1 for 33 ,,	3 for 8 ,,	1 for 2 ,,
3 for 20 ,,	2 for 7 ,,	10 for 1 week
2 for 18 ,,	3 for 6 ,,	

amounting to a total of 429 weeks. The five budgets from regular labourers were accepted for purposes of comparison....

C

The general level of income in the families studied may be summed up by stating that of the 27 budgets kept for four weeks and upwards

2 had an average income of over	£2	
1	ditto	32s. 4d.
5	ditto	from 25s. to 30s.
7	ditto	20s. to 25s.
8	ditto	15s. to 20s.
4	ditto	under 15s.

Taking the husbands' earnings only in the same families,

3 men averaged over 25s.

2 men averaged over 20s.

12 men averaged between 15s. and 20s.

10 men averaged below 15s.

The highest amount recorded in any one week is the 48s. of the one week budget, no. 39, the next highest 34s. None of the men, except no. 39, seem therefore to have belonged to that aristocracy of dock labourers whose high, though irregular, earnings are said to attract outsiders to Liverpool....

D

In sixteen out of the forty budgets, the wives added something to the family income by charing, washing, sewing or hawking. Several others kept lodgers....With some half-dozen exceptions, however, the sums recorded are trifling and do not form any considerable proportion of the income. Many of the women, in spite of the young children with which they are burdened, would gladly do more work if they could get it....

E

The immense importance of the part played by the pawn-broker and the money-lender in the lives of most casual labourers is perhaps the fact most strongly brought out by this enquiry.... The security being good, the rate of interest charged [*by the pawnbroker*] is only moderate

—usually $\frac{1}{2}d$. on 2s. (or less) on pledging and $\frac{1}{2}d$. on redeeming. The articles most generally pawned are the Sunday clothes of the whole family. These often go in quite regularly every Monday and come out again on Saturday, irrespective of the family's being in any special straights, and the pawnshop serves as a wardrobe for them. Families who have nothing left of their own to pawn will often borrow a bundle from a neighbour....But the real evil of pawning only comes in when articles essential to the well-being of the family—bedding, necessary clothes and furniture—are taken and the house left bare and comfortless. It is the ease with which this can be done to get money for drink, as well as for more legitimate needs, that has given the pawnshop the slight odour of discredit which undoubtedly hangs about it....From the pawn-shop to the money-lender is, however, a distinct step downwards....The money-lender, usually a woman, having in most cases no security whatever for her loans, secures her profits first, by charging an exorbitant rate of interest, and secondly, by using personal terrorism to enforce repayment. The usual rate charged is 2d. per shilling for the first week, sometimes rising to 3d. in subsequent weeks. A few money-lenders charge only 1d. per week. This, however, does not always represent the full cost of the transaction to the debtor. Some money-lenders keep small shops and others hawk fish or more rarely meat, and part of the loan has to be taken in kind. Thus, in order to obtain 2s. in cash a woman has often to take 1s. worth of fish as well... Her debt is then entered as 3s. 4d. One informant was in the habit of throwing away most of this fish for fear her husband should guess where she got it from. In a good many instances the husband was unaware of the wife's dealings with the money-lender and the latter could then exert extra pressure by threatening exposure. To disgrace the debtor in the eyes of the neighbours by making a row on the doorstep is another favourite method of enforcing claims....

F

The following real instance (not a budget-keeper) illustrates well most of the forms of debt commonly incurred by the poor.

Mr *X* is a labourer in regular work at 24*s.* per week. The family consists of eight people—father, mother, grandmother, and five children. The grandmother gets 2*s.* 6*d.* a week from the Parish and a lodger pays 2*s.* The total income is thus 28*s.* 6*d.* They pay 7*s.* rent. They are decent people, well thought of by the clergyman of the parish, but Mrs *X* is not a good manager.

In October, 1908, *X*'s liabilities were as follows:

Balance still due of loan of £4 from well-to-do friend in 1907 to meet debt contracted during illness	1	2	0
Paying at rate 1s. or 6d. a week; no interest			
Balance still due of loan from Loan Company, borrowed when out of work in 1908 at 8s. interest on whole	2	5	0
Paying at rate of 2s. 6d. a week, plus 6d. a week towards arrears			
Debt to Money lender contracted by wife when *X* was on half time	1	0	0
Paying 3s. 4d. a week interest			
Owing to Doctor	1	8	0
Paying 4s. a month by order of Court			
Back Rent	1	10	0
Paying 1s. a week			
Interest on lodger's shawl, usually pawned on Monday for 7s. 4d., redeemed on Friday for 7s. 8d.	0	0	4
Interest on friend's bundle, usually pawned on Monday for 6s. 4d., redeemed on Friday for 6s. 8d.	0	0	4
Six weeks arrears on Weekly Burial Club, subscription 1s. 10d.		13	0
No payment being made at date			
Coal Bill		3	6
No payment being made at date			
Boots		4	0
No payment being made at date			

Thus the weekly repayments amounted to 9*s.* 6*d.* or 10*s.*, of which about 4*s.* 3*d.* was what the poor call 'dead interest'....

G

It is however, difficult to convey by means of any general statement a correct picture of a diet of which the most marked feature was its fluctuations of plenty and scarcity, according to the quantity of the family income. In the matter of food even less than the other necessaries of life, an irregular supply is not the equivalent of its average, since neither physiologically nor in any other way can privation at one time be compensated by a surfeit at another. . . .

In most of the budgets, especially the poorer ones, the week forms a sort of cycle, the fare being particularly generous on Sunday and decreasing through the week till Saturday when pay day brings sufficiency again. The housewifely instincts of the mother can be judged to some extent from the distribution of her weekly purchases, the better managers buying everything but the more perishable articles on Saturday, and the less foreseeing everything in pennyworths, daily or twice daily as it is wanted. The lack of cupboards and facilities for keeping food no doubt makes the expensive practice of buying in small quantities in many cases almost inevitable. . . .

H

If. . .any employers of casual labour in Liverpool read this report, they can hardly feel quite satisfied with the picture it gives of the conditions of life among those by the help of whose labours their fortunes are being built up. Some of the studies describe homes in which an orderly self-respecting home life is being carried on and a very moderate standard of comfort maintained in spite of difficulties. Others are too meagre to leave much definite impression. But the majority are depressing records of poverty and failure, of the decadence of families who have seen better days, of the hopeless struggle of the women with problems in housewifery too hard for them, and for which they have received no adequate training, of the squalid and unabashed poverty of those who have given up or never made the effort. . . . The question, however, is not whether the conditions of casual employment are the sole cause of the unsatisfactory conditions of life among the labourers, but whether they do not aggravate and perpetuate those conditions, by making the upward path as difficult and the downward as easy as possible. Everything about the system of employment seems to foster the formation of bad habits and nothing to encourage the formation of good ones. The alternations of hard work and idleness disincline the men to steady exertion. The uncertainty of earnings encourages concealment from the wife and by accustoming the family to existence at the standard of bad weeks sets the surplus of good ones free for self-indulgence. The fluctuations of income make the problem of house-keeping impossibly difficult for most of the women, and the consequent discomfort and privations of the home drive the man to the public-house, wear out the health, the spirit, and the self-respect of the women, and injure the health and the happiness of the children....

...one is sometimes surprised that the results are not worse and that so much virtue is still left to smell sweet and blossom in the dust and wreckage of the casual labourer's life.

I

No. 16—Dock Labourer

Family known to visitor for some years.

Household (9)—Father over 60; Mother; 7 children: eldest son 20, a builder's labourer; girl 17, in service; 2 girls, 15, 12; 3 boys, 9, 7 and 5.

The house (3s.) is a three-roomed cellar, consisting of a small kitchen and two tiny bedrooms—one a mere cupboard. This they shared with a married daughter and her husband. When asked how eleven persons managed in such a space, Mrs P said she really could not say how they did manage. The window curtains were always clean and tidy, and the cellar had an outward air of cleanliness, but did not bear closer inspection.

The son-in-law paid the rent, and Mrs P contributed what she could towards it.

Mr P gets practically no work, though his wife says he goes to the Docks every morning to look for it. His age, as she says, is against him, but besides this he has the look of a permanent 'out-of-work', and no foreman would be likely to pick him unless very short of men.

Mrs P has a good deal of intelligence, and caught at the hope that by keeping a book [*of her household expenditure*] she might be helping somehow or other to make things better in the future. She is a managing woman, and makes the most of a little—e.g. when a shop was burnt down she picked up several skeins of wool in very short lengths. These she knotted together, and knitted them into two pairs of socks for the boys. In bad weeks the family had often only one or two meals a day. On Sunday 'none' was entered at all four meals.

The investigator got the eldest daughter a situation at 4s. a week, and as soon as she had repaid her outfit she began taking her meals home. She quickly gets homesick if placed far from her home, but is now doing well near by. Since the Budget was stopped, the family have moved to a larger house.

The loan entries were from a money lender. The married daughter and her husband had separate meals and are not included in the Budget.

[*Table of purchases in the week omitted*]

Menu of Meals during week 2

	Breakfast	Dinner	Tea	Supper
Sunday	Bread Margarine Tea Fish 9	Meat Potatoes 8	Bread Margarine Tea 9	—
Monday	Bread Margarine Tea 9	Cold Meat Potatoes 9	Bread Margarine Tea 8	—
Tuesday	Bread Margarine 5	Soup 5	Bread Margarine 6	—
Wednesday	Bread Margarine 5	—	Bread Margarine 8	—
Thursday	—	Bread Margarine 8	Bread Margarine 7	—
Friday	—	Bread Margarine 6	Bread Margarine 8	—
Saturday	—	Bread Margarine 8	Bread Margarine 8	—

104. THE FARM WORKER ON THE EVE OF WAR

Source: B. Seebohm Rowntree and May Kendall, 'How the Labourer Lives' (1913), pp. 22–4, 26–7, 30–2, 243–7.

There was much discussion of the "land question" in the early 1900's. Much of this turned upon land costs and land ownership in and about the expanding cities. But in so far as it concerned wages, it sprang from a feeling that in the big Edwardian boom, the incomes of the rural population were being left behind and that living standards in the country-

side were seriously low. Seebohm Rowntree turned the methods of inquiry developed by Booth and himself for the study of urban poverty in this direction and made a careful study of the incomes and expenditure of farm workers' families. The effect of this inquiry, taken together with official evidence, was to suggest that the average of farm labourers' wages was insufficient for primary wants. The minimum wage, which was accepted by the Liberal administration of the day as the remedy for this state of affairs, did not arrive until during the First World War. For the state of rural housing, which also entered into the debate, W. G. Savage, 'Rural Housing' (1915).

IN 1907 the weekly earnings of ordinary agricultural labourers in England averaged 17s. 6d. Those of horsemen, cattlemen, and shepherds were a little higher, and if they are included in the general average the figure is raised to 18s. 4d. It should be noted that these figures refer not to cash wages but to *total earnings*, including payment in kind, such, for instance, as free cottage, milk, potatoes, etc., and they take into account all extra payments, such as those for harvest and hay time. It should also be noted that the figures *refer solely to able-bodied male adult labourers in regular employment;* bailiffs, foremen, and stewards are not included, nor are old and infirm men and casual labourers, or women and young persons....

Earnings vary enormously from county to county. To simplify, we may confine ourselves to the earnings of ordinary agricultural labourers. These vary from 14s. 11d. in Oxfordshire to 20s. 10d. in Derbyshire....

It is not possible to go further back than 1898 to obtain general figures, but figures of the wages paid to ordinary labourers on 156 farms in different parts of England and Wales show that, if we take the wages for the year 1900 as equal to 100, they were 92·6 in 1880, remained almost stationary until 1894, when they stood again at 92·6, rose between 1894 and 1900 to 100, since when they have risen to 103·1 in 1910.... Thus we see that in the last ten years for which statistics are given, there has been a rise of 3 per cent in the wages of ordinary labourers in England and Wales. But the cost of living has, during that period, advanced by about 10 per cent[1] and by a further

[1] All figures showing the rise and fall in the price of foodstuffs must be regarded as rough estimates only, and the same remark applies to estimates of general wages based on those paid on so small a number as 156 farms. But though the

five per cent between 1910 and 1912, with *the result that the real wages of agricultural labourers have actually diminished since 1900.*

. . . It may be taken as an established fact that a family of five persons whose total income does not exceed 20s. 6d., and whose rent is 2s., is living below the 'poverty line'.

We wish to make it perfectly clear that this estimate only allows for expenditure *necessary for the maintenance of physical efficiency.* That a reasonable 'living wage' would have to include a further amount for recreation, a more varied dietary, for emergencies, and, generally, to render life less austere, few will deny. But in attempting to estimate how much should be allowed for these purposes we enter a region of controversy where personal opinions must take the place of scientific data. We prefer, therefore, to adopt the above minimum, and merely to state our own strong conviction that such a minimum does not by any means constitute a reasonable living wage.

If we now turn to the actual wages of ordinary agricultural labourers, we find that notwithstanding the fact that we have assumed a poverty line so low as to be open to the criticism of serious inadequacy, yet, with five exceptions (Northumberland, Durham, Westmorland, Lancashire and Derbyshire), the average earnings in every county of England and Wales are below it.

It is not, of course, suggested that every family is living below this line. Often there are subsidiary earnings by other members of the family which, added to those of the chief wage earner, raise the general level. Often also the number in the family is less than five; and again, many labourers have gardens or allotments on which they can raise an important proportion of their total food requirements. It would, however, be quite misleading to add the value of the produce so raised to the wage. It is raised by the worker's own labour, in his spare time, upon land for which, directly or indirectly, he pays rent, and it does not affect the conclusions to which we are driven that *the wage paid by farmers to agricultural labourers is, in the vast majority of cases, insufficient to maintain a family of average size in a state of merely physical efficiency.* . . .

figures here given are subject to some criticism, they confirm the conclusion to which many other facts point, that real wages have fallen during recent years. See Board of Trade Gazette, January 1913, p. 4.

Study No. XXXIV—Berkshire

Man, wife; four sons, aged fourteen, nine, six, and two; and five daughters, aged twelve, eleven, seven, four, and four months.

Total Weekly Earnings of Family

Wages—	s.	d.
Man	13	0
Son	6	0
	19	0
Perquisites—		
Cottage and garden, say	2	0
	21	0

Extra earnings in the course of the year, £3 15s.

Mrs Warren is a very reserved, scrupulously clean woman, of a type often called superior. Probably she will never be frank enough about her troubles to get much help from the charitably disposed; and her husband, if possible, is more reserved than she is....

Mr Warren gets 13s. a week, with the house. He starts work at 5 a.m.—he is a carter—and comes home to breakfast a little after 6. He is back at work at 7, taking a slice of bread and cheese with him, and goes on till 3, when he has an hour for dinner. At present he gets back finally at about 5.45 p.m. The boy works with his father, and has the same hours....

There is some Sunday work, but only about three hours.

We asked their opinion on the matter of debts incurred by labourers with young families, and Mrs Warren spoke out of her own hard experience....She thought that debts could very seldom amount to £15, or even £10.

'One shop tells another—I've heard them doing it—about other people. They tell us such as we *must* pay ready money, for if we can't pay this week, it isn't likely we can pay next'....

She manages to get a piece of meat for the two breadwinners every day, or nearly every day. Like many another, she apportions out the meat at the beginning of the week, and keeps back so much 'to look at'. It is said in this neighbourhood of the women and children, 'they eat the potatoes and look at the meat'....

'But of course there is extra money?'

'Yes. This Michaelmas we had 50s. I don't know what we shall get next spring; we haven't been here long enough; but once he earned 25s. extra going with the binder. It's then we try to pay off all that has got behind. I do my best to put 1s. by one week for clothes and another week for shoes; but now that we're using more coal and oil it's almost impossible. We go to a second-hand shop sometimes.... But the shoes—I can never get straight with the shoes'....

There is a deficiency of 35 per cent of protein in this family's dietary, and of 22 per cent of energy value. One tenth of the food consumed is home produce.

105. THE CHECK TO REAL INCOMES

Source: Arthur L. Bowley, 'The Change in the Distribution of the National Income, 1880–1913' (Oxford, 1920), reprinted in "Three Studies on the National Income": No. 6 of 'Series of Reprints of Scarce Works on Political Economy' (L.S.E., London, 1938), pp. 26–7.

The controversy over the distribution of incomes was often conducted without regard to the growth of the national income. This tended to be taken for granted. The nation had seen its aggregate income grow faster than its numbers throughout most of the nineteenth century and had come to accept this as part of the natural order of things. Between 1906 and 1914 the economic difficulties of the middle classes tended to be blamed on taxation and foreign tariffs; those of wage-earners, on the cost of living. It was, however, a significant fact, that industrial expansion was not taking place at a rate which would have allowed incomes to keep pace with and to outstrip rising prices. The first to point out that the great nineteenth-century expansion of incomes came to an end, not with the First World War, but half a generation before it, was A. L. Bowley. He assigned no causes. The late Victorian controversy over the distribution of wealth began while economic expansion still persisted, in the last quarter of the nineteenth century. Its Edwardian phase, and the industrial disputes which went with it, took place when incomes were almost stationary.

THE broad results of this investigation are to show that the national dividend increased more rapidly than the population in the generation before the war, so that average incomes were quite one-third greater in 1913 than in 1880; the increase was gained principally before 1900, since when it barely kept pace with the diminishing value of money. The increase was shared with remarkable equality among the various economic classes. Property obtained a diminishing share of the home product, but an unchanged share of the whole income when income from abroad is included.

The only marked alteration that has been found is the increase of the intermediate class that contains persons with small salaries, profits, or earnings in other forms than wages. These include clerks and others in retail and wholesale and distributive trade, and the younger or less successful persons in teaching and other professions. This class is no doubt mainly recruited from the sons and daughters of artisans and labourers; though their incomes are not greater than the earnings of skilled artisans, yet when they are regarded as part of the class from which they came, they appear in the vanguard of that class, increasing the relative number of educated and skilled labour whether manual or clerical. The progress of labour cannot reasonably be considered without reference to this movement. Manual labourers have been a diminishing proportion of the population. More of the whole effort of the population has turned to direction, distribution and exchange, and relatively less to production. This has been rendered possible, it may reasonably be presumed, by the increasing services of capital to production, and probably also by the increased intelligence of labour.

The constancy of so many of the proportion and rates of movement found in the investigation seems to point to a fixed system of causation and has an appearance of inevitableness. The results of the system have not produced a satisfactory livelihood to the bulk of the population, and its working in the generation before the war afforded no promise of any rapid improvement; indeed, in the early years of this century real income increased little faster than the population. Statisticians writing at or before the date of the beginning of the Fiscal Controversy (1902) could reasonably dwell with a certain satisfaction on the progress that had been made, and the slackening in the years that followed was masked by rising prices and years of good trade; but before the war it had become evident that the progress of real wages was checked, and it now appears that this check was not on wages alone.

CHAPTER 7

THE WAGES BARGAIN

Early in the 1870's, British political opinion, such as it was on the wider but still restricted franchise introduced in 1867, conceded that trade unions neither had been made by the law nor could be abolished by it. After nearly half a century of reluctant toleration, Parliament granted them for the first time full legal standing, together with wide scope within the law for their special industrial activities and methods, including the strike and the picket.

The legislation enacted between 1871 and 1876 recognized the consequences of a whole generation of union expansion and industrial growth. For trade unions, as the Victorians came to know them, were the result of the radical transformation of industrial relations which followed the decline of the small workshop and the general development of factory production. Collective bargaining succeeded individual bargains as a natural consequence of the change in scale. Rule-makers there clearly had to be in the new industry. The recognition of trade unions was a step towards the admission that it might be better for the rules and even for the output of industry if those who had to obey them were given some share in making them.

But trade unions were not the product of large-scale industry only. They were not strictly speaking a product at all. They were the reply of a great number of persons to the situation in which they found themselves, as the conditions of their work changed. A concern for wages, hours and working conditions animated them, together with a no less deep concern for social and industrial status, so far as that depended upon or appeared to depend upon income. For the rest, trade unionists varied greatly among themselves. Brought together by the works, the mine, the public house, the railway carriage and the chapel, they were very much men of their time, members of the active, labouring, talking, arguing, quarrelling industrial society of Victorian and Edwardian Britain.

The essential business of the trade unions was to find an adequate income for their members within the labour market. The idea which had had so much influence among working people, even trade unionists, in the 1830's and the 1840's that the market might one day be escaped from or superseded by some form of co-operative commonwealth had retreated to the back of men's minds. It was far from dead and was to come back, in altered form, before the end of the century.

But it had been replaced during the booming years of the 1850's and 1860's by the longing to be able to bargain from a position of strength within the market, even to modify and control it. Trade unionists wished above all not to be weak in the competitive struggle, not to survive by the grace and favour of another's superior strength. 'Freedom in union' had become the ideal and the improvement of wages which had taken place in many trades, affording a margin available for trade union subscriptions, provided the means.

The change from early Victorian living conditions was both social and economic. The better paid wage-earners of the late 1860's and 1870's were and knew themselves to be in some ways different people from their parents and grandparents.[1] The personal link with their country forbears had been broken. They and their families had become integrated with the new communities of the industrial towns. During thirty years, modest improvements in wages, leisure time, schooling, access to books and newspapers and railway travel, had bred a type of working man who knew his way around the industrial life of his day far better than the confused working population of the Chartist era ever could have done. His experience was different, his expectations and those of his wife and children were different. Brought up in the hardest possible school of practical experience, he had become a fair judge of the risks of industrial life for those who lived on a weekly wage. Knowing the strength and the weakness of his position, he was prepared to take some action to protect himself, if vigorously led. Behind the legislation of 1871–6 and what followed lay the emergence of this new type of working man—the inhabitant, with his family, of an infinity of new streets in the towns and mining villages of Victorian Britain. The typical trade unionist of the nineteenth century belonged to a working class which was socially self-conscious long before it was politically active.

Equally novel since the Chartist day was the rise of a characteristically Victorian type of industrial leader, varied in personal quality, against the general background of chapel, factory, mine and public house, willing and able to lead according to his lights. The lack of education and of prospects of advancement for many men undoubtedly increased the chances of such leadership being found in what was really a new artisan elite.

The mid-Victorian trade union world was extremely small. The best of the Victorian historians of trade unions[2] thought it doubtful

---

[1] The many small changes which had helped to educate a new generation since the Chartist days were ably summed up by J. M. Ludlow and Lloyd Jones, *Progress of the Working Class, 1832–1867* (1867).

[2] Sidney and Beatrice Webb, *History of Trade Unionism* (revised edition, 1920), pp. 748–9.

whether in 1842 there had been as many as 100,000 enrolled and contributing members. The long years of good trade and industrial development in the mid-century, ending in the high boom of the early 1870's, brought membership up possibly as high as a million. Then came the trade recession, leading to unemployment and loss of subscriptions. Perhaps the million mark was reached again in the business revival of 1885. Membership doubled by 1900, a year of good trade, when over two million members were registered. It doubled again by 1914, rising to over four millions on the crest of the industrial boom just before the First World War.[1] Trade unionists at that date were organized in over twelve hundred unions.

The first great expansion of numbers, between 1871 and 1900, had been reached in a period of slackening economic growth, marked by recurrent unemployment, although with real wages still rising. But it had had the weight and the drive, the idealism and the bread-and-butter calculation, of the mid-Victorian era of high capital formation and improving conditions behind it. The second expansion, between 1901, the year of the Taff Vale decision, and the opening of the First World War, took place when the long Victorian rise in real wages had faltered and when the consequences of a generation of reduced industrial investment had to be faced in a lack of new industries competing for labour. In the current state of earnings, with real wages almost stagnant, there was only too much to argue and fight about.

These were the broad economic conditions under which trade unions first rose to a position of power in British industry and collective bargaining became part of the day-to-day routine of an industrial society. In the last quarter of the nineteenth century, trade union activity began to spread far beyond the comparatively narrow range of the mid-Victorian unions. The most successful of these had been skilled, apprenticed men, organized, sometimes locally, sometimes in national bodies. They were able to use the relative scarcity of their type of labour to defend and improve their standard of living. The last quarter of the century saw a swift extension of union among unskilled and semi-skilled men, the so-called 'New Unionism'. The strike among the London dockers in 1889, an event much discussed at the time, was a notable symptom. It represented the surprising success under new and slightly more favourable conditions of attempts at union among the unskilled which had been seen before.

By the end of the century, an exceedingly wide variety of organizations existed which had as their prime aim the negotiation with employers of collective agreements relating to wages, hours and

[1] Figures of membership after 1892 in B. R. Mitchell and Phyllis Deane, *Abstract of British Historical Statistics* (1962), p. 68.

conditions of work, including sometimes entry of labour into the trade. They followed other important objects too. Before the pensions legislation of 1908 and the national health and unemployment insurance law of 1911, many trade unions found it important to provide by mutual convenience benefits for their members against the risks of sickness, loss of work, funeral expenses, and so forth.

United only in their general functions, trade unions varied enormously in the quality and character of their leadership. They differed in their methods and outlook from trade to trade and from one industrial region to another. A concentration on local and specific industrial problems and an unwillingness to think beyond their district or outside the range of their own membership came naturally to most of them. But in 1901 their strong tendencies to self-centredness and separation received a severe shock. A sense of common interest was reborn perforce owing to a legal judgment.

The echoes of the Taff Vale decision were to be heard for many years, long after the Trade Disputes Act passed by the Liberal government in 1906 had reversed the judgment. For the opinion of the judges in the case brought by the owners of a small South Wales railway against the Amalgamated Society of Railway Servants had the effect of depriving striking trade unionists of the protection of the law, in the event of damage to the employer arising out of the strike. Legal action of a civil kind, involving heavy penalties, could, it appeared, make the conduct of any industrial dispute a matter of serious risk to trade unions, by exposing their fighting funds to crippling damages. For some years Taff Vale overshadowed and held up the process, which in the past quarter of a century had moved very fast indeed, towards the spread of collective agreements and their influence through the whole vast structure of British industry.

Taff Vale had also political consequences of the highest importance. The court judgment and the failure of parliamentary opinion to respond to the conviction of trade unionists that it must be reversed turned votes. In 1906 many trade unionists, hoping for a change in the law, helped to sweep the Conservatives out of office and put a Liberal government into power, although there were many other conditions working towards that result. Taff Vale reinforced the belief which had been growing among some working men for years that they must have a political party of their own in Parliament, to bring pressure to bear on the existing Liberal and Conservative parties. It was in this way that many trade unionists found themselves supporting with their contributions and votes the parliamentary candidates of the Labour Representation Committee after 1900, although the Taff Vale judgment was but one element among many in the new political development. The political interests of some trade unionists, it is worth remembering, had been strong for forty years before Taff Vale.

In 1906 the new Liberal administration recognized that the practical effect of the Taff Vale judgment, however reasonable it might be as law, had been to make the normal course of industrial collective bargaining virtually impossible. In reversing the judgment, Parliament gave to the unions a privileged position at law, in the interests of the proper discharge of their duties. The unions could now get on with their work of securing collective agreements on standard conditions of work and pay. Sometimes they worked with the active support or acquiescence of employers, making use of negotiating machinery which had been created both by employers and employed. They took advantage of the methods of industrial arbitration and conciliation, commonplace now but new then, which had come into existence between 1860 and 1896.

The economic purpose of the trade unions was to enable their members to get the best income they could, by securing the best terms for their labour. It was the market within which this had to be done, rather than the whole wide social structure of their day, that the mid-Victorian pioneers of trade unionism had accepted. It was the market which their successors set out to dominate with a skill that increased with time. The test of their success was the number of workpeople whose wages, hours and conditions of work were controlled by the agreements they reached with employers and the stability of those agreements. What place the labour market could or ought to occupy in a civilized society, when they thought about such matters, trade union leaders could and did differ about. But they could in 1910 point out with a satisfaction varying with their temperament that some 2,400,000 people, or rather less than a quarter of the gainfully employed population of the United Kingdom, mainly in mining, textiles, transport, metals, engineering, shipbuilding, building, clothing and printing, were covered by collective agreements, including arbitrations and awards.[1] They could also assert with truth that the influence of such agreements was felt far and wide in industry among those who were not, as well as those who were, members of trade unions and employers organizations. The movement had spread to include clerical and other white collared workers and women workers.

Some trade unions, including the largest, were much interested in securing legislation on behalf of their members. The most striking example of this tendency was the series of laws—the Coal Mines (Eight Hours) Act 1908, the Coal Mines (Regulation) Act 1911, and the Coal

[1] *Board of Trade, Report on Collective Agreements between Employers and Workpeople in the United Kingdom 1910* (Cd. 5366).

Mines MinimumWage Act 1912—which came to govern hours, safety and wages in the enormous coal-mining industry. Some observers[1] of this and other legislation at the time supposed that the final aims of the trade unions could only be realized within a vast system of state regulation of industry. But the coal-industry laws were well inside a characteristically British legal tradition, which combined specific remedies for specific evils with the minimum of respect for general principles. The pressure of the trade unions for law was important. Equally important, however, was their, and the employers', reluctance to bring the state in, so to speak, at shop floor level or to allow it to control the sphere of collective bargaining. They preferred to stand on their own feet and look after their own interests, wherever they could. If trade unionists as a body possessed an ideal, it has been said, it was not so much collectivist as collectivist *laissez faire*.[2] Their ideal required maximum freedom for the great negotiating bodies.

The very success of the redoubtable pragmatists who controlled the trade unions and who faced men on the other side of the table as empirical as themselves, living in and for the immediate situation, created new problems and risks which could not have been foreseen. These problems might even come in time to threaten what they prized most, the fabric of free collective bargaining.

One most urgent worry grew out of the national character of the area within which negotiation had now to be carried on and the serious impact of major trade disputes upon the various sectors of industry. Both self-interest and self-protection suggested the need for a further extension of trade union unity. An alliance of large unions— the miners, railwaymen and transport workers—to pursue their policies jointly came into being after 1912. The stage of 'collectivist *laissez faire*', which had now been reached, seemed to bring within the bounds of possibility a general strike. It also inevitably posed the question, although this seems not to have been deeply considered at the time, what the attitude of the State, the supreme force in the land, was likely to be in such an event, towards an act of power which could scarcely fail to be construed as a challenge to its own. The last few years of peace and of industrial boom, from 1911 on, were a time of growing confusion in industrial relations. The rise of prices and cost of living produced much trade union activity. The new and very interesting demand for workers' control, which helped to create the shop steward movement after 1910, added to the confusion and the

[1] E.g. Sidney Webb, in his article on 'The Economic Theory of a Minimum Wage', in the *Journal of Political Economy* for 1912. This was in line with opinions which Webb had formed many years before.

[2] O. Kahn-Freund, in *Law and Opinion in England in the Twentieth Century*, ed. M. Ginsberg (1959), p. 224.

bitterness. Much of the tension which existed must be judged to have been healthy, despite strikes and violence. A much more even and reasonable balance between the bargaining power of the employer and that of the employed now existed than in Victorian times. It is, however, the fundamental business of law to ensure that the powerful tensions which always stir at the heart of any growing society shall be stripped, as far as possible, of their danger; that they shall become creative and remain peaceable, neither degenerating into open war nor turning insidious and corrosive. There seemed little ground for optimism on that score.

Britain was ceasing to be the land of uncontrolled, individualist economy which it had been for so many years. But despite active legislation after 1906 and the personal intervention of leading politicians, such as Winston Churchill and Lloyd George, in industrial affairs, she had not discovered the guiding lines of a satisfactory new system of industrial relations. If relations between managements and men were in some industries very good, in others, including some of the largest in the country, such as coal, they were poor and deteriorating. If those large industries should ever have to face a time of rapid and unfavourable economic change, their failure to handle their human relations well might exact a heavy price, both from the industries themselves, and from the rest of the nation.

FURTHER READING

The history of trade unions has been written more often than that of industrial relations. E. H. Phelps Brown, *The Growth of British Industrial Relations* (1959) deals mainly with the years 1906–14. For the course of real wages, A. L. Bowley, *Wages and Income in the United Kingdom* (1937). There is room for far more study in depth of particular industrial situations and for a careful identification of the many elements which went to their making. There is also much need for more local studies, such as S. Pollard, *History of Labour in Sheffield* (1959).

Two great studies of trade union development were written during the period and remain monuments to late Victorian thought and scholarship. They are Sidney and Beatrice Webb's *History of Trade Unionism* (1894) and *Industrial Democracy* (1898). They concentrate too much on formal constitutional things, to the neglect of general economic and social conditions, to be wholly satisfactory now. G. D. H. Cole's *The World of Labour* (1913) and *Short History of the British Working Class Movement* (first published 1925–7) should be compared with B. Pribićević, *The Shop Stewards Movement and Workers' Control 1910–1922* (1959, with introduction by G. D. H. Cole). For a recent sketch, H. M. Pelling, *History of British Trade Unionism* (1963).

The history of trade unions and of trade union leaders has suffered from hagiography, too often combined with a failure to relate particular events to their wider setting. It is worth comparing the fortunes of trade unions in the different branches of the national economy, to see where and why they were weak or strong or had special difficulties to meet. See for agriculture, F. E. Green, *A History of the English Agricultural Labourer 1870–1920* (1920) and E. Selley, *Village Trade Unions in Two Centuries* (1919); for the builders, R. W. Postgate, *The Builders' History* (1923); for railwaymen, P. S. Bagwell, *The Railwaymen* (1963); for engineers, J. B. Jefferys, *The Story of the Engineers* (1945); for the coal miners, R. Page Arnot, *The Miners 1889–1945* (1949–61); for clerical workers, F. Hughes, *By Hand and Brain: the Story of the Clerical and Administrative Workers' Union* (1953). Within a large industry, the fortunes of trade unions could vary greatly: see, e.g. E. W. Evans, *The Miners of South Wales* (1961) and J. E. Williams, *The Derbyshire Miners* (1962). The organization of the smaller occupational groups deserves study as much as that of the big, although they received less public notice. See, e.g. C. J. Bundock, *The Story of the National Union of Printing, Bookbinding and Paper Workers* (1959); T. J. Connelly, *The Woodworkers 1860–1960* (1960); M. H. Cuthbert, *The Lace Makers Society* (1960); A. Fox, *The History of the National Union of Boot and Shoe Operatives* (1958); A. E. Musson, *The Typographical Association* (1954); W. H. Warburton, *The History of Trade Union Organisation in the North Staffordshire Potteries* (1931).

What qualities made a successful trade union leader in late Victorian and Edwardian conditions? There are a number of autobiographies and biographies which throw some light, although few. Many of the men concerned have become shadows of shades. For agricultural labourers, Joseph Arch, *The Story of His Life Told by Himself* (1898) and George Edwards, *From Crow-Scaring to Westminster: an Autobiography* (1922); a brassworker, W. A. Dalley, *Life Story of W. J. Davies* (1914); a carpenter, A. W. Humphrey, *Robert Applegarth* (1913); coal miners, A. Watson, *A Great Labour Leader, the life of the Rt. Honourable Thomas Burt* (1908), John Wilson, *Memories of a Labour Leader, the autobiography of John Wilson* (1910); dockers and water-side workers, H. Gosling, *Up and Down Stream* (1927), Sir James Sexton, *Sir James Sexton, Agitator: an Autobiography* (1936), B. Tillett, *Memories and Reflections* (1931); a gas worker, Will Thorne, *My Life's Battles* (1925); a stone mason, Henry Broadhurst, *Henry Broadhurst, M.P., the Story of his life from a stone mason's bench to the Treasury Bench. Told by himself* (1901); women workers, M. A. Hamilton, *Mary Macarthur* (1925).

An enormous mass of information on the state of industrial relations at the end of the nineteenth century is to be found in the *Report and Minutes of Evidence of the Royal Commission on Labour*, published between

1891 and 1894. The practical results of this inquiry were negligible. It led, however, to the Conciliation Act of 1896, out of which a number of systems of industrial conciliation and arbitration developed. For these, see the *Second Report on Rules of Conciliation and Arbitration Boards* (1910) (by G. R. Askwith).

For the relations of the Trade Unions with Parliament, B. C. Roberts, *The Trades Union Congress 1868–1921* (1958).

106. THE TRADE UNION BILL, 1871

Source: 'The Economist', 1 February 1871, pp. 193–4.

Important organs of political opinion such as the 'Economist' and 'The Times' gave a highly qualified approval to the trade union legislation of the early 'seventies. Compare Charles Reade's popular novel of 1870. 'Put Yourself In His Place', written around the Sheffield outrages, which might be said to have been based on the view that trade unionists were more prone to crime than other men. This more extreme view was going out. The bill discussed in the 'Economist' leader was introduced early in 1871 by H. A. Bruce, home secretary in the Gladstone administration, but soon withdrawn in order to make way for the Trade Union Act, 1871, and the Criminal Law Amendment Act, 1871. For the course of events, as seen by one who played a considerable part at the time on the trade union side, see George Howell, 'Labour Legislation, Labour Movements and Labour Leaders' (1902).

THE Bill introduced by Mr Bruce on Tuesday evening to regulate Trades' Unions is a characteristically English measure. It cannot be praised for theoretical completeness; on the contrary, it has every sort of theoretical defect. But it removes or alleviates many practical evils; it introduces many practical improvements; it is suited to the present temper of men's minds, and to the stage of the discussion which its subject has reached. And therefore probably it ought to pass, and will pass....

To this defective state of opinion Mr Bruce's Bill is very nicely adapted. It removes the worst evils, and does as much as could now be hoped for; and in English legislation it is no new thing to have to wait long for consistent principle and real completeness. The points of the Bill are these.

First,—it abolishes altogether the common law superstition that Trades' Unions are not to be recognized by law because they are 'in restraint of trade'. This doctrine was invented by a very learned and acute Judge, at a time when 'Trades' Unions' were thought to be necessarily pernicious, and when also it was thought possible to put them down. 'As you take any stick to beat a dog with', so this old doctrine was looked out of the law books, and applied to the societies which it was wished to dissolve. But now, to go into no disputable considerations, everyone is agreed that Trades' Unions cannot be put down, and that they are, for good and evil, an inseparable as well as most living part of our present society, and therefore this ingenious application of ancient doctrine must be dismissed as useless and pernicious.

Secondly,—it establishes a system of registration for Trades' Unions analogous to that which now exists for Friendly Societies, and it gives all Trades' Unions so registering the power to sue and be sued, a special and quick remedy against defaulting officers, the power to hold land or erect buildings necessary for their objects—in a word, all the usual privileges of a Friendly Society. This is consistent with present opinion, and we do not wish to object to any decent compromise of an irritating question. Still the evils of the proposal should be seen. A special registration is in the nature of a special endorsement: it gives a sanction of special goodness to those societies, which other societies side by side with them have not. The Friendly Societies have traded on it for years. Their late Registrar, Mr Tidd Pratt, was one of the best known men by name in England among the saving poor. The universal impression was that so good and excellent a man would not have 'certified' any society which was not solvent and would deceive the poor. Now a 'Trades' Union' is, as we once before said, 'a Strike Society tied to a Friendly Society'. Certain funds, not, actuaries tell us, at all more than enough, are subscribed by the poor to support them in sickness and old age, and these funds are used by the 'Strike Society' to raise the rate of wages, to prevent the rate from falling, and to enforce many other conditions on masters. But it is plain that such a joint society is insolvent *upon principle*. A bare minimum of subscriptions being raised for one purpose, large parts of them are upon occasion taken for another purpose. No working man can ever be sure that a majority of the Union may not use for present fighting the money he saved for future maintenance, and we do not like the State to endorse this.

Of course we in no way object to the foundation of such societies. If working men prefer this kind of combination let them try it. But the State should give what is so radically vicious no special favour, sanction or approval. Trades' Unions should be *legal* clubs, but they should not be *privileged* clubs.

Thirdly,—the Bill enacts that no workman shall use violence to anyone, or intimidate or molest anyone for Trades' Union purposes, and sends him to prison for three months if he does.

In theory no doubt this enactment ought to be part of the penal code. If we had such a code, with clear definitions and sufficient doctrines, these penalties would follow from it, and would need no special enactment. There would be a general head 'Molestation' in which this offence would be included with many others. And this would be a great gain, because it is not very easy to say what is molestation and what is not, and the delicate discussion on that nice question is more likely to be rightly decided upon a general and abstract argument than in a particular and irritating instance. But as we have now no such code, some definition is necessary, and therefore Mr Bruce has rightly given it. There will be much controversy about its terms but we think, upon the whole, they will be sufficient for their purpose —at least we cannot mend them!

107. THE INCREASING POWER OF TRADE UNIONS, 1878

Source: George Howell, ' The Conflicts of Capital and Labour' (1878), p. xii.

The "legal enfranchisement" referred to in this extract is the Trade Union legislation passed by Parliament in the years 1871–5. George Howell (1833–1910) acted in the early 1870's as secretary to the parliamentary committee of the trade union congress.

WHATEVER may be said with regard to trade-unions, either as to their policy, their objects, or the means which they employ, one great fact cannot be ignored, namely, that they wield a vast power, socially and politically, and whether for good or for evil, it is daily increasing. They are, moreover, public institutions in Great Britain to-day, exercising great authority by reason of their extent, their wealth, their organisation, and the numbers within the pale of their influence, and they are as deeply rooted in the minds and affections of the working people as almost any institution in the country. It is useless to abuse them, to put them down is impossible; the only sensible way of dealing with them has been done by legally enfranchising them; they are now protected by law, as well as being amenable to the law, and their future action will show that this policy is as wise as it is just.

108. ARBITRATION IN THE COAL INDUSTRY

Source: 'Durham Coal Trade Arbitration': February 1876 (1876). pp. 94–5.

Much of the work of trade unions after the emancipatory legislation of 1871–6 as before it consisted in promoting machinery for conciliation and arbitration on wage claims. This machinery came frequently into action during the price falls of the late nineteenth century, it being commonly assumed in industry that selling price ought to determine wage levels. The coal-mining industry had passed through a state of high boom and inflated prices at the beginning of the 1870's, and was in the middle of a spate of wage reductions when this award was made. In effect, conciliation machinery had become geared to the nineteenth-century trade cycle.

Copy of Mr Hopwood's Award

Whereas differences have arisen between the Coal Owners of the County of Durham, and the men employed in or about the Collieries of the said County as to a proposed reduction in the rate of wages to be paid to the said men: and whereas it was agreed between the Durham Coal Owners' Association, representing the said Owners, and the Durham Miners' Association, representing the said men, that the questions, as to whether any reduction should be made in such rate of wages, and if so, what should be the amount of such reduction, should be referred to Arbitration: and whereas it was agreed between the said Associations that Messieurs William Armstrong and David Dale should be Arbitrators for the said Owners, and Messieurs Lloyd Jones and William Crawford should be Arbitrators for the said men: and it was further agreed that the said Arbitrators should appoint an Umpire, to whom the above-mentioned questions should be referred, if the Arbitrators should not be able to come to an agreement thereupon: and whereas I, CHARLES HENRY HOPWOOD, was chosen as Umpire by the said Arbitrators: and whereas the Arbitrators have been unable to agree upon the questions referred to them, and have therefore called upon me to act as Umpire: and whereas they have agreed that my Award shall apply to all underground and surface men employed in or about the above-mentioned collieries, except Enginemen, Firemen, Joiners, Smiths, Masons, and Masons' Labourers, and also except the Cokemen, who are dealt with in a separate Arbitration and Award.

Now, having duly considered the various statements and arguments laid before me, I make this my Award on the questions so referred:—I do decide and award that there shall be a reduction of seven per cent in the present rate of wages paid to the underground men employed in or about the said collieries, and a reduction of four per cent in the present rate of wages paid to the surface men employed in or about the said collieries. And I award and direct that the said reductions shall take effect and begin with and from the commencement of the next pay which shall happen after the date of this my Award.

Without presuming to dictate to men so competent to judge for themselves as the parties to the present Arbitration are, I would express the hope that some self-adjusting principle or standard may be discovered for the regulation of the rate of wages, at once more simple, ready, and less expensive, than Arbitration. If both sides will apply themselves heartily to this problem, there is little doubt it may be solved.

Dated this 16th day of February, 1876.

CHAS. H. HOPWOOD

3 Paper Buildings, Temple, London

109. THE ACCEPTANCE OF COLLECTIVE BARGAINING: PRINTING

Source: E. Howe, 'The London Compositor' (1947), pp. 290–2.

Printing was a very good example of an industry in which the importance of the skilled, apprenticed man made it comparatively easy to bring in trade unionism at an early date. By the 1880's, the London trade had been accustomed to collective agreements for many years, as this letter shows.

To the Members of the London School Board

PRINTING CONTRACTS

23, Abchurch Lane, London
October, 1889

Gentlemen,—I beg with all respect, as a Master-Printer of old standing, to lay before you a few remarks bearing upon the question of what are called 'fair' and 'unfair' houses in the Printing Trade, and upon the effect of the Trade Union among Printers.

I am strongly of opinion that the Trade Union, with all its imperfections, is a necessary institution, good for the employers, good for the workmen, and good for the general welfare. It should always be remembered that the present scale of prices is not one-sided, imposed by the workmen upon their unwilling employers; but a compact settled by mutual agreement, and varied, as occasion required, from the year 1810 to 1874....

I have mentioned these successive changes to prove that from 1810, up to now, there has been a continuity of agreement between employers and workmen. Such mutual agreements have had a most beneficial effect upon the peacefulness of the trade, and I think it would be a great calamity were they now ignored, in favour of a free fight between Labour and Capital. Indeed, no better plan for the welfare of the trade could be devised than the appointment of a truly representative Committee of Employers, to arrange with a Committee of the Union, a scale, which could be accepted and adhered to by all parties.

I would like to add that while unable to endorse all that has been said about 'sweating', I have no hesitation in repeating that the Union is advantageous to both sides. It does not, as some people accuse it of doing, 'reduce the good and the bad workman to one dead level'. It does its best to prevent the employer obtaining work at a lower scale than he or his representatives have agreed to pay, but it only fixes a *minimum*, below which no man ought to work, and above which many Compositors are now paid. I refer to men on weekly wages, irrespective of what they really earn; and here, although 36s. is the lowest wage, the cases are numerous in which the same roof covers men receiving, as abler journeymen. 38s., 40s., or 42s.

The benefit of a Trade Union to the employers is, to me, patent. In these days of severe competition, when a long schedule of work is given out to be tendered for, it is of vital importance for an employer to know that his competitors must pay for the workmen's labour the same price as he does. Not unfrequently it happens that anxiety to get work induces an employer to put in a tender which he finds, too late, will not pay. His great aim then is to pare down cost, and wages is naturally the first thing which tempts him. In such a case the workman, unsupported by his Union, would be at the mercy of the employer, and reduction would slowly succeed reduction, until 'sweating' would really be reached. The employer who wished his men to be paid fairly would be compelled to follow suit or see his trade collapse. Then would ensue a series of strikes, and the formation of fresh Trade Unions—there would be friction everywhere, and renewed war between Capital and Labour, a certain result of what is called Freedom of Contract. This word 'freedom' is perhaps the most ill-used word in our language. Obedience to a generally-received scale is not curtailing the employer's freedom of contract with his men. On the contrary, it is the absence of such laws that would surely intensify unnatural competition, and lead to tyranny on the one hand and hate on the other.

But do the so-called 'unfair' houses pay their men 'sweating' wages? To no great extent, at present, because the Union rate of wages working all around them keeps up the wage of the Non-Unionist workman to the same, or nearly the same, level as the Unionist. To force down wages much below the Union standard would certainly drive the Non-Unionist into the Union ranks; but should the Union ever be thrown over, through the opposition or apathy of the majority of Employers, the system of 'sweating' would soon be reached. All employments prove the truth of the axiom: 'Where Unionism is weak, wages are low.'

As to the effect of the Union on its members, I have no doubt that its moral influence is good. No man found guilty of crime is allowed to remain a member, and therefore cannot be employed in any Printing Office where Union rules are in force. The inner rules of the Union, by which members must abide, tend to promote foresight, brotherhood, self-respect, and a feeling of corporate responsibility, thus fostering in the mind a true sense of manhood. Unrestrained competition, whether Capital against Capital, or Labour against Labour, leads to social cannibalism, so that the less scrupulous a man is, the better chance there is of rising upon the body of his brother. To avoid this a scale of wages accepted and adhered to by both Employers and Employed seems the real remedy.

As an old Master Printer, whose business lies outside such Contracts as are now under debate, and whose position will be unaffected by a decision either way, I have ventured to address you, feeling strongly that your action in this question will have an important effect upon the future of both Employers and Workmen.

WILLIAM BLADES

(*Firm:* Blades, East and Blades)

IIO. THE NEW UNIONISM: THE AGRICULTURAL LABOURERS

Source: '*Joseph Arch the Story of His Life Told by Himself*' (*1898*), *pp. 68–9.*

Joseph Arch (1826–1919), an itinerant hedge-cutter and local Dissenting preacher, addressed farm-workers at Wellesbourne, a village in Warwickshire near Stratford-on-Avon. This was the beginning of the National Agricultural Labourers' Union.

THE day was February 7th, 1872. It was a very wet morning, and I was making a box. My wife came in to see me and said, 'Joe, here's three men come to see you. What for, I don't know.' But I knew fast enough. In walked the three; they turned out to be labourers from over Wellesbourne way. I stopped work, and we had a talk. They said they had come to ask me to hold a meeting at Wellesbourne that evening. They wanted to get the men together, and start a Union, directly. I told them that, if they did form a Union, they would have to fight hard for it, and they would have to suffer a great deal; both they and their families. They said the labourers were prepared both to fight and suffer. Things could not be worse; wages were so low, and provisions were so dear, that nothing but downright starvation lay before them unless the farmers could be made to raise their wages....

When I reached Wellesbourne, lo, and behold, it was as lively as a swarm of bees in June. We settled that I should address the meeting under the old chestnut tree; and I expected to find some thirty or forty of the principal men there. What then was my surprise to see not a few tens but many hundreds of labourers assembled; there were nearly two thousand of them. The news that I was going to speak that night had been spread about: and so the men had come in from all the villages round within a radius of ten miles. Not a circular had been sent out nor a handbill printed, but from cottage to cottage, and from farm to farm, the word had been passed on; and here were the labourers gathered together in their hundreds. Wellesbourne village was there, every man in it; and they had come from Moreton and Locksley and

Charlecote and Hampton Lucy, and from Barford, to hear what I had
to say to them. By this time the night had fallen pitch dark; but the
men got bean poles and hung lanterns on them, and we could see well
enough. It was an extraordinary sight, and I shall never forget it, not
to my dying day. I mounted an old pig-stool, and in the flickering
light of the lanterns I saw the earnest upturned faces of these poor
brothers of mine—faces gaunt with hunger and pinched with want—
all looking towards me and ready to listen to the words, that would
fall from my lips.... We passed a resolution to form a Union then and
there, and the names of the men could not be taken down fast enough;
we enrolled between two and three hundred members that night. It
was a brave start, and before we parted it was arranged that there
should be another meeting at the same place in a fortnight's time. I
knew now that a fire had been kindled which would catch on, and
spread, and run abroad like sparks in stubble; and I felt certain that this
night we had set light to a beacon, which would prove a rallying point
for the agricultural labourers throughout the country.

III. THE LOCK OUT IN AGRICULTURE

Source: Frederick Clifford, 'The Agricultural Lock-Out of 1874'
(1875), pp. v, 12, 13, 23–4, 166–7, 169.

    Frederick Clifford, a barrister, acted as special correspondent of 'The
Times' newspaper during the lock-out in the Eastern counties which
followed the organization of the National Agricultural Labourers' Union
in 1872.

I

THE Letters which have here been woven into a narrative were
published in 'The Times' during the year 1874. They describe the
first great struggle between the farmers and the agricultural labourers
of England—or, as the farmers prefer to say, between themselves and
the Trade-Union leaders—and the first important symptoms in rural
society of an antagonism between capital and labour, with which
Artisan Trade-Unions have made us familiar in the towns. A struggle
so prolonged, and so novel in many of its conditions, will always be
remarkable in our industrial history, and has been thought worthy of
some permanent record.

II

March 1, 1873

Dear Sir,—The agricultural labourers of this branch of the National Agricultural Union in your employ beg respectfully to inform you that, on and after March 7, they will require a rise in their wages of 3s. a week—a week's work to consist of   hours. Being desirous of retaining good relations between employers and employed, and to assure you that no unbecoming feelings prompt us to such a course, we invite you (if our terms are not in accordance with your views) to appoint an early time to meet us, so that we may fairly consider the matter and arrange our affairs amicably. Your obedient servants, The Committee, Exning Branch.

III

On March 10 [*1874, following a request that year for a rise, the minimum wages being at the time 13s. a week, with extras*] the Newmarket farmers held a general meeting, at which resolutions were come to that no other alteration should be made, either in the rate of wages or the hours of labour. Further, they resolved, on the ground that they might otherwise be beaten in detail, 'that all Union men be locked out, after giving one week's notice, such notice to begin the next pay-day of each of the members respectively, and that such lock-out continue so long as the men continue on strike'.

IV

On the whole, the conduct of the labourers throughout the lock-out was exemplary. There were isolated attempts at intimidation, and a few cases of personal violence; but considering that the lock-out extended over a great portion of the county of Suffolk, and included parts of Cambridgeshire, the men were orderly and well-behaved. Great moral pressure[1] was no doubt brought to bear upon non-Unionists by men who had joined the body, and still more by women. In villages men are more constantly under the influence of their fellows than in towns, have greater difficulty in escaping from the social pressure

---

[1] 'The "moral pressure" in my parish,' says a farmer, 'developed into stone-throwing, hooting, and other forms of annoyance. Many of our men who continued at work were afraid to go from one village to another, and quite afraid to stir out after dark.'

brought to bear upon them and their families, and find it harder to live under the stigma that they are not 'standing by their order'. Still, moral force of this kind is a legitimate thing, against which nothing can be said.

V

After seeing and hearing a good deal of the 'Defence' movement at Newmarket, Bury, and in East Suffolk, I cannot resist the conclusion that the mass of the farmers were fighting 'squarely', not against one, but against any and every Union.... The fact is, that to many of the farmers of the old school the very notion of combination among farm labourers and their alliance with agitators from a distance was strange and unnatural. Yet, if the right and the necessity of trade combinations are admitted anywhere and in any calling, I think they would be admitted in rural communities and among farm-labourers, who, as units widely scattered, with most imperfect means of intercommunication, are, or have hitherto been, powerless against bad masters.

VI

If the labourers, then, failed, as no doubt they did fail, solely through want of unanimity, the farmers were still more divided; and it was a material fact that even during the heat of the late struggle, about one-half of the Union labourers in Suffolk were kept in work by their masters. We must bear in mind, then, that the struggle was waged not by classes, but only by sections of each class. Both men and masters may become more united hereafter; but union will do more for the men than for the masters, and will make them more formidable as a fighting power than the masters.

112. THE NEW UNIONISM: THE GAS STOKERS

Source: Will Thorne, 'My Life's Battles' (n.d.), pp. 67–9.

One of the signs of the "new unionism" of the last years of the nineteenth century was the successful organization of the stokers in the works of the main London gas companies. Will Thorne (1857–1946) reported, many years after, the speech in which he, then a gas stoker, announced the formation of the National Union of Gas Workers and General Labourers, at an open air meeting in Canning Town on 31 March 1889.

The Wages Bargain

I KNOW that many of you have been working eighteen hours under very hard and difficult circumstances, that many of you must be dead tired; often have I done the eighteen-hour shift. I am under the impression that the resident engineer knew that I had arranged this meeting, and that he deliberately kept you working late. This sort of thing has gone on for a long time; we have protested, but time after time we have been sneered at, ignored and have secured no redress. Let me tell you that you will never get any alteration in Sunday work, no alteration in any of your conditions or wages, unless you join together and form a strong trade union. Then you will be able to have a voice and say how long you will work, and how much you will do for a day's work.

In my opinion, you have a perfect right to discuss all these matters with your employer through your chosen spokesman. Why should any employer have the power to say you must do this, that, and the other thing? By your labour power you create useful things for the community, you create wealth and dividends, but you have no say, no voice, in any of these matters.

All this can be altered if you will join together and form a powerful union, not only for gas workers, but one that will embrace all kinds of general labourers. Some of you only work in the gas works in the winter; when the warm weather comes, you are dismissed, to find what work you can get at the docks, in the brickfields, navvying, or anything that comes along.

Stand together this time; forget the past efforts we have made to form you into a union, when we failed only because you did not respond to our call. Some of you were afraid of your own shadows, but this morning I want you to swear and declare that you mean business and that nothing will deter you from your aim.

It is easy to break one stick, but when fifty sticks are together in one bundle it is a much more difficult job. The way you have been treated at your work for many years is scandalous, brutal and inhuman. I pledge my word that, if you will stand firm and don't waver, within six months we will claim and win the eight-hour day, a six-day week, and the abolition of the present slave-driving methods in vogue not only at the Beckton Gas Works, but all over the country. Now, will you do this?

Who Gained by Change?

113. THE ORIGINS OF THE STRIKE AT THE LONDON DOCKS, 1889

Source: H. Llewellyn Smith and Vaughan Nash, 'The Story of the Dockers' Strike, told by two East Londoners' (1889), pp. 29–33.

The organization of the dock strike owed much not only to the docker Ben Tillett (1859–1943), here described at work, but also to John Burns (1858–1943) and Thomas Mann (1856–1941), both of whom were members of the Amalgamated Engineers' Society. The authors of this description, young men at the time, became notable public servants later on, Llewellyn Smith (1864–1945) at the Board of Trade, Vaughan Nash (1861–1932) as private secretary to two Prime Ministers, Campbell-Bannerman and Asquith.

FOR many years discontent has been sullenly smouldering among the dockers. Employment has been shrinking, and what has remained has become more uncertain and irregular. The dock labourer does not, as a rule, reason very deeply about the causes of the change. He knows but little of the effect of the Suez Canal on the trade routes of the world, or of the rights and wrongs of the internecine war between the rival dock companies which has driven the shipping lower down the Thames. All he knows is that the waiting at the dock gates has become longer and more hopeless, and that times have been harder and harder, and a vague feeling of injustice has grown up, which has only waited for a spark to burst into a blaze.

Before now, indeed, this inarticulate discontent has broken out into strikes. In 1872 there was a successful strike for a rise in wage from 4d. to 5d. an hour, but the result is said to have been a large extension of casual employment and of the contract system. In 1880 the casuals of London and St Katharine Docks demanded and obtained the recognition of a minimum rate of 6d. an hour for contract work. But of late years a spirit of apathy seemed to have settled down upon the dock labourers, and though now and again a socialist speaker tried to stir the embers of discontent, little impression seemed to be made at the time.

But all this while, the course of events was being keenly watched by a young man named Benjamin Tillett, then working for his living at the wharves and docks. Tillett's life had been a chequered one. He was born in Bristol in 1859. Before the age of thirteen he had been three times a runaway from home, and had passed six months on a fishing smack, and had imbibed a smattering of bootmaking, and some knowledge of the rougher side of the world. He continued to indulge his West Country instinct for roving and fighting, first in the Navy, then on a trading vessel, where he was always ready for a contest with the skipper; and when more than nine years ago he had settled down to steady work at the riverside, those who knew him might have predicted that he would not be long before scenting a grievance and setting himself to put it right. Of slight and delicate physique, but of a restless and energetic temperament, with indomitable pluck and a strong vein of ambition, he was just the man to inspire restlessness in others.

He found his opportunity nearly three years ago, when a dispute at Cutler Street Tea Warehouse led to the formation of the 'Tea Operatives' and General Labourers' Union'. He was first asked for advice, then put on the committee, in a few weeks he was made general secretary, and settled down to the tremendous task of organising the heterogeneous mass of men around him. It was slow and laborious work. There were scarcely any funds, beyond the proceeds of the weekly subscription of 2*d*., and a few pounds subscribed from outside, and the men were new to the idea of combination. A strike organised at Tilbury last autumn for an advance of wage from 4*d*. to 5*d*. an hour dragged on for a month and then flickered out. The labourers lost heart, and when Tillett recovered from illness, brought on by exposure during the strike, he found his work undone, the Union disorganised, and the men harder to move than ever. Though sorely tempted to abandon the task, he nevertheless set to work again, but little advance seemed to be made until the formation of the Gas Workers' Union in the spring of the present year. The gas workers demanded and obtained an alteration of the twelve hours' shift to one of eight hours. There was no actual strike, but large meetings were held, addressed among others by John Burns and Tom Mann, and Tillett himself had a share in drafting the rules of the Union. In this way the future leaders of the dock strike became familiar with many sections of East London workers, and began to gain their confidence.

The formation of the Gas Workers' Union marks an epoch in the labour movement in East London. By this time, also, the general revival of trade was in full swing. Many who had lost heart regained their confidence in combined action, and some of the dock labourers wanted to come out on strike in the early summer; but the Union was still weak, and for various reasons many labourers held aloof. A further step was taken, when a permanent labourer, named Harris, determined to form a new Union for permanent hands, and induced John Burns and others to address a meeting with this view.

The wisdom of this step has been variously judged, but, without a doubt, it helped to force on the strike. The prospect of a fresh Union infused new vigour into Tillett's organisation, and the men were already ripe for a contest, when, on August 12th, a dispute at the South West India Dock served as the spark which kindled the blaze.

The nature of the dispute—about the division of the 'plus' on a certain cargo—is of little importance, for it was avowedly only the pretext for a revolt against all the grievances which had long rankled in the minds of the dock labourers. The men wanted to come out at once, and their leader only managed to restrain them until he had formulated their demands in writing, and sent them to the dock authorities. The demands were as follows: No man to be taken on for less than four hours at a stretch, contract and piecework to be abolished, and wages to be raised to 6*d*. an hour and 8*d*. overtime. The letter was written on Tuesday, August 13th, and an answer requested by twelve o'clock next day.

The executive was elected by the councils of the Amalgamated and United Societies of Stevedores, and after the first day met regularly at the Wade's Arms, in Jeremiah Street, Poplar. James Toomey, the massive chairman of the Amalgamated who had hitherto acted as chief marshal of the strike processions, was soon chosen to preside at the daily meetings—a difficult and often stormy position, which needed a strong arm in more senses than one. An appeal was issued from the Wade's Arms asking for financial support from other trades.

Meanwhile another committee was sitting at Wroot's dingy little coffee tavern, only a few minutes' walk off, which had been chosen by Ben Tillett as the headquarters of the old Dockers' Union, and collecting-boxes in aid of the strike were issued from that centre also, as well as from Wade's Arms, an arrangement which caused some little confusion and friction.

It is a matter of some interest to trace the early history of these two strike councils, and the circumstances which led to their amalgamation, and formation of a separate committee for finance. From Sunday onwards funds began to come in from outside—chiefly to Benjamin Tillett. The money was welcome, but how was it to be used? It would not be much good to shower it in sixpences among the crowd, but there was not enough as yet to admit of an organised distribution of relief, and, moreover, the hands of the leaders were too full with adding to the number of the strikers to give much attention to the work of feeding them. So things drifted, and for the first few days no one but the pickets received any share of the proceeds of the collections.

The first step towards coping with the difficulty was taken on Tuesday, when, at the usual afternoon gathering outside the dock gates, John Burns invited all sections of waterside labourers affected by the strike, to send representatives to a great meeting at the Assembly Hall, in the Mile End Road, the same evening, for the purpose of electing a finance committee to organise relief. John Burns was to be secretary, Tom Mann treasurer, and five members were to be chosen by the meeting, with power to add seven to their number.

The meeting was packed and enthusiastic, and a good deal of enrolling of new members of the Union was got through. The five members of committee were also duly elected, but—alas, for human nature—only one of the five, Henry Kay, put in an appearance next day at Wroot's. He, therefore, with Burns and Mann, constituted for a time the finance committee. Mr Champion, the well-known editor of the *Labour Elector*, gave a great amount of useful help in their work, but was never formally added to the committee. Some few days later, a docker turned up and inquired if a strike was going on, as he was told he had been elected on a committee at the Assembly Hall. He explained that he was not quite clear about it, having had a drop too much at the time. He was politely bowed out. So far did the paper constitution of the finance committee differ from the reality.

Who Gained by Change?

114. THE SIGNIFICANCE OF THE DOCK STRIKE

Source: 'The Times', 16 September 1889.

After five weeks, the London dock strike ended in a resounding victory for the dockers. Settlement was reached on 15 September and 'The Times' newspaper in a leader the next morning tried to sum up the importance of what had occurred.

GENERAL rejoicing will hail the announcement that the strike is a thing of the past. It is an announcement which has been deferred so long that people had almost ceased to expect it. Now that it has come it is hardly less welcome to those concerned than the news of the conclusion of peace after an exhausting war. How much longer the strike might have dragged on but for the gallant efforts of CARDINAL MANNING, the LORD MAYOR, and MR SIDNEY BUXTON, can only be conjectured. It can only be affirmed that both sides appeared to be well-matched in pertinacity, and that there were few symptoms in either of a disposition to yield when this small band of mediators came on the scene. All the more richly they deserve the public thanks for persevering, in the face of somewhat acrimonious treatment by the strike leaders, until they brought the contending parties into agreement. The result is that, so far as regards the precise questions at issue, the dock labourers and their allies have won a remarkable victory. The dock companies have granted all the more important of their demands....

But, although the victory of the dock labourers is discounted by other considerations, the strike will remain a most significant event in the relations between capital and labour. There is first the fact that the despised dock labourers, possessed of no special skill, industry, or strength, and in regard to the last two qualifications often singularly ill equipped, have been able to combine—combination hitherto having been considered a weapon only available for the skilled labourer. But even this, although a remarkable, was by no means the most remarkable, phenomenon of the strike. If the dock labourers and their employers had been left severely alone to fight it out the dock labourers could not have held out a week. Here we have what differentiates this strike from all others. The hard case of the men elicited the sympathy of all the various categories of riverside labourers without exception. These among them made up a compact industry army, without whom the shipping trade of London could not proceed; and it accordingly stood still. More than that, the case of the dock labourers took a powerful hold upon public opinion. It drew sympathy and material support from all quarters; for some yet unexplained reason, from Australia above all. Thus the men were placed beyond the reach of starvation. They were enabled to bargain on equal terms with their employers: and they were eventually successful. The hints afforded by the great strike will probably not be neglected in the future. It would not be too much to say that we may look for a large development of them in future conflicts between capital and labour. The fortuitous alliance of riverside labourers, possessing various grades of skill and social standing, will probably be taken as an encouragement to carry into effect those wider federations of labour which have hitherto been treated as visionary. Nor must employers expect too confidently in future that public opinion will observe a strict neutrality whilst their labourers are adopting that process of adjusting the market price of their labour which is called a strike.

115. THE BROOKLANDS AGREEMENT

Source: 'Board of Trade Report on Wages and Hours of Labour, Part II, Standard Piece Rates', 1894, C. 7567—I, vol. XXXI, pp. 9–11.

The contemporary historians of late Victorian trade unionism Sidney and Beatrice Webb, thought the machinery for collective bargaining developed by the cotton operatives "approaches the ideal" ('Industrial Democracy', 2nd ed., 1902, p. 203). The machinery had been severely tested in 1892–3, a time of severe depression and slender profit margins in cotton spinning. The employers demanded a 10 per cent reduction in wages to bring their costs into line with the state of the market, while the operatives urged short-time working until better times came round. Over three hundred firms closed their mills to enforce the wage reduction and between 45,000 and 50,000 cotton workers were locked out. After a twenty weeks' stoppage of work, some thirty or forty representatives of employers and employed met at a country inn and after an all-night sitting brought the dispute to an end with the following agreement, which governed the cotton spinning trade down to 1905.

THAT the pending dispute be settled by a reduction of (sevenpence) in the (pound) in the present wages of the operative cotton spinners, card and blowing room hands, reelers, winders, and others, such reductions to take effect forthwith, and the mills resume work on Monday next, the 27th instant.

That when the employers and employed next agree upon an increase in the standard wages of the operative cotton spinners, card and blowing room hands, and others who participated in the last advance in wages, such increase shall not exceed the reduction now agreed upon, unless in the meantime, there shall have been a further reduction of such wages, in which case, should an advance be agreed to, the employed shall be entitled to an advance equal in amount to the last preceding reduction, plus the reduction of sevenpence, in the £, now agreed upon, provided always that no application for an increase or reduction of such wages as now agreed upon shall be made for a period of six calendar months from the date hereof.

That subject to the last preceding clause, and with the view to prevent the cotton spinning trade from being in an unsettled state too frequently from causes such as the present dispute, to the disadvantage of all parties concerned, no advance or reduction in such wages as aforesaid shall in future be sought for by the employers or the employed until after the expiration of at least one year from the date of the previous advance or reduction, as the case may be; nor shall any such advance or reduction, when agreed upon, be more or less than five per cent upon the then current standard wages being paid. Notwithstanding anything herein-before contained in this clause, whenever a general demand for an advance or decrease of wages shall be made, the wages of the male card and blowing room operatives may be increased or decreased to such an extent as may be mutually agreed upon.

That the Secretary of the Local Employers' Association and the Secretary of the Local Trade Union shall give to the other of them, as the case may be, one calendar month's notice, in writing, of any and every general demand for a reduction or an advance of the wages then being paid.

That in future no Local Employers' Association, nor the Federated Association of Employers, on the one hand, nor any Trade Union or Federation of Trade Unions, on the other hand, shall countenance, encourage, or support any lockout or strike which may arise from or be caused by any question, difference, or dispute, contention, grievance or complaint with respect to work, wages, or any other matter, unless and until the same has been submitted in writing, by the Secretary of the Local Employers' Association to the Secretary of the Local Trade Union, or by the Secretary of the Local Trade Union to the Secretary of the Local Employers' Association, as the case may be, nor unless and until such Secretaries or a Committee, consisting of three representatives of the Local Trade Union, with their Secretary, and three representatives of the Local Employers' Association, with their Secretary, shall have failed after full inquiry, to settle and arrange such question, difference, or dispute, contention, complaint, or grievance within the space of seven days from the receipt of the communication, in writing, aforesaid. Nor unless and until failing the last mentioned settlement or arrangement (if either of the said Secretaries of the Local Trade Union or Local Employers' Association shall so deem it advisable) a Committee consisting of four representatives of the Federated Association of Employers, with their Secretary, and four representatives of the Amalgamated Association of the Operatives' Trade Union, with their Secretary, shall have failed to settle or arrange, as aforesaid, within the further space of seven days from the time when such matter is referred to them. Provided always that the Secretaries or the Committees herein-before mentioned, as the case may be, shall have power to extend or enlarge the said period of seven days whenever they may deem it expedient or desirable to do so.

Every Local Employers' Association or the Federated Association of Employers on the one hand, and every Local Trade Union or the Federation of Trade Unions on the other hand, shall, with as little delay as possible, furnish to the other of them, in writing, full and precise particulars with reference to any and every question, difference or dispute, contention, complaint or grievance, with a view to the same being settled and arranged at the earliest possible date, in the matter herein-before mentioned.

It is agreed that in respect of the opening of new markets abroad, the alteration of restrictive foreign tariffs, and other similar matters which may benefit or injure the cotton trade, the same shall be dealt with by a Committee of three or more from each Federation, all the Associations undertaking to bring the whole of their influence to bear in furthering the general interests of the cotton industry in this country. The above Committee shall meet whenever the Secretary of either

Federation shall be of opinion that questions affecting the general interests of the cotton trade should be discussed.

The representatives of the employers and the representatives of the employed in the pending dispute do hereby mutually undertake that they will use their best endeavours to see that the engagements hereinbefore respectively entered into by them are faithfully carried out in every respect.

This agreement is signed on behalf of the Federation of Master Cotton Spinners' Associations, the Amalgamated Association of Operative Cotton Spinners, the Amalgamated Association of Card and Blowing Room Operatives, and the Amalgamated Northern Counties Association of Weavers, Warpers, Reelers and Winders.

116. INDUSTRIAL WAR IN SHIPBUILDING

Source: 'Memoirs of John Wigham Richardson': privately printed (Glasgow, 1911), pp. 323–5.

John Wigham Richardson has appeared before in these documents as one of the successful business-men of his day (No. 29). At the time when this dialogue was written by him, in September, 1894, he was one of the more prominent employers in shipbuilding, which was much disturbed in its industrial relations.

A Colloquy on Strikes and Trade Unions

Interviewer. How is it that you masters display so much indifference when a perfect civil war of industry is being waged?

Employer. You use the word *master*, an appellation which often gives offence to artisans. We are sometimes called tyrants, sometimes plutocrats, sometimes captains of industry, and so forth. If you accept the last appellation as being most applicable to what you call a war, you will realise that in the thick of the strife, officers rarely enter into abstract discussions as to the causes or justification of a war. They think more of their own immediate duty and of their promotion. The more reflecting may realise the horrors of the war and the injuries inflicted on the country, but their duty is to overcome the obstacles in front of them and not to philosophize....

Interviewer. You will hardly go so far as to say that trade unions have not raised wages?

Employer. I certainly think they have not only *not* raised, but actually lowered wages. To speak more accurately, they have prevented them from rising so much as they would otherwise have done. That a ring of men may for a time force up the rate of wages, no one will deny; but it does not follow that those men will be better off as they will probably get less employment in consequence. You have also to consider the great waste caused by strikes. The strikes or locks-out for 1892 alone must have involved a direct loss of three or four millions in wages, besides the loss on machinery stopped from producing. I am willing to grant that wages have doubled, or increased threefold, or even if you like sixfold, within the last hundred and twenty years. But still we must wonder that the working classes are not better off. Consider for a moment what the power of machinery means, and what must be the effect on the national wealth, when production is increased, thirty or forty or a hundred fold.

Interviewer. You say that the workmen have not profited so much as they ought to have done by the national prosperity. What is the main cause of this in your opinion?

Employer. It is hardly necessary for either of us to discuss this! Have we not both lived all our lives in the atmosphere of philanthropic efforts to promote temperance, thrift, foresight and industry?

Interviewer. What in your opinion is the principal cause of strikes?

Employer. Undoubtedly it is the belligerent nature of man. The worst strikes which we have had on the Tyne in recent years have been caused by the quarrels between different classes of workmen, in which the masters were not directly concerned.

117. THE TAFF VALE DECISION, 1901

Source: 'Law Reports, Appeal Cases' (1901), pp. 429–31, taken from the judgement of Justice Farwell.

The transfer by the Taff Vale Railway Company in South Wales of a signalman, J. Ewington, from one district to another, against his wishes, was the act which led to a strike on that railway in August 1900. At first unauthorized, later supported by the Amalgamated Society of Railway Servants, the strike was tumultuous and there were acts of an unlawful character. The general manager of the company, A. Beasley, brushed aside the advice of the company's solicitors and applied for a legal injunction against the trade union officials concerned. He also began a civil suit against the union in its corporate capacity for damages for wrongful acts. Justice Farwell granted the injunction and the damages. His judgment was reversed on appeal but upheld by the Law Lords in the House of Lords. The decision in the House of Lords, given in July 1901, was extremely important. It exposed the Amalgamated Society to the damages which were later awarded against it, together with the legal costs. More important, it reversed the impression generally held since the legislation of the early 1870's that, while trade unions could sue for recovery of funds, for example, against defaulting officials, they could not themselves be sued for damages for actions committed by their members in the course of a trade dispute. As an interpretation of the law, the Taff Vale judgment was probably technically correct. But it made almost impossible trade union activity that might lead to a strike and imperilled the whole procedure of collective bargaining. For an example of the kind of problem it created, see the case Denaby and Cadeby Main Collieries Ltd. v. The Yorkshire Miners Association and others. In a bitter strike, between June 1902 and March 1903, the mining company instituted proceedings against the Yorkshire miners union and claimed £150,000 in damages. The union won its case after a long fight. 'Law Reports, Appeal Cases' (1906), pp. 384–408.

...although a corporation and an individual or individuals may be the only entity known to the common law who can sue or be sued, it is competent to the Legislature to give to an association of individuals which is neither a corporation nor a partnership nor an individual a capacity for owning property and acting by agents, and such capacity in the absence of express enactment to the contrary involves the necessary correlative of liability to the extent of such property for the acts and defaults of such agents. It is beside the mark to say of such an association that it is unknown to the common law....

Now the Legislature in giving a trade union the capacity to own property and the capacity to act by agents has, without incorporating it, given it two of the essential qualities of a corporation—essential, I mean, in respect of liability for tort, for a corporation can only act by its agents, and can only be made to pay by means of its property. The principle on which corporations have been held liable in respect of wrongs committed by its servants or agents in the course of their service and for the benefit of the employer...is as applicable to the case of a trade union as to that of a corporation. If the contention of the defendant society were well founded, the Legislature has authorized the creation of numerous bodies of men capable of owning great wealth and of acting by agents with absolutely no responsibility for the wrongs that they may do to other persons by the use of that wealth and the employment of those agents.... If, therefore, I am right in concluding that the society are liable in tort, the action must be against them in their registered name. The acts complained of are the acts of the association. They are acts done by their agents in the course of the management and direction of a strike; the undertaking such management and direction is one of the main objects of the defendant society, and is perfectly lawful; but the society, in undertaking such management and direction, undertook also the responsibility for the manner in which the strike is carried out. The fact that no action could be brought at law or in equity to compel the society to interfere or refrain from interfering in the strike is immaterial; it is not a question of the rights of members of the society, but of the wrong done to persons outside the society. For such wrongs, arising as they do from the wrongful conduct of the agents of the society in course of managing a strike which is a lawful object of the society, the defendant society, is in my opinion, liable.

118. TRADE UNIONISM AFTER TAFF VALE

Source: S. and B. Webb, 'Industrial Democracy', Introduction to the 1902 edition, pp. xxvi–xxvii.

At first sight there would seem little or nothing to complain about. The judgment professes to make no change in the lawfulness of Trade Unionism. No act is ostensibly made wrongful which was not wrongful before. And if a Trade Union, directly or by its agents, causes injury or damage to other persons, by acts not warranted in law, it seems not inequitable that the Trade Union itself should be made liable for what it has done. The real grievance of the Trade Unions, and the serious danger to their continued usefulness and improvement, lies in the uncertainty of the English law, and its liability to be used as a means of oppression. This danger is increased, and the grievance aggravated, by the dislike of Trade Unionism and strikes which nearly all judges and juries share with the rest of the upper and middle classes. The public opinion of the propertied and professional classes is, in fact, even more hostile to Trade Unionism and strikes than it was a generation ago. In 1867–75, when Trade Unionism was struggling for legal recognition, it seemed to many people only fair that, as the employers were left free to use their superiority in economic strength, the workmen should be put in a position to make a good fight of it against the employers. Accordingly, combinations and strikes were legalised, and some sort of peaceful picketing was expressly authorised by statute....It all belonged to the conception of a labor [*sic*] dispute as a stand-up fight between the parties, in which the State could do no more than keep the ring. Gradually this conception has given way in favour of the view that, quite apart from the merits of the case, the stoppage of work by an industrial dispute is a public nuisance, an injury to the commonweal, which ought to be prevented by the Government. Moreover, the conditions of the wages contract are no longer regarded only as a matter of private concern. The gradual extension of legislative regulation to all industries, and its successive application to different classes of workers and conditions of employment, decisively negatives the old assumption of the employer that he is entitled to hire his labor [*sic*] on such terms as he thinks fit. On the other hand, public opinion has become uneasy about the capacity of English manufacturers to hold their own against foreign competition, and therefore resents, as a crime against the community, any attempt to restrict output or obstruct machinery, of which the Trade Unions may be accused. And thus we have a growing public opinion in favour of some authoritative tribunal of conciliation or arbitration, and an intense dislike of any organised interruption of industry by a lock-out or a strike, especially when this is promoted by a Trade Union which is believed— often on the strength of the wildest accusations in the newspapers—to be unfriendly to the utmost possible improvement of processes in its trade.

119. THE TRADE DISPUTES ACT, 1906

Source: 'The Law Reports. The Public General Statutes passed in the sixth year of...Edward VII' (1906), vol. XLIV, 6 Edw. VII, ch. 47. An Act to provide for the regulation of Trades Unions and Trade Disputes.

The Taff Vale judgment opened a period of uncertainty and agitation.

*The issue arising was essentially political. Was Parliament prepared to
reverse the decision of July 1901? The question was answered, after the
General Election of 1906, by the Trade Disputes Act of the same year.
This was the result of considerable political excitement and the adherence
of the trade unions to the Labour Representation Committee in order to
secure a change in the law. For Taff Vale in politics F. Bealey and
H. Pelling, 'Labour and Politics 1900–1906' (1958).*

4–(1) An action against a trade union, whether of workmen or of
masters, or against any members or officials thereof on behalf of themselves and all other members of the trade union in respect of any
tortious act alleged to have been committed by or on behalf of the
trade union, shall not be entertained in any court.

120. RAILWAYS: THE NON-RECOGNITION
OF TRADE UNIONS

*Source: G. W. Alcock, 'Fifty Years of Railway Trade Unionism'
(1922), p. 376.*

*The process of collective bargaining made slow headway in some
industries, including one of the largest, the railways. Several railway
trade unions existed, including the Amalgamated Society of Railway
Servants, founded in 1871. The railway managements were adamant,
however, against recognizing them, usually on the plea that to do so would
weaken staff discipline and that staff discipline was bound up with public
safety. The speaker here was Sir Alexander Henderson, addressing the
shareholders of the Great Central Company, in 1907. Recognition was
substantially granted in 1911, when new conciliation machinery was set
up. By 1914 terms between the railway managements and the unions
had become more or less amicable.*

IN common with other companies who have been approached by the
Amalgamated Society of Railway Servants, who demand recognition as the representatives of our men, we doubt their right to formulate
such a demand, and we certainly cannot entertain it for one moment.
We believe that so far the action of the society has been detrimental to
the interests of those they are supposed to serve. A reasonable amount
of overtime which the men appreciated has been taken from them,
mainly, I believe, owing to the action of this self-constituted body.
No doubt the agitation has been cleverly engineered and made to appear of portentous magnitude, but we are confident of the justice with

which we treat our workmen, and we are equally sure that our employés recognise our fairness, and require no intermediary to act for them, and resent the attempt that is being made to foster ill-will.

121. THE COAL MINES REGULATION ACT, 1908

Thomas Ashton reporting to the International Miners Federation, 'I.M.F. Quarterly Report' (March 1909), quoted J. E. Williams, 'The Derbyshire Miners' (1962), p. 384.

An eight hours' day in the coal mines had been agitated for by the Miners' Federation of Great Britain for many years before 1908. Legislation was delayed by differences of opinion among the miners themselves, the Northumberland and Durham men being not in favour because they were themselves employers of labour, boy-labour, and it did not suit their arrangements to change. When the change came, it was the result both of trade union pressure, now united, and the influence of the miners' M.P.s in the Liberal majority of the House of Commons, after 1906. The bank was the pit-bank, i.e. the top of the pit-shaft.

THE Act is a long way short of what was asked for, but it may be considered a foundation upon which we can now begin to build. It is the first instalment of an eight hours' working day by legal enactment. The agitation will still continue until that which the Federation set out for is obtained, a Mines Act limiting the working hours at not more than eight per day from bank to bank.

122. MINIMUM WAGES IN THE COAL INDUSTRY, 1912

Source: 'The Law Reports. The Public General Statutes passed in the 2nd and 3rd years of the Reign of King George V' (1913), vol. L, 2 and 3 Geo. V, ch. 2.

The Coal Mines (Minimum Wage) Act of 1912 was passed after a strike of five weeks, which involved all the British coalfields. The dispute began with representations in South Wales about the difficulties of men working "abnormal places". Here owing to physical conditions at that place in the mine and not through any fault of his own, the miner could not earn a normal wage. But this was in effect a side issue. What led to the strike was the desire of miners in many fields for a "living wage", i.e. a minimum wage independent of the fluctuations of the market. The current rise in the cost of living lent force and fire to this demand. See J. W. F. Rowe, 'Wages in the Coal Industry' (1923).

The Wages Bargain

1. (1) It shall be an implied term of every contract for the employment of a workman underground in a coal mine that the employer shall pay to that workman wages at not less than the minimum rate settled under this Act and applicable to that workman....

2. (1) Minimum rates of wages and district rules for the purposes of this Act shall be settled separately for each of the districts named in the Schedule to this Act by a body of persons recognised by the Board of Trade as the joint district board for that district....

(2) The Board of Trade may recognise as a joint district board for any district any body of persons, whether existing at the time of the passing of this Act or constituted for the purpose of this Act, which in the opinion of the Board of Trade fairly and adequately represents the workmen in coal mines in the district and the employers of those workmen, and the chairman of which is an independent person appointed by agreement between the persons representing the workmen and employers respectively on the body, or in default of agreement by the Board of Trade....

(3) The joint district board of a district shall settle general minimum rates of wages and general district rules for their district (in this Act referred to as general district minimum wages and general district rules), and the general district minimum rates and general district rules shall be the rates and rules applicable throughout the whole of the district to all coal mines in the district and to all workmen or classes of workmen employed underground in those mines....

[*The Schedule attached to the Act lists the twenty two coal mining districts subject to its provisions.*]

123. SYNDICALISM IN THE COAL FIELDS

Source: 'The Miners' Next Step' (Tonypandy, 1912), pp. 8, 9, 19, 20.

This celebrated penny pamphlet arose out of the Cambrian Combine strike in the South Wales coalfield in 1911. A sharp difference of opinion arose over the direction of the strike, between the leaders of the South Wales Miners' Federation and the members of the local Cambrian Strike Committee. The pamphlet set out with great force a gospel which spread swiftly through the South Wales coal valleys, although many men did not accept it, and it became nationally famous. This was the doctrine of syndicalism or the transfer of the means of production and exchange from the capitalist, not to the state, but to the workers in industry, organ-ized in their unions. Here it meant "the mines for the miners", as a first step towards a nation organized on the syndicalist basis. Syndical-ism represented a mood of revolutionary idealism much stronger in French and American industry before the First World War than it was here. But its appearance in Britain was important. It was a force to be reckoned with between 1912 and 1926. See B. Pribićević, 'The Shop Stewards' Movement and Workers' Control 1910–1922' (1959).

HERE is perhaps after all our strongest indictment. The policy of 'collective bargaining' will be dealt with later on. But we have here to point out why there is discontent with 'leaders'. The policy of conciliation gives the real power of the men into the hands of a few leaders. Somebody says 'What about conferences and ballots?' Con-ferences are only called, and ballots only taken when there is a differ-ence of opinion between leaders. The conference or ballot is only a referee. Can this be denied? In the main, and on things that matter, the Executive have the supreme power. The workmen for a time look up to these men and when things are going well they idolise them. The employers respect them. Why? Because they have the men—the real power—in the hollow of their hands. They, the leaders, become 'gentlemen', they become M.P.'s, and have considerable social prestige because of this power. Now when any man or men assume power of this description, we have a right to ask them to be infallible. That is the penalty, a just one too, of autocracy. When things go wrong, and we have shown that they have gone wrong, they deserve to be, and are blamed. What really is blameworthy, is the conciliation policy which demands leaders of this description. For a moment let us look at this question from the leaders' standpoint. First, they are 'trade unionists by trade' and their profession demands certain privileges. The greatest of all these are plenary powers. Now, every inroad the rank and file make on this privilege lessens the power and prestige of the leader. Can we wonder then that leaders are averse to change? Can we wonder that they try and prevent progress? Progress may arrive at such a point that they would not be able to retain their 'jobs', or their 'jobs' would become so unimportant that from their point of view, they would not be worth retaining. The leader then has an interest—a vested interest—in stopping progress. They have therefore in some things an antagonism of interests with the rank and file. The conditions of things in South Wales has reached the point when this difference of interest, this antagonism, has become manifest. Hence the men criticise and are discontented with their leaders. But the remedy is not new leaders. But—well, we shall see....

PROGRAMME

Ultimate Objective

One organisation to cover the whole of the Coal, Ore, Slate, Stone, Clay, Salt, mining or quarrying industry of Great Britain, with one Central Executive.

That as a step to the attainment of that ideal, strenuous efforts be made to weld all National, County, or District Federations, at present comprising the Miners' Federation of Great Britain, into one compact organisation with one Central Executive, whose province it shall be to negotiate agreements and other matters requiring common action. That a cardinal principle of that organisation be: that every man working in or about the mine, no matter what his craft or occupation—provisions having been made for representation on the Executive—be required to both join and observe its decisions.

Immediate steps—industrial

I. That a minimum wage of 8s. per day, for all workmen employed in or about the mines, constitute a demand to be striven for nationally at once.

II. That subject to the foregoing having been obtained, we demand and use our power to obtain a 7 hour day.

Programme—political

That the organisation shall engage in political action, both local and national, on the basis of complete independence of, and hostility to all capitalist parties, with an avowed policy of wresting whatever advantage it can for the working class.

In the event of any representative of the organisation losing his seat, he shall be entitled to, and receive, the full protection of the organization against victimization.

Who Gained by Change?

General

Alliances to be formed, and trades organisations fostered, with a view to steps being taken, to amalgamate all workers into one National and International union, to work for the taking over of all industries, by the workmen themselves.

The Programme is very comprehensive, because it deals with immediate objects, as well as ultimate aims. We must have our desired end in view all the time, in order to test new proposals and policies, to see whether they tend in that direction or not. For example, the working class, if it is to fight effectually, must be an army, not a mob. It must be classified, regimented and brigaded, along the lines indicated by the product. Thus, all miners, etc., have this in common, they delve in the earth to produce the minerals, ores, gems, salt, stone, etc., which form the basis of raw material for all other industries. Similarly the Railwaymen, Dockers, Seamen, Carters, etc., form the transport industry. Therefore, before an organised and self-disciplined working class can achieve its emancipation, it must coalesce on these lines.

It will be noticed that nothing is said about Conciliation Boards or Wages Agreements. The first two chapters will, however, have shown you that Conciliation Boards and Wages Agreements only lead us into a morass. As will be seen when perusing the policy and constitution, the suggested organisation is constructed to fight rather than to negotiate. It is based on the principle that we can only get what we are strong enough to win and retain.

124. INDUSTRIAL RELATIONS BEFORE THE WAR

Source: Lord Askwith, 'Industrial Problems and Disputes' (1920), pp. 348–9.

The years immediately before the First World War were years of rising investment at home and abroad and much business activity. But they were at the same time years of intense unrest in the sphere of industrial relations. Sir George Askwith (1861–1942) was from 1911 Comptroller-General of the Labour Department of the Board of Trade and Chief Industrial Commissioner, therefore the government's chief conciliation officer at the time. He was speaking to the Cavendish Club in Bristol, in November 1913.

The Wages Bargain

THERE is a spirit abroad of unrest, of movement, a spirit and a desire of improvement, of alteration. We are in, perhaps, as quick an age of transition as there has been for many generations past. The causes of this are manifold. I am only going to indicate a few. One is that the schoolmaster has been abroad in the land, and that, as education improves, the more a man wishes to get to a better and higher position. Another is that the competition in life increases, and must increase, year by year.... Again, every man, whatever the actual cost of his livelihood may be, if he has arrived at a particular standard of life, not only desires to improve it, but also would struggle hard before he would give it up. When you come to certain standards of wages and livelihood, and find that particular things that you particularly use rise greatly in price, it affects the amenities of life and the margin of life to such an extent that there is disenchantment and a desire to keep to the standard which may have been achieved. Then there is the spirit of movement throughout the world. We quicken day by day means of transport. You have your tramways, railways, motors, taxis, and fast ships; and more and more a movement from place to place, and a movement that is taken advantage of by the people at large in increasing millions year by year. In addition to that you have in this country for some years past what I may call political equality. One man's vote is as good as another—sometimes better. If a man has got educated up to the view of considering himself politically equal to another man, he is far more anxious to achieve a greater amount of economic equality; a desire to reach that economic equality must necessarily exist in his mind. Upon platform after platform there has been preached the doctrine of Imperial possessions and their importance, and men to whom these Imperial possessions have been given are not inclined to think they are nobody in the world. There is also a vast amount of going backwards and forwards to dominions beyond the seas. Men come back from Canada and Australia, and come back imbued with ideas they find there; and leaven the local feeling in particular localities in this country. That, shortly, sums up some of the reasons why there is unrest, unrest that nobody can be surprised at, and which is bound to continue. Are men to remain in a backwater and do nothing, or to be cast out of the stream and remain as flotsam and jetsam on the bank?

Who Gained by Change?

125. THE TRIPLE ALLIANCE

Source: R. Smillie in 'The Labour Year Book' (1916), pp. 103–4.

Robert Smillie (1857–1940), President of the Miners' Federation of Great Britain between 1912 and 1921, describes the motives, as he saw them, which led the coalminers, the railwaymen and the transport workers to agree to work together in formulating and putting forward wage demands. For the formal terms of the alliance, see R. Page Arnot, 'The Miners: Years of Struggle' (1953), pp. 177–8.

ONE definite concrete result of the industrial unrest of recent years is the formation of the Triple Industrial Alliance proposed at a conference of the Miners' Federation of Great Britain, the National Union of Railwaymen, and the National Transport Workers' Federation, held on April 23rd, 1914.

The idea of such a conference was first brought into prominence at the Miners' Annual Conference in 1913, when a resolution was passed,

'That the Executive Committee of the Miners' Federation be requested to approach the Executive Committees of other big Trade Unions with a view to co-operative action and the support of each others demands.'

The miners contented themselves in the first place with securing a joint meeting with the representatives of the two industries most comparable to their own—railways and transport. It was felt that if a working arrangement could first be concluded with a few of the larger sections, afterwards extensions to other groups could be made.

The three bodies have much in common. Their membership is considerable, the miners numbering 800,000, the railwaymen 270,000, and the transport workers 250,000. The miners have done much fighting in the past sectionally and generally; the railwaymen on more than one occasion have come through struggles similar to our own; and the transport workers are famed for their fighting spirit and fighting qualities. But while we have achieved a great deal by our industrial struggles, and while we can hardly calculate the benefit conferred upon our people by these three bodies, it must be admitted that a great deal of suffering and privation has been caused. A strike on the railway system immediately affects the miners and the transport workers, as well as others. Though these for the moment may not have any quarrel with their respective employers, yet within a few days they are placed in the same position as though they had. They are idle and are thrown upon the funds of their unions. The same result follows if the miners or the transport workers are on strike. When the miners struck in 1912 the cost to the railwaymen alone was about £94,000. Whenever any of these three great sections have [*sic*] struck the others have had to stand by and suffer in silence.

The meeting of the three Executives, held in April, 1914, to consider ways and means of working in common and so avoiding the evils of disjointed action, was enthusiastic and unanimous. It resolved that a working agreement should be drawn up, and appointed a committee, consisting of the presidents and secretaries of the three organisations, for the purpose. The idea behind this agreement is not in any way the formation of a federation. The new body is not to be a rival to any other. Nor is it to be sectional in any sense. There is no suggestion, for instance, that if one section of the miners determines to strike they will receive the assistance of the new alliance. Action is to be confined to joint national action. Further, no action will be taken until all three partners have met in conference and have agreed upon the course to be adopted. Sympathetic action, in fact, is no longer to be left to the uncontrolled emotions of a strike period, but is to be the calculated result of mature consideration and careful planning. The predominant idea of the alliance is that each of these great fighting organisations, before embarking upon any big movement, either defensive or aggressive, should formulate its programme, submit it to the others, and that upon joint proposals joint action should then be taken.

It is clear to everyone acquainted with industrial development that capital is now organised for the purpose of attacking Trade Unionism and for defence against Trade Union advance. Should the occasion arise, each section of the alliance must be ready to render sympathetic action, deliberately thought out and agreed upon, should any one of the partners in the scheme be the object of attack.

While the scheme at the moment is not intended to include more than the three trades referred to, it may well be found advisable later on to extend the scope of the alliance in the general interests of Labour as a whole. Even now, indeed, it has already been discussed whether the Triple Alliance might not be in a position to assist our fellow workers in the textile industry if, at an adverse moment, they were threatened with a lock-out. Under such circumstances there is every probability that a stoppage of production would cause an immediate settlement. In every case the results of joint action on a large scale should be rapid and decisive, and all the suffering and loss inseparable from trade troubles of the past could be prevented in the future.

The mere calling of our conference caused somewhat of a sensation among the capitalists on the one hand, while, on the other, it created a new hope in the ranks of the industrial forces throughout the country. With the coming of war, however, the scheme had to be laid aside for a time, but already the annual meeting of the Railwaymen and the Transport Workers have signified their approval, and it now remains to be considered by the Miners' Conference at Nottingham in October, 1915. If the approval of the miners is forthcoming, and, in view of the scheme being their original suggestion, there is little likelihood of any other decision, the committee will then be at liberty to go ahead with the details. It will be wise, indeed essential, to have the working agreement ready for the days of peace after the war. It is then that we may expect an attack on Labour by the employers; it is now, in the midst of war, that we must prepare for the industrial conflicts that the military peace will bring.

CHAPTER 8

THE CONCEPT OF THE MINIMUM

What do we mean if we say that Victorian society was, as regards the distribution of wealth, individualist? Presumably what is intended is that it was the sort of society in which certain dominant beliefs about the economic rights and duties of the private person prevailed, and that these laid special stress upon what the individual or the head of the family could and ought to do for himself in the way of earning an income, as distinct from what the community should or could do for him and his family. Those beliefs may have been perhaps imposed upon rather than accepted by many people. But prevailed they must have done to make an individualist society.

The years between the reform of the Poor Law in 1834, just before Victoria came to the throne, and the great stir of social thought which came in with the 1880's, were the period when ideas of this kind were held and preached and accepted, not exclusively among the educated classes, but with special fervour by them. The central doctrine of those years on the matter of social obligation in the way of making an income was that it was a man's duty to provide for himself and all his dependents, both for the ordinary purposes and the contingent risks of life, including sickness and the want of work, old age and death. He should not only earn such an income. He should so lay it out between saving and expenditure as to meet all these needs in the best possible way.

These views reflected well enough the conventional beliefs and habits of the land-owning and land-tenanting classes in the counties, of the commercial and industrial middle classes in the towns, who did so much to provide Britain down to the First World War with its social and political leadership. Centuries of slowing expanding economic opportunity had taught these men, a small property-owning minority, how to make the most of their resources; how to save and invest, how to spend; how to adjust their financial means to ends and their ends to financial means. It was in this sense that the governing classes of Bagehot's day liked to regard themselves as above all practical. They were business-like and knew what business standards were, even when they lived unbusinesslike lives and rebelled against the values of the market place.

So was the trade unionist business-like, despite the disapproval of the middle classes, as he steered his collective course to avoid the bitter poverty which existed in every Victorian town. The will and the willingness to be financially independent, to look after one's own, extended deep down into the nation. It had strengthened with the economic development of the country in the previous generation. The Britain of the railway age had seen an enormous multiplication of jobs, a huge extension of the labour market, adequate to take up and provide some kind of an income even for a swiftly increasing population. Men were beginning a little to forget what it had once meant to live in a crowded, only partly industrial country, with plenty of concealed unemployment about.

Individualism did not scorn collective action of a voluntary sort. This was perhaps particularly true of the working classes, although mutual clubs and insurance societies for various purposes existed at every social level. Savings banks (State run, through the Post Office), friendly societies, trade unions with a benefit side, industrial assurance societies, abounded, although they were not always carefully thought out or well managed or always run for the benefit of those for whom they were ostensibly invented. They were the chief means by which people provided, if they did so at all, against the unavoidable and potentially disastrous expenses of sickness, lack of employment and burial—against everything except the day's needs, which had the first claim on weekly income.

Individualism was never unqualified, if only because personal incomes could always be trusted to break down from time to time. Hard weather or bad trade reduced many thousands of families to a state of destitution, where what furniture there was might have to be sold for food, if the worst came to the worst. At some periods of life, in old age, sickness and childhood, income was not earned. The propriety of community help was not denied on these occasions. There were recognized lines of defence which could be manned. Members of the family, in a rather extended sense, took the strain first; then friends and neighbours; then the charity of strangers. In the last resort, public action in the shape of the Poor Law stepped in. But all this did not impair the central doctrine, little relevant as this might seem to be to the sort of people whose lives were examined by Henry Mayhew or Charles Booth.

There can be no doubt about the individualism of the Victorians. Equally, like all such social characteristics, it was far from being unchanging. It represented a scheme of social values which was very old, profoundly modified by the experience of industrialization. What has been described as individualism was really an amalgam of personal and communal elements, in which the communal side had at one time almost certainly been much stronger. In earlier times, among a relatively thin population, following largely agricultural occupations and living for the most part, although not exclusively, in small and slow-moving communities, the ties of kinship and neighbourhood had been powerful. In that kind of society, in Tudor and Stuart England, the personality of the individual had been as much part of the community around him as the ore is part of the rock. His making of an income, like other aspects of his life, seemed very much part of the lives of other people. It was a situation from which he sometimes longed to escape. But the rock was even then breaking up, under many influences, not all of them economic. Population growth, industrial development and the growth of towns shivered the old pattern of social life in Britain. What the Victorians contributed to this process was an enormous expansion of the labour market in the railway age, an unheard-of mobility of residence and occupation at all levels of society, and the harsh common-sense of those who came out best in the struggle for income in the middle years of the century. They wished to know why everyone else was not so successful as they were.

It was to circumstances as comparatively recent as these and to classes in society newly formed that Victorian Britain owed the immense exaggeration of the role of the individual in its social thinking and the temporary discredit of the community. Many men genuinely believed that in creating his family income a man had discharged all his obligations to the community, owing nothing more to it and the community nothing to him. They were the ratepayers and taxpayers whose reluctance to admit that they had any duty to light the streets for their neighbours or to pay for the schooling or the health of other people formed an obstacle to social legislation in the 1850's and 1860's.

By the 1880's, that period is at an end. In the cities and towns which had become the new mould of British social life, economic individualism in the sense that it has been defined here was the target of criticism and subject to dissolution. This happened from two general causes. Both were connected with the scale and speed of the changes which were going on in the heart of Victorian society.

The first was the continued decline of the older social ties of family and locality. In a larger and longer-living population, crowded in great cities, this created evils which although not new in kind were certainly new in scale. By the end of the nineteenth century, for example, the situation of old people who had lived beyond the ability to make an income for themselves and for whom no relative or neighbour would accept responsibility, had become a problem of the first magnitude in the big towns.[1] This was a personal problem before it became social and social before it became political. The centre of it was still old age. But surroundings urban and industrial made it almost a new kind of problem. It was not solved by a doctrine which seemed to suppose

[1] See Edith Sellers, 'Old Age Pensions and the Belongingless Poor', *Contemporary Review* (1908), pp. 147 ff.

that the unskilled man in the town could save enough to keep himself and his wife till death. If the last years could not be provided for by him and were not a matter for family or neighbours, for whom were they a problem? Tradition said, for the charitable rich and the poor law. But late nineteenth-century opinion, quickened by political democracy, thought otherwise.

The other cause of the weakening of the fashionable individualism was the reverse and more positive side of this social process. It was the emergence of new forms of community life and a new scale of social values. This represented the adaptation of an old civilization to the new conditions of social life. In the light of it, the defiant individualism of the railway age began to look a transient and anachronistic thing.

The period after 1870, when expanding local government, collective bargaining and the increased efficiency of central administration were altering the character of social life, was also the age in which socialist ideas began to play for the first time a role in British politics. From the 1880's onwards, the influence of all the many forms of socialism, Marxist and non-Marxist, which flourished in this country was thrown, broadly speaking, on the side of collectivism, not individualism. At any time before 1914, however, socialism was decidedly a minority view, although the growth of its influence was rapid. Great changes in outlook and law had to be effected by a public opinion which, such as it was, was for the most part satisfied with conservative or liberal politics, or with no politics at all, and through the institutions of the day, such as they were.

Three great institutions were particularly important in the period 1880–1914 for the part which they played in modifying the individualism of the mid-Victorians and substituting for it a pattern of social life which was significantly different from that of the England of Marx and Mill.[1] They were the cities; the trade unions; and the civil service or as any Continental observer would have called it, the bureaucracy.

The cities were particularly significant in their widening influence. Ideas of social welfare which in the twentieth century became important in the life of the nation and the State had often begun their career on a municipal stage thirty and forty years before. The role of the cities between the 1860's and the end of Victoria's reign was that of forcing beds of social experiment. This was so, because so much of the life of the age poured through them. Liverpool in the 1860's, Birmingham in the 1870's, London in the 1890's, became successively the current pattern of good city government. By their sanitation and public health services, their education, their transport systems, municipal gas, water and electricity works, they set new standards of communal

[1] John Stuart Mill died at Avignon in 1873, Karl Marx in London in 1883.

life. City life as it is known today began to emerge as a result of long and hard fought local battles.

The cities began in the last thirty years of the nineteenth century the business of levelling up living standards irrespective of personal income. They made the first great inroads upon the narrow and self-satisfied individualism of the early industrial age. In doing so, they brought something new into the mind of the nation. It has been suggested[1] that when Sismondi, the Swiss historian and economist, launched the criticism of the British classical economists which made him famous in the early years of the nineteenth century, he did so partly under the influence of Italian thinkers who in turn owed something of their thought to the welfare provision of the great cities of Italy. However that may be, the cities of late Victorian Britain certainly assisted to bring new views of economic welfare into British economic thinking. In much earlier days, under the simpler conditions of the Britain of Adam Smith and Ricardo, the growth of output itself had seemed a sufficient contribution to welfare. But in dealing with their day-to-day problems, the Victorian towns and cities raised a general question. Were there not certain basic elements of a civilized life which all citizens ought to enjoy? If there were, and if some citizens did not possess the income with which to obtain those elements, it seemed right and proper to make a certain transfer of incomes, in the form of services, from the richer citizens. It also seemed right that the city as a body should own and possess property, out of which a community income could be raised. These were the ideas of what was coming to be called in the 1880's and 1890's municipal socialism. They were also the ideas which two municipal reformers of practical genius, Joseph Chamberlain and Sidney Webb, were fighting to import into national politics, each in his own very different way, towards the end of the century.

If the influence of the towns and cities worked towards the recognition of a right to the provision of a minimum of welfare, or of whatever the community chose to regard as welfare, so too did big industry and its habit of collective bargaining foster similar habits of mind. The negotiations between trade unions and employers, pursued annually in scores and hundreds of industries, became a search for common minimum standards of wage, hours of employment and conditions of work. These standards left considerable freedom to both employers and employed, but the minimum condition was applicable to everybody in that particular trade. Factory and mining law, becoming a complicated code of industrial legislation about this time, shared the same general character. It laid down, and enforced, not always very

[1] See the very interesting discussion in H. O. Pappe, *Sismondis Weggenossen* (Geneva, 1963).

satisfactorily, a minimum provision of welfare in factory, workshop, quarry and mine. By the 1880's, industries which escaped the factory and workshops acts and which were not subject to the rules of collective industrial agreements, stood the risk of being described as sweated industries. They were disapproved of by public opinion.

The opening of permanent appointments in nearly all departments of the state to competitive examination in 1870 coincided with the first beginnings of political democracy. Between them, manhood suffrage and the reformed civil service transformed the conditions of government as an earlier generation had known them. A flow of able men was attracted into the central administration of the country, just when public opinion was more disposed to legislation than ever before. Reform of the civil service did not begin the adaptation of the State to the altered society that was growing up—that had started with the controversies over factory law and public health in the 1830's and 1840's—but did help to carry it much further. The mid-Victorian machinery of State never could have borne the weight and complexity of legislation in education, public health, national insurance and a hundred other spheres which distinguished the next half century.

National legislation worked in the same direction as town government and the trade unions. It set up standards below which the citizen was not to be allowed to fall, whatever his income. What the standards were and how they were set depended upon the pressure of many social groups acting upon one another. This was part of the political history of the age. But they were imposed and accepted to an increasing extent, especially after 1900.

Between them, the cities, the unions and the legislative action of the state brought into national politics what was essentially a new idea. This was the belief that somewhere or other there existed a standard of what the basic elements of a civilised life ought to be, that that standard could be found and that when found law and custom should enforce it. This was much more than an economic idea. It represented rather a new phase in the development of industrial and urban civilization within Great Britain. But it carried distinct and far-reaching economic implications. It seemed to imply that if individuals did not possess the income necessary to purchase these indispensable elements of a decent human existence for themselves, then it would be right and proper for the community to use its authority (*a*) to see whether an adequate income could not somehow be found for them in the market, (*b*) to direct income, via taxation, from the more fortunate citizens towards those who tended to fall below the minimum.

No idea could enter on the British political scene complete or all at once. A few men might and did hammer out for themselves philosophical positions but the nation's approach to its problems was resolutely pragmatic. The Poor Law, the product of an earlier society, more authoritarian, socially and politically, than late Victorian Britain could be, began to fall into disrepute from the 1890's onwards. This way of dealing *en bloc* with the economic risks of life no longer satisfied. The royal commission on the Poor Law of 1905–9 failed to pull off the major reform which many people by that time desired. One by one, the chief risks of working class life were isolated and dealt with in other ways. They left the Poor Law standing side by side with what was substantially a new system of social policies run on different principles. Industrial accident was handled through employer's liability law (1894, 1897); old age by State pensions, non-contributory (1908); sickness, by national insurance, contributory (1911).

This process of transforming or supplementing incomes went beyond the beginning of a break up of the Poor Law and its replacement by social services. The State recognized for the first time since 1813 a certain responsibility for the level of wages. This was clearly implied in the Trade Boards Act of 1909. It was aimed at the sweated trades but provided an object lesson for the coal and the farming industries, which were far larger employers.

The further the State travelled along this road, the more clear it became that to undertake responsibility for income was also to take it for the employment by which income was earned. Unemployment provided the biggest problem of all. Its mere existence challenged the basic Victorian assumption that employment was always there for those who wanted it. The devastating effect of unemployment on incomes was approached indirectly by legislation in 1905, 1909 and 1911 on unemployment and public works, labour exchanges and unemployment insurance. The 1911 National Insurance Act brought unemployment within the new insurance scheme. But the unemployment which was in the legislator's mind was seasonal and cyclical. It was not the unemployment proceeding from structural change in industry and its markets which became the unemployment problem of the 1920's and 1930's. Nor was there for another generation after 1911 any question of the State assuming a general responsibility for the level of employment and the use of national resources.

At this point, pre-1914 economic thinking halted. If we revalue the figures of the total public expenditure of a social service kind, including education, borne out of taxes and rates at the prices of 1900, to give a standard of comparison, it appears that in 1870, this stood at something like 6s. 3d. per head of the United Kingdom population of those days. In 1910 it was something like £1.4s.9d.; in 1920, when the national insurance legislation had become fully operative, at £1.9s.5d. Of every pound in the average income per head of 1870 (national income divided by population) 3d. had been diverted from the taxpayer and ratepayer to meet public expenditure of this kind. In 1910 7*d*. was diverted; in 1920 between 7*d*. and 8*d*. This modest degree of economic effort, where it was aimed at supplying income, provided it only at the low level of the unskilled man of the day. It did something, not perhaps very much, to modify the conviction, so powerful in Victorian times, that the man without possessions was scarcely a person and could not expect the same treatment in the arrangements of society as the man whose property gave him a title to superior consideration.

FURTHER READING

The legislative and administrative changes of the middle years of the nineteenth century, which were important in themselves as well as a basis for later action, have been studied by D. Roberts, *The Victorian Origins of the British Welfare State* (New Haven, 1960).

Victorian charity and social work need more study. See, however, M. Simey, *Charitable Effort in Liverpool in the nineteenth Century* (1951); C. L. Mowat, *The Charity Organization Society 1869–1913* (1961); K. Woodroofe, *From Charity to Social Work in England and the United States* (1962); and E. Moberley Bell, *Octavia Hill* (1942). See also A. F. Young and E. T. Ashton, *British Social Work in the nineteenth Century* (1956).

The institutions of the Poor Law have received much attention, especially from S. and B. Webb, *English Local Government: English Poor Law History: Part II, The Last Hundred Years* (1929) and the same authors' *English Poor Law Policy* (1910). The Minority Report of the Royal Commission on the Poor Laws, 1909, still repays reading as a study in transitional thought.

For the cities and their influence on British social life, Asa Briggs, *Victorian Cities* (1963) and W. A. Robson, *A Century of Municipal Progress 1835–1935* (1935). On their economic activities, the contemporary Leonard Darwin, *Municipal Trade* (1903). See also S. Webb, *The London Programme* (1891).

For the influence of the trade unions as standard-setters in an industrial society, S. and B. Webb, *Industrial Democracy* (1897 and later editions). For the influence of the State in the same line, B. Hutchins and A. Harrison, *A History of Factory Legislation* (1903 and later editions). For the special problem of low wages in the 'sweated trades' and others, Clementina Black, *Sweated Industries* (1907).

The Civil Service as such lacks a history. There are lives of two important administrators in R. Lambert, *Sir John Simon 1816–1904 and English Social Administration* (1963) and B. M. Allen, *Sir Robert Morant* (1934).

The Fabian Socialists, who played an important part in formulating a concept of the minimum but whose influence on law has sometimes been exaggerated, are the subject of a recent study, A. M. McBriar, *Fabian Socialism and English Politics 1884–1918* (1962). They are best studied in their own *Fabian Tracts* and *Fabian Essays* (1889). For Marxian-type Socialism C. Tsuzuki, *H. M. Hyndman and British Socialism* (1961) and for the popular Socialism which was neither Marxian nor Fabian, L. V. Thompson, *Robert Blatchford, the Portrait of an Englishman* (1951).

On changes of thought and law from the 1890's, leading up to the social security legislation, (Lady) Gertrude Williams, *The State and the Standard of Living* (1936) presents an economist's view. M. Bruce, *The Coming of the Welfare State* (1961) and K. de Schweinitz, *England's Road to National Security* (1943) are general accounts. Both E. Halevy, *A History of the English People in the Nineteenth Century* in the fifth and sixth volumes of the paperback edition and R. C. K. Ensor, *England 1870–1914* (1936) devote much space to the social legislation of the period and have the interest of having been written by men who lived through it. The processes by which economic thinking and social values came to be changed still need much examination. The modification of economic thought may be judged from A. C. Pigou, *Wealth and Welfare* (1912), particularly part III, chapter 12, on A National Minimum. Compare another Cambridge economist, writing in mid-Victorian times, H. Fawcett, *Manual of Political Economy* (2nd ed. 1865), ch. VIII, on Popular Remedies for Low Wages.

126. THE POSITION OF WAGE-EARNERS

Source: J. T. Danson, 'The Wealth of Households' (Oxford, 1886), pp. 7, 331.

John Towne Danson (1817–98) was a Liverpool businessman and statistician. His book was originally a series of lectures on political economy at Queen's College, Liverpool, delivered in 1875–6. This statement of mid-Victorian orthodoxy does not appear to have been intended to be controversial.

A

They share the food-security of a well-ordered community; and they share many other of its advantages. But, as mere earners of weekly wages, awaiting a constant supply from others of the means of life, they are still about as near the condition of slavery as the public opinion of their time will permit them to be.

Who Gained by Change?

[Danson elsewhere explains what is presumably meant by 'the food-security of a well-ordered community'.]

Attendant on individualism, as on every other form of human policy yet tried, is beggary. This comes of the fact, as yet apparent in every form of human society, that there are some who are wholly unable, and some who are inveterately unwilling, to provide for themselves. Where slavery prevails, this tendency leads to some of its most revolting features. Where there is personal freedom, public compassion, protesting against permitted starvation, provides a remedy: either in tolerated begging, or in legal means of relief for the destitute.

127. THE CAB-HORSE STANDARD

Source: 'General' William Booth, 'In Darkest England and the Way Out' (1890), pp. 18–20.

The Salvation Army, which adopted its title in 1878, was perhaps the one religious movement of Victorian England that addressed itself directly and exclusively to the poor of the great towns. William Booth (1829–1912), its founder, adapted a title for his book, 'In Darkest England', from the narrative of the explorer, H. M. Stanley, 'In Darkest Africa', also published in 1890. The two books were best sellers of the year. Booth, who was assisted in writing his tract by the journalist W. T. Stead, was appealing for money for work among the destitute. The book owed something to Charles Booth's survey, but far more to personal experience and impatience with complacent respectability. For William Booth and his social attitude, see K. S. Inglis, 'The Churches and the Working Classes in Victorian England' (1963).

...The denizens in Darkest England, for whom I appeal, are (1) those who, having no capital or income of their own, would in a month be dead from sheer starvation were they exclusively dependent upon the money earned by their own work; and (2) those who by their utmost exertions are unable to attain the regulation allowance of food which the law prescribes as indispensable even for the worst criminals in our gaols.

I sorrowfully admit that it would be Utopian in our present social arrangements to dream of obtaining for every honest Englishman a gaol standard of all the necessaries of life. Some time, perhaps, we may venture to hope that every honest worker on English soil will always be as warmly clad, as healthily housed, and as regularly fed as our criminal convicts—but that is not yet. . . .

What, then, is the standard towards which we may venture to aim with some prospect of realisation in our time? It is a very humble one, but if realised it would solve the worst problems of modern Society.

It is the standard of the London Cab-Horse.

When in the streets of London a Cab-Horse, weary or careless or stupid, trips and falls and lies stretched out in the midst of the traffic, there is no question of debating how he came to stumble before we try to get him on his legs again. . . .

These are the two points of the Cab Horse's Charter. When he is down he is helped up, and while he lives he has food, shelter and work. That, although a humble standard, is at present absolutely unattainable by millions—literally by millions—of our fellow men and women in this country. Can the Cab Horse Charter be gained for human beings? I answer, yes. The Cab Horse standards can be obtained on the Cab Horse terms. If you get your fallen fellow on his feet again, Docility and Discipline will enable you to reach the Cab Horse ideal, otherwise it will remain unattainable. But Docility seldom fails where Discipline is intelligently maintained. Intelligence is more frequently lacking to direct, than obedience to follow direction. . . . Some, no doubt, like the bucking horse that will never be broken in, will always refuse to submit to any guidance but their own lawless will. They will remain either the Ishmaels or the Sloths of Society. But man is naturally neither an Ishmael nor a Sloth.

128. HOW FAR IS IT SAFE TO ABANDON THE MARKET?

Source: 'The Economist' (10 November 1883), p. 1306.

The newspaper was commenting upon an address by G. J. Goschen the day before to the Edinburgh Philosophical Institution on Laissez-Faire and Government. G. J. Goschen (1831–1907) had been President of the Poor Law Board and First Lord of the Admiralty in the first Gladstone administration. He was one of the more prominent members of the Liberal party and M.P. for Ripon.

THE question which is at present being discussed with so much interest, of the duty of the State in reference to the housing of the poor of our large towns, was touched on by Mr Goschen, and affords an excellent illustration and test of the principles which he laid down. Public feeling has been justly shocked by the horrible revelations, to which a wide publicity has recently been given, of the unsanitary and degrading condition of the houses of the urban poor. It is character-istic of the temper of the times that a demand is at once raised by men of the most different parties and political creeds for the beneficent intervention of the State, and the provision of decent dwellings for the lowest stratum in the community is assumed, almost without argu-ment, to fall within the scope of the legitimate functions of Govern-ment. This is a case in which, as it appears to us, the true limit to the responsibilities of the State is singularly easy to define. To prevent the erection of dwellings which are unfit for habitation, to compel the repair and improvement of dwellings which have become unfit, to punish all forms of nuisance, and all omissions on the part either of owners or occupiers which are hurtful to the general health—these are clearly matters of police, and they are all amply provided for by existing legislation. The Public Health Act of 1875 contains a sanitary code more minute and elaborate than any that has ever been adopted by a civilised country, and the real cause of much the larger part of the scandals which are now distressing us is to be sought, not in the defects of the law, but in the impossibility of administering it in the large towns. That impossibility arises partly from the lethargy of the local authorities, whose members, it is to be feared, are often personally interested in the continuance of the present state of things, and still more from the characters and habits of the population which has to be dealt with. Nothing short of an army of inspectors and policemen kept at work night and day would suffice to enforce the law in this metropolis.... But no case whatever has been made out for the proposal that the State, acting either by its central or local authorities, should itself take in hand the building and letting of workmen's dwellings. There is not the least reason why, if the State is to provide good lodgings cheap, it should not also be required to supply food and clothing (which are under existing conditions very unequally distri-buted) upon the same terms.

129. THE PRINCIPLES OF CHARITY

*Source: 'Eighth Annual Report of the Charity Organisation Society',
1876, appendix IV, pp. 24–5.*

*Victorian charity spoke with many voices. They ranged from that of
genuine friendship to unintelligent cruelty. Much of the charity which
helped was based upon kinship and neighbourhood and was between
people of the same class and income-level. Periods of trade depression
saw many families helping one another, sometimes to their mutual
destruction. Charity between the classes had a semi-official spokesman
from 1869 in the powerful London Charity Organisation Society and in
Charles Loch (1849–1923), the Society's secretary from 1875 to 1914.
The general principle of the Society's work is here stated by one of its
district committees. This heroic view, standard in the 1870's, ran into
increasing difficulties in the next quarter century, if only because the
Booth and Rowntree investigations made clear the national extent of
inadequate wages among the unskilled.*

THE principle is, that it is good for the poor that they should meet
all the *ordinary* contingencies of life, relying not upon public or
private charity, but upon their own industry and thrift, and upon the
powers of self-help that are to be developed by individual and collective effort. Ample room will still be left for the exercise of an abundant
charity in dealing with exceptional misfortune, and also in connection
with large schemes for the benefit of the working classes which may
require, in the first instance at all events, the fostering of wealth and
leisure. But it is a hurtful misuse of money to spend it in assisting the
labouring classes to meet emergencies which they should themselves
have anticipated and provided for. The working man does not require
to be told that temporary sickness is likely now and then to visit his
household; that times of slackness will occasionally come; that if he
marries early and has a large family, his resources will be taxed to the
uttermost; that if he lives long enough, old age will render him more
or less incapable of toil—all these are the ordinary contingencies of a
labourer's life, and if he is taught that as they arise they will be met by
State relief or private charity, he will assuredly make no effort to meet
them himself. A spirit of dependence, fatal to all progress, will be
engendered in him, he will not concern himself with the causes of his
distress, or consider at all how the condition of his class may be
improved; the road to idleness and drunkenness will be made easy to

him, and it involves no prophesying to say that the last state of a population influenced after such a fashion as this will certainly be worse than the first. One thing there is which true charity does require the working man to be told, and it is the aim of this Society to tell him, not in words merely, but in acts that cannot be confuted. We desire to tell him that those who are born to easier circumstances sympathise with the severe toil and self-denial which his lot imposes upon him; that many are standing beside him ready and even eager to help if proper occasion should arise; and that if he, or wife, or child should be stricken with *protracted* sickness, or with some special infirmity, such as we all hope to escape, there are those at hand who will gladly minister to his necessities, and do their best at least to mitigate the suffering which it may be beyond their power to remove.

130. THE CONDITIONS OF CHARITY

Source: 'Form No. 28, Notice to Persons Applying for Assistance' in collection of 'Charity Organisation Forms, Papers, Investigation Tickets, Bye-laws, Almanack, etc. 1877–90', in possession of the Family Welfare Association (formerly C.O.S.), Denison House, London, reprinted in K. Woodroofe, 'From Charity to Social Work in England and the United States' (1962), p. 41.

The London Charity Organization Society and its helpers worked out in the nineteenth century the basis of what is known today as social case-work; but its aid to persons had to be given within the limits of Victorian economic individualism.

1. The Society desires to help those persons who are doing all they can to help themselves, and to whom temporary assistance is likely to prove a lasting benefit.

2. No assistance should be looked for without full information being given in order that the Committee may be able to judge:

(1) Whether the applicant ought to be helped by charity.

(2) What is the best way of helping them....

3. Persons wishing to be assisted by Loans must find satisfactory security, such as that of respectable householders....Loans have to be paid back by regular instalments.

4. Persons who have thrown themselves out of employment through their own fault ought not to count upon being helped by charity.

5. Persons of drunken, immoral or idle habits can not expect to be assisted unless they can satisfy the Committee that they are really trying to reform.

6. The Society does not, unless under exceptional circumstances, give or obtain help for the payment of back rent or of funeral expenses. But when help of this sort is asked for, there may be other and better ways of assisting.

7. Assistance will not, as a rule, be given in addition to a Parish Allowance.

By Order,

C.O.S.

.........Committee.

131. THE PRINCIPLE OF PUBLIC ASSISTANCE

Source: Helen Bosanquet, ' The Poor Law Report of 1909: a Summary explaining the Defects of the Present System and the Principal Recommendations of the Commission, as far as relates to England and Wales' (1909), pp. 1–3.

Helen Bosanquet played a leading part in the Charity Organization Society and was a member of the Royal Commission on the Poor Law, 1905–9.

WHAT is the Poor Law, and who are the people to whom it applies?

Every civilised country has a different answer to give to this question, but in their main outlines all answers will coincide.

In the first place, the law which we in England call the Poor Law, but which receives more appropriate names in other countries, is that law which regulates the administration or distribution of assistance from public funds to private individuals on the ground of their failure to provide for themselves.

In the second place, the ultimate fact upon which all systems of public assistance are based is the fact that there are in every country persons who, for one reason or another, are found to be without the necessaries of life, whether provided by their own exertions or by their friends and relations. In the absence of any legal provision, these persons either die or are maintained by the charity of the benevolent. In most Christian communities it has originally been considered that the charity either of private persons or of religious communities should be sufficient to meet the need, and under these conditions begging has become a recognised means of obtaining a living. In a small community, where begging is only an appeal from one neighbour to another, the arrangement may serve well enough; but it leads to intolerable evils, both of fraud and neglected suffering, where it prevails in larger communities; and sooner or later it has always been considered necessary for the law to intervene and regularise the situation. That has been done by defining where the responsibility for the maintenance of these people lies, and by making the responsibility one to be enforced by law.

In England the duty was laid in the first instance upon the family, and failing this upon the parish, until at the beginning of last century it was found that for many reasons the parish was too small an area for effective administration. Under the Poor Law Amendment Act of 1834 parishes were then grouped into unions, and each union of parishes became responsible first for administering, and finally for providing, the necessary funds within their area. Since then the responsibility of administration has remained with the union, but there has been a constant tendency to widen the area of financial responsibility by means of subsidies from various sources until at the present time the percentage of expenditure on poor relief which is not met from local sources is about 20 per cent....

Thus the legal responsibility lies in the first place upon the individual —if capable—to maintain himself; in the second place it lies upon the family; and failing both these it lies ultimately upon the ratepayers of the union and county, and the taxpayers of the country.

132. PUBLIC ASSISTANCE IN THE 1890's

Source: G. Lansbury, 'My Life' (1931), pp. 135–7.

A sharp change in the administration of the Poor Law arrived in the 1890's. Under the Local Government Act, 1894, the conditions of election to the boards of guardians were altered. Multiple voting according to property was abolished. Women and working-men became eligible as candidates for the first time. George Lansbury (1859–1940) became a guardian of the poor in Poplar, a densely populated dockside parish of East London, in 1892. Together with William Crooks (1852–

1921), a cooper, he entered upon a local reform of poor relief. He describes the bad side of the Poor Law. There were other sides. For Lansbury, R. Postgate, The Life of George Lansbury (1951).

My first visit to the workhouse [*at Poplar*] was a memorable one. Going down the narrow lane, ringing the bell, waiting while an official with a not too pleasant face looked through a grating to see who was there, and hearing his unpleasant voice—of course he did not know me—made it easy for me to understand why the poor dreaded and hated these places, and made me in a flash realize how all these prison or bastille sort of surroundings were organized for the purpose of making self-respecting, decent people endure any suffering rather than enter. It was not necessary to write up the words 'Abandon hope all ye who enter here'. Officials, receiving ward, hard forms, white-washed walls, keys dangling at the waist of those who spoke to you, huge books for name, history, etc., searching, and then being stripped and bathed in a communal tub, and the final crowning indignity of being dressed in clothes which had been worn by lots of other people, hideous to look at, ill-fitting and coarse—everything possible was done to inflict mental and moral degradation.

The place was clean: brass knobs and floors were polished, but of goodwill, kindliness, there was none. There is a little improvement in the ordinary workhouse of today, but not much. Most of them are still quite inhuman, though infirmaries, hospitals and schools are all vastly improved. But thirty years ago the mixed workhouse at Poplar was for me Dante's *Inferno*. Sick and aged, mentally deficient, lunatics, babies and children, able-bodied and tramps all herded together in one huge range of buildings. Officers, both men and women, looked upon these people as a nuisance and treated them accordingly. Food was mainly skilly, bread, margarine, cheese, and hard, tough meat and vegetables, and occasionally doses of salted dried fish. Clothing was of the usual workhouse type, plenty of corduroy and blue cloth. No undergarments for either men or women, no sanitary clothes of any sort or kind for women of any age, boots were worn till they fell off. The paupers, as they were officially styled, were allowed out once a month and could be visited once a month. Able-bodied men were put to stone-breaking or oakum picking. No effort was made to find work for men or women. Girls came to be delivered of their babies, went out, and in course of time came back again. On one visit I inspected the supper of oatmeal porridge. On this occasion the food was served up with pieces of black stuff floating around. On examination we discovered it to be rat and mice manure. I called for the chief officer, who immediately argued against me, saying the porridge was good and wholesome. 'Very good, madam,' said I, taking up a basinful and a spoon, 'here you are, eat one mouthful and I will acknowledge I am wrong.' 'Oh dear, no' said the fine lady, 'the food is not for me, and is good and wholesome enough for those who want it.' I stamped and shouted around till both doctor and master arrived, both of whom pleaded it was all a mistake, and promptly served cocoa and bread and margarine.

133. THE REPORT ON THE POOR LAW, 1909

*Source: The diaries of Beatrice Webb, in B. Webb, 'Our Partnership',
ed. B. Drake and M. Cole (1948), pp. 425–6.*

*The years between 1905 and 1909 saw an important public inquiry
into the Poor Law, the most comprehensive and searching since 1834.
The findings of the royal commission were not, however, unanimous.
The commissioners divided themselves into majority and minority bodies,
writing separate reports. Their lack of agreement postponed any important
administrative reform of the law for another twenty years. Beatrice
Webb, who had been the leader of the minority, describes the press
reception of the two reports.*

February 18th. The day after the reception of the reports of the Poor Law Commission. We turned out to be quite wrong as to the reception of the Majority Report. So far as the first day's reviews are concerned, the majority have got a magnificent reception. We have had a fair look in, but only in those papers which had got to know of the existence of a Minority Report before the issue late on Wednesday night. If we had not taken steps, we should have been submerged completely, by the great length of the Majority Report, coupled with their revolutionary proposals, the largeness of the majority and the relative weight of their names. Roughly speaking, all the Conservative papers went for the majority proposals, and the London Liberal papers were decidedly for ours. We secured, in fact, belligerent rights, but not more than that. The majority hold the platform. Perhaps we feel a trifle foolish at having crabbed the Majority Report to our family and intimate friends, and exalted our own. That has certainly not proved to be the estimate of public opinion.

February 22nd. I am recovering my equilibrium slowly. It is always interesting to analyse one's mistakes and successes. In our depreciation of the Majority Report and our false expectation of its failure to catch on, we overlooked the immense step made by the sweeping-away of the deterrent poor law, *in name, at any rate,* and, to some extent in substance, by municipalising its control. Every now and again, I realised this; but then, when I considered the chaotic proposals of the Majority Report, I lost sight of it in my indignation at their attempt to present a new appearance whilst maintaining the old substance under-neath. In a sense the Majority Report meant success to our cause, but not victory to ourselves. However, I am inclined to think the distinc-tion between the two reports—the fact that only by re-distribution of the services can you obtain curative and restorative treatment—will become gradually apparent to the nation. What is certainly most surprising is the absence of any kind of protest from the adherents of the old order—the believers in the principles of 1834—against the iconoclastic effect of the Majority Report. That the principles of 1834 should die so easily is certainly a thorough-going surprise. Even the *Spectator* acquiesces.

134. THE CASE FOR POOR LAW REFORM

Source: S. and B. Webb, 'English Poor Law Policy' (1910), pp. 313–17.

The Minority Report on the Poor Laws, 1909, merits comparison with the Poor Law Commissioners' Report of 1834. Both are extremely able statements of a case, well argued by persons who had a firm grasp on the first principles of their inquiry. They measure the distance which social thought in Great Britain had travelled since the early Victorian age. Much of the change of opinion was also reflected in the report of the majority of the commissioners, among whom the Charity Organization Society was well represented. Sidney and Beatrice Webb, then engaged in an active campaign on behalf of the minority, here sum up what they conceived the issues to be between themselves and the majority. They took their stand on the rapid growth of institutions and policies outside of the Poor Law, dealing with particular groups of persons who had once been looked after by the Poor Law alone. They wished to carry these

*developments much farther and were prepared to abolish the Poor Law in
favour of the new social services. The majority thought that the minority's
proposals stood in danger of breaking up the unity of the family along
with the Poor Law. But the main difference ran between those who
regarded destitution as a sign of some defect of personality and those who
thought of it as a kind of social disease, abolishable by collective effort.
For an independent view of the dispute, Una Cormack, ' The Welfare
State: the Royal Commission on the Poor Laws, 1905–1909, and the
Welfare State, Loch Memorial Lecture' (1953).*

THE Majority Commissioners hold, on the assumption that every
case of pauperism implies a moral defect, that there should be, in
each locality, one Authority and only one Authority to deal with
persons requiring maintenance from public funds. They, therefore,
recommend the establishment of a new 'Destitution Authority' to
deal only with persons who are destitute, and only when they are
destitute; and for such persons to provide, from birth to burial, in
distinctively Poor Law Institutions, or under distinctively Poor Law
officials, all that is required. It is admitted that this involves the repeal
of the unemployed Workmen Act and the Education (Provision of
Meals) Act. We must leave politicians to judge whether it is practicable
to thrust the unemployed workman, and the child found hungry at
school, back into the Poor Law, even if the Poor Law is called by
another name. But even if this were done, the Majority Report would
still leave the overlap as regards the destitute aged which is involved in
the Old Age Pensions Act; the overlap as regards the destitute sick
which is involved in the evergrowing activities of the 700 rate-main-
tained municipal hospitals of the Local Health Authorities; the overlap
with regard to destitute children which is involved by the activities of
the Local Education Authorities and the Home Office under the
Industrial Schools Acts, and now under the Children Act. And the
Majority Commissioners cannot, it appears, make up their minds
whether or not they wish the recommendations of the Royal Commission on the Feeble-minded to be carried into law, and thus end the
overlap between the Poor Law Authority and the Lunacy Authority.

The Majority Report purports to give the new 'Public Assistance
Authority' some guidance as to policy. It is to relieve none but those
at present entitled to relief, and therefore, in all cases, to wait until
destitution has set in. Thus the aid will, as now, come too late to

prevent or to cure. On the other hand, the 'deterrent' attitude of 1834 is to be given up; the workhouse is to be abolished; and 'curative and restorative treatment', at home or in an appropriate institution, is to be afforded to every case. Yet in order to afford to certain classes of applicants methods of relief and treatment more suitable than any Public Assistance Authority is to be allowed to afford, a complete system of Voluntary Aid Committees is to be set up, and to such Committees these particular applicants are to be required to apply, whether or not they prefer charity to public aid....

The only effective substitute for deterrence is, the Minority Commissioners suggest, the Principle of Prevention—prevention, that is, not merely of pauperism, but of the very occurrence of destitution. This negatives the very idea of a Destitution Authority, whatsoever its designation or its policy. It is in vain to hope that any Poor Law, or any Destitution Authority, however improved, can ever prevent or even diminish destitution; because, confined as it is to dealing with a destitution which has occurred, it is inherently precluded by its very nature from attacking any of the causes which produce the destitution that is perpetually coming on its hands. Thus, the twenty millions sterling now spent annually in the United Kingdom on the mere relief of destitution do practically nothing to prevent the creation, year by year, of new masses of destitution. Even the educational work which the Poor Law Authorities do for the Poor Law children is largely vitiated by their inherent disability to exercise any supervision over the life of the child before and after the crisis of destitution. The greater part of expenditure on the Poor Law Medical Service is, so far as any gain to the health of the nation is concerned, wasted because no sick person can legally be treated in the incipient stage of his disease when it may still be curable; the Poor Law doctor must always wait until destitution has set in! This—so the Minority Commissioners claim—must necessarily be the same in the case of the 'Public Assistance Authority', proposed in the Majority Report, or, indeed, in the case of anybody set to administer a Poor Law. On the other hand, the fact that universal provision of some services to all persons, whether destitute or not, has been adopted by Parliament, has led to a duplication and confusions of functions between the old Poor Law Authority and the new Preventive Authorities. This daily increasing overlap and duplication can only be ended by either stripping the new Preventive Authorities of functions entrusted to them within the last few years by Parliament—which is plainly impossible—or by abolishing the Poor Law. Hence, the only safe, as well as the only advantageous way out of this confusion is to go forward on the Principle of Prevention. This Principle of Prevention may take the form, on the one hand, of altering the environment, on the other, of treating the individual. But if the cost of curative treatment, or even of altering the environment, is to be borne by the community, it is essential, on grounds of economy, that there should be a searching out of all incipient cases and such a disciplinary supervision as will prevent persons from becoming destitute through neglected infancy, neglected childhood, preventable illness, and voluntary unemployment.

In this disciplinary supervision over those who repeatedly fall into the morass of destitution, or who, by failing to fulfil their social obligations, show signs of entering upon the descent into that morass, we see a more humane, as well as a more effective form of 'deterrence' than that of the 1834 Poor Law. The new preventive authorities deter from falling into destitution, not by fear of what will happen when the fall has taken place, but by timely insistence on the performance of the social duties that will prevent the fall. The parents who, under the pressure of the Local Education Authority, are induced and compelled to send their children to school from 5 to 14 years of age are not only effectually 'deterred' from living on their children's earnings, but are also prevented from so far neglecting their offspring as to fail to get them to school regularly and punctually, or to fail to maintain them in a state fit for admission to school, according to a standard that is constantly rising. In some districts the Local Education Authority has even gone far, by means of inspection, instruction, exhortation, and, in the last resort, prosecution, towards effectually 'deterring' parents from letting their children become verminous. Deterrent action of this kind by the Local Education Authority has been accompanied by corresponding action by the Local Health Authority, which has—again by inspection, instruction, exhortation, and, in the last resort, prosecution—induced many occupiers of tenement dwellings to prevent these from remaining verminous or otherwise grossly below the current standard of sanitation. This form of deterrence it is that lies at the base of all our Public Health and Factory Legislation; a deterrence that leads the owners and occupiers to bestir themselves to keep their dwellings up to the current local standard of healthiness, the occupiers of factories to maintain these in accordance with the requirements of the law, and the operatives in unhealthy trades to observe the precautions prescribed against disease. The same idea of a preventive deterrence will inspire the Local Lunacy Authorities, once they are made responsible for the feeble-minded, to insist on proper care and control for those helpless girl mothers whom the Poor Law must perforce leave free to propagate a feeble-minded race. In the same way the Minority Commissioners believe that the new National Authority for Unemployment, of which we may detect the beginnings in the National Labour Exchange, will be able to 'deter' men from becoming unemployed, not only by actually preventing many unnecessary breaches of continuity in employment (by equalising, year by year, the aggregate demand for labour, regularising employment in the seasonal trades, and 'decasualising' the casual labourer in the ways elaborately described in the Report), but also by putting the necessary pressure on the will of those who are 'born tired' or who have become 'unemployable', either to accept and retain the situations that will be definitely offered to them, or else to submit themselves to disciplinary training, with the reformatory Detention Colony in the background.

135. LONDON WAGES AT THE TURN OF THE CENTURY

Source: Charles Booth, 'Life and Labour of the People in London (1903 edition), 2nd Series: Industry', vol. v, pp. 266–7, 268, 270.

The inquiries of men like Charles Booth and Seebohm Rowntree into the incidence of destitution and the numbers of families which were trying to live off inadequate incomes, below 'the poverty line', were read by contemporaries in the light of what they knew about the average of wages paid. What were representative wages? They varied with the occupation, class of labour, and district. Booth himself tried to provide figures for the London area.

I TAKE 21s. as the bottom level for adult male labour in London. The employments in which less than 21s. a week (or 3s. 6d. a day) is paid are exceptional in character. When the rate is 18s. or 20s. the work is not only characterized usually by great regularity and constancy with no slack seasons or lost days, but is generally such as a quite young or quite old man could perform—men who probably have only themselves to keep. It is work which demands but little experience or muscular strength. Thus, many mailcart drivers and a considerable number of one horse carmen are paid on this basis. Railway goods porters are another instance, but these men are transferred from one part of England to another, and the rates paid are affected by other than London conditions. There are also a proportion of 18s. or 20s. men amongst the unskilled labourers employed in flour mills, rope works, etc. Many of these, and still more those employed in market gardening, live in the outskirts of London and share, more or less, the position of country labour....

More than 21s. will always be paid when the work demands any special powers. The qualification may be very slight, but, if the work ceases to be that which every man can perform, an extra wage is paid; and if his services are needed at all, the man who possesses the additional qualification may be said to command a wage of 22s., 23s., or 24s. But his chance of obtaining work of the kind for which he possesses special aptitude, may perhaps be no better than that which the man who is only worth 21s. has of obtaining such work as he can do....

Most labourers are paid weekly, but the day's work is usually the basis of remuneration, and very many of those who appear amongst the poorly paid on our lists have not had a full week's work. When men are employed permanently, the weekly wages are often calculated on a rather lower basis. Payment by the hour is not usual for unskilled, or semi-skilled, specialized labour, but when paid in this way, the rate is commonly 6d.

Skilled work, on the other hand, is very commonly paid by the hour, and receives from 8d. to 10d. or 1s. In most of the skilled trades competent steady men work nearly full time on the average, that is, overtime and short time about balance each other. Full time, however, varies from forty to more than sixty hours per week. As a rule the higher the rate of pay the shorter the day—forty hours at 1s. are equal to sixty hours at 8d. and 40s. a week is, in effect, the basis of remuneration for skilled work in London, men earning a little more or a little less than this according to the combination they may make of rates and hours within the limits given above.

136. WHAT IS SWEATED INDUSTRY?

Source: 'Fifth Report from the Select Committee of the House of Lords on the Sweating System 1890' (169), vol. XVII, paras. 5–6, 40–1, 91–3, 175–8.

Late in the 1880's, public opinion became excited about what were described as sweated trades. It appeared that in certain markets, for example, for matchboxes, clothes, chains, nails and cutlery, there was an easy supply of cheap labour, often that of married women, and a great demand for cheap goods. The result was to encourage employers to use the incessant competition of those seeking work to beat down prices. Extremely low wages and bad conditions of work were the consequence. Much of the work was done at home, in London and elsewhere, under conditions of domestic industry which had once been general. It was consequently out of the reach of the Factory Acts. It was also outside the limits of the trade unions, which found labour of this forlorn type quite unorganizable. Attention having been drawn by a report of the Board of Trade, Earl Dunraven moved in the House of Lords, 28 February 1888, for a select committee. No legislation followed the report of 1890, although Sydney Buxton proposed an amendment of the Factory Acts to cover part of the problem. For his proposals, see S. and B. Webb, 'Problems of Modern Industry' (1898: new edition 1902), pp. 152–5. There was nothing new about the industrial conditions investigated by the committee. The description of domestic industry in the Black Country may be compared with Disraeli's 'Sybil' (1845) a generation earlier.

Tailoring: (1) London

Every cause which tends to produce and perpetuate sweating is at work in the most concentrated form in the clothing trades. In reference to those trades, therefore, we have found it necessary to take a large body of evidence, much of which is of the greatest interest and importance.

It is stated that some years ago a tailor, who was properly trained in his calling, could make either a complete suit of clothes, or any part of it: he knew his business throughout. Sweating has been known for 50 years. The parcelling out of work must have had its origin in the fact that the journeyman tailor took his work home to be done by himself, and possibly by other members of his family. There were obviously advantages to the journeyman tailor and employer in this arrangement. There was little subdivision, the tailor made the garments

from end to end; the only subdivision then being that the least important part of the work was put into the hands of the workmen's own
apprentices. In the opinion of many witnesses the gradual lapse of the
system of thorough apprenticeship increases the sweating, and is
extremely prejudicial to the interest of trade and to the public. Now,
excepting in the very best bespoke trade, a man generally confines
himself to one particular kind of garment, or to a certain portion only
of a garment, the making of which is easily learnt. Now, instead of
the thoroughly practical tailor being employed, the trade is divided
into different sections. There are foremen or cutters, basters, machinists,
fellers, buttonholers, pressers, and general workers, one witness indeed
stating that there were 25 subdivisions. 'Sub-division is so minutely
carried out that a man who can press a coat cannot necessarily press a
waistcoat, and a waistcoat presser is equally unqualified to press trousers.
If the labour was not so much subdivided there would not be half the
evils connected with sweating.' This is borne out by Mr Burnett,
Labour Correspondent of the Board of Trade. 'Except for the best
kinds of clothing, the old-fashioned tailor has been crushed out; and
although for the highly skilled man the rates of remuneration may be as
high, or higher than before,' (and this high remuneration is shown to
exist), 'the great bulk of the cheap clothing is in the hands of a class who
are not tailors at all in the old sense of the term;' the trade is governed
by no rules at all, at least as regards the lower grades; the hours are
anything a sweater likes to make them; each sweater has his own
method of engaging and paying his workers. The question as to what
is a day, or half a day, is differently interpreted by different masters.
It is the usual thing for seven and a half, eight, and nine hours to be
regarded as half a day....

Chain and nail-making

These industries do not give employment to a great number of
persons, but in scarcely any that have come under our notice is so
much poverty to be found, combined with such severe work and so
many hardships. We have taken a great deal of evidence in regard to
the circumstances of the people, and we now proceed to give a
summary of the more important of the facts that have been brought
before us. Some general information was furnished by Mr R. Juggins,

secretary of the Midland Counties Trades Federation, which consists of a combination of trade societies, such as the chain-makers, nail-makers, rivet-makers, and other workers in iron. Chain-making is carried on chiefly at Cradley Heath, and in villages comprised within an area of three or four miles. It is a small industry, not more than from two to three thousand persons being engaged in it. The larger descriptions of chains, known as cable chains, are made in factories; block chains, cart-horse back bands, dog-chains, and other smaller kinds are made in the district, in small shops attached to the home of the workers. In most cases there is a workshop at the back of the house, fitted up with an anvil, a stone block, and other appliances. The occupier of the shop may let it out, wholly or in part, to four or five other persons. A shop of the kind described, with a dwelling-house attached to it, lets from 3s. to 3s. 6d. a week.

The business is carried on in this way: the worker receives a certain weight of iron, and he has to return a corresponding weight of chain, less an allowance, which is, or ought to be, four pounds in the bundle weighing half a hundredweight, for the waste in working. It is stated that workmen can occasionally save some iron out of the allowance for waste, which they work up on their own account, and sell to 'foggers' at low rates, to the general detriment of the trade. One of the most common charges, however, brought by the workers is, that the necessary weight for waste is not allowed them, and consequently they are unable to return the requisite weight of chain.

The sweater in these trades is known as the 'fogger'. He goes to the master, takes out the work, and distributes it among the men and women. When it is done he takes it back to the master. Sometimes the fogger works himself, but more frequently he acts merely as a go-between. It is also stated in evidence that the workpeople are compelled in many cases to buy the provisions and other things they require at the fogger's shop, or at a shop kept by his relations or friends; in fact, that he manages to get the workers into his power, and obliges them to deal at his shop, under the penalty of refusing to give them work. When the fogger has a shop, the prices he charges for his wares are said to be of an exorbitant character. For American bacon, which an ordinary tradesman sells for 5½d. a pound, they charge 8d.; for sugar they make their customers pay a halfpenny per pound above the usual price; for tea they charge more by 50 per cent than other shops. It is also stated that the fogger does not always wait for orders, but sends in articles to the men, which they are compelled to take, for fear of losing their work.

...we are of opinion that, although we cannot assign an exact meaning to 'sweating', the evils known by that name are shown in the foregoing pages of the Report to be—

1. A rate of wages inadequate to the necessities of the workers or disproportionate to the work done.
2. Excessive hours of labour.
3. The insanitary state of the houses in which work is carried on.

These evils can hardly be exaggerated.

The earnings of the lowest classes of workers are barely sufficient to sustain existence.

The hours of labour are such as to make the lives of the workers periods of almost ceaseless toil, hard and often unhealthy.

The sanitary conditions under which the work is conducted are not only injurious to the health of the persons employed, but are dangerous to the public, especially in the case of the trades concerned in making clothes, as infectious diseases are spread by the sale of garments made in rooms inhabited by persons suffering from small-pox and other diseases.

When we come to consider the causes of and remedies for the evils attending the conditions of labour which go under the name of sweating, we are immediately involved in a labyrinth of difficulties. First, we are told that the introduction of sub-contractors or middle-men is the cause of the misery. Undoubtedly, it appears to us that employers are regardless of the moral obligations which attach to capital when they take contracts to supply articles and know nothing of the condition of the workers by whom such articles are made, leaving to a sub-contractor the duty of selecting the workers and giving him by way of compensation a portion of the profit. But it seems to us that the middleman is the consequence, not the cause of the evil; the instrument, not the hand which gives motion to the instrument, which does the mischief. Moreover, the middleman is found to be absent in many cases in which the evils complained of abound.

Further, we think that undue stress has been laid on the injurious effect on wages caused by foreign immigration, inasmuch as we find that the evils complained of obtain in trades, which do not appear to be affected by foreign immigration.

We are of opinion, however, that certain trades are, to some extent, affected by the presence of poor foreigners, for the most part Russian and Polish Jews. These Jews are not charged with immorality or with vice of any description, though represented by some witnesses as being uncleanly in their persons and habits. On the contrary, they are represented on all hands as thrifty and industrious, and they seldom or never come on the rates, as Jews support by voluntary contributions all their indigent members. What is shown is that the Jewish immigrants can live on what would be starvation wages to Englishmen, that they work for a number of hours almost incredible in length, and until of late they have not easily lent themselves to trade combinations.

Machinery, by increasing the sub-division of labour, and consequently affording great opportunities for the introduction of unskilled labour is also charged with being a cause of sweating. The answer to this charge seems to be, that in some of the larger clothing and other factories, in which labour is admitted to be carried on under favourable conditions to the workers, machinery, and sub-division of labour to the greatest possible extent, are found in every part of the factory.

With more truth it may be said that the inefficiency of many of the lower classes of workers, early marriages, and the tendency of the residuum of the population in large towns to form a helpless community, together with a low standard of life and the excessive supply of unskilled labour, are the chief factors in producing sweating. Moreover, a large supply of cheap female labour is available in consequence of the fact that married women working at unskilled labour in their homes, in the intervals of attendance on their domestic duties and not wholly supporting themselves, can afford to work at what would be starvation wages to unmarried women. Such being the conditions of the labour market, abundant materials exist to supply an unscrupulous employer with workers helplessly dependent upon him.

Who Gained by Change?

Source: Charles Booth, 'Life and Labour of the People of London'
(1903), 2nd series, 'Industry', vol. II, p. 265.

Charles Booth, in making his survey of incomes in London, found his
attention drawn to the relation between the special lowness of some wages
and certain industries characteristic of East London. These were, in particular, work at the docks and domestic labour carried on at home or in
small domestic workshops in the making of cheap clothes, paper and
cardboard-boxes, boots and shoes, and so forth. His descriptions did much
to focus public opinion on the problem of 'sweated trades', although he
had no remedies to suggest for these domestic industries.

W OMEN and girls make the boxes from the materials prepared by
the men and boys. Comparing the condition of these workers
as represented in the returns now obtained with that found when the
previous inquiry was made (1888), little difference is seen. The same
methods of learning obtain, and the earnings of the girls do not differ
materially. The ordinary worker's weekly earnings are still about
10s. to 13s., but the proportion of young girls may have slightly
increased, the number receiving less than 10s. being rather greater
in 1893-4. Home workers still play as important a part in the trade,
small boxes of all kinds being almost entirely made outside the work-
rooms. The material is cut and prepared, and then given out, usually
to married women who have worked in one of the factories before
marriage. A few minutes spent outside one of these establishments any
afternoon towards the end of the week will give an observer an idea
of the extent of this trade. Numbers of women and children may be
seen returning the finished work to the warehouse, carried in carefully
covered parcels or wheeled thither in perambulators.

Source: 'Sweated Industries being a Handbook of the "Daily News"
Exhibition compiled by Richard Mudie Smith' (1906), pp. 118–19.

From 1905 an Anti-Sweating League existed. The 'Daily News'
newspaper organized in 1906 an exhibition of sweated goods and
industries in the Queen's Hall in London. There was nothing new about
the conditions disclosed. The ex-machinist's letter might be compared
with Thomas Hood's 'Song of the Shirt' 1843, although the invention

of the sewing machine had intervened. The dominant influence here in producing bad conditions was not technical innovation but the peculiar and enduring conformation of the labour market (see above, no. 136).

THE following letter, addressed to the Organising Secretary, is printed because it represents the experience of a host of similar sufferers. The name and address of the writer are, for reasons needless to name, withheld, but for every statement made she is prepared to produce chapter and verse.

April 17th, 1906

Sir,

The following is an account of my past experience as a City machinist. I sought work from firms now in existence, and obtained work at these prices:

Flannel and cotton chemises, plain bands with trimming on them and on sleeves	1s.	doz.
Flannel and cotton small children's chemises and knickers, no trimming	8d.	„
Flannel and cotton nightdresses, with insertion and frills on neck and sleeves	2s. 9d.	„
Flannelette bathing gowns, trimmed with braid	3s.	„
Ladies' flannel and cotton shirts, plain	1s. 9d.	„
The velvet ones	2s. 3d. and 2s. 9d.	„
Ladies' white muslin shirts, trimming down fronts, 1 row each side, tucks in between, making about 20 tucks	3s.	„
Pinafores, with tucked yoke lace insertion let in, tucked frills round yoke and sleeves, skirt with broad hem insertions and lace let in	3s.	„
Dressing gowns, flannelette and cotton, with Watteau pleat pointed collar with lace and stitched band	5s. 6d.	„
Or yoke top with frill of same down front as far as band	3s. 6d.	„
Buttons on both buttonholes made at warehouse, sateen slips plain	10d.	„

After paying for cotton and railway journey, I had 7s. per week on an average, sometimes less, and paid 5s. for rent; I worked from six a.m. in morning till ten at night, only taking about one hour for my meals. While at warehouses I saw some had notices up that work kept longer than four days would not be paid full price. Work must be counted before taken away, or any deficiency must be paid for. A difficult matter to measure trimmings and count parts in a hurry, especially when you sometimes only had the floor to pack up on. Some could not understand why the Inspector never called on them, but some thought they never had their full number of outdoor workers until the Inspector had been. I myself never had a visit unless I put a bill in a window to try and get a girl. The home workers who get on the best are those who have a number of machines and take learners whom they send off when their time is up and have fresh ones.

I had some flannelette shirts, lined, sent me at 1s. 9d. I could stand it no longer; took them to St Pancras Vestry; showed them to the lady Inspector, who sent me to the Working Women's League, who could do nothing then unless the workers would strike.

Yours truly,

AN EX-MACHINIST

139. THE TRADE BOARDS ACT, 1909

Source: 'The Law Reports. The Public General Statutes passed in the ninth year of the Reign of King Edward VII' (1909), vol. XLVII. 9 Edward VII, ch. 22.

In the early 1900's political opinion was feeling its way round to the argument that legislation might be justified in relation to the 'sweated trades'. The choice seemed to lie between a system of licensed manufacture and a direct attempt to fix wages statutorily, hoping that this might stimulate employers and employed to organize themselves. A model of minimum wage law had existed since 1896 in the state of Victoria, Australia. Since 1900 Sir Charles Dilke (1843–1911) had introduced annually into the House of Commons a Wages Boards' Bill copied from Victoria. In 1908 a new government inquiry reported in favour of the minimum wage principle. The President of the Board of Trade, Winston Churchill, took charge of the subsequent bill. The Act applied to four trades only; tailoring, making of paper boxes, lace-making and chain-making. They included some 200,000 workers, mostly women and girls. Five more trades were included in 1913.

[*Section One of the Act states that it should apply to the trades specified in the schedule to the Act. The Board of Trade may make a provisional order applying this Act to other trades if necessary. The second Section states that where practicable the Board of Trade shall establish one or more Trade Boards according to regulations given in this Act for any trade to which this Act applies. Then continues:*]

3. A Trade Board for any trade shall consider, as occasion requires, any matter referred to them by a Secretary of State, the Board of Trade, or any other Government department, with reference to the industrial

conditions of the trade, and shall make a report upon the matter to the department by whom the question has been referred.

Minimum rates of wages

4. (1) Trade Boards shall, subject to the provisions of this section, fix minimum rates of wages for timework for their trades (in this Act referred to as minimum time-rates), and may also fix general minimum rates of wages for piecework for their trades (in this Act referred to as general minimum piece-rates), and those rates of wages (whether time- or piece-rates) may be fixed so as to apply universally to the trade, or so as to apply to any special process in the work of the trade or to any special class of workers in the trade, or to any special area.

If a Trade Board report to the Board of Trade that it is impracticable in any case to fix a minimum time-rate in accordance with this section, the Board of Trade may so far as respects that case relieve the Trade Board of their duty.

(2) Before fixing any minimum time-rate or general minimum piece-rate, the Trade Board shall give notice of the rate which they propose to fix and consider any objections to the rate which may be lodged with them within three months.

(3) The Trade Board shall give notice of any minimum time-rate or general minimum piece-rate fixed by them.

(4) A Trade Board may, if they think it expedient, cancel or vary any minimum time-rate or general minimum piece-rate fixed under this Act, and shall reconsider any such minimum rate if the Board of Trade direct them to do so, whether an application is made for the purpose or not:

Provided that the provisions of this section as to notice shall apply where it is proposed to cancel or vary the minimum rate fixed under the foregoing provisions in the same manner as they apply where it is proposed to fix a minimum rate.

(5) A Trade Board shall on the application of any employer fix a special minimum piece-rate to apply as respects the persons employed by him in cases to which a minimum time-rate but no general minimum piece-rate is applicable, and may as they think fit cancel or vary any such rate either on the application of the employer or after notice to

the employer, such notice to be given not less than one month before cancellation or variation of any such rate.

5. (1) Until a minimum time-rate or general minimum piece-rate fixed by a Trade Board has been made obligatory by order of the Board of Trade under this section, the operation of the rate shall be limited as in this Act provided.

(2) Upon the expiration of six months from the date on which a Trade Board have given notice of any minimum time-rate or general minimum piece-rate fixed by them, the Board of Trade shall make an order (in this Act referred to as an obligatory order) making that minimum rate obligatory in cases in which it is applicable on all persons employing labour and on all persons employed, unless they are of opinion that the circumstances are such as to make it premature or otherwise undesirable to make an obligatory order, and in that case they shall make an order suspending the obligatory operation of the rate (in this Act referred to as an order of suspension).

[*The Act goes on to say that an order of suspension of rates shall take effect until an obligatory order is made by the Board of Trade. It continues:*]

6. (1) Where any minimum rate of wages fixed by a Trade Board has been made obligatory by order of the Board of Trade under this Act, an employer shall, in cases to which the minimum rate is applicable, pay wages to the person employed at not less than the minimum rate clear of all deductions, and if he fails to do so shall be liable on summary conviction in respect of each offence to a fine not exceeding twenty pounds and to a fine not exceeding five pounds for each day on which the offence is continued after conviction therefor.

[*The Act continues with other details on the setting up, organisation, and members of these Trade Boards, and ends with the following:*]

Schedule: Trades to which the Act applies without provisional order

1. Ready-made and wholesale bespoke tailoring and any other branch of tailoring in which the Board of Trade consider that the system of manufacture is generally similar to that prevailing in the wholesale trade.

2. The making of boxes or parts thereof made wholly or partially of paper, cardboard, chip, or similar material.

3. Machine-made lace and net finishing and mending or darning operations of lace curtain finishing.

4. Hammered and dollied or tommied chain-making.

[*Certain details follow, concerning, e.g. contracts involving employment, to which a minimum rate is applicable, given by a government department or local authority.*]

140. A MINIMUM WAGE FOR AGRICULTURAL WORKERS?

Source: R. Lennard, 'Economic Notes on English Agricultural Wages' (1914), pp. 63–5, 143.

The position of the farm-worker came in for much attention in the years of high living costs just before the First World War. Part of the interest was frankly political, as illustrated by the two volumes of the 'Liberal Land Inquiry', vol. I (1913) and vol. II (1914); part came from an extension to the country of methods of social survey first worked out for the towns. Seebohm Rowntree came to the conclusion that the 'poverty problem', i.e. under-nourishment, was no less serious in villages than in industrial cities. Reginald Lennard, an economist writing from Heyford in North Oxfordshire, examined the case for and against a minimum wage in the farming industry. The fixing of minimum wages for agricultural workers came three years later, during the war, to counter war prices.

IT is now time to attempt some summary of the conclusions toward which the arguments of this chapter have been tending.

In the first place, it seems that agricultural labour in England is peculiarly cheap—that English agricultural labourers sell their labour for a smaller proportion of its value to their employers than is obtained by labourers in other trades. The weakness of farm labourers in bargaining is not remedied by peculiar mobility in flight to other employments.

Secondly, as agricultural labour in general is cheap, the presumption is that the dearest labour in agriculture is cheaper than the dearest labour in other industries. This may at least be supposed until definite evidence to the contrary is produced.

Thirdly, the advantage of this cheap labour must go to some one. And as the prices of most agricultural products depend on the conditions of the world's markets, it can hardly be maintained that this advantage goes to the consumer. It can scarcely be denied that foreign competition would prevent the cost of a rise in wages from being transferred to the consumer in augmented prices, except in the case of a few 'sheltered' products, among which milk may perhaps be included. On the whole, then, it appears that either the farmer or the landlord or both gain by the cheapness of agricultural labour.

Fourthly, in so far as the advantage goes to the landlord in augmented rents, the removal of the advantage would not affect the agricultural entrepreneur, but would simply lead to a fall in the rent of agricultural land. At the same time, the establishment of a Land Court would be advisable to prevent the tenant farmer suffering from any deficiency in his power of bargaining with the landlord for a reduction of rent.

Fifthly, defects in competition make it likely that in fact the advantage of the cheap labour is to a great extent reaped by the farmer. Its removal therefore would tend to mean (1) that those to whom semi-monopolistic privilege brings a large income would have their incomes reduced; (2) that farmers who accept the advantage as an opportunity for idleness would be stimulated to greater effort; and (3) that those who are too inefficient to gain large incomes under shelter, or to improve their methods when the shelter was taken away, would be driven over the margin into bankruptcy.

Sixthly, it appears that various measures might be adopted to throw the career of farming more open to talents. Thus the place of the inefficient might be taken by better men.

There is no need to attempt a formal summary of the conclusions towards which the arguments of the preceding pages have been tending. They suggest that a rise in agricultural wages is possible, and that the rise should, as a rule, be greater in the low-wage than in the high-wage districts. They point to unemployment as the one danger against which safeguards require to be provided; but at the same time they indicate that a tendency towards a reduction in the volume of agricultural employment may very well be only the 'shadow side' of a progress which means improvement in the efficiency of farm labourers and an augmentation of the national dividend. It appears too that the danger of unemployment might be mitigated and even reduced to insignificance by supplementary measures, of which the chief aim should be the development of agricultural science and enterprise and the encouragement of small holdings. As to the extent to which agricultural wages might be raised, either generally or in different districts, nothing has been said. That can best be discovered, not by the reasoning of the economist, but by daring and yet careful and sympathetic experiment, carried out either through the agency of Wages Boards established for each county, or by the determination of some central authority after careful inquiry into local conditions.

141. THE INADEQUACY OF A MINIMUM WAGE

Source: Mrs Pember Reeves, 'Round About a Pound a Week' (2nd ed. 1914), pp. 216–18.

While some social reformers thought in terms of a minimum wage, others pointed out that a minimum wage could not do everything. This passage comes from a report on a four-year investigation carried out by a group of professional women. Its subject was the domestic economy of working class families in a particular area of London—'the district stretching north to Lambeth Road, south to Lansdowne Road, and east to Walworth Road' with particular reference to infantile mortality and the rearing of the children. The line of thinking here, continued by Eleanor Rathbone, 'The Disinherited Family' (1924) led many years later to the Family Allowances Act of 1945.

THE first remedy for this state of things [*the inability of nearly one third of the men employed in regular occupations in the United Kingdom to maintain their families adequately nourished and cared for on the wages they received, i.e. something less than 25s. a week*] which springs to the mind of the social reformer is a legal minimum wage. The discussion of a minimum wage, which is at the same time to be a family wage, is exceedingly difficult. We realise that wages are not now paid on a family basis. If they were we should not have 2,500,000 adult men receiving for full-time work a sum which the writer has no hesitation in saying is less than sufficient for the proper maintenance, and that on the lowest scale, of one adult person. To pay wages in future, on an adequate family basis, to every adult worker who could possibly have helpless children dependent upon him or her would be a startlingly new departure. There are none, in fact, who advocate it. And yet if we are really attempting to solve the problem of hungry children by minimum wage legislation, we ought to aim at no less....

Moreover, to keep the children of the nation in health and strength is too important and vital a responsibility to be placed entirely on the shoulders of one section of the community—namely, the employers of labour. It is a responsibility which should be undertaken by the only authority which is always equal to its complete fulfilment—the State.

142. OLD AGE IN STEPNEY

Source: Charles Booth, 'Pauperism and the Endowment of Old Age' (1892), pp. 133, 164, 241.

Old people who became destitute were relieved by the Poor Law. The maintenance of the old became more difficult in the nineteenth century, with the growth of population, industry and urban life. The ties of kinship and of the small rural community declined in force. Meanwhile, towards the end of the century the expectation of life began to rise. Savings out of incomes which were low and irregular came nowhere near to meeting the financial need. The Friendly Societies occupied only a small part of a field largely given over to the Guardians of the Poor. Charles Booth put the discussion of the matter on a new basis in a paper read before the Royal Statistical Society in December 1891. In the course of a study of old age, charity and public relief in two districts of London, Stepney and St Pancras, he attempted an estimate of the national volume of destitution due to old age and came out in favour of a system of State pensions. Stepney Poor Law Union consisted of the Thames waterside parishes of Limehouse, Shadwell and Wapping. Its population found employment mainly at the wharves and on the docks.

... Where out-relief is freely given there may not be very many poor who do not come more or less, sooner or later, upon the rates. But where out-relief is withheld, and especially in towns, we find numbers of people struggling on, working a little, begging a little, helped by their friends or helped by the Church; people who would be glad enough to accept parish relief if given outside, but who manage to keep above ground somehow by these other means if out-relief is denied. So hardly do they do this, so nearly do they sail to the rocks, that in the year of our inquiry at Stepney burial was provided for 76 individuals of whom very few had received anything [*from the Poor Law*] when alive, or at any rate during that year. Seventy-six such deaths must imply a very large population living on the same miserable terms, without having themselves provided for death, and without friends who care enough for them to bury them. Such people probably live in greater discomfort than those who frankly accept pauperism.

Besides paupers, as we count them, and occasional paupers, and those who refuse to become such, except on their own terms, there is a large class of the respectable poor who ask for nothing, but are nevertheless very poor. Out of their ranks painfully drop those whose best efforts fail to make headway against sickness or loss of work....,

It may meanwhile be accepted as probable that the ratio of paupers to population [*for the nation as a whole*], if on the average it is 4½ per cent, will be for those from 16 to 60 (the naturally self-supporting years of life), less than 4 per cent, but that for those between 60 and 65 the rate will rise to about 8 per cent, while for those over 65 it is probably more than 25 per cent....

It is not in the name of the people, but to the people, that I would speak, in advocating the endowment of old age as at once a practical and possible means of giving a surer footing to those who now, trying to stand, too often fall and sometimes sink altogether. I advocate it as bringing with it something of that security necessary to a higher standard of life. A security of position which will stimulate rather than weaken the play of individuality on which progress and prosperity depend.

143. ASQUITH ON OLD AGE PENSIONS, 1908

Source: 'Parliamentary Debates', 4th series, vol. 188, col. 471–2.

That old age, as well as sickness, should be insured against by everybody compulsorily under a State scheme had been suggested in the 1870's by the Rev. W. L. Blackley (1830–1902), 'The Nineteenth Century' (1878), pp. 834–57. His plan was examined by a select committee of the House of Commons, 1885–7, and reported upon adversely. Old age pensions became in the 1890's a political issue, largely owing to the intervention of one of the most powerful politicians of the day, Joseph Chamberlain, who advanced proposals for a contributory scheme. For the course of the discussion see A. Wilson and G. S. Mackay, 'Old Age Pensions' (1941). Nothing emerged out of much inquiry and calculation until 1908. Then the Liberal administration brought in a pensions scheme intended to apply to rather more than half a million people. H. H. Asquith was delivering, on the 7 May 1908, his third Budget speech. By this time he was Prime Minister.

THE proposals that we make having regard to these various considerations are as follows: First, the income limit, apart from pension, should be fixed at £26 a year, subject to reduction in the case of married couples living together from £52 to £39 a year. I say a year because, as many of these old people are in more or less casual employment, now with a job and now without one, it is very much better to take the whole income for the preceding year than the weekly income from time to time. Secondly, we think that the age limit, having regard to the figures which I quoted to the House a short time ago, at which a pension should accrue should, in the first instance at any rate, and for the purpose of our present proposal, be fixed at seventy. Thirdly, there is no substantial difference of opinion, I believe, as to the amount of the pension, which should be £13 a year and in the case of married couples living together £9.15s. per head. Fourthly, we think that stringent conditions should be provided— and by stringent I mean effective—for forfeiture or suspension, follow- ing in the main those which prevail in New Zealand. A much more difficult question, and one as to which I am bound to confess that my own opinion and that of many of my colleagues in considering this matter has fluctuated, is whether or not we are to follow the example of New Zealand and Denmark and adopt a sliding scale, and propor- tion the amount of the pension given to the means of the pensioner— that is to say, if a man has only 2s. a week, give him 5s.; and if he has 10s., give him only 1s. We have come to the conclusion, on the whole, to do nothing of the kind. I quite agree there is an apparent paradox in a man with 10s. getting the same pension as one who has nothing at all, but as the sums with which we are dealing are relatively so small, we are inclined to the conclusion that it is not desirable to introduce any sliding scale, and that we should have a fixed pension of 5s. for everybody who satisfies the prescribed conditions. Then, further, to make clear what I have already stated about the *status* of the candidates, we think that all persons should be disqualified who have within, say, five years of their application been convicted of serious crime or of such offences as desertion, habitual vagrancy, and so on.

144. LOOKING FOR WORK IN THE 1870's

Source: George Haw, 'From Workhouse to Westminster: the Life Story of Will Crooks M.P.' (1907), pp. 47–8, 51–2.

About the year 1876, Will Crooks (1852–1921) a young Londoner recently out of his apprenticeship as a cooper, twice tramped, carrying his

*trade union card, from London to Liverpool and back, seeking work. He
eventually found it in London.*

I
T is a weird experience, this, of wandering through England in search
of a job.... You keep your heart up so long as you have something
in your stomach, but when hunger steals upon you, then you despair.
Footsore and listless at the same time, you simply lose all interest in the
future....

Nothing wearies one more than walking about hunting for employment which is not to be had. It is far harder than real work. The
uncertainty, the despair, when you reach a place only to discover that
your journey is fruitless, are frightful. I've known a man say 'Which
way shall I go today?' Having no earthly idea which way to take, he
tosses up a button, If the button comes down on one side, he treks east;
if on the other, he treks west.

You can imagine the feeling when, after walking your boots off,
a man says to you, as he jingles sovereigns in his pocket, 'Why don't
you work?' That is what happened to me as I scoured the country
between London and Liverpool, asking all the way for any kind of
work to help me along....

[*Crooks finally sought work in London again*]

One typical day of tramping for work in London he described to me
thus:

I just went down to the river-side at Shadwell. No work was to be
had there. Then I called at another place in Limehouse. No hands
wanted. So I looked in at home and got two slices of bread in paper
and walked eight miles to a cooper's yard in Tottenham. All in vain.
I dragged myself back to Clerkenwell. Still no luck. Then I turned
towards home in despair. By the time I reached Stepney I was dead
beat, so I called at a friend's in Commercial Road for a little rest. They
gave me some Irish stew and twopence to ride home. I managed to
walk home and gave the twopence to my wife. She needed it badly.

That year I know I walked London until my limbs ached again.
I remember returning home once by way of Tidal Basin and turning
into the Victoria Docks so utterly exhausted that I sank down on a
coil of rope and slept for hours.

Another day I tramped as far as Beckton, again to no purpose. I must have expressed keen disappointment on my face, for the good fellows in the cooperage there made a collection for me, and I came home at night with one and sevenpence.

There are few things more demoralizing to a man than to have a long spell of unemployment....No one cares whether he gets a job or goes to the dogs. If he goes to the dogs the nation is the loser in the double sense. It has lost a worker and therefore a wealth-maker. Secondly, it has to spend public money in maintaining him or his family....

A man who is out of work for long nearly always degenerates. For example, if a decent fellow falls out in October and fails to get a job say by March, he loses his anxiety to work. The exposure, the insufficient food, his half-starved condition, have such a deteriorating effect upon him that he becomes indifferent whether he gets work or not. He thus passes from the unemployed state to the unemployable state. It ought to be a duty of the nation to see that a man does not become degenerate.

145. A PUBLIC WORKS PROGRAMME FOR THE UNEMPLOYED, 1886

Source: '16th Annual Report of the Local Government Board 1886–87, 1887', C. 5131, vol. XXXVI, *appendix no. 4, pp. 5–7.*

Theoretically, according to the provision of the Victorian Poor Law, no unemployed man or woman capable of work could be granted public money without going to the workhouse for it. In practice, the fluctuations of industry caused unemployment to recur on a great scale at more or less regular intervals. This created a situation extremely difficult for the Poor Law administrators to cope with. Joseph Chamberlain, when President of the Local Government Board in 1886, suggested a method of dealing with unemployment outside of the Poor Law. This was by municipal public works. They became a standard although unsatisfactory resort at such times.

Pauperism and Distress: Circular Letter to Boards of Guardians—Local Government Board, Whitehall S.W.

15th March 1886

Sir,

The enquiries which have been recently undertaken by the Local Government Board unfortunately confirm the prevailing impression as to the existence of exceptional distress amongst the working classes. This distress is partial as to its locality, and is no doubt due in some measure to the long continued severity of the weather.

The returns of pauperism show an increase, but it is not yet considerable; and the numbers of persons in receipt of relief are greatly below those of previous periods of exceptional distress.

The Local Government Board, have, however, thought it their duty to go beyond the returns of actual pauperism which are all that come under their notice in ordinary times, and they have made some investigation into the condition of the working classes generally.

They are convinced that in the ranks of those who do not ordinarily seek poor law relief there is evidence of much and increasing privation, and if the depression in trade continues it is to be feared that large numbers of persons usually in regular employment will be reduced to the greatest straits.

Such a condition of things is a subject for deep regret and very serious consideration.

The spirit of independence which leads so many of the working classes to make great personal sacrifices rather than incur the stigma of pauperism, is one which deserves the greatest sympathy and respect, and which it is the duty and interest of the community to maintain by all the means at its disposal.

Any relaxation of the general rule at present obtaining, which requires as a condition of relief to able-bodied male persons on the ground of their being out of employment, the acceptance of an order for admission to the workhouse, or the performance of an adequate task of work as a labour test, would be most disastrous, as tending directly to restore the condition of things which, before the reform of poor laws, destroyed the independence of the labouring classes and increased the poor rate until it became an almost unsupportable burden.

It is not desirable that the working classes should be familiarised with poor law relief, and if once the honourable sentiment which now leads them to avoid it is broken down, it is probable that recourse will be had to this provision on the slightest occasion....

What is required in the endeavour to relieve artizans and others who have hitherto avoided poor law assistance, and who are temporarily deprived of employment is:

1. Work which will not involve the stigma of pauperism;

2. Work which all can perform, whatever may have been their previous avocations;

3. Work which does not compete with that of other labourers at present in employment;

And, lastly, work which is not likely to interfere with the resumption of regular employment in their own trades by those who seek it.

The Board have no power to enforce the adoption of any particular proposals, and the object of this circular is to bring the subject generally under the notice of boards of guardians and other local authorities.

In districts in which exceptional distress prevails, the Board recommend that the guardians should confer with the local authorities, and endeavour to arrange with the latter for the execution of works on which unskilled labour may be immediately employed.

These works may be of the following kinds, among others:

(*a*) Spade husbandry on sewage farms;

(*b*) Laying out of open spaces, recreation grounds, new cemeteries, or disused burial grounds;

(*c*) Cleansing of streets not usually undertaken by local authorities;

(*d*) Laying out and paving of new streets, etc.

(*e*) Paving of unpaved streets, and making of foot-paths in country roads;

(*f*) Providing or extending sewerage works and works of water supply.

It may be observed, that spade labour is a class of work which has special advantages in the case of able-bodied persons out of employment. Every able-bodied man can dig, although some can do more than others, and it is work which is in no way degrading, and need not interfere with existing employment.

In all cases in which special works are undertaken to meet exceptional distress, it would appear to be necessary, 1st, that the men employed should be engaged on the recommendation of the guardians as persons whom, owing to previous condition and circumstances, it is undesirable to send to the workhouse, or to treat as subjects for pauper relief, and 2nd, that the wages paid should be something less than the wages ordinarily paid for similar work, in order to prevent imposture, and to leave the strongest temptations to those who avail themselves of this opportunity to return as soon as possible to their previous occupations.

When the works are of such a character that the expenses may properly be defrayed out of borrowed moneys, the local authorities may rely that there will be every desire on the part of the Board to deal promptly with the application for their sanction to a loan.

I shall be much obliged if you will keep me informed of the state of affairs in your district, and if it should be found necessary to make any exceptional provision, I shall be glad to know at once the nature of such provision, and the extent to which those for whom it is intended avail themselves of it.

I am, etc.,

(*Signed*) J. CHAMBERLAIN

The Clerk to the Guardians.

146. UNEMPLOYMENT THE MAIN RISK OF WORKING-CLASS LIFE

Source: H. S. Foxwell, "Irregularity of Employment and Fluctuations of Prices", in ' The Claims of Labour' (ed. J. Oliphant, 1886), pp. 273–5.

Herbert Somerton Foxwell (1849–1936) an economist of the younger generation, was taking part as a lecturer in a series of addresses, delivered in 1886, arising out of the Industrial Remuneration Conference of January 1885. For the Industrial Remuneration Conference, which brought representatives of capital and labour together in London under the chairmanship of Sir Charles Dilke, to debate the division of wealth, see the 'Report of Proceedings and Papers' (1885). The year 1886 was one of heavy unemployment and deep trade depression.

I RETURN, then, in conclusion, to the contention with which I started. The precarious nature of employment is a social evil of the first magnitude, which we can and must in some degree remove. After analysing the fluctuations of price which give rise to it, we have seen that the evil is at least not beyond relief. There are many minor remedies which may be applied to the various causes of disturbance.... But I say without hesitation that we ought not to rest content, till in one way or another we have succeeded in giving to the artisan and labourer as much social security as is commonly enjoyed by the salaried and professional classes. It will be an extremely difficult task. There is no royal road to this goal, no one simple panacea. The problem must be attacked at all points and in many ways. I have tried this evening, however, imperfectly, to indicate some of the means by which we may hope to attain success. As to the means, I may well be mistaken; but I do not think I am mistaken as to the end. It is my most rooted and settled conviction that, of all the many claims of labour, the most grave, the most pressing, and the most just, is the claim I have brought before you tonight, the claim for more regular employment.

147. THE UNEMPLOYED WORKMEN ACT, 1905

Source: 'The Law Reports. The Public General Acts passed in the Fifth year of the reign of Edward VII' (1905), vol. XLIII, 5 Edw. VII, ch. 18.

The middle of the first decade of the present century saw the beginnings of a sharp decline of the home boom of the previous few years. Meanwhile, the coming activity in foreign investment and exports of 1906 onwards still hesitated. At this time of falling general investment and slack trade the Unemployed Workmen Act 1905 was passed. It represented a coming together of the Poor Law, the towns and organized charity to cope with distress arising from unemployment. The method was temporary local relief work. W. H. Beveridge later carefully studied the records collected and the whole administration of the Act. He concluded that local relief work 'generally implies something that degrades the name of work and disregards the principles of relief'. 'Unemployment' (3rd ed. 1912), p. 190.

[*Organisation for London*]

  1. (1) For the purposes of this Act there shall be established, by order of the Local Government Board under this Act, a distress committee of the council of every metropolitan borough in London, consisting partly of members of the borough council and partly of members of the board of guardians of every poor law union wholly or partly within the borough and of persons experienced in the relief of distress, and a central body for the whole of the administrative county of London, consisting partly of members of, and selected by, the distress committees and of members of, and selected by, the London County Council, and partly of persons co-opted to be additional members of the body, and partly, if the order so provides, of persons nominated by the Local Government Board, but the number of the

persons so co-opted and nominated shall not exceed one-fourth of the total number of the body, and every such order shall provide that one member at least of the committee or body established by the order shall be a woman.

(2) The distress committee shall make themselves acquainted with the conditions of labour within their area, and when so required by the central body shall receive, inquire into and discriminate between any applications made to them from persons unemployed:

Provided that a distress committee shall not entertain an application from any person unless they are satisfied that he has resided in London for such period, not being less than twelve months, immediately before the application, as the central body fix as a residential qualification.

(3) If the distress committee are satisfied that any such applicant is honestly desirous of obtaining work, but is temporarily unable to do so from exceptional causes over which he has no control, and consider that his case is capable of more suitable treatment under this Act than under the poor law, they may endeavour to obtain work for the applicant, or, if they think the case is one for treatment by the central body rather than by themselves, refer the case to the central body, but the distress committee shall have no power to provide, or contribute towards the provision of, work for any unemployed person.

(4) The central body shall superintend and, as far as possible, co-ordinate the action of the distress committees, and aid the efforts of those committees by establishing, taking over, or assisting labour exchanges and employment registers, and by the collection of information and otherwise as they think fit.

(5) The central committee may, if they think fit, in any case of an unemployed person referred to them by a distress committee, assist that person by aiding the emigration or removal to another area of that person and any of his dependents, or by providing, or contributing towards the provision of, temporary work in such manner as they think best calculated to put him in a position to obtain regular work or other means of supporting himself. . . .

[*Organisation outside London*]

2. (1) There shall be established by order of the Local Government Board for each municipal borough and urban district with a population,

according to the last census for the time being, of not less than fifty thousand, and not being a borough or district to which the provisions of section one of this Act have been extended, a distress committee of the council for the purposes of this Act, with a similar constitution to that of a distress committee in London, and the distress committee shall, as regards their borough or district, have the same duties and powers, so far as applicable, as are given by this Act to the distress committees and central body in London....

148. CASUAL LABOUR IN LONDON BUILDING

Source: N. B. Dearle, 'Problems of Unemployment in the London Building Trades' (1908), pp. 97–8.

The prevalence of ill-paid casual labour in many towns and cities was an important element in the demand for what was called 'the organization of the labour market' between 1905 and 1909. As events turned out, the most effective work of the Labour Exchanges between 1909 and 1914 was done not among casual workers but among those who possessed some skill.

IN respect of the large casual fringe that it possesses, the building trade shares with dock and waterside labour an unenviable pre-eminence. In part this fringe is a thing apart from the trade as a whole, being confined to certain branches of it, and to a certain type of work, and is recruited from sources peculiar to itself. For it is made up very largely of half-trained and untrained men who have slipped down into it. They largely serve employers engaged on very small work, who have not means or ability to obtain large or steady contracts, and are compelled to take work and consequently labour as they can get it. Many of the men, therefore, so live because they have never known any other form of life, and perhaps are not fit for any other kind of work; and live from day to day a sort of hand-to-mouth existence. Quite different from this is the case of those who belong to the higher ranks of labour—men who usually are steadily employed, and who suffer periods of unemployment, not as a regular thing because always casually employed, but from the more regular and calculable changes. Those who suffer from purely seasonal causes, those who are out because trade is depressed, those who are displaced by changes in the methods of the trade, have little in common with the men whose unemployment is nearly always chronic. At the same time, these two divisions shade off into one another. Every depression leaves behind it a trail of those who have sunk from the ranks of the steadily-employed to those of the casual labourer; and often when they fall they do not rise again, but becoming and remaining 'casual', their places are quickly taken by new men. Casual work usually brings casual life and often degradation and inefficiency, and they continue to swell the number of casual labourers, even after trade has resumed its normal dimensions....

Part of this tendency to drive men into the casual labour market may be seen in other trades; but in London, except with waterside labour and part of the transport trade, there is nothing approaching the great reserve of it that the distress committee returns [*i.e. returns of the Distress Committee set up in London under the Unemployed Workmen Act, 1905*], among other things, show for the building trade. Even here it is confined largely to certain branches. With masons, plumbers and plasterers, even allowing for the smallness of the numbers, there is little of it; with bricklayers and carpenters there is more of it....But it is with labourers and still more with painters that 'casual' labour is rife, the number of casual painters, especially, being immense....

149. CHURCHILL ON LABOUR EXCHANGES

Source: 'Parliamentary Debates', 5th series, vol. 5, cols. 500–3.

The President of the Board of Trade, Mr Winston Churchill, spoke in the House of Commons, 19 May 1909. A motion introduced by Mr E. H. Pickersgill had drawn attention to the Minority Report of the Royal Commission on the Poor Laws and asked that steps should be taken to decasualize casual labour and to absorb the surplus labour thereby thrown out of employment, also to regularize the demand for labour and develop trade union insurance against the risks of unemployment. The Labour Exchanges Bill (no. 150) was introduced the following day.

THERE is high authority for such a measure. The Majority and Minority Reports of the Poor Law Commission, differing in so much, agreeing in so little, are agreed unanimously in advocating a system of labour exchanges as the first step which should be taken in coping with the problem of poverty and unemployment. Conferences were held in London the other day by delegates who represented 1,400,000 trade unionists who passed a resolution in favour of this policy. The Central (Unemployed) Body, who are equally concerned in these matters, have approved of that policy. The delegates of the Labour party who went to Germany a few months ago returned greatly impressed with the Exchanges which they saw at work in Germany. Economists as diverse in their opinions as Professor Ashley, of Birmingham, and Professor Chapman, of Manchester—leading exponents of Tariff Reform and of Free Trade—have all publicly testified in favour of such proposals; and several prominent Members of the Front Opposition Bench have in public, either in evidence before the Commission or in speeches in the country, expressed themselves as supporters of such a policy. The argument from authority is reinforced by the argument from example, because as early as 1904 Germany, Austria, Switzerland, France and Belgium all exhibited the system of public labour exchanges and public labour bureaux in full working order; and since 1904 Norway has also adopted some application of that system. . . .

With such argument from authority and example it is hardly necessary to submit the case upon its merits, but there are two general defects in the industrial position of this country which are singled out by the Royal Commission, the lack of mobility of labour and the lack of information about all these questions of unemployment. For both of these defects the policy of labour exchanges is calculated to afford a remedy. Modern industry is national. The facilities of transport and communication knit the country together as no country has ever been knitted before. Labour alone has not profited by this improved organisation. The method by which labour obtains its market to-day is the old method, the demoralising method of personal application, hawking labour about from place to place, and treating a job as if it were a favour—looking at it as if it were a favour, as a thing which places a man under an obligation when he has got it. Labour exchanges will increase the mobility of labour, but to increase the mobility of labour is not to increase the movement of labour. To increase the mobility of labour is only to render the movement of labour when it has become necessarily [*sic*] less painful. The movement of labour when it is necessary should be effected with the least friction, the least suffering, the least loss of time and of status to the individual who is called upon by the force of economic conditions to move. It would be a great injustice to the policy of labour exchanges if it were supposed that it would be the cause of sending workmen gadding about from pillar to post throughout the country, whereas the only result of the policy will be, not to make it necessary for any man to move who does not need to move to-day, but to make it easy for him to move the moment the ordinary economic events arise which make movement necessary. There is another thing in connection with labour exchanges. They will not to any large extent create new employment. In so far as facilities for getting labour on particular occasions sometimes leads to extra men being taken on, they will increase employment. That, however, is only a very small result. They will not directly add to the volume of employment. I never contemplated that they should. It would be to invest the policy with an air of humbug if we were to pretend that labour exchanges are going to make more work. They are not. What they are going to do is to organise the existing labour, to reduce the friction which has attended the working of the existing economic and industrial system, by reducing the friction of that system we cannot help raising the general standard of economic life....

I am quite sure that those who know the sort of humiliation to which the genuine working man is subject, by being very often indistinguishable from one of the class of mere loafers and vagrants, will recognise as of great importance any steps which can sharply and irretrievably divide the two classes in our society. Lastly, labour exchanges are indispensable to any system of unemployment insurance, or, indeed, I think to any other honourable method of relieving unemployment, since it is not possible to make the distinction between the vagrant and the loafer on the one hand and the *bonâ fide* workman on the other, except in conjunction with some elaborate and effective system of testing willingness to work such as is afforded by the system of labour exchanges. I shall to-morrow have an opportunity of asking the permission of the House to introduce this Bill, and we present it to the House as a piece of social machinery, nothing more and nothing less, the need of which has long been apparent, and the want of which has been widely and cruelly felt by large numbers of our fellow countrymen.

Who Gained by Change?

150. LABOUR EXCHANGES ACT, 1909

Source: 'The Law Reports. The Public General Statutes passed in the Ninth year of Edward VII' (1909), vol. XLVII, 9 Edw. VII, ch. 7.

An Act to provide for the establishment of Labour Exchanges and for other purposes incidental thereto

Be it enacted by the King's most Excellent Majesty, by and with the advice and consent of the Lords Spiritual and Temporal, and Commons, in this present Parliament assembled, and by the authority of the same, as follows:

1. (1) The Board of Trade may establish and maintain, in such places as they think fit, labour exchanges, and may assist any labour exchanges maintained by any other authorities or persons, and in the exercise of those powers may, if they think fit, co-operate with any other authorities or persons having powers for the purpose.

(2) The Board of Trade may also, by such other means as they think fit, collect and furnish information as to employers requiring workpeople and workpeople seeking engagement or employment....

2. (1) The Board of Trade may make general regulations with respect to the management of labour exchanges...and such regulations may, subject to the approval of the Treasury, authorise advances to be made by way of loan towards meeting the expenses of workpeople travelling to places where employment has been found for them through a labour exchange....

5. In this Act the expression 'labour exchange' means any office or place to be used for the purpose of collecting and furnishing information, either by the keeping of registers or otherwise, respecting employers who desire to engage workpeople and workpeople who seek engagement or employment.

6. This Act may be cited as the Labour Exchanges Act, 1909.

151. NATIONAL INSURANCE THE FIRST STEP TO A NEW SOCIAL POLICY

Source: 'Lloyd George's Ambulance Wagon being the Memories of William J. Braithwaite 1911–1912', ed. Sir Henry N. Bunbury (1957), pp. 121–2.

412

The Concept of the Minimum

Lloyd George, Chancellor of the Exchequer, was engaged in preparing the new National Insurance Bill for its first reading. The extract is a note which he passed, on 7 March 1911, to R. G. Hawtrey, one of the civil servants assisting him.

INSURANCE necessarily temporary expedient. At no distant date hope State will acknowledge a full responsibility in the matter of making provision for sickness breakdown and unemployment. It really does so now, through Poor Law, but conditions under which this system had hitherto worked have been so harsh and humiliating that working-class pride revolts against accepting so degrading and doubtful a boon.

Gradually the obligation of the State to find labour or sustenance will be realized and honourably interpreted.

152. UNEMPLOYMENT AN INSURABLE RISK

Source: "Summary of the Scheme of Unemployment Insurance embodied in Part II of the National Insurance Act, 1911, issued by the Board of Trade", in W. H. Beveridge, 'Unemployment' (3rd ed. 1912), appendix F, pp. 307–8.

Unlike sickness insurance, unemployment insurance, when it came, did not apply generally. The National Insurance Act, 1911, on this side was selective and experimental. About a half-a-dozen industries employing two and a quarter million people were chosen for the new type of insurance. These were trades with a marked tendency to fluctuate, being closely connected with capital construction. They had suffered severely from loss of work in the previous two or three years, following the American crisis of 1907. The national extension of the system came later, during and after the First World War. For a study of unemployment in York in the year preceding the Act, see B. Seebohm Rowntree and B. Lasker, 'Unemployment a Social Study' (1911).

SUMMARY OF SCHEME

I. *Introduction*

The scheme of insurance against unemployment which is contained in Part II of the National Insurance Act is to be administered by the Board of Trade, and comes into operation on Monday, 15 July 1912. The object of the scheme is twofold.

In the first place provision is made for the payment of contributions by all employers and workpeople in the trades mentioned below, and for the payment of benefit to the workpeople when unemployed. This part of the scheme is compulsory. In the second place provision is made for the encouragement of voluntary insurance against unemployment by means of money grants from State funds to associations of persons, in all trades and occupations, which pay out-of-work benefits.

II. *The Compulsory Insured Trades*

On and after Monday, 15 July, 1912, all workpeople (whether men or women) over 16 years of age who are engaged wholly or mainly by way of manual labour in the following trades will be compulsorily insured against unemployment and have contributions towards the Unemployment Fund deducted from their wages:

(1) Building; that is to say, the construction, alteration, repair, decoration, or demolition of buildings, including the manufacture of any fittings of wood of a kind commonly made in builders' workshops or yards.

(2) Construction of Works; that is to say, the construction, reconstruction or alteration of railroads, docks, harbours, canals, embankments, bridges, piers, or other works of construction.

(3) Shipbuilding; that is to say, the construction, alteration, repair or decoration of ships, boats, or other craft by persons not being usually members of a ship's crew, including the manufacture of any fittings of wood of a kind commonly made in a shipbuilding yard.

(4) Mechanical Engineering; including the manufacture of ordnance and firearms.

(5) Ironfounding; whether included under the foregoing headings or not.

(6) Construction of vehicles; that is to say, the construction, repair, or decoration of vehicles.

(7) Sawmilling (including machine woodwork); carried on in connection with any other insured trade or of a kind commonly so carried on.

Foremen other than manual workmen, clerks, indentured apprentices, and persons under 16 years of age are excluded....

On and after the 15 July 1912, no employer may engage a workman in one of the insured trades unless the latter holds, or at once applies for, an Unemployment Book. An Unemployment Book can be obtained by making application after 1 June at any Labour Exchange or other Local Office of the Unemployment Fund. For the address of the nearest Labour Exchange or Local Office enquiries should be made after 1 June at any Post Office.

153. LLOYD GEORGE ON NATIONAL INSURANCE, 1911

Source: 'Parliamentary Debates', 5th series; vol. 25 cols. 611–13.

Provision against sickness and its attendant loss of income among wage-earners, had been the business in Victorian times of the Friendly Societies, which were mutual benefit associations, often with a distinctly convivial side, and the Poor Law. But the Friendly Societies covered the ground most inadequately, while for many years Poor Law reformers had recognized that medical care for those with low incomes fitted awkwardly into a deterrent Poor Law intended to frighten men and women from asking too readily for public assistance. The majority of the royal commission on the Poor Law reported in 1909 in favour of a system of invalidity insurance modelled on Belgian practice, in which both the Friendly Societies and the State would take part. On 4 May 1911 the Chancellor of the Exchequer in the Liberal Government, Lloyd George, introduced a bill to provide insurance against loss of health and for the prevention and cure of sickness. The extract is from his speech that day. For the friendly societies, P. H. J. H. Gosden, 'The Friendly Societies in England 1815–1875' (1961). For a stringent criticism of their short-comings in the field of burial insurance, A. Wilson and H. Levy, 'Industrial Assurance' (1937). And for an analysis of the National Insurance Act, A. S. Comyns Carr, W. H. Stuart Garrett and J. H. Taylor, 'National Insurance' (1912).

Now comes the question, which leads up to the decision of the Government to take action. What is the explanation that only a portion of the working-classes have made provision against sickness and against unemployment? Is it they consider it not necessary? Quite the reverse, as I shall prove by figures. In fact, those who stand most in need of it make up the bulk of the uninsured. Why? Because very few can afford to pay the premiums, and pay them continuously, which enable a man to provide against those three contingencies. As a matter of fact, you could not provide against all those three contingencies anything which would be worth a workman's while, without paying at any rate 1s. 6d. or 2s. per week at the very lowest. There are a multitude of the working classes who cannot spare that, and ought not to be asked to spare it, because it involves the deprivation of children of the necessaries of life. Therefore they are compelled to elect, and the vast majority choose to insure against death alone. Those who can afford to take up two policies insure against death and sickness, and those who can afford to take up all three insure against death, sickness and unemployment, but only in that order. What are the explanations why they do not insure against all three? The first is that their wages are too low. I am talking now about the uninsured portion. Their wages are too low to enable them to insure against all three without some assistance. The second difficulty, and it is the greatest of all, is that during a period of sickness or unemployment, when they are earning nothing, they cannot keep up the premiums. They may be able to do it for a fortnight or three weeks, but when times of very bad trade come, when a man is out of work for weeks and weeks at a time, arrears run up with the friendly societies, and when the man gets work, it may be at the end of two or three months, those are not the first arrears which have to be met. There are arrears of rent, arrears of the grocery bill, and arrears for the necessaries of life. At any rate he cannot consider his friendly society only. The result is that a very considerable number of workmen find themselves quite unable to keep up the premiums when they have a family to look after.

Undoubtedly there is another reason. It is no use shirking the fact that a proportion of workmen with good wages spend them in other ways, and therefore have nothing to spare with which to pay premiums to friendly societies. It has come to my notice, in many of these cases, that the women of the family make most heroic efforts to keep up the premiums to the friendly societies, and the officers of friendly societies, whom I have seen, have amazed me by telling the proportion of premiums of this kind paid by women out of the very wretched allowance given them to keep the household together. I think it is well we should look all the facts in the face before we come to consider the remedy. What does it mean in the way of lapses? I have inquired of friendly societies, and, as near as I can get at it, there are 250,000 lapses in a year. That is a very considerable proportion of the 6,000,000 policies. The expectation of life at twenty is, I think, a little over forty years, and it means that in twenty years' time there are 5,000,000 lapses; that is, people who supported and joined friendly societies, and who have gone on paying the premiums for weeks, months, and even years, struggling along, at last, when a very bad time of unemployment comes, drop out and the premium lapses. It runs to millions in the course of a generation. What does that mean? It means that the vast majority of the working men of this country at one time or other have been members of friendly societies, have felt the need for provision of this kind and it is only because they have been driven, sometimes by their own habits, but in the majority of cases by circumstances over which they have no control—to abandon their policies. That is the reason why, at the present moment, not one half of the workmen of this country have made any provision for sickness, and not one-tenth for unemployment. I think it necessary to state these facts in order to show that there is a real need for some system which would aid the workmen over these difficulties. I do not think there is any better method, or one more practicable at the present moment, than a system of national insurance which would invoke the aid of the State and the aid of the employer to enable the workman to get over all these difficulties and make provision for himself for sickness, and, as far as the most precarious trades are concerned, against unemployment.

CHAPTER 9

THE ECONOMICS OF EMPIRE

Our habit of describing the late Victorian and Edwardian age as 'Imperialist' descends from the men of the time. They often described themselves and one another, in praise or disapprobation, as 'Imperialists'. What did they mean by the word? Were they describing something, some trait of the society they lived in, which still appears important?

Any attempt to answer such questions lands us back at once into the maze of events among which these men passed their lives, with its difficulties of interpretation, of linking one event causally with another. It also leads us back into the shifting sands of language, where things change and words change with them, not always at once. The words empire, imperial, imperialist, have signified many different things to men of different races and nations at different times in the world's history. To sort out the meanings and to study their relation to historical situations is a major task.

The words imperialism and imperialist were already undergoing a significant change in the 1870's and early 1880's of last century. There had been a mid-Victorian usage, which employed them to describe the system of government by centralized authority in Continental states. For the upper-class Englishman of Palmerston's day, imperialism might mean the methods of administration and control of the Emperor of the French, Napoleon III. The French Emperor vanished from history with his defeat by the German armies in 1870, although there were still emperors German and Austrian and Russian. After that date, this use of the word became old-fashioned. Another and ancient employment of the terms empire, imperial, imperialism, was one which attached them to colonies and to dominion exercised outside of Europe, overseas. In the 1870's and 1880's, this usage returned in force. It spread and propagated itself strikingly in the last quarter of the century. This was a period of great colonial acquisitions and of a heightened, self-conscious, even aggressive, imperialism in British public opinion. It was then that controversies began in reference to the colonies about imperial defence, imperial consolidation and imperial reciprocity, which lasted in one form or another to 1914 and beyond. Why was this? What experiences of the men of the time can possibly have led to this change? Why, not least, the strong emotional content of the words, suggestive of changes going on about which people felt deeply?

For the adherents of Marxian sociology, who were numerous in

Europe from the 1890's on, the final explanation was discovered by V. I. Lenin, before he came to power in Russia, writing as an exile in Switzerland, during the First World War.[1] He was concerned to solve two problems—the long postponement of the proletarian revolution foretold by Karl Marx and the war then raging, which had arrived before the Marxian revolution. For Lenin, all the developments described by the late Victorians' use of the words empire and imperialism—the expansion of colonies, the partition of Africa among the European powers in the 1880's, the struggle for spheres of influence in China in the 1890's, most of them events in which Great Britain had taken a leading part—were the inevitable consequence of a capitalist economy. Founded in the accumulation of capital by the possessing classes and in the exploitation of the workers, to whom any improvement in their conditions was denied, advanced capitalism with its great powers of production could only end in one way. With the gradual exhaustion of investment opportunities at home, monopolies would first strive to annex the home market, then a search would begin for new investment opportunities abroad. As these, too, threatened to become exhausted, the forcible seizure of lands suitable for investment and exploitation must lead to colonial wars and these in turn to war between the colonizing powers. Imperialism was the last, or as he put it, highest stage of capitalism. This created the deadly competition of rival monopolies in the world and at last the European war itself, the final crisis in which world revolution would be born.

Marxian doctrine as expounded by Lenin had some limited support in British economic thinking. Both Robert Torrens[2] and Gibbon Wakefield, early in the nineteenth century, had argued that suitable investment opportunities at home might from time to time fail. In such a situation, colonies, for example, in Australia and New Zealand, would be a proper outlet for idle savings and surplus population. They saw this, however, as a temporary, perhaps a recurring, need, not as the impending bankruptcy of the economic system. Early in the 1900's, J. A. Hobson,[3] writing as a critic of the South African war of 1899–1902 and of the policies which led to it, described the conflict of Boer and Briton as the product of an ill-managed economic system which could not or would not build up consumption at home, consequently was forced to find employment for its capital in Africa, including the goldmines of the Transvaal. Hobson was quoted with approval by Lenin.

[1] V. I. Lenin, *Imperialism the Highest Stage of Capitalism* (2nd English edition, London 1934).

[2] L. Robbins, *Robert Torrens and the Evolution of Classical Economics* (1958).

[3] J. A. Hobson, *Imperialism* (1902). Hobson's book was part of a large literature arising out of the war and the crisis it caused in British political opinion.

Who Gained by Change?

How much light do these interesting historical speculations throw upon our problem? Did the new social values which lay behind the 'imperialist' discussions and the new use of words rise out of an economic situation of this kind? Certainly the British economy had capital to spare and invested abroad on a great scale in these years. Certainly too Great Britain added largely to her colonial possessions in the same period. Certainly, again, those who had investments abroad, in South Africa and elsewhere, influenced from time to time in a decided manner the policies of British governments. But it is noticeable that the area of largest territorial expansion, tropical Africa, was not the one most favoured by investors. That part of the world was rather avoided by them. Moreover, influence was not control, even where British investments stood far higher than they did in Africa north of Capricorn. The history of the South African war is incomparably better known today than it was when Hobson wrote.[1] Foreign capital on the Rand, most of which was British capital, had an interest in modifying the policies of the South African Republic and used its considerable influence with the British government from time to time. But no one now would argue that it controlled, in any realistic sense, the British High Commissioner in South Africa, Sir Alfred Milner, or the Colonial Secretary, Joseph Chamberlain, or the Cabinet in London. The war in South Africa was a grave reflexion on the wisdom of British policies, both in London and in South Africa, but not in quite the way that Hobson, writing as a contemporary and in all good faith, had supposed.

The theory which regards the imperialism of the late nineteenth century as economic imperialism and economic imperialism as the product of a search for investment opportunities has had a long run. It directs our attention to an important figure, the investor, and to a distinct strand in events, overseas investment. But it is clearly inadequate to explain the course of empire in two great areas of the world, where European, including British, colonial expansion was most active and where at the same time European capital movements were on a relatively modest scale compared with economic developments elsewhere—tropical Africa and the Western Pacific.[2] Neither does it seem necessary on theoretical grounds to invoke a breakdown, actual or potential, of capital accumulation in order to account for the flow of

[1] See especially J. S. Marais, *The Fall of Kruger's Republic* (1961), and R. H. Wilde, *Joseph Chamberlain and the South African Republic 1895–1899*, Archives Year Book for South African History (1956), vol. I.

[2] On the failure of the pattern of colonization to conform to the pattern of investment, M. Barratt Brown, *After Imperialism (1963)*; also S. H. Frankel, *Capital Investment in Africa* (1938). The European partition of the Pacific has been described by W. P. Morrell, *Britain in the Pacific Islands* (1960) and J. D. Legge, *Britain in Fiji 1858–1880* (1958).

capital abroad at that time. The period in which home capital formation in this country was depressed, between the mid-1870's and the end of the century, while it was a great foreign investing age, never saw such a mania for foreign lending as marked the years immediately before and immediately after it, during the early 1870's and again in the Edwardian time. It may one day be a matter of curiosity that a theory suffering from such defects as an explanation of events should ever have been so widely and so implicitly accepted.

Both colonization and foreign investment were old, not new, in 1870. The economic side to the colonial expansion which went on at almost all periods of the nineteenth century cannot be understood from a consideration of foreign investment alone. The fundamental process was the industrialization of Great Britain and the demand for food-stuffs and raw materials for her industrial population which this set up. This made it worth while to invest money in the production of such things overseas. It laid the foundation of the incessant movement abroad of savings, people and export commodities in the century before 1914. The economic links established in this way between Great Britain and every part of the world often led to no imperial expansion at all. This was particularly true of the vast trading area of the Americas, North and South. On the other hand, the rising system of world economic exchanges certainly contributed to the building up of a long list of settlements and colonies which was already immense by 1870. From this point of view, an expanding British empire was a function of the expansion of an economy of extraordinary power.

But if this was so, how are we to account for the heightened self-consciousness of the empire-building after 1880? Why the contemporary haste and anxiety and, what went with it, the aggressiveness? There were influences at work which were broadly economic and which made themselves felt at this time, not only in Great Britain but throughout western Europe. One of these was the pressure on economic resources produced by large and growing populations, themselves the product of the European population 'explosion'. The other was the emergence of competitive national industrial economies, such as Germany, the United States and Great Britain, depending upon their position in the world market for the purchase of the raw materials and foodstuffs which they needed and for the sale of industrial goods with which to buy them. This kind of international economic competition is accepted now. It was new and unheard of then. It seemed to suggest, not least to British opinion, that there might be advantages in the exclusive possession of particular markets.[1] Economic imperialism of

[1] Compare a Cambridge economist who wrote in 1923—'how deny in the gross that there is a real competition between the teeming industrial populations

this kind did not determine the foreign and colonial policies of Great Britain. But it seemed to carry a logic of its own in the post-Cobden age, in the Britain of Joseph Chamberlain and Alfred Harmsworth, subject as it was to strident international competition, a modern newspaper industry, and a concerned public opinion. It was part of the 'imperialism' of the age, although by no means the whole.

As the world economy expanded in the nineteenth century, with Great Britain playing a leading part in the expansion, it ran up against a system of sovereign states which it had not created. Many of these political structures were ill-fitted to stand the stresses and strains set up in old societies by the new methods of making income. Much which one reads of the imperialism of the late nineteenth and early twentieth centuries arose in this way. Traditional sovereigns might fail to save themselves from the temptations and dangers which went with the onward sweep of two distinct yet related things, the spread of new ways of making and spending an income, and the incessant rivalry of the European powers. To join the new world economy could bring immense gains to societies fortunate enough to possess a strong government. For a weak State, it could mean disaster, even or perhaps especially if the joining was confined to generous loans from the more developed countries. There was a problem here of a substantially new kind. Mid-Victorian wisdom had supposed that international free trade, the economic policy championed by Great Britain, would, by strengthening the liberal elements in the societies concerned, call out reforming energy to reconstruct the State from within. Economic intercourse would then go on all the more favourably between countries and governments which had modernized themselves. The experience of the late nineteenth century suggested that this was an optimistic view. To States in a condition of economic underdevelopment and political weakness, the spread of European enterprise, not least powerful new methods of obtaining finance, could be a danger as much as a help. The cases of European Turkey and of Egypt before and after the British occupation in 1882, were much in point.[1]

Similar problems arising out of the inescapable relation between economic development and political control were encountered in other parts of the world during the remainder of the century. In South Africa they led to a final conflict of authority between the Boer Republics and the British government, for which British investments

for limited markets and limited sources of supply, or that exclusive possession, if it could be obtained without continuous menace to international peace, would be a real material advantage?' D. H. Robertson, *Economic Fragments* (1931), p. 160.

[1] D. C. Blaisdell, *European Financial Control in the Ottoman Empire* (1929); D. Landes, *European Financiers and Egyptian Pashas* (1958).

on the Rand were rather the occasion than the cause. Above all, they helped to determine that extraordinary event, the European partition of Africa. When we speak of the colonial imperialism of the late nineteenth century, it is usually African destinies that we have in mind.

The speed with which the partitioning of the African continent was carried through after 1884, contrasted with the laggard economic development of its tropical regions, must suggest some lively doubts about the nature of the relationship between the two. How economic was European empire-building in Africa? Much of the European commerce with the tropical parts of that continent down to the 1880's had deliberately eschewed political intervention, over a long period of time. There appears to have been no quickening of the pace of Africa's economic growth between 1880 and 1900 which would account for the rapidity of the political change. Africa was being increasingly drawn into the world economy by a rising demand in the industrial States of Europe for her mineral and vegetable products. But she joined it at her own slow gait. The pace of African annexations after 1880 was not slow at all.

What broke the pattern of European behaviour? It is, of course, possible to point to the disparity between the knowledge and the economic expectations of Europeans in the days of the 'scramble for Africa'. There was a distinct El Dorado[1] element in their attitude towards the resources of a continent which was still 'the Dark Continent' to English readers in the 1870's. There was room for every sort of speculation, from the most intelligent and the most honest to the most stupid and the most greedy. Still, the contrast between economic realities and hope, while it will account for much, will hardly explain the taking-over of a continent, including vast tracts too remote or too desert to encourage illusions of gain of any kind. There was no revolution in economic expectations concerning tropical Africa in the 1880's. Expectations only became stronger and better-informed.

The key to much that happened in the last quarter of the century in Africa and elsewhere is to be found in Europe itself. It can be and has been argued that—'The relations of the Great Powers have determined the history of Europe'.[2] This is, one might say, the classical view (among historians) of the causes of historical change in Europe during the four centuries of modern times. In the nineteenth century the sovereign States of Europe conducted their relations within a network of communications, of population movements, of trade, which was

[1] Salisbury's phrase about both the German and the British mind during the 1890 negotiations on East Africa. W. R. Louis, *Ruanda-Urundi 1884–1919* (1963), p. 97.

[2] A. J. P. Taylor, *The Struggle for Mastery in Europe 1848–1918* (1954), p. xix.

world-wide. Their policies, with or against their will, became ecumenical. Western society, which was expanding so fast in its relations with the rest of mankind, possessed no political unity or stability of its own. On the contrary, a European system of independent States, each dependent for survival upon its own armed force, tended historically to drift towards the hegemony of a single State. This in turn could only be countered by the building up of the power of other States and by the traditional sanction of war. Such a fundamental disturbance of the European political equilibrium took place in the last quarter of the century with the decline of France and the rise of Germany as the dominant power, economic, military, political, upon the European continent. Much that happened in the African continent is to be understood only partly in economic terms, much more as a consequence of the European political drift. The losses to French authority in Europe and the Mediterranean, as a result of the war of 1870–1 and the British occupation of Egypt in 1882, were particularly serious. These events made it seem urgent to French governments to build up balancing power outside of Europe, wherever the spread of French emigration, trade, investment and missionary work suggested a path. Part of England's colonial activity in these years was directed to countering the moves of other European countries, particularly France and Germany. But she also established colonial positions which were new, and protected those which were old, especially India and the routes to India, even to the extent of new annexations.[1] In all this, what was at stake was not so much the making of incomes, although developed resources have their own political and military value, as the rivalry of the chief European States in a world which they dominated, but which was radically without law and security. It was not only Africa's potential wealth but also, and above all, her political weakness which exposed her to partition in the years between the French defeat at Sedan and the building up of the European alliances which fought the war of 1914–18.

It would be a great mistake, however, to seek the imperial consequences of the European system solely in colonies of exploitation of the African type. The business end, so to speak, of British colonial imperialism in the age before 1914 lay not with them but with the colonies of settlement, Australia, New Zealand, Canada, South Africa. This was partly for reasons which lay with the great resources and the value of the trade of these nations, but partly in the recurrent threats to

[1] This is a severely compressed account of a tangled story. European expansion in tropical Africa had its political roots partly west of the Rhine, partly much further east in Europe. It can be and has been represented as an extension of the Eastern question of the 1870's, i.e. as an aspect of the decline of Turkish power. R. Robinson, J. Gallagher, A. Denny, *Africa and the Victorians* (1963).

peace in Europe and the help they could give in a crisis. To English men interested in foreign policy and defence, the self-governing colonial empire with its rapidly developing national economies presented the supreme attraction of a system of many nations under the direction of one. The defence and foreign policy of the whole empire were settled in London. Much of the talk of imperial unity, from the Imperial Federation League of 1884–92 to the Colonial Conferences of 1907 and 1911, turned in the long run upon the question of war or peace in Europe and upon conflicts of interest in other parts of the world arising out of the unstable character of the European system. Looked at from this point of view, the political economy of empire was part of the economics of British defence and a contribution towards war-potential. Considerations of strategy and communications played a great role in two contrasting features of British imperial policy—the willing acceptance of colonial nationality outside of Europe and the resolute refusal to admit the existence of an Irish nation.

Exceptional economic and political pressures after 1870, to do with the rapid industrialization of the main countries of the West, and the tilting of the see-saw of power in Europe as Germany rose at one end of it and the once great Ottoman empire sank at the other, involving in its fall not only Austria and Hungary but European relations with Asia and Africa, account for much of the empire-building of this period. There were, it appeared, solid economic and political advantages to be had through colonies and out-posts. The Industrial Revolution, now Europe-wide, created new occasions of quarrelling among the European peoples in the competition for incomes and power, and it put novel weapons into the hands of those who were the parties to old disputes. To the fixed hostility of Frenchman and German on the Rhine and the equally historic enmity of German and Slav in Eastern Europe was added a brand-new quarrel between Britain and Germany, the one the greatest power at sea, the other the greatest power on land, each disposing of the most formidable equipment that their highly industrial economies could provide. The decisions of policy were often although not always, taken by men of the old ruling classes in Europe,[1] whose hereditary preoccupation with foreign policy and defence helped them to maintain their social position in a fast-changing world. But while they might come out of a feudal past, as Salisbury and Bismarck and Lansdowne and Grey undoubtedly did, there was nothing out-moded or antique about their methods or about the objects of

[1] As J. A. Schumpeter, with an eye on Berlin and Vienna, acutely observed, although he made too much of it. See his essay, 'Zur Soziologie der Imperialismen', originally published in 1919 in the *Archiv für Sozialwissenschaft und Sozialpolitik* (vol. 46), translated by H. Norden and edited by P. M. Sweezy, in J. A. Schumpeter, *Imperialism and Social Classes* (1951).

pursuit. The European argument was about power and income in their latest, most up-to-date and desirable forms, sought by the most rational methods that were known, in what had become an unacknowledged contest for supremacy.

While the growth of competing interests will account for the widening area of potential conflict and for the rising tension of European relations in the years before the First World War, they will not account for the eruption into violence and all the passions of war. For that, we must look beyond the policies of the powers and the calculations of the market, where means were so carefully fitted to end, to the ends themselves. Here the character of European society is to be remembered and the conditions under which those ends had to be pursued in accordance with the nature of existing institutions. The competition of the market, including the international market, and the competition of states require, if they are to be tolerable and justifiable, the control and the security of law. Within the nation and the nation-state, such governing rules were taken for granted. But a framework of rules, over and above what individuals and nations could find for themselves, Europe had never known. Europe politically speaking was merely a geographical expression. It was a matter of unfortunate accident that it happened also to be a civilization. In such circumstances, lacking the guidance of a sense of common interests, even where those interests were real, and of a wider loyalty, men were handed over to the control of the institutions which they had themselves created. The market, with its keen but limited concentration on income, and the nation-state, with its ceaseless striving for power, were poor guides to a correct sense of values in a world where economic interdependence was not matched with political security. War was the recognized final way out of a difficult situation and the European situation in these years had become increasingly difficult. Only in some such way, it appears, can we account for the unquestioned fact that in the great European capitals men above the average in intellect and in their sense of the public good, confusing the rationality of the means they employed with the validity of the ends they pursued, temporarily blind to any other interests and loyalties than those of the States to which they belonged, chose war in 1914, when they might have had peace. So they frustrated their own intentions as well as those of others and in the moment when they thought themselves to be acting most freely bound themselves slaves to war's uncertainty and the evils even more profound of the years which followed.

FURTHER READING

Relations between economic development and political sovereignty, in relation to colonies and the undeveloped parts of the world, were discussed at some length by the classical economists, such as Adam Smith and Robert Torrens. With the two world wars, the break-up of European colonial empires and the world-wide growth of population and industry, the problems have completely changed their shape. From the period of transition between the wars, two theoretical studies, by a British and an American scholar, R. G. Hawtrey, *Economic Aspects of Sovereignty* (1930) and 'Economics and War', in A. A. Young, *Economic Problems New and Old* (1927), are still worth reading.

For the general diplomatic background of the period 1870–1914, W. L. Langer, *The Diplomacy of Imperialism* (2nd ed. 1951), A. F. Pribram, *England and the International Policy of the European Great Powers* (1931) and A. J. P. Taylor, *The Struggle for Mastery in Europe 1848–1918* (1954).

Much of the debate of the past half-century on international history has turned on the interpretation of diplomacy. What did international relations signify in terms of the economic or political sociology of Europe? What were the real stakes of diplomacy, in terms of wealth and power? Were they rational stakes at all, or a game or a terrible rite, like that of King of the Forest by Lake Nemi, in Roman times? Economics has played a role in this discussion which has varied at different periods. Compare, e.g. the change in terminology between L. Woolf, *Empire and Commerce in Africa* (1919) and R. Robinson, J. Gallagher and A. Denny, *Africa and the Victorians* (1963).

The changes in historical situation and in political values which are perpetually altering the meaning of words have been studied with profound learning by R. Koebner, *Empire* (1961) and R. Koebner and H. D. Schmidt, *Imperialism* (1964). The second volume of this great posthumous work deals with the nineteenth century.

More particularly concerned with British developments are C. A. Bodelsen, *Studies in Mid-Victorian Imperialism* (1924), J. E. Tyler, *The Struggle for Imperial Unity 1868–1895* (1938), B. Semmel, *Imperialism and Social Reform: English Social-Imperial Thought 1895–1914* (1960) and A. P. Thornton, *The Imperial Idea and Its Enemies* (1959). It is well to read the Victorians themselves. C. W. Dilke's *Greater Britain* (1868) and J. R. Seeley, *The Expansion of England* (1880) were contemporary and influential. Dilke brings out the racial, 'Anglo-Saxon' side of Late Victorian Imperialism, which had a part to play in Milner's South African policies, just before the Boer War. See L. M. Thompson, *The Unification of South Africa* (1960).

Who Gained by Change?

The volume of the *Life of Joseph Chamberlain* by J. L. Garvin and J. Amery covering the Tariff Reform agitation has not yet been published. Richard Jebb was one of the few Englishmen of that day who grasped the significance, political and economic, of rising nationalism within the Empire; see his *Studies in Colonial Nationalism* (1905). For the trading system of the Empire, as a part of world trade, S. B. Saul, *Studies in British Overseas Trade 1870–1914* (1960).

The generalizations about Imperialism of half a century ago—Lenin, Rosa Luxemburg, Schumpeter—concentrated on what were conceived to have been the directing forces in Europe. Since then, two things have happened. The diplomatic and political records of Europe have been searched and the history of countries outside of Europe has begun to be written, often by non-Europeans, with documentary care. African and Arab appear as having had will and intention of their own and the European 'man on the spot' has ceased to be a figure of legend. See for British tropical Africa, K. O. Diké, *Trade and Politics in the Niger Delta, 1830–1885* (1956), J. D. Hargreaves, *Prelude to the Partition of West Africa* (1963), M. Perham, *Lugard* (1956) and *Diaries of Lord Lugard* (1960), J. E. Flint, *Sir George Goldie and the Making of Nigeria* (1960), R. Oliver, *Sir Harry Johnston and the Scramble for Africa* (1957). But the man on the spot was not always administrator or soldier. He might be trader or missionary. The broad effect of these inquiries, often unrelated to one another, is to dissolve general views into a vast web of particular situations with particular actors in them, holding varying degrees of initiative at different times. The results for our views of imperialism have still to be reckoned with. For one thing, ignorance, contingency and error seem to be in process of being restored to what one conceives to be their true place in human affairs, not only among 'men on the spot'.

154. THE ARMED PEACE IN EUROPE

Source: Henry Howard Molyneux, fourth earl of Carnarvon, 'Essays, Addresses and Translations', ed. Sir R. Herbert (1896), vol. III, p. 26.

Lord Carnarvon (1831–90), who had been colonial secretary in Disraeli's second administration since 1874, had resigned his office in January 1878. He was speaking in Edinburgh on 5 November 1878, amid the tension created by the Russo–Turkish war and the fear of general war arising out of the conflicting ambitions of the Powers in eastern Europe. Note the use of the word imperialism.

FOREIGN Imperialism means vast standing armies; and at this moment we have before our eyes the nations of Europe divided into hostile and suspicious camps. The 350,000 men who in the earlier period of the Roman Empire were sufficient to guarantee the peace of the world, have now grown into something like 6,000,000 of armed men. It is the day of great empires casting their colossal shadows over the smaller States; and through the gloom of that shadow those small States look up and, as they may well do, tremble. It is the day of reckless intrigue and of reckless expenditure.

155. THE INSTITUTION OF WAR AND THE ECONOMY OF EUROPE

Source: T. E. Cliffe Leslie, "Political Economy and Sociology" (1879) in 'Essays in Moral and Political Philosophy' (1897), pp. 402, 409.

Thomas Cliffe Leslie (1827?–1882), an Irish economist, was writing in the shadow of the successive European wars and rumours of war of the 1860's and 1870's. He was, as he says in the preface to his book, strongly of the opinion that " the economy of modern Europe—including therein the occupations of its inhabitants, the motives determining the directions of their energies, and the constituents, amount and distribution of their wealth—cannot be adequately interpreted without reference to the warlike tendencies of the age and their causes".

At no period of the middle ages was so large a proportion of the population of the Continent trained to war as at the present day. An immense part of the wealth of modern Europe, England included, consists of weapons, warlike structures and stores, and the appliances of armies and fleets.... The very improvements in manufacture and the military art which tended in Adam Smith's view to wean the mass of mankind from war, the very agencies represented by steam and gunpowder to which Buckle triumphantly traced its extinction in the civilized world, have brought nations so close together, and armed them with such deadly weapons, that every man may almost be said now to sleep with arms at his side, ready to do battle in the morning. Science and industry themselves, along with pacific tendencies, have others of the opposite character, both in the effects already referred to, and in the higher pride, rivalry, ambition, and patriotism of nations developed by intellectual and industrial progress.

156. BRITAIN'S ECONOMIC GAIN FROM COLONIES

Source: J. S. Jeans, 'England's Supremacy: its Sources, Economics and Dangers' (1885), pp. 301–2 and 305.
The weight which the "Empire argument" carried in economic and political discussion in the 1880's and 1890's owed much to the expansion of colonial populations and trade since the early years of the century.

...That the colonies are a source of strength and power is generally admitted; but the extent to which they confer these attributes, and the why and wherefore of their possession, are not so clearly appreciated.

We may, at the outset, appropriately consider the question, What is the real magnitude of the British Empire? Its area is upwards of eight millions of square miles, being about seventy times the size of the mother country. Its population is over 300 millions, or eight and a half times that of the United Kingdom. Other countries have possessed colonies before England, and other countries possess colonies now; but no country has ever before had colonies distinguished at once by such magnitude and such progress, by such far-reaching extent and such fecundity. Nothing is more calculated to strike the imagination than a study of the growth of our colonial empire. In population, in commerce, in revenue, in debt, and, generally, in all the elements of material development, that growth has been stupendous. Between 1860 and 1884, the population of our colonies (including India and Canada) increased from 152½ to 300 millions. In the same interval, the annual value of their commerce rose from 190½ to 370 millions sterling. The same quarter of a century witnessed a growth of revenue from 51 to 110 millions, and of debt (largely incurred on behalf of railways) from 125 to 320 millions. Some colonies have, of course, been developed at a much more rapid pace than others. Our African possessions have been developed more rapidly than all. Between 1860 and 1880, the population of our dominions in South Africa increased by 251 per cent, and in western Africa by 148 per cent. Within the same period, the commerce of the former has increased by 320 per cent and of the latter by 245 per cent. The largest amount of advance has, as might be expected, taken place in India, where the population has increased by 71 millions, or about twice the total number of inhabitants in the United Kingdom. Over our empire beyond the seas, regarded as a whole, there has been an increase in the last twenty years of 50 per cent in population and 90 per cent in commerce. Whither will this enormous expansion ultimately lead us? At the same rate of growth, if continued for less than another half century, England would, in 1930, have an empire of between seven and eight hundred million souls—that is to say, of more than twice the population of Europe, and nearly nine times the population of the American continent at the present time. It does not seem as if there were any physical limitations to this prospect. . . .

Subject to obvious and not infrequent limitations, which need not here be dwelt upon, there are few maxims of business more generally true than that which predicates that 'the trade follows the flag'. The aphorism is, however, peculiarly applicable to the trade of the United Kingdom. . . .

The next largest colonising and colony-owning countries after the United Kingdom are Portugal, Holland, France, Spain, and Denmark. The colonies of these five countries have unitedly a population of about 47½ millions, or about a fifth of the population of the colonial possessions of Great Britain. But while the total value of the import and export trade of the nations just named amounts to approximately 700 millions, only 35 millions, or 5 per cent of the whole trade, is carried on with their several colonies. Great Britain, on the other hand, has a total trade, including imports and exports, officially valued at about 715½ millions sterling, of which fully 186½ millions, or 26 per cent, is carried on with her own possessions abroad. Obviously, therefore, our colonies confer upon the mother country, from a commercial point of view, advantages of the most substantial and exceptional character.

157. THE 'FAIR TRADERS'

Source: W. Farrer Ecroyd, "Fair Trade", 'The Nineteenth Century', vol. x (1881), pp. 589–90 and 592–3.

The 1880's saw a decided reaction against the economic policy of free trade. Farrer Ecroyd was one of the spokesmen of this "Fair Trade" movement. He held that the measures he recommended would assist the economy by enabling manufacturers to obtain a larger share of the home market. Food prices would be only slightly increased. Meanwhile, the colonies would expand their demand for British manufactured goods with

Who Gained by Change?

incomes earned from supplying the British market with foodstuffs. For the "Fair Traders", who remained a minority group, see B. H. Brown, 'The Tariff Reform Movement in Great Britain 1881–1895' (1943).

OUR manufacturers are more and more excluded from the markets of the civilised world, not by fair competition, but by oppressive tariffs. At home they are met by the unrestricted competition of every article which can be made more cheaply in any country by dint of longer hours of work, lower wages, and a meaner style of living on the part of the workers. They enjoy the one advantage of cheap food, it is true; but that is purchased, as they are finding to their cost, by the ruin of those dependent upon agriculture, and the consequent paralysis of the home trade in the rural districts.

Under these circumstances, it has been proposed to establish an import duty of 10 per cent on all foreign manufacturers, not for protection, but to regain our power of bargaining with other nations, whose manufactures we buy, to admit ours as freely and fairly as we wish to admit theirs. And, to leave our hands free to do this, it is urged that we ought not to make or renew any commercial treaties but such as either establish free trade in manufactures on both sides, or are terminable at a year's notice.

As a matter of necessity, all raw materials of our manufacturing industries must be admitted duty free from every quarter.

It has been further proposed to impose a duty, not exceeding 10 per cent on a low range of values, upon all articles of food imported from foreign countries, whilst admitting the same duty free from every part of our own Empire; the object, here again, being clearly not protection, but the diversion of the food-growing into our own colonies, with whose inhabitants experience teaches us we enjoy a return trade in our manufactures at least twenty times larger per head than with the Americans and Russians, from whom, at present, we are unfortunately obliged to buy most of our food, though they do their best to exclude our manufactures by oppressive import duties....

For myself, I am firmly convinced that we could, and should by the means proposed, obtain (1) a greatly enlarged and more equal interchange of our manufactures with countries like France; and (2) and far more important, a free, or substantially free, exchange of our manufactures for food within our own empire; and (3) both these results at so modest and temporary a cost that we should promptly regain it tenfold.

[*Farrer Ecroyd goes on to argue that the net effect of these fiscal measures would be far from harmful to the British economy. Prices would be very little affected by the proposed tariff upon manufactured products. On the other hand, this proposal would enable our manufacturers to obtain a large share of the home market. Food prices would only be slightly increased. Our intention must be to enable our colonies to capture more of the British market, and thereby encourage them to expand their demand for British manufactured goods.*]

158. A LETTER ON UGANDA

Letter from the Reverend G. A. Sowter, dated 18 October 1892, to Lord Rosebery, quoted by A. Low, "British Public Opinion and the Uganda Question: October–December 1892", 'The Uganda Journal', vol. 18, no. 2 (1954), p. 88.

The establishment of the Uganda protectorate in April 1893 was a turning point in Liberal attitudes towards the Empire, for it was the Rosebery administration which took the step. But it was also a singularly good illustration of the complexity of motives which lay behind the policy of annexation. The Uganda question arose out of the gradual expansion of British missionary, commercial and political interests in that part of East Africa late in the nineteenth century. Sir William Mackinnon (1823–93), a founder of the British India Steam Navigation Company, trading on the Indian Ocean, had formed the Imperial British East Africa Company in 1888, with a charter from the crown to develop trade in the Lakes region of East Africa. The company also gave aid and protection to British missionaries working there. It acquired a forceful servant in Captain Frederick Lugard, who was to play a leading part in extending British influence both in East and West Africa. But financially the company failed. Then the question of its withdrawal from Uganda arose and Parliament and Cabinet had to decide whether Company rule there should be succeeded by Colonial Office rule. This was "the Uganda issue" as it was discussed by Victorian public opinion in the autumn of 1892. For the African background, D. Johnson and A. S. Baxendale, "Uganda and Great Britain", 'University of Birmingham Historical Journal' (1962), pp. 162–88.

I HAVE the honour to lay before your Lordship a copy of two resolutions adopted unanimously at a well-attended meeting in St Silas' School, Bristol, last night. I do so with the greater pleasure because I believe your Lordship is keenly alive to the terrible results which will

Who Gained by Change?

not improbably follow the withdrawal of the representatives of the Imperial British East Africa Company from that country. I recognize the fact that the exact course to pursue must be left to those in responsible positions in the state who are better informed of all the circumstances of the case, and in so difficult a matter as this, your Lordship has the fullest sympathy of many. But there can be little doubt that the evacuation of Uganda in March next will retard the civilization of that important country, perhaps for centuries, besides imperilling the lives of many native Christians and giving a fresh impetus to the slave trade now largely held in check.

159. UGANDA: THE CHAMBERS OF COMMERCE

Source: M. W. Beresford, 'The Leeds Chambers of Commerce' (1951), p. 115.

This resolution was passed in November 1892. It was one of a large number of Uganda resolutions passed by the Chambers of Commerce of the cities and towns in the autumn of that year.

THE British Africa Company contemplates giving up Uganda. This Chamber is glad to hear that the British Commission is taking over in the name of trade, humanity and good government. Most countries are now building up a hostile tariff wall against our commodities, and it is of the utmost importance to preserve as much of the world as possible for our trade.

160. 'PEGGING OUT CLAIMS FOR POSTERITY'

Source: 'Foreign and Colonial Speeches by the Rt. Honourable J. Chamberlain, M.P.'(1897), pp. 113–15.

Joseph Chamberlain, speaking from the opposition benches in the House of Commons, 20 March 1893. The question at issue was the future of Uganda. Henry Labouchere, a well-known Liberal M.P., had just condemned the decision of the Gladstone government to send a mission to that part of Africa to decide whether the British occupation of the country should continue.

BUT I must put another question to my honourable friend....He is opposed to all expansion of the Empire, on the ground, as I understand, that we have enough to do at home.

434

Now, suppose this view, which he puts before the Committee...
had been put fifty or one hundred years ago, and suppose it had been
accepted by the Parliament of that day. I ask myself what would now
be the position of this country, what would be the position of persons
in the slums for whom my honourable friend has so much sympathy
and feeling? (Hear, hear.) Does my honourable friend believe, if it
were not for the gigantic foreign trade that has been created by this
policy of expansion, that we could subsist in this country in any kind
of way—I do not say in luxury, but in the condition in which, at the
present time, a great part of our population lives. Does he think that
we could support in these small islands forty millions of people, without the trade by which a great part of our population earns its living—
a trade which has been brought to us by the action of our ancestors,
who in centuries past did not shrink from making sacrifices of blood
and treasure, and who were not ashamed—if I may borrow the expression which has been referred to more than once to-night—to peg
out claims for posterity?...If this idea of closing all the doors through
which all new trade is to come to us is to be accepted by this House, at
least we ought to adopt some means by which our population can be
kept stationary....

What are we asked to do to-night? This is not a question of Uganda
only; but we are asked to reverse the whole policy of this country...
to relinquish the vast advantages which have accrued to us by the
surrender of Heligoland, and by the treaties and engagements with
foreign States, and to secure which our country has made sacrifices,
in the belief that we were, in return, getting a *quid pro quo*. That *quid
pro quo* we are now asked to sacrifice, and are asked to give up all share
in what has been called the partition of Africa. (Cheers).

161. UGANDA: GIVING UP TO WHOM?

Source: 'Reports Relating to Uganda by Sir Gerald Portal' (C. 7303),
*1894, pp. 31-2. Sir Gerald Portal to the Earl of Rosebery, dated
Zanzibar, 1 November 1893, received in London 6 December.*

*Gerald Portal (1858-94), British agent in Zanzibar, headed the mission
sent to Uganda by the Liberal government. Rosebery was Foreign
Secretary in the Gladstone administration. Declaration of the Uganda
Protectorate followed in 1894 when Rosebery had become Prime Minister.*

Who Gained by Change?

For the terms of the Protectorate, Sir E. Hertslet, ' The Map of Africa by Treaty' (1909).

THE strategical importance of the position of Uganda, as controlling the head-waters of the Nile and the three great lakes of Victoria, Albert, and Albert Edward, can perhaps be better estimated in England than in Uganda; this is, moreover, a question of wide and general policy which it is outside my province to discuss.

I may, however, be allowed to call attention to the fact that an evacuation of Uganda means a great deal more than a mere withdrawal of a few officers and a flag from a distant and partly-known country in Central Africa. It means, practically, the renunciation of the whole of that vast territory reserved by the Anglo-German Convention for the sphere of British influence. The country lying between Lake Victoria and the east coast is valuable chiefly as being the road to Uganda, and the evacuation of the latter would soon be recognized as being equivalent to the restriction of British influence and British commerce to the coast-line and to the ports of the Zanzibar Sultanate.

So long as the race of Waganda continue to exist as a homogeneous people, they must, in virtue of their higher civilization, and of their greater intelligence and initiative, occupy a leading position among the natives of Central Africa, and the European Power which exercises a controlling influence over Uganda will ultimately be able to control the politics and to guide the commerce of an immense section of the richest part of the continent. I have already stated the reasons for my conviction that the withdrawal of English influence must be followed by the establishment of the control of some other European Power, and I venture to repeat that such control would almost inevitably extend, not only over Uganda and its immediate dependencies, but would embrace all the neighbouring countries, the great lakes, the Nile Valley, and the natural highways of the interior. The control of Uganda means, in the course of a few years, a preponderance of influence and of commerce in the richest and most populous section of Central Africa; a withdrawal from Uganda entails, besides the legacy of war and bloodshed left to that country itself, a renunciation on the part of England of any important participation in the present work of development, in the suppression of slavery, and in the future commerce of East and Central Africa.

436

For the above, as well as for other reasons which need scarcely be detailed here, I venture to submit to your Lordship that all question of a complete evacuation of Uganda, at all events for the present, should be set aside.

162. UGANDA: THE NILE INTEREST

Source: 'Parliamentary Debates', 4th series, vol. 79, cols. 880–81.

The speaker was William St John Brodrick (1856–1942), Parliamentary Secretary to the Foreign Office in the Salisbury administration, the date 22 February 1900.

IT has been suggested that we have undertaken in Uganda liabilities which will prove an incubus to this country, but I challenge that statement altogether. I believe that, so far, the object for which these protectorates were first taken up were not merely that they should become civilising mediums, not because there was a mere desire to acquire territory for the process of expansion, but the considerable liabilities attaching to them were undertaken in the pursuance of a definite policy of securing territory which had to do with the head waters of the Nile, which are absolutely necessary for the control of Egypt and the Soudan. I regard it, therefore, not as a question of national advantage, but as a question of Imperial necessity. If we are to hold Egypt and be masters of the Soudan as we are, it is absolutely necessary that the head waters of the Nile should be in the hands of the power which controls those two countries; and we have no intention whatever of giving way in the position we have taken up. Every year it becomes more and more obvious that the life of Egypt is the Nile....

163. UGANDA: THE INDIAN INTEREST

Source: 'Report of His Majesty's Special Commission on the Protectorate of Uganda' (Cd. 671), 1901, p. 7.

The British Special Commissioner in Uganda was Sir Harry Johnston (1858–1927). The relation between India and East Africa was already centuries old, although the spread of steamship and railway services was giving it a new scale about this time.

I HAVE made a rough computation, and I estimate that our dealings with Uganda since the establishment of the Protectorate in 1894 have cost us 1,394,000 l. for our administration and its resulting wars for the protection of the country, and 4,900,000 l. for the construction of the Uganda Railway. What justification is there for this outlay, and what hope of ever recovering the sums advanced, either by direct payments to Imperial Treasury or indirect profit to British commerce?

I am inclined to look at the whole question from the point of view of a caviller. Why, in the first place, do we hold Uganda? We do so for political and philanthropic reasons. The political reasons are that the lands comprised within the Uganda Protectorate contain the headwaters of the River Nile. The Power which holds Uganda—whether European or African—might, by means of relatively simple engineering works, withhold the main source of the Nile supply from the irrigation of Egypt. It is a disputed point whether the Nile floods by which Egypt is kept alive, derive their volume equally or disproportionately from the lake and rivers of Abyssinia or the lakes and rivers of Uganda. But the Abyssinian source of supply is not under British control, and should any circumstances cause interference with the water-supply coming from Abyssinia it would be certainly necessary that the other contribution from the main source of the Nile should be completely under our control. We take a peculiar interest in the welfare of Egypt because that country is at present such an important stage on the way to India. The maintenance of our control, therefore, over the East African and Uganda Protectorates is necessitated by our regard for the political future of India. There is a secondary reason, moreover. On account of our Indian Empire we are compelled to reserve to British control a large portion of East Africa. Indian trade, enterprise, and emigration require a suitable outlet. East Africa is, and should be, from every point of view, the America of the Hindu. We do not naturally desire to see all the Indian enterprise in Eastern Africa sheltered by a flag that is not British. I am aware that British Indian subjects carry on a brisk trade in German and Portuguese East Africa, and have little or nothing to complain of at the hands of the Portuguese or German authorities; but at the same time I regard it as a political necessity that a portion (and, happily, it is the richest portion) of East Africa should be open to Indian enterprise under the British flag.

The philanthropic reasons for our holding Uganda may not be considered sufficient justification at the present day for the expenditure of the British tax-payer's money, so that I will not dwell on them unduly. These reasons, however, in 1890 and 1894, weighed almost more with the British Governments of those days than the political and commercial motives which I have brought forward. They were sufficiently powerful to cause both political parties who alternately govern the Empire to pledge themselves respectively to the maintenance of the British Protectorate, and this pledge must, within reasonable limits, be held to bind us to the task, even at the cost of a few million pounds.

164. DEATH DUTIES AND DEFENCE

Source: A. G. Gardiner, 'The Life of Sir William Harcourt' (1923), vol. II, pp. 293, 298–9.

Mounting naval expenses, arising out of the defence of the Empire, forced a major innovation in public finance in 1894. This was the reform of the taxes on inherited property. The State had recognized different kinds of property—real (i.e. landed) and personal, different types of succession, and different degrees of relationship between the beneficiaries of an estate. The existing taxes were complicated and ineffective. Other statesmen had looked at the problem. It was left to Sir William Harcourt (1827–1904), Chancellor of the Exchequer in the Liberal Rosebery administration of the 1890's, to replace them by a simpler and more fruitful system. Harcourt was himself a member of the landed class. But he had made up his mind that the great landed estates and the great houses of Victorian England—Chatsworth, Longleat, Blenheim, Hatfield and many others—did not play their proper part in meeting the rising cost of public finance. The Prime Minister, Lord Rosebery, was opposed to Harcourt's proposals when they were introduced in the Cabinet, but the Chancellor of the Exchequer pushed them through. Within a generation, the reformed death duties, as they were called, had become a mainstay of the system of national finance, yielding a sum much larger than Harcourt had ever contemplated. The first extract is from the Chancellor of the Exchequer's speech defending his bill against strong attack in the House of Commons, on 10 May 1894. The second is from a letter by Harcourt to Queen Victoria. She had expressed her alarm at his proposals and the Parliamentary rough weather which they created. For the details of his budget, Bernard Mallet, 'British Budgets 1887–1913' (1913). A. J. Balfour had been first lord of the Treasury, C. J. Goschen Chancellor of the Exchequer in the preceding Salisbury administration.

Who Gained by Change?

Given the necessity for raising large sums for national defence by increased taxation, how is the money to be got? We affirm and you deny that the powerful and wealthy liquor interests should make a further contribution. Secondly, we affirm and you deny that for the purposes of the death duties realty and personalty should be treated alike. (*Mr Balfour*,—No, I did not deny it.) Then why do you want to throw out the Budget? We affirm and you deny (Opposition laughter) —I do not know which of you is going to deny—that taking a moderate system of graduation immense wealth should pay at a higher rate than smaller fortunes. That is a clear issue. We affirm and you deny—it remains to be seen how long you will venture to deny—that if great expenditure requires a high rate of income-tax, the burden should fall more lightly on the humbler incomes, (*Mr Balfour*,—I asserted it) and until the late First Lord of the Treasury and the late Chancellor of the Exchequer can make up their minds on the subject of finance you are not entitled to throw out the Budget. These are the clear issues which divide our principles from those of the Tory Party. (*Mr Balfour*,—No, they do not)....If you should defeat the Budget, you will not defeat the principles on which it is founded, those principles being founded on just and equal taxation, adjusted to the capacity of the various classes to bear the burden.

[*Harcourt to Queen Victoria*]

11 Downing Street, Whitehall, S.W., *June 9, 1894*—Sir W. Harcourt presents his humble duty to your Majesty, and begs leave to report that in the last few days solid progress has been made with the clauses of the Budget Bill in Committee.

Sir William desires to assure the Queen that the outcry which has been made by the landed interest on the subject of extraordinary pressure upon them in the Budget is grossly exaggerated if not entirely unfounded. Lord Salisbury's statement that it will absorb four years' income is entirely contrary to the fact. In the case of a man with £100,000 the additional taxation will be 1 per cent, and in that of a man with a million 4 per cent, and in the case of the last it might amount to 2 years' income payable in eight years. The truth is that the land-owners have been so long accustomed to exemption from their fair share of the taxation borne by the other classes of the community that they resent as a great injustice that they should be treated on an equal footing.

It is no doubt a great misfortune that owing to the immense expenditure upon armaments it should be necessary to raise an additional sum of 4 millions by taxation, but that can only be done by imposing the burthen equally upon all classes with a regard to the ability of the several parties to bear it....

165. BRITISH TRADE AND THE EMPIRE

Source: 'Foreign and Colonial Speeches by the Rt. Honourable J. Chamberlain, M.P.' (1897), pp. 141–4.

Speech delivered by Joseph Chamberlain at a banquet given to him by the Birmingham Chamber of Commerce, 13 November 1896. Chamberlain had become Colonial Secretary in the Salisbury administration the year before. The special character of his audience needs to be remembered.

ALL the great offices of State are occupied with commercial affairs. The Foreign Office and the Colonial Office are chiefly engaged in finding new markets and in defending old ones. (Hear, hear.) The War Office and Admiralty are mostly occupied in preparations for the defence of these markets, and for the protection of commerce. (Hear, hear.) The Boards of Agriculture and of Trade are entirely concerned with those two great branches of industry. Even the Education Department bases its claims to the public money upon the necessity of keeping our people well to the front in the commercial competition which they have to sustain; and the Home Office finds the largest scope for its activity in the protection of the life and the health, and in the promotion of the comfort, of the vast army of manual labourers who are engaged in those industries. Therefore, it is not too much to say that commerce is the greatest of all political interests—(hear, hear)—and that that Government deserves most the popular approval which does most to increase our trade and to settle it on a firm foundation....

...I think I may claim, perhaps with the assent of some of my political opponents, credit to the Government for doing all in their

power to increase and to develop those great free markets in the world
to which we look now, to which we shall have in future to look still
more, for outlets for British trade—for the trade which, I am sorry to
say, foreign nations, and even some of our own colonies, are threatening by hostile and restrictive tariffs. (Hear, hear.) Attention was
called the other day, in a very able and a very powerful speech delivered by Lord Rosebery in Edinburgh, to the fact that during the last
few years we have added 2,600,000 square miles to the territories which
are either dominions of the Queen or over which the Queen exercises
her influence....

I should be perfectly prepared to admit that, if other nations would
only stand aside, it might have been wiser that we should have proceeded more gradually....But there was no appearance of such an
inclination on the part of other nations. (Laughter). I can truly say
that we were not the first or the most eager to move; but, if we had
remained passive, what would have happened? Is it not as certain as
that we are sitting here that the greater part of the continent of Africa
would have been occupied by our commercial rivals, who would have
proceeded, as the first act of their policy, to close this great potential
market to British trade? (Cheers).

Let me make one remark here, the proper consideration of which
would, I think, do very much to modify that jealousy with which
undoubtedly foreign nations regard our extension. My remark is this
—that we, in our colonial policy, as fast as we acquire new territory
and develop it, develop it as trustees of civilisation for the commerce
of the world. (Cheers) We offer in all these markets over which our
flag floats the same opportunities, the same open field to foreigners
that we offer to our own subjects, and upon the same terms. (Hear,
hear.)

166. EMPIRE AN OUTLET FOR CAPITAL?

Source: J. A. Hobson, 'Imperialism' (1902), pp. 60–1, 62, 85–6.

*The war in South Africa, 1899–1902, provoked a great public debate,
for and against the policies which led to conflict with the Boers. Hobson's
book was a contribution to this discussion. J. A. Hobson (1858–1940)
visited South Africa and his book, interpreting the war in terms primarily
of the interests of British investors on the Rand, was an able statement of
a case. It influenced for many years the views of those who were critical*

of the war and enjoyed a further lease of life from being taken up and quoted with approval by Lenin during the First World War, as evidence of the economic character of imperialism. There can be no doubt however that Hobson, over-influenced by South African experience, seriously exaggerated the importance of investment opportunities as an incentive to empire. The pattern of foreign investment was very far from being the same as the pattern of colonial expansion. For a critical view, D. K. Fieldhouse, "Imperialism", an Historiographical Revision, 'Economic History Review', vol. XIV (December 1961).

IT is not too much to say that the modern foreign policy of Great Britain is primarily a struggle for profitable markets of investment. To a larger extent every year Great Britain is becoming a nation living upon tribute from abroad, and the classes who enjoy this tribute have an ever-increasing incentive to employ the public policy, the public purse, and the public force to extend the field of their private investments, and to safeguard and improve their existing investments. This is, perhaps, the most important fact in modern politics, and the obscurity in which it is wrapped constitutes the gravest danger to our State.

What is true of Great Britain is true likewise of France, Germany, the United States, and of all countries in which modern capitalism has placed large surplus savings in the hands of a plutocracy or of a thrifty middle class. A well-recognised distinction is drawn between creditor and debtor countries. Great Britain has been for some time by far the largest creditor country, and the policy by which the investing classes use the instrument of the State for private business purposes is most richly illustrated in the history of her wars and annexations. But France, Germany, and the United States are advancing fast along the same path....

Aggressive Imperialism, which costs the tax-payer so dear, which is of so little value to the manufacturer and trader, which is fraught with such grave incalculable peril to the citizen, is a source of great gain to the investor who cannot find at home the profitable use he seeks for his capital, and insists that his Government should help him to profitable and secure investments abroad.

If, contemplating the enormous expenditure on armaments, the ruinous wars, the diplomatic audacity of knavery by which modern Governments seek to extend their territorial power, we put the plain, practical question, *Cui bono*? the first and most obvious answer is, The investor....

Over-production in the sense of an excessive manufacturing plant, and surplus capital which cannot find sound investments within the country, force Great Britain, Germany, Holland, France to place larger and larger portions of their economic resources outside the area of their present political domain, and then stimulate a policy of political expansion so as to take in the new areas. The economic sources of this movement are laid bare by periodic trade-depressions due to an inability of producers to find adequate and profitable markets for what they can produce. The Majority Report of the Commission upon the Depression of Trade in 1885 put the matter in a nut-shell. 'That, owing to the nature of the times, the demand for our commodities does not increase at the same rate as formerly; that our capacity for production is consequently in excess of our requirements, and could be considerably increased at short notice; that this is due partly to the competition of the capital which is being steadily accumulated in the country.' The Minority Report straightly imputes the condition of affairs to 'over-production'. Germany is at the present time suffering severely from what is called a glut of capital and of manufacturing power: she must have new markets; her Consuls all over the world are 'hustling' for trade; trading settlements are forced upon Asia Minor; in East and West Africa, in China and elsewhere the German Empire is impelled to a policy of colonisation and protectorates as outlets for German commercial energy.

Every improvement of methods of production, every concentration of ownership and control, seems to accentuate the tendency. As one nation after another enters the machine economy and adopts advanced industrial methods, it becomes more difficult for its manufacturers, merchants, and financiers to dispose profitably of their economic resources, and they are tempted more and more to use their Governments in order to secure for their particular use some distant undeveloped country by annexation and protection.

The process we may be told is inevitable, and so it seems upon superficial inspection. Everywhere appear excessive powers of production, excessive capital in search of investment. It is admitted by all business men that the growth of the powers of production in their country exceeds the growth in consumption, that more goods can be produced than can be sold at a profit, and that more capital exists than can find remunerative investment.

It is this economic condition of affairs that forms the taproot of Imperialism.

167. WORLD TRADE AND THE ROLE OF NAVAL POWER

Source: 'The Times', Thursday, 20 October 1902.

Captain A. T. Mahan (1840–1914), quoted here, was the American naval historian whose book, 'The Influence of Sea Power on History' (1890) had a wide effect on political and service opinion in this country about the turn of the century. 'The Times' leader, discussing naval questions, appears to have been written under the combined influence of great political events, the emergence of the United States as a world power and the beginnings of the arms race with Germany, following the German navy laws of 1898 and 1900, and the export drive of newly industrialized nations, notably the Germans, Americans and Japanese. In the close relation which the newspaper sought to establish between trade opportunities and armed power, it was hardly characteristic of British public opinion as a whole; but it did represent a point of view which had exponents on both sides of the North Sea. Compare the vision of a new mercantilist age in G. Schmoller, M. Sering and A. Wagner, 'Handels— und Machtpolitik' (Stuttgart, 1900), 2 vols. For Anglo-German relations at this date see R. J. S. Hoffmann, 'Great Britain and the German Trade Rivalry 1875–1914 (1933)' and, more critical, E. L. Woodward 'Great Britain and the German Navy' (1935).

IN other words, naval expansion is an inexorable and inevitable necessity, alike for the United States and for any other Power which aspires to take its due share in that political and commercial future which the march of events is preparing for the nations of the Western world. Whither it is all tending no man can tell fully as yet, but the tendency itself is unmistakable. The 'extension of commerce by political pressure', says Captain Mahan, in a pregnant sentence, 'is a leading element in the spirit of the times'. In Germany the same thing has been said in different words—'Unsere Zukunft liegt auf dem Wasser'—and the proposition is unquestionably true of any nation which aspires to hold its own in the modern commercial struggle for existence. Commerce nowadays means for the most part transmarine commerce—the interchange of commodities otherwise unobtainable, or obtainable only at increased and often prohibitive cost, between nations and peoples separated by the seas. Nearly every commercial Power, except England, seems bent on securing for itself, as far as may be, a monopoly in the distant markets which are still open to its enterprise. For this reason the legitimate and, in itself, salutary impulse of commercial expansion too often entails either territorial acquisition or the exercise in the region affected of a dominant, if not exclusive, political influence on the part of the Power which is seeking to establish its monopoly. Where the field is still open, this entails, in its turn, the rivalry, and even antagonism, of other Powers equally interested and claiming equal rights; and the result is that each Power so affected must either withdraw from the contest or be prepared, in the last resort, to assert its rights and defend its interests—not necessarily by going to war, but by showing itself to be so powerful that its just demands must needs be treated with respect.... It is determined, not by the abstract defensive needs of this Power or that, but by the resolve of each Power in turn, not to allow any other Power to acquire exclusive influence in any sphere of commercial activity still open to all the world. There are, of course, other influences and forces at work that make for naval expansion, but we are considering the matter, for the moment, from a purely commercial and economic point of view....

Such is the argument, and it is undoubtedly a very cogent, as well as a very comprehensive, argument. It touches not only the United States, but every naval and commercial Power in the world, and it opens out a prospect of universal naval expansion to which it seems hardly possible to set any assignable limit. Is there no escape from this conclusion? None, we fear, so long as the premises remain unchanged. But it may, perhaps, some day occur to the Powers which seek to establish a commercial monopoly in their own favour that even a monopoly can be too dearly purchased at such a price as, to all appearance, they will have to pay for it.... From the economic point of view, it is not to be disputed that the aggregate profits of the world's commerce, if based on an absolute and universal system of free exchange, must be far greater than they can be on any system of fiscal barriers and restrictions, and the partial monopolies that result from them, although they might be very differently distributed. This being so, it must always be a question whether the advantage which any nation derives from the maintenance of such restrictions is not more than balanced by the expenditure on warlike preparation, chiefly naval, which is inexorably entailed by the assumed necessity of maintaining them. Experience shows that such expenditure tends incessantly to increase.

168. THE BASIS OF TARIFF REFORM

Source: J. Chamberlain, 'Imperial Union and Tariff Reform: Speeches delivered from 15 May to 4 November, 1903' (1903), pp. viii–x.

Joseph Chamberlain, then Colonial Secretary in the Balfour administration, launched his Tariff Reform programme in a speech at Birmingham on 15 May 1903. He resigned from the government in the following September, to lead an agitation which divided British political life from top to bottom, until it was temporarily settled by the general election of 1906. The following paragraphs were written by Chamberlain after his resignation. They served as an introduction to a collection of his opening speeches on Tariff Reform and were dated 9 November 1903. The timing of Chamberlain's initiative, in the years of trade depression just after the South African war, and at a period when public opinion was beginning to be seriously concerned at what it felt to be the exposed British position in a world of rising international tensions, needs to be remembered. The general character of his proposals was for a measure of protection for the British manufacturer and a system of preference on the goods of those British colonies which controlled their own import duties.

THE changes that have taken place, since the adoption of Free Trade nearly sixty years ago, in the conditions of international exchange, in the comparative position of foreign nations, and, above all, in our relations with our own Colonies, seem to point conclusively to the necessity of a reconsideration of our fiscal system. It is not desirable to postpone this review to a time of depression, which many close observers think to be imminent, when the pressure of exceptional distress may compel us to hasty and ill-considered reforms.

The original object of Mr Cobden and his colleagues was to secure a free exchange of products between the nations of the world at their natural price, but for many years the example of the open door set by the United Kingdom has not been followed by other countries, and hostile tariffs have everywhere interfered with the natural course of trade.

Who Gained by Change?

These tariffs, avowedly designed to exclude British manufactures, have been supported by the operation of bounties, subsidies and trusts; while foreign producers have been enabled, partly by the same means, and partly by the lower standard of living, to which their working classes are accustomed, to undersell the British manufacturer in neutral markets and even seriously to attack his home trade.

The doctrinaire Free Traders have no remedy to propose for this state of things, which, indeed, they either deny, or else ascribe to the want of enterprise and intelligence on the part of our manufacturers, to the ignorance and incapacity of our people, or to the tyrannical action of the Trade Unions.

The Tariff Reformers, on the other hand, believe that by recovering our freedom of action, and by re-arming ourselves with the weapon of a moderate tariff, we may still defend our home market against unfair competition, and may, at the same time, secure a modification of foreign tariffs which would open the way to a fairer exchange of our respective products than we have hitherto been able to obtain.

But they attach even greater importance to the possibility of securing by preferential and reciprocal arrangements with our Colonies a great development of trade within the Empire and a nearer approach to a commercial union, which in some shape or another, must precede or accompany closer political relations, and without which, as all history shows, no permanent co-operation is possible.

They believe that these objects can be promoted, without loss to any class or any individual, by a slight transfer of existing taxes which will not increase national burdens, but will raise the revenue required for defence and administration in such a way as to develop our inter-Imperial trade to the mutual benefit both of the Colonies and the Mother Country, while adding greatly to the amount of employment for our ever-growing population.

The questions thus raised, although they interest every class, are more vitally important to working men than to any other, since they alone depend upon their daily employment for their daily subsistence.

To the manufacturer and the capitalist the essential consideration is security for his investments which, under present conditions, are always liable to a kind of interference against which it is impossible for him to provide. His foreign competitor, unassailable in his home market, can safely issue forth to attack him, while he is incapable of retaliation, and powerless to defend himself against the new methods of foreign competition.

169. THE PROGRAMME OF TARIFF REFORM

Source: 'Mr Chamberlain's Speeches', ed. C. W. Boyd (1914), vol. II, pp. 156–9, 161–2.

In a speech delivered at Glasgow, 6 October 1903, Chamberlain under-took to give in some detail the measures which he thought necessary to bring foreign tariffs down and to weld the Empire into an economic union. The political significance of these plans was that they involved a de-parture in principle from the Free Trade, i.e. non-protective policies which had governed Great Britain's external economic relations for half a century past. Hence the disturbance of public opinion and the confused state of politics in the years which followed.

CAN we invent a tie (to keep the Empire together) which must be a practical one, which will prevent separation, and I make the same answer as Mr Rhodes, who suggested reciprocal preference (twelve years ago), and I say that it is only by commercial union, reciprocal preference, that you can lay the foundations of the con-federation of the Empire to which we all look forward as a brilliant possibility. Now I have told you what you are to gain by preference. You will gain the retention and the increase of your customers. You will gain work for the enormous number of those who are now un-employed; you will pave the way for a firmer and more enduring union of the Empire. What will it cost you? What do the colonies ask? They ask a preference on their particular products. You cannot give them, at least it would be futile to offer them, a preference on manufactured goods, because at the present time the exported manu-facture of the colonies is entirely insignificant. You cannot, in my opinion, give them a preference on raw material. It has been said that I should propose such a tax; but I repeat now, in the most explicit terms, that I do not propose a tax on raw materials, which are a necessity of our manufacturing trade. What remains? Food.

...I recognise that you have a right to call upon me for the broad outlines of my plan, and those I will give you if you will bear with me. You have heard it said that I propose to put a duty of 5s. or 10s. a quarter on wheat. That is untrue. I propose to put a low duty on foreign corn, no duty at all on the corn coming from our British possessions. But I propose to put a low duty on foreign corn not exceeding 2s. a quarter. I propose to put no tax whatever on maize, partly because maize is a food of some of the very poorest of the population, and partly also because it is a raw material for the farmers who feed their stock with it. I propose that the corresponding tax, which will have to be put on flour should give a substantial preference to the miller, and I do that in order to re-establish one of our most ancient industries in this country, believing that if that is done not only will more work be found in agricultural districts, with some tendency, perhaps, operating against the constant migration from the country into the towns, but also because by re-establishing the milling industry in this country, the offals, as they are called—the refuse of the wheat—will remain in the country and will give to the farmers or the agricultural population a food for their stock and their pigs at very much lower rates....I propose to put a small tax of about 5 per cent on foreign meat and dairy produce. I propose to exclude bacon, because once more bacon is a popular food with some of the poorest of the population. And, lastly, I propose to give a substantial preference to our colonies upon colonial wines and perhaps upon colonial fruits....

But I propose also some great remissions. I propose to take off three-fourths of the duty on tea and half of the whole duty on sugar, with a corresponding reduction on cocoa and coffee. [*Chamberlain argues that the net effect of all these changes will reduce the food budget of the agricultural labourer by 2d. a week and that of the town artisan by 2½d. a week.*]...these advantages to the consumer will involve a loss to the Exchequer...the loss to the Exchequer will be £2,800,000 per annum. How is it to be made up? I propose to find it, and to find more, in the other branch of this policy of fiscal reform, in that part of it which is sometimes called 'retaliation' and sometimes 'reciprocity'. Now I cannot deal fully with that subject to-night. I shall have other opportunities, but this I will point out to you, that in attempting to secure reciprocity we cannot hope to be wholly successful. Nobody, I imagine, is sanguine enough to believe that America or Germany and France and Italy and all those countries are going to drop the whole of their protective scheme because we ask them to do so, or even because we threaten.

What I do hope is that they will reduce their duties so that worse things may not happen to them. But I think we shall also have to raise ours. Now a moderate duty on all manufactured goods, not exceeding 10 per cent on the average, but varying according to the amount of labour in these goods—that is to say, putting the higher rate on the finished manufactures upon which most labour would be employed—a duty, I say, averaging 10 per cent would give the Exchequer, at the very least, £9,000,000 a year, while it might be nearer £15,000,000 if we accept the Board of Trade estimates of £148,000,000 as the value of our imports of manufactured and partly manufactured goods. Nine millions a year—well, I have an idea that the present Chancellor of the Exchequer would know what to do with a full purse. For myself, if I were in that onerous position—which may Heaven forfend—I should use it in the first place to make up this deficit of £2,800,000 of which I have spoken; and, in the second place, I should use it for the further reduction both of taxes on food and also of some other taxes which press most hardly on different classes of the community.

170. IMPERIAL UNION

Source: 'Mr Chamberlain's Speeches', ed. C. W. Boyd (1914), vol. II, pp. 255–6.

Speech by Joseph Chamberlain at Cardiff, 20 November 1903. Political opinion was much impressed by the argument, at the time, that the coming century would be an age of large states and big economic unions.

IT is no commercial repose we want, it is commercial activity. It is time to change our system. We are losing our old customers. We have set them a good example. They do not follow it. Let us try whether a gentle pressure may not be found still more convincing, and, above all, let us draw closer the ties between ourselves and our colonies by accepting offers of advantage which no other country can give to us. Let us meet their requests in the spirit which dictated them, not in a peddling or huckstering spirit, which would be as discreditable to us as their action is creditable to them. They are not animated merely by selfish interests. They see as we ought to see—as I think we do—that our future history depends upon the extent to which we can weld the different parts of the Empire together. What Washington did for the United States of America, what Bismarck did for Germany, it is our business to do for the British Empire.

171. FREE TRADE BY RETALIATION?

Source: Arthur James Balfour, 'Economic Notes on Insular Free Trade' (1903), pp. 3–4, 8–9, 19–21, 23–4, 28–31.

When Joseph Chamberlain began his campaign for Tariff Reform, he both precipitated an immense public controversy and put his Prime Minister, Balfour, in a difficulty. Balfour was not prepared to tie himself to a system of tariffs. At the same time, he believed a Free Trade Britain lacked the power to bring pressure to bear upon the tariffs of other nations. Therefore, he asked for a free hand, with the authority to impose tariffs in the interest of a policy of retaliation and reciprocity. His arguments failed to satisfy either his own followers or public opinion, as the results of the 1906 election showed. But they were published by him, in September 1903, in what was at first a Cabinet paper, later a pamphlet, of high lucidity and analytical power and an agreeable wit. It is this document which is partly reproduced here. For the politics of the situation, K. Young, 'Arthur James Balfour' (1963).

IT may be as well to premise that I approach the subject from the free trade point of view: though the free trade is perhaps not always that which passes for orthodox in the House of Commons or on the platform. There is indeed a real danger of the controversy degenerating into an unprofitable battle of watch-words, behind which there is nothing deserving to be called independent reflection at all. Popular disputation insists on labels; and likes its labels old. It therefore divides the world, for purposes of fiscal controversy, into protectionists and free traders. Those who are protectionists are assumed to be protectionists after the manner of Lord George Bentinck. Those who are free traders are assumed to be free traders after the manner of Mr Cobden. Does a man question the dogma that taxation must always be for revenue? Then evidently he hankers after the fiscal system of 1841 and a twenty-shilling duty on corn. Does he admire the tariff reforms of sixty years ago? Then evidently he regards the simple and unqualified doctrine of 'free trade' as so fundamental in its character, so universal in its application, so capable of exact expression, that every conclusion to which it logically leads must be accepted without hesitation or reserve.

I am a 'free trader', but not, it must be acknowledged, precisely after this pattern....

[*Balfour then discusses the proposition that there is no pre-established harmony between economic world interests and national well-being. Recognition of this implies an abandonment of 'laissez faire' as absolute dogma, and acceptance of the view that our fiscal policy should vary with varying circumstances. No plan should be regarded as perfect because it is simple, unartificial and familiar. He continues:*]

...we must now accept the fact that while our own free trade is rather insular than imperial, the most advanced of our commercial rivals are not only protectionist now, but in varying measure are going to remain so. Other nations have in the past accepted the principle of free trade; none have consistently adhered to it. Irrespective of race, of polity, and of material circumstances, every other fiscally independent community whose civilisation is of the western type has deliberately embraced, in theory, if not in practice, the protectionist system. Young countries and old countries, rich countries and poor countries, large countries and small countries, free countries and absolutist countries, all have been moved by the same arguments to adopt the same economic ideal. In circumstances so little foreseen we are driven to ask whether a fiscal system suited to a free trade nation in a world of free traders, remains suited in every detail to a free trade nation in a world of protectionists...

[*Balfour considers what have been the alleviating circumstances in the economic position of Great Britain as a free trade country in a protectionist world. They are, in the first place, that 'foreign countries owe us a great deal of money, which they pay by means of imports into the United Kingdom', because in no other way can they obtain the sterling money required to make interest payments; secondly, that large areas of the world, both within and outside the Empire, remain unprotected or largely so, because imported manufactures are essential to them, as in South America, or their tariff is subject to international control, as in Turkey, or their tariff policy is settled in London, as in the non-self-governing parts of the Empire. He continues:*]

The third reason which prevents Britain from suffering the full penalty which might and would befall a free trade community in a completely protectionist world is that tariffs, even in the most protectionist countries, are not absolutely exclusive. In some of those countries, and for some of our main industries, indeed, no loophole is permitted. The barrier is impregnable. Bradford goods do not go to America, nor does bleach to Russia. Yet on the whole there is a large import into the protected area of the commercial world; protectionist nations and protectionist colonies are still our most important customers.

In order, however, to form an exact estimate of our industrial relation to those communities, we have to consider not merely what is, but what is to be. The tendency of trade, not its momentary position, is what chiefly concerns us. And this gives food for thought.

It is, I think, clear that our export trade, which should, other things remaining the same, have grown with our growth and with the yet more rapid growth of some of our customers, has, in fact, done neither one nor the other. Absolutely it may have increased, but its rate of increase has on the whole seriously diminished; in some important departments no increase is perceptible, in others there are symptoms of decay.

The cause of this is commonly set down to the 'industrialisation' of the world. How, it is asked, can we expect to provide foreign nations with ever-increasing quantities of our manufactures, since they have learned, at our feet, so amply to provide for themselves? Britain had formerly an undisputed primacy in the industrial world; she has it no longer; she could not hope to have it. But, after all, the roots of this great change lie deep in the nature of things; why complain of the inevitable?

But this argument is wide of the mark. No complaint is made of the relative growth in wealth, population and prosperity of other nations. This ought, on the contrary, to be a matter of rejoicing. We might expect[1] on the free trade theory to gain, not to lose by it. It should increase, not diminish, the rate at which we get richer; and the tide of international commerce ought to flow, not merely without slackening, but in a volume proportionate to the growing numbers and wealth of the different populations to which it ministers.

If neither this nor anything like this is happening, it is not simply because 'in the nature of things' and by the operation of some inevitable law it is impossible; but because it has been made impossible by the

---

[1] Though not with absolute certainty.

operation of hostile tariffs.[1] National industries have not been allowed to become mutually supplementary; they have been compelled to become mutually exclusive. Fiscal contrivances have forced them out of co-operation into competitive channels.[2]

That this is the true theory, on ordinary free trade principles, of what is now taking place, it seems to me impossible to deny. But there are two circumstances accompanying the diminishing rate of increase in our export trade by which some observers are greatly consoled.

They say, in the first place, that if we are losing our predominance in foreign markets, the home market is making corresponding gains. They say, in the second place, that if our staple industries are stationary or retrograde, this is more than made up for by the variety of goods we now manufacture for the foreign consumer. From neither circumstance can I derive much satisfaction. These are precisely the signs which would accompany the struggle of a free trade country so to modify its industries as to pierce the barrier of foreign tariffs. They are presumably, therefore, in part the consequences of protection. If so, the industrial changes in which they consist must surely involve an economic loss. It would be impossible to hold a version of the free trade theory so perverse as one which assumed that while any artificial diversion of industry due to home protection must necessarily be pernicious, the foreign protectionist accidentally confers upon us a benefit which we cannot confer upon ourselves....

If, then, an examination of the quantity and character of our exports to tariff-protected countries confirm [*sic*] the unsatisfactory conclusion which theory independently suggests, we have to ask ourselves whether there is reason to anticipate any improvement in the future. Are we to be permitted to take our fair share in the growing industrial labours of the world, and to reap our fair share of their reward; or is our

---

[1] The Board of Trade estimate the *ad valorem* equivalent of the duties levied on our principal exports to be in the case of Russia, 130 per cent; of the U.S.A., 72 per cent; of Austria-Hungary, 32 per cent; of France, 30 per cent; of Italy, 27 per cent; of Germany, 25 per cent; of Canada, 16 per cent; of Belgium, 13 per cent; of New Zealand, 9 per cent; of Australia, 7 per cent; of the South African Customs Union, 6 per cent.

[2] I do not, of course, mean that under a system of international free trade there would have been no competition between industrial nations; but only that there would have been much less competition and much more co-operation.

position going to worsen relatively to that of other nations, or even to worsen absolutely?

I see no satisfactory symptoms. The highly developed industrial countries, like Germany, America, and France, give no sign of any wish to relax their protectionist system. The less developed protectionist communities, like Russia and some of our own self-governing colonies, are busily occupied in building up protected interests within their borders—a process which is doubtless costly to them, but is not on that account the less injurious to us.

Nor has it, I think, been sufficiently noted that the injury in these cases, is or tends to become, a double one. The effect of any artificial stimulus to manufacturers in a country like the United States of America, or Russia, or Canada, is to ante-date the period when their food supplies will be required for internal consumption. Protection of manufactures diverts the supply of capital and labour from agriculture to manufactures. It diminishes the relative number of those who grow corn, and increases the relative number of those who eat it without growing it. To us, who not only wish to export manufactures but to import food or (if you prefer it) who have to export manufactures largely because we have to import food, this may become a serious matter; and in the interests of cheap bread, it is eminently desirable that the produce of the wheat-growing areas available for exportation should be kept at the highest possible level....

I have now said enough to indicate the grounds of my difference with our commercial optimists. At first sight their case seems a good one. Judged by all available tests, both the total wealth and the diffused well-being of the country are greater than they have ever been. We are not only rich and prosperous in appearance, but also, I believe, in reality. I can find no evidence that we are 'living on our capital', though in some respects we may be investing it badly. Why then, it is asked, do we trouble ourselves to disturb a system which has been so fruitful in happy results?

I will not take up the barren challenge contained in the last phrase, or add to the profitless and inconclusive dispute as to whether the growth of our prosperity is due to a good financial system, and the still greater growth in the recent prosperity of some other nation has been reached in spite of a bad one. The point to which I desire to direct attention is a different one. I ask the optimists to study tendencies—the dynamics not the statics of trade and manufactures. The ocean we are navigating is smooth enough, but where are we being driven by its tides? Does either theory or experience provide any consolatory answer to this question? Consider some of the points on which I have commented in these notes: the injury which foreign protection is calculated to inflict on a free trade country; its need for open markets; the threatened contraction of existing free trade areas; the increasing severity of tariffs in protectionist areas; the building up of vested protected interests in new countries, which may be discouraged now, but not hereafter; the effect of this protection on our future corn supply; the uncertainty and loss which tariff-protected trusts are inflicting, and may hereafter inflict, upon British capital invested in Britain.

One and all of these evils, actual and prospective, are due to protection. The man who says that their cumulative effort is so small as to be negligible, can hardly describe himself as a 'free trader'—at least he can attach but a very small value to free trade. The man who, admitting their reality, does not anticipate their increase has (it seems to me) not learned the lesson which theory and experience agree in teaching. The man who admits their present reality and the probability of their increase, and yet is too contentedly prosperous even to consider whether any mitigation is practicable, appears little short of reckless.

I cannot accept any of these positions. It seems to me clear that we are bound to seek for some mitigation; and that only in one direction can we hope to find it.

The source of all the difficulty being protective tariffs imposed by fiscally independent communities, it is plain that we can secure no concession in the direction of a freer exchange, except by negotiation, and that our negotiators can but appeal to self-interest or, in the case of our colonies, to self-interest and sentiment combined.

Now, on the free trade theory self-interest should have prevented these tariffs being originally imposed. But it did not; and if argument failed before powerful vested interests were created, it is hardly likely to be effective now.

The only alternative is to do to foreign nations what they always do to each other, and instead of appealing to economic theories in which they wholly disbelieve, to use fiscal inducements which they thoroughly understand. We, and we alone, among the nations are unable to employ this means of persuasion, not because in our hands it need be ineffectual, but because in obedience to 'principle' we have deliberately thrown it away.

The 'principle' to which we pay this strangely incongruous tribute is, of course, the principle of 'free trade'. But what a curious view of free trade it implies. The object which these fiscal inducements are intended to attain is increased free trade and nothing else; yet simply because the 'fiscal inducement' may, *if it fails of its effect but not otherwise,* involve duties not required for revenue purposes, or in certain cases even carry with it some element of protection to home industries, we are to turn away from it as from an accursed thing.

This seems to me, and has always seemed to me, extraordinarily foolish. It is certainly quite inconsistent with rational free trade. There is one, and only one, standard by which we can measure the free trade merits of any policy, and that is the degree to which it promotes free trade. This to be sure is as near a tautology as anything well can be, yet seemingly there are free traders to whom it presents itself as heresy, if not as a paradox. They regard the maxim 'thou shalt not tax except for revenue' not as the concise description of a fiscal ideal, but as a moral imperative of binding force. In their judgment it admits of no qualification or exception. It is, in school jargon, 'universal' and 'necessary', and could you prove to them that by risking the imposition of the most trifling protective tariff at home, it was possible to secure the greatest relaxation of protective tariffs abroad, they would only answer that we must not do evil that good may come of it!

This attitude of mind seems to me absurd. I hold myself to be in harmony with the true spirit of free trade when I plead for freedom to negotiate that freedom of exchange may be increased. This freedom to negotiate, like all other freedoms, may of course be abused. But are we therefore in a mood of irrational modesty to declare ourselves unfitted to enjoy it? I think myself that it ought not to be difficult to devise a method of turning it to most useful account. But were I proved to be wrong, my opinion on the fundamental question would remain unchanged. Where we fail others may succeed. It cannot be right for a country with free trade ideals to enter into competition with protectionist rivals, self-deprived of the only instrument by which their policy can conceivably be modified. The first and most essential object of our national efforts should be to get rid of the bonds in which we have gratuitously entangled ourselves. The precise manner in which we should use our regained liberty is an important, yet after all only a secondary, issue. What is fundamental is that our liberty should be regained.

172. THE FREE TRADE CASE IN THE NEW CENTURY

Source: A. Marshall, "Memorandum on the Fiscal Policy of International Trade (1903)" in 'Official Papers by Alfred Marshall', ed. J. M. Keynes (1926), pp. 394-5, 401-4, 405-6, 406-9, 410.

Alfred Marshall, the economist, was requested by the Treasury to advise them, in 1903, on two questions arising out of the Tariff Reform controversy. They were, first, who bore the incidence of import duties and second, how far and in what directions had the circumstances altered which formerly made Free Trade the best policy for Great Britain? Marshall's memorandum represented his reply to both questions. He declined to print it in 1903, although given permission to do so, because he felt it to be incomplete, but agreed that it should be printed as a parliamentary paper, with some slight revisions, in 1908. The memorandum was undoubtedly the most thorough and acute restatement of the case for Free Trade since the time of Cobden and Peel. On the other hand, Marshall's subtlety and caution of treatment show many traces of the great economic and political changes which had come over the world since their day. The extracts from this lengthy document come from the part of it which deals with the Treasury's second question. The subheadings are Marshall's own. For Marshall, his experience and personality, see J. M. Keynes, 'Essays in Biography' (1933), pp. 150 ff.

England's Fiscal Policy assumes the Relative Maturity of her Industries

[Marshall begins his discussion of the problem whether the Free Trade policy needs to be changed by discussing the bases of England's fiscal policy sixty years ago. He emphasizes the Free Trade argument that protective taxes lessen aggregate employment and profits, while the free importation of goods does not displace labour, only changes the direction of its employment. The basic economic doctrine was that all wages and profits depend on the aggregate efficiency of national production and on the free import of foreign goods in exchange for exports. He points out that when the English economists were preparing the way for Free Trade, England had a partial monopoly in *many of her exports. She could then hope—she cannot now—to throw a share of the burden of her import duties on foreigners. Moreover, the economists did not condemn all import duties. Marshall goes on to consider whether the widely different conditions at the time of his writing necessitate a change in this policy.*]

It seems to me that the policy adopted in England sixty years ago remains the best, and may probably remain the best, in spite of increasingly rapid economic change, because it is *not* a device, but the absence of any device. A device contrived to deal with any set of conditions must become obsolete when they change. The simplicity and naturalness of Free Trade—that is, the absence of any device—may continue to outweigh the series of different small gains which could be obtained by any manipulation of tariffs, however scientific and astute.

I proceed to consider some of the changes which may be urged as affording a *prima facie* case for reconsidering the fiscal policy adopted by England sixty years ago. They may be roughly classified thus:

(i) The increase in the strength and purity of Government in its administrative machinery, and the broadening of the functions which it is expected to perform, and does perform, with general approval.

(ii) The advance of the United States, Germany, and other countries.

(iii) The tendency to an increase in the taxes levied both by old and new countries on the importation of manufactured produce.

(iv) Changes affecting England's industrial leadership.

(v) The growth of powerful industrial aggregations and combinations, fostered by tariffs and other Government favours, whose power to manipulate trade gives cause for anxiety.

(vi) The new possibilities of closer relations between England and other English-speaking countries, resulting partly from the development of electrical and steam communication....

[*Marshall expands upon the first of these changes and comes to the conclusion that nothing further should be done to overload the government in a modern age which demands more constructive work from it than it can get through. Moreover, he would not like to see an increase in the money value of political power, in the influence of rival interested parties in Parliament. He then deals with the advance of the United States and Germany. The United States is not dependent on foreign trade, so protection cannot harm her. The recent increase in Germany's foreign trade, Marshall concludes, has been with the countries of Eastern Europe, ready to use Western goods, but not to make them themselves. It is therefore due to advantages which scarcely any fiscal policy could destroy. Marshall continues:*]

England is undoubtedly in a worse position than she would be if the commodities for which she has a special aptitude were not generally liable to heavy taxes abroad. But the taxes on her imports levied by a country in the same industrial phase with herself will always be of relatively small importance to her. It is generally to the advantage of both that they should exchange textiles or metal goods whenever merchants see their way to a profitable exchange. But if England made things for home consumption with the capital and labour with which she makes her exports to (say) Germany, and Germany acted in like manner, neither of them would be seriously injured. To put an artificial obstacle in the way of the trade would be unwise; but its total economic consequences would be small after the immediate effect of the disturbance had passed away.

Nor could England be very seriously injured even by a concurrent imposition of taxes on her imports on the part of all countries in the same industrial phase with herself. She might indeed then be unable to market abroad any great quantity of those refined machines and other implements, for which there is little demand except in highly advanced countries; and, therefore, she would be a little restricted in the economies of production on a large scale in this important group of manufactures. But her own markets would afford scope in almost every branch of such work for several establishments of the largest size which can advantageously be controlled by single management; and therefore her loss under this head, though considerable, would not be very great. She would give more attention to products suitable for sparsely peopled countries; and this would help her in obtaining such crude mineral and agricultural products as she needed.

Nor is there any very urgent danger to be feared *in the near future* from the concurrent imposition of heavy import duties on manufactures by sparsely peopled countries. For most of those countries are still in urgent need of capital; and they cannot afford to divert much of it from developing their abundant resources to setting up modern steel and other industries, which may absorb a thousand pounds' worth of capital or more for each person to whom they give employment.

Consequently, many manufactured products will long continue to be imported on a large scale even into the more highly developed new countries. And there will also long remain large areas of the world in which there are no organised industries, and where the door must be kept fairly open to the large majority of Western products.

But the world is being peopled up very quickly. It is but a century since Britain accumulated her great Public Debt; and before another century has passed the scene may have changed. There may then remain but a few small areas of fertile soil, and of rich mineral strata, which are not so well supplied with both population and capital as to be able to produce most of the manufactured products which they require, and to be able to turn to a tolerably good account most of their raw products for their own use. When that time comes, those who have surplus raw products to sell will have the upper hand in all international bargains. Acting concurrently, whether by mutual agreement or not, they will be in the possession of an unassailable monopoly; and any taxes, however oppressive, which they may choose to impose on the only products which densely peopled countries can offer to them will be paid mainly by those countries. It is this consideration, rather than the prospect of any immediate danger, which makes me regard the future of England with grave anxiety.

Changes affecting England's Industrial Leadership

The progress of the arts and resources of manufacture had benefited England more than almost any other country in one important but indirect way. It has so reduced the cost of carriage by land and sea that raw materials and food can come to her, even from the centres of great continents, at a less cost than they could come from the near neighbourhood of the sea-shores and great rivers of the Continent sixty years ago; and the 300,000 miles of railways which have been built during the last sixty years in America, Asia, Africa, and Australia are rendering greater service to Englishmen than to any other people, except those in whose lands the several railways are placed.

In almost every other respect the progress of the arts and resources of manufacture has benefited England less than any other country. For, even sixty years ago, the excess of the cost of the manufactures needed for her own consumption over that of the raw material by which they were made was small. If it could have been reduced to nothing, she would have gained by the change very much less than she has gained by the lowering of the cost of imported food and raw material for her own use.

On the other hand, countries which used to be dependent on imported manufactures have gained all round: they have gained by lowered cost of transport, and they have gained by the lowered cost of manufacture of commodities for direct use; and that almost equally, whether these goods are manufactured by themselves or imported. For competition compels England, Germany, and other Western countries to give to consumers almost at once the full benefit of any economy in manufacturing processes which they have obtained.

In so far as the increasing economy of transport and manufacture enables Western goods to be disposed of in backward countries where before they could not compete with hand-made products, the exporting country gets a great share of the benefit. But people's most urgent needs for some classes of manufactures are now satisfied by manufactures which, with modern processes, absorb very little labour, and therefore sell under competition very cheaply. For instance, further economies in the manufacture of pins might diminish rather than increase the total value of the export of pins, and the number of people to whom that industry gives employment.

Therefore, England's gains from the further progress of manufacture, except in so far as it led to yet further cheapening of long-distance transport, might be less than those of most other countries, even if that progress made a proportionately increasing demand for those industrial faculties by which England obtained her leadership. But it does not.

For the very perfection of the textile and other machinery by which England won her industrial leadership has enabled it to be worked fairly well by backward races. That combination of liberty with order, and of individual responsibility with organised discipline, in which England excelled, was needed for pioneer work in manufactures; while little more than mere order and organised discipline will go a long way towards success, where the same tasks are performed by modern machinery 'which does most of the thinking itself'. Thus England is at a steadily increasing relative disadvantage in trading not merely with people like the Japanese, who can assimilate every part of the work of an advanced factory; but also with places where there are abundant supplies of low-grade labour, organised by a relatively small number of able and skilled men of a higher race. This is already largely done in America, and it certainly will be done on an ever-increasing scale in other continents.

Consequently, England will not be able to hold her own against other nations by the mere sedulous practice of familiar processes. These are being reduced to such mechanical routine by her own, and still more by American, ingenuity that an Englishman's labour in them will not continue long to count for very much more than that of an equally energetic man of a more backward race. Of course, the Englishman has access to relatively larger and cheaper stores of capital than anyone else. But his advantage in this respect has diminished, is diminishing, and must continue to diminish; and it is not to be reckoned on as a very important element in the future. England's place among the nations in the future must depend on the extent to which she retains industrial leadership. She cannot be *the* leader, but she may be *a* leader. . . .

[*Sixty years ago England had leadership in most branches of industry. The finished commodities and, still more, the implements of production, to which her manufacturers were giving their chief attention in any one year, were those which would be occupying the attention of the more progressive of Western nations two or three years later, and of the rest from five to twenty years later. It was inevitable that she should cede much of that leadership to the United States. It was inevitable that she should yield a little of it to Germany. It was not inevitable that she should yield so much of it as she has done.*]

The greatness and rapidity of her loss is partly due to that very prosperity which followed the adoption of Free Trade. She had the full benefit of railways, and no other country at that time had. Her coal and iron, better placed relatively to one another than elsewhere, had not begun to run short, and she could afford to use largely Bessemer's exacting but efficient process. Other Western nations partially followed her movements towards Free Trade, and in distant lands there was a rapidly increasing demand for manufactures, which she alone was able to supply in large quantities. This combination of advantages was sufficient to encourage the belief that an Englishman could expect to obtain a much larger real income and to live much more luxuriously than anybody else, at all events in an old country; and that if he chose to shorten his hours of work and take things easily, he could afford to do it.

But two additional causes of self-complacency were added. The American Civil War and the successive wars in which Germany was engaged, partially diverted the attention of these countries from industry: it checked the growth of their productive resources; and it made them eager to buy material for war, including railway plant and the more serviceable textile materials, at almost any cost. And lastly, the influx of gold enriched every English manufacturer who could borrow money with which to buy materials, could apply moderate intelligence in handling them, and could then sell them at a raised level of prices and discharge his debt with money of less purchasing power than that which he had borrowed.

This combination of causes made many of the sons of manufacturers content to follow mechanically the lead given by their fathers. They worked shorter hours, and they exerted themselves less to obtain new practical ideas than their fathers had done; and thus a part of England's leadership was destroyed rapidly. In the 'nineties it became clear that in the future Englishmen must take business as seriously as their grandfathers had done, and as their American and German rivals were doing; that their training for business must be methodical, like that of their new rivals; and not merely practical, on lines that had sufficed for the simpler world of two generations ago; and lastly that the time had passed at which they could afford merely to teach foreigners and not learn from them in return.

The estimate of leadership is different from, almost antagonistic to, measurement of a country's leadership by the volume of her foreign trade without reference to its *quality*. Measurement by mere quantity is misleading.

[*Of course, the statistics of foreign trade are specially definite and accessible; and since the fluctuations of business confidence and activity are reflected in foreign trade among other things, the habit has grown up of using export statistics as a* prima facie *indication of the time and extent of such fluctuations*

Who Gained by Change?

Export statistics are not very trustworthy; while for broader purposes they are quite untrustworthy.]

Other things being equal, an increase in the efficiency of those industries in which a country is already leading will increase her foreign trade more than in proportion. But an increase in the efficiency of those in which she is behind will diminish her foreign trade.

England has recently (1903) been behind France in motor-car building, and behind Germany and America in some branches of electrical engineering. A great relative advance on her part in those industries would enable her to make for herself things which she had previously imported, and would thus diminish her foreign trade. On the other hand, even a small advance in her power of spinning very high counts of cotton yarn would increase her foreign trade considerably; because that is a thing for which other nations have an elastic demand, and are at present almost wholly dependent on England.

England's export trade, though still very much larger in proportion to population than that of Germany and America, is not (in 1903) increasing as fast as theirs. But this fact is not wholly due to causes which indicate relative weakness.

The chief cause of it is that the improvements in manufacture and in transport, aided by Free Trade, enable England to supply her own requirements as regards food, clothing, etc., at the cost of a continually diminishing percentage of her whole exports. Her people spend a constantly diminishing percentage of their income on material commodities; they spend ever more and more on house-room and its attendant expenses, on education, on amusement, holiday travel, etc. Present censuses show a progressive increase in the percentage of Englishmen who earn their living by providing for these growing requirements. That is to say, the number of Englishmen who devote themselves to producing things which might be exported in return for foreign products increases very slowly. Of course, if her foreign trade be measured by the quantity of things exported and imported, it is increasing fast; for a man's daily labour now deals with a much larger volume of goods in almost every industry than formerly. But still it is not increasing (in 1903) as fast as that of Germany and America. How far is this really an evil?

American conditions are very dissimilar to ours. But if anyone compares in detail German and English trade statistics, he will find it difficult to point out desirable foreign commodities with which England is not the better supplied. The earnings of England's capital invested in foreign countries and in ships on the ocean enable her to bring home about a hundred and fifty millions' worth of commodities for her own consumption, in addition to those which she buys with her nominal exports. Her people think that these, taken together, are enough; and prefer expensive summer holidays to increasing still further above the German level their consumption of oranges or silk. Who shall say that they are wrong? It is useless to point out things which England might export and does not: unless it can be shown that the extra things, which she would be able to import by so doing, are more desirable than the things and services which she is providing for herself and which she would need to give up in order to make those things for export.

The real test of relative progress which foreign trade offers lies in the opportunity afforded by it for measuring the skill with which each nation applies her industry to producing great results with small manual effort; or, in other words, in making commodities cheap relatively to effort, and effort dear relatively to commodities. In view of her failing stores of iron ore, England rightly exports an ever-increasing proportion of machinery and implements which are of small bulk relatively to their value, and that is an indication of the qualities of leadership; but her imports of electrical plant and aniline dyes show that her hold on leadership is insecure, and can be retained only by renouncing the easy self-complacency engendered by abnormal prosperity in the third quarter of the last century.

For England, though not for America, Free Trade is Essential to Leadership

The position, then, is this. On the one hand, England is not in a strong position for reprisals against hostile tariffs, because there are no important exports of hers, which other countries need so urgently as to be willing to take them from her at a considerably increased cost; and because none of her rivals would permanently suffer serious injury through the partial exclusion of any products of theirs with which England can afford to dispense.

And, on the other hand, it is not merely expedient—it is absolutely essential—for England's hopes of retaining a high place in the world, that she should neglect no opportunity of increasing the alertness of her industrial population in general, and her manufacturers in particular; and for this purpose there is no device to be compared in efficiency with the plan of keeping her markets open to the new products of other nations, and especially to those of American inventive genius and of German systematic thought and scientific training.

Further, it is more necessary for her manufacturers than for any others that they should be able to buy cheaply, and without friction, any foreign products—whether technically described as 'manufactured' or not—which they may want at any stage of their complex and varied work....

Though it be true that the import duties of Western nations inflict greater loss on England than they did sixty years ago, it seems that she stands to gain little and to lose much by any attempt to coerce them into lowering their tariffs. Especially does it seem contrary to England's interests to levy import duties with the object of giving English diplomatists something to bargain with when discussing foreign tariffs. English business would be disturbed by the opinion that such a duty was probable; and again by its actual imposition, and again by the probability that it would be removed, and again by its actual removal. It would disturb business in every way; and it would set particular classes of business men on influencing Government, as it has done in other countries where diplomats are intrusted with a power of this kind. Protective duties are easy to impose, and hard to remove; and the suggested plan would lead to a number of protective taxes based on no scientific system, and conducive neither to the material nor the moral prosperity of the country.

173. THE STRATEGIC CASE FOR FREE TRADE

Source: Memorandum (by Mr later Sir, Eyre Crowe, Senior Clerk, Foreign Office) on the Present State of British Relations with France and Germany, 1 January 1907, F.O.371/257, in G. P. Gooch and H. Temperley, 'British Documents on the Origins of the War 1898–1914', vol. III (1928), appendix A.

This survey of Great Britain's external policy was written by a high Foreign Office adviser, Eyre Crowe (1864–1925), during the Liberal

Campbell-Bannerman administration, which had been formed in 1905. The style of argument he employed vividly illustrates the importance of political values in political economy, especially in practical application. Free Trade had often been defended, in the middle years of the nineteenth century, when political and economic conditions favoured a detachment of British interests from the Continent of Europe, as the natural instrument of a pacific and isolationist foreign policy. When Crowe was writing, after the changes of sixty years, Free Trade began to look like the best foreign economic policy for a country which found itself drawn increasingly into the groupings and rivalries of European politics and the naval and military race which went with deepening quarrels.

THE general character of England's foreign policy is determined by the immutable conditions of her geographical situation on the ocean flank of Europe as an island State with vast overseas colonies and dependencies, whose existence and survival as an independent community are inseparably bound up with the possession of preponderant sea power. The tremendous influence of such preponderance has been described in the classical pages of Captain Mahan. No one now disputes it. Sea power is more potent than land power, because it is as pervading as the element in which it moves and has its being. Its formidable character makes itself felt the more directly that a maritime State is, in the literal sense of the word, the neighbour of every country accessible by sea. It would, therefore, be but natural that the power of a State supreme at sea should inspire universal jealousy and fear, and be ever exposed to the danger of being overthrown by a general combination of the world. Against such a combination no single nation could in the long run stand, least of all a small island kingdom not possessed of the military strength of a people trained to arms, and dependent for its food supply on oversea commerce. The danger can in practice only be averted—and history shows that it has been so averted—on condition that the national policy of the insular and naval State is so directed as to harmonize with the general desires and ideals common to all mankind, and more particularly that it is closely identified with the primary and vital interests of a majority, or as many as possible, of the other nations. Now, the first interest of all countries is the preservation of national independence. It follows that England, more than any other non-insular Power, has a direct and positive interest in the maintenance of the independence of nations, and therefore must be the natural enemy of any country threatening the independence of others, and the natural protector of the weaker communities.

Second only to the ideal of independence, nations have always cherished the right of free intercourse and trade in the world's markets, and in proportion as England champions the principle of the largest measure of general freedom of commerce, she undoubtedly strengthens her hold on the interested friendship of other nations, at least to the extent of making them feel less apprehensive of naval supremacy in the hands of a free trade England than they would in the face of a predominant protectionist Power. This is an aspect of the free trade question which is apt to be overlooked. It has been well said that every country, if it had the option, would, of course, prefer itself to hold the power of supremacy at sea, but that, this choice being excluded, it would rather see England hold that power than any other State.

History shows that the danger threatening the independence of this or that nation has generally arisen, at least in part, out of the momentary predominance of a neighbouring State at once militarily powerful, economically efficient, and ambitious to extend its frontiers or spread its influence, the danger being directly proportionate to the degree of its power and efficiency, and to the spontaneity or 'inevitableness' of its ambitions. The only check on the abuse of political predominance derived from such a position has always consisted in the opposition of an equally formidable rival, or of a combination of several countries forming leagues of defence. The equilibrium established by such a grouping of forces is technically known as the balance of power, and it has become almost an historical truism to identify England's secular policy with the maintenance of this balance by throwing her weight now in this scale and now in that, but ever on the side opposed to the political dictatorship of the strongest single State or group at a given time.

174. THE QUARREL WITH GERMANY

Source: 'Journals and Letters of Reginald, Viscount Esher', ed. M. V. Brett (1934), vol. II, p. 267.

The language of this private diary deserves study. On both sides of the North Sea, a kind of old-fashioned mercantilism sometimes did duty for economic thinking in high official circles before the 1914 war. The writer, the second Viscount Esher (1852–1930), was an original member of the Committee of Imperial Defence, 1904, a supporter of the army reforms of Lord Haldane and a man of influence behind the scenes on all defence questions. He had talked that day to Sir Ernest Cassel, the banker, who had recently met the German Kaiser. The Committee of Imperial Defence was at this time brooding upon the possibilities of invasion from the Continent. The year was 1907.

ORCHARD LEA, December 3rd...Meanwhile the Germans proceed unabashed on their way, and have their objectives clearly in view. The German prestige, rising steadily on the continent of Europe, is more formidable to us than Napoleon at his *apogee*. Germany is going to contest with us the Command of the Sea, and our commercial position. She wants sea-power, and the carrying trade of the world. Her geographical grievance has got to be redressed. She must obtain command of the Ports at the mouths of the great rivers which tap the middle of Europe. She must get a coastline from which she can draw sailors to man her fleets, naval and mercantile. She must have an outlet for her teeming population, and vast acres where Germans can live, and remain Germans. These acres only exist within the confines of our Empire. Therefore, *l'Ennemi c'est l'Allemagne.*

INDEX OF DOCUMENTS

Note. For extracts from:
Acts of Parliament, *see* Law Reports
Blue-books, etc., *see* Government publications
Newspapers, etc., *see* Periodicals
Parliamentary debates *see* Hansard
Reports of Commissions, *see* Commissions
Reports of Committees, *see* Committees

Index of Documents

Index of Documents

Index of Documents

Report on Wages and Hours of Labour (Brooklands Agreement, 1894), 343–6
Summary of Scheme of Unemployment Insurance embodied in Part II of the National
    Insurance Act (1911), 413–15

Haggard, H. Rider, *Rural England* (1902), 53–9
Haldane, Lord, to House of Lords, on scarcity of industrial scientists (1916), 173–6
Hall, A. D., *A Pilgrimage of English Farming* (1913), 59–62
Hansard: *Parliamentary Debates: House of Commons*
    Asquith on old age pensions (1908), 399–400
    Broderick on Uganda (1900), 437
    Chamberlain on expansion of Empire (1893), 434–5
    Churchill on labour exchanges (1909), 409–11
    Lloyd George on national insurance (1911), 415–17
Hansard: *Parliamentary Debates: House of Lords*
    Haldane on scarcity of industrial scientists (1916), 173–6
Harcourt, Sir William, *Life of* (Gardiner, 1923), 439–41
Harford, John, *A Voyage to the African Oil Rivers Twenty-five Years Ago* (in *West
    African Studies*, by Mary Kingsley, 1899), 202–3
Haw, George, *From Workhouse to Westminster: the Life Story of Will Crooks, M.P.*
    (1907), 400–2
Hobson, C. K., *The Export of Capital* (1914), 228–9
Hobson, J. A., *Imperialism* (1902), 442–5
Hogg, Ethel M., *Quintin Hogg: a Biography* (2nd ed., 1904), 169–71
Hogg, Quintin, life of (1904), 169–71
Hopwood, C. H., *Durham Coal Trade Arbitration* (1876), 329–30
Howe, E., *The London Compositor* (1947), 330–3
Howell, George, *The Conflicts of Capital and Labour* (1878), 328–9

Ince, Richard, *see* Ferranti, G. Z. de
International Miners' Federation: *Quarterly Report* of (March, 1909), 352–3
Irish Landowners' Convention (1902), and Irish Land Conference (1903)
    Resolutions and Statement adopted by, 68–70

Jeans, J. S., *England's Supremacy: its Sources, Economics, and Dangers* (1885), 430–1
Jeans, W. T., *Creators of the Age of Steel* (2nd ed. 1885), 98–100
Jenks, J. W., *Industrial Combination in Europe* (*Reports of the U.S. Industrial
    Commission*, 1901), 244, 252–9
Jevons, H. S., *The British Coal Trade* (1915), 95–6
Jevons, W. S., *The Coal Question* (2nd ed. 1866), 91–2
John, A. H., *A Liverpool Merchant House, being the History of Alfred Booth and
    Company 1863–1958* (1959), 203–5

Kendall, May, *see* Rowntree
Keynes, J. M. (ed.), *Official Papers by Alfred Marshall* (1926), 20, 459–68
King, Bolton, *see* Ashby
Kingsford, P. W., *F. W. Lanchester* (1960), 153–4
Kingsley, Mary, *West African Studies* (1899), 202–3
Kingzett, C. T., *The History, Products, and Processes of the Alkali Trade* (1877), 163–4

Index of Documents

Index of Documents

The Electrician (1878), on football by electric light, 123–4; (1881), on electric lighting, 126–9

Internal Combustion Engineering (1913), on the assembly line, 156–60

The Ironmonger (1895), on retail price maintenance, 247–9; (1904), on crisis among cycle-makers, 148–9

The Times (1888, 1889), on the Salt Union, 245–7; (1889), on the dock strike, 342–3; (1893), on a national plan for coal, 249–52; (1900), prospectus of Associated Portland Cement Manufacturers, 259–61; (1901), on imports from U.S.A., 208–13; (1902), on world trade and naval power, 445–7; (1904), on the Regent Street Polytechnic Institute, 169–71

Pigou, A. C. (ed.), *Memorials of Alfred Marshall* (1925), 20–2

Playfair, Lyon, letter to Schools Inquiry Commission (in *Report*, 1897), 167–9; *Subjects of Social Welfare* (1889), 164–5

Portal, Sir Gerald, *Reports relating to Uganda by* (1894), 435–7

Rathbone, Eleanor, *How the Casual Labourer Lives* (1909), 304–12

Reeves, Mrs Pember, *Round About a Pound a Week* (2nd ed. 1914), 397–8

Reid, Sir Charles, and others, *Coal Mining: Report of the Technical Advisory Committee* (1944–5), 92–5

Reid, Wemyss, *Memoirs and Correspondence of Lyon Playfair* (1900), 164–5

Rew, R. H., *An Agricultural Faggot* (1913), 49–51

Richardson, A., *The Evolution of the Parsons Steam Turbine* (1911), 109–11

Richardson, John Wigham, *Memoirs of* (1911), 107–9, 171–2, 346–7

Rolls, C. S., *Motor Vehicles* (in *Encyclopaedia Britannica*, 1911), 154–5

Rowntree, B. Seebohm, *Poverty: a Study of Town Life* (3rd ed. 1902), 299–304

Rowntree, B. Seebohm, and May Kendall, *How the Labourer Lives* (1913), 312–16

'Rutherford, Mark' (William Hale White), life of (Maclean, 1955), 113

Schulze-Gaevernitz, G. von, *The Cotton Trade in England and on the Continent* (1895), 116–19

Smillie, R., in *The Labour Year-book* (1916), 358–60

Smith, H. Llewellyn, and Vaughan Nash, *The Story of the Dockers' Strike...* (1889), 338–41

Smith, Richard Mudie, *Handbook of Daily News Sweated Industries Exhibition* (1906), 390–2

Sowter, Rev. G. A., letter to Lord Rosebery on Uganda (1892), 433–4

Spender, J. A., *Weetman Pearson, First Viscount Cowdray* (1930), 234–8

Swan, Joseph, letter to *Nature* (1880), 124–5; *Memoir of* (1929), 125–6, 172–3

Swan, Mary E., and Kenneth R., *Sir Joseph Swan F.R.S.: A Memoir* (1929), 125–6, 172–3

Tariff Commission: *Report of the*, 1904, 103–7

Taylor, F. Williams, *Canadian Loans in London* (in *United Empire: the Journal of the Royal Colonial Institute*, 1912), 230–4

Temperley, H., *see* Gooch

Thorne, Will, *My Life's Battles* (1889), 336–7

Index of Documents

United States of America: Commissioner of Corporations, *Report on the Tobacco Industry* (1909), 262–5; Industrial Commission, *Report on Industrial Combination in Europe* (1901), 252–9

Van Oss, S. F. (ed.), *Fenn on the Funds* (16th ed. 1898), 228

Ward-Jackson, C. H., *A History of Courtaulds* (1941), 144–6

Waterhouse, Rachel E., *The Birmingham and Midland Institute 1854–1954* (1954) 163; *A Hundred Years of Engineering Craftsmanship (a short history of Tangyes Ltd)* (1957), 162–3

Watts, John I., *The First Fifty Years of Brunner, Mond and Company 1873–1923* (1923), 136–40

Webb, Beatrice, *Our Partnership* (1948), 378–9

Webb, Sidney and Beatrice, *English Poor Law Policy* (1910), 379–83; *Industrial Democracy* (1902), 349–50

Webb, Sidney and Arnold Freeman, *Seasonal Trades* (1912), 149–51

White, Sir William, *Life of* (Manning, 1923), 112–13, 113–14

White, William Hale ('Mark Rutherford'), life of (Maclean, 1955), 113

Williams, J. E., *The Derbyshire Miners* (1962), 352–3

Woodroofe, K., *From Charity to Social Work in England and the United States* (1962), 374–5

Wolff, Sir Henry Drummond, *Rambling Recollections* (1908), 218–20

GENERAL INDEX

Abyssinia, 438

accounts, farmers', 46, 54, 56, 61

aeroplanes, 84, 154

Africa, British possessions in, 430; Germany and, 444; investment in, 419, 420; partition of, 419, 423, 435, 442; *see also* East Africa, South Africa, Uganda, West Africa

Agamemnon, S.S., 198, 199 n.

Agricultural Depression, Commission on, 43–5

Agricultural Derating Act (1896), 44

Agricultural Holdings Acts (1875), 39, 42; (1883), 38

agricultural labourers, 34, 35–6, 46; in Ireland, 67, 286, 287; lock-out of, 52, 334–6; minimum wage for, 395–7; scarcity of, 54; trade unions of, 35, 395, 333–4; wages of, 34, 40, 51–3, 61, 286, 287, 295–7, 312–16, 333

Agricultural Labourers' Union, 295, 333–4

agricultural machinery, American, 210–13

agriculture, changes in, 33–77, 165; depression in, 18, 19, 34–5, 38–43, 62–6, 206, 432; investment in, 8; prices of products of, 18, 19, 28, 29, 43–5, 49; share of national income supplied by, 33, 35, 287

Agriculture, Board (later Ministry) of, 38, 43

Agriculture, (Richmond) Commission on, 38, 63

Aitken, W. C., 163

Algeria, 192

alkali trade, 163–4

American Tobacco Co., 262–6

ammonia-soda process (Solvay's), 137, 138

Anglo-American Brush Light Corporation, 128

Anglo-German Convention (on Africa), 436

Anglo-Persian Oil Co., 112

Anti-Sweating League, 390

anti-trust legislation, in British Dominions, 274; in U.S., 243

arbitration, 322; in the coal industry, 329–30

Arch, Joseph, 333

Argentina, export of locomotives to, 210; imports from, 178, 190, 194; loans to, 29, 31, 229; railways in, 16

armaments, empire and, 425, 428–9; expenditure on, xvi, 283, 443; taxation for, 439–41

Ashby, Joseph, 295

Ashley, William J., 26, 213

Ashton, Thomas, 352

Asia Minor, 444

Askwith, Sir George, 356

Asquith, H. H., 399–400

assembly line, in motor-vehicle industry, 156–60

Associated Portland Cement Manufacturers Ltd., 260–1

Australia, colonial imperialism and, 424; gold from, 32; help for London dockers from, 343; imports from, 178, 190, 194; industrial growth in, 31; Japanese coal for, 96; land boom and financial crisis in, 220–5; loans to, 81, 229–30; minimum wage in (Victoria), 392; 'over-development' in, 228; tariffs of, 455 n., voyages to, by sail and steam, 197

Australian Direct Steam Navigation Co., 197

Austria–Hungary, financial crisis in (1873), 15; industrial growth in, 31; labour exchanges in, 410; loans to, 29; railways in, 16, 228; steel industry of, 105; tariffs of, 455 n.;

480

Exchanges, merchants', in London, 196

Exhibitions, of 1851 and 1862, 168; Paris, (1867) 168, (1900) 172–3

expectations, economic, 3–32, 282, 423

expenditure, of labourers' families, 297, 306, 309; public, on social service, 367–8

explosives industry, combination in, 242

exports from U.K., booms in, (1870–4) 207, (1906–14) 83, 121; coal, 91, 93, 95–6; coal-tar, 141–2; cotton textiles, 118, 121–3; cotton yarn, 119–20; 'invisible', 181, 467; iron and steel, 16, 17, 194–5; machinery, 119, 185, 213–14; statistics of, 465–6; total, 16, 178, 179, 180, 431, 454; wool, 194–5

Factory Acts, 385

'Fair Trade', 431–3

Family Allowances Act (1945), 397

farmers, tenant, 33–4, 45–6, 60; in Ireland, 62, 63, 66, 68

Feeble-Minded, Commission on, 380

feeding-stuffs, supply of, 39, 450

Fenn on the Funds, 228

Ferranti, S. Z. de, 129, 130

fertilizers, imported, 39; synthetic, 166

Firth (Thomas) and Sons, Sheffield, 112

'Fiscal Controversy' 185–6, 317, 459

fishing, as supplementary to farming, 67, 70, 72, 75

Fleming, Sir Ambrose, 134

'foggers', in the chain and nail trades, 387–8

food, of farm labourers, 298–9, 315, 316; imports of, 38, 48–9, 177–8, 179, 180, 182, 184–5, 456; prices of, 13, 26–7, 28, 39, 313; proposed import duties on, 450; of town labourers, (Liverpool) 309–10, 311, 312, (London), 294, (York) 302, 303; in workhouse, 377; *see also* meat, wheat, etc.

Food, Supply of Raw Materials and, in Time of War, Commission on, 188–92

football, by electric light, 123

Ford cars, 156

Foxwell, H. S., 405

France, British factory in, 215; colonies of 431, 443, 444; decline of, 424; foreign investment by, 29; imports of U.S. agricultural machinery by, 210; labour exchanges in, 410; motor-vehicle manufacture in, 151, 155, 466; naval rivalry with, 111; payment of indemnity by, 15; shipbuilding in, 112; syndicalism in 354; tariffs of, 456; technical education in, 168, 169, 173; wages in, 27; wool re-exported to, 195

Franco-Prussian War, 14, 15, 168

Free Trade policy, Balfour on, 452–9; of British Empire, 442, 446; economic case for, 446; legislation for, 178; Marshall on, 459–68; reaction against, 180, 431; strategic case for, 468–9

Friendly Societies, 362, 398, 415, 416; trade unions as, 321, 327

fruit, imports of, 49

fruit-farming, 54, 55

gas industry, competitive with electricity, 126, 130

gas stokers, 336–7, 339

Gas Workers and General Labourers, National Union of, 336, 339

Gellatly, Hankey, Sewell and Co., shipowners, 199

general strike, 323

Germany, British factories in, 213; coal production in, 95, 96; colonies of, 438, 443, 444; competition with, 7, 160, 161–2, 206, 207, 421; copying of U.S. manufactures by, 212; cotton industry of, 122; dominance of, in Europe, 424, 425; dye industry of, 141–2; electrical engineering in, 131, 466; as enemy of Britain, 471; export drive of, 445, 460–1, 466, 468; foreign investment by, 29; French indemnity and, 15; industrial growth in, 6, 7, 31, 79, 80, 460, 464;

General Index

Uganda, 433–9

Unemployed Workmen Act (1905), 380, 406–8

unemployment, (1830's) 287, (1885–6) 19, 289, (1920's and 1930's) 83, 367; in, agriculture, 396; insurance against 367, 411, 413–17; in Ireland, 64; Labour Exchanges and, 383; in London, 292; main risk of working-class life, 405–6; miners' fear of, 94; trade cycle and, 6; Will Crooks's experience of, 400–2

United States of America, agricultural machinery from, 210–13; British factories in, 215; Civil War in, 189, 465; coal production of, 95, 96; competition with, 7, 160, 162, 421; cotton industry of, 122; electrical engineering in, 126, 131, 466; exports to, (wool) 195, (leather) 203–4; financial crises in, 15, 231, 413; imports from, (cotton) 121, 188–9, (food) 165, 190, 191, 192, 432; industrial growth in, 6, 7, 31, 79, 80; industrial innovation in, 180, 468; loans to, 15, 16, 229, 421; oil (petroleum) from, 189; locomotives from, 208–10; range-cattle industry in, 225–7; silver agitation in, 23, 29; steel industry of, 99, 160, 162, 193; syndicalism in, 354; tariffs of, 455 n., 456; technical education in, 174; wages in, 27, 107; as world power, 443, 445, 460, 464; and world trade, 177–8, 466

Uruguay, 178

vegetables, growing of, 41, 51; imports of, 49

vehicle-building, unemployment insurance in, 414

veterinary science, 50

Victoria, Queen, 439

viscose process for artificial silk, 144, 145

wages, 27–8, 285; of agricultural labourers, 34, 40, 51–3, 61, 286, 287, 295–7, 312–16, 333; of cotton-workers, 343–6; of dock labourers, 338, 340; of Liverpool labourers, 307; in London, 286, 383–4; of machinist (home-worker), 391–2; of miners, 329–30; real, 317, 320; of skilled labour, 384; in sweated industries, 389, 390, 391; the State and, 367; trade unions and, 318–60; for unemployed on public works, 404; in United States, 106, of unskilled labour, 284, 302, 373, 383–4; in York, 299–304; see also minimum wage

Wales, farm wages in, 286; iron and steel industry of, 103; miners in, 352

Wantage, Lord, 47, 129

Warder Brushnell and Glessner Co., Springfield, Ohio, 211

wars, and national debts, 228

Webb, Sidney, 323 n., 365, 379

Webb, Mrs Sidney (Beatrice Potter), 305, 378, 379

welfare, social, discussion of, xvi, 280–1; factors favouring, 364–7; obstacles to legislation for, 363; proportion of national income spent on, 367–8

West Africa, trade by barter in, 202–3

Westmorland, farm wages in, 314

wheat, alternatives to, 47–9; home-grown, 191; imports of, 33, 48, 190–2; price of, 17, 45, 191, 295; production of, in U.S., 165

Wheatstone, Charles, 164

whisky industry, combination in, 242

'whisky money', allotted to educational purposes, 167, 170

White, Sir William, 112

White, William Hale ('Mark Rutherford'), 112

Wilson (Thomas), Sons and Co, ship-owners, 199

wireless telegraphy, 134–6

wire-making, 101

Wolff, Sir Henry Drummond, 218